X-RAY

X-RAY

Ray Davies

THE OVERLOOK PRESS
WOODSTOCK • NEW YORK

First published in the United States in 1995 by
The Overlook Press
Lewis Hollow Road
Woodstock, New York 12498

Library of Congress Cataloging-in-Publication Data

Davies, Ray
X-ray : the unauthorized autobiography / Ray Davies.
p. cm.
1. Davies, Ray, 1944-. 2. Rock musicians–England–Biography.
3. Rock music–England–History and criticism.
I. Title.
ML420.D25A3 1995
782.42166'092–dc20
[B] 95-17328 CIP
ISBN: 0-87951-611-9
First American Edition
135798642

For my family

I was born in a welfare state

My name is of no importance. In fact it is of no concern to anyone except those who have loved and befriended me during my somewhat limited tenancy on this earth. It is a matter between me and my employers. Suffice to say that I am nineteen years of age, and I am about to embark on my first major journalistic enterprise, for a Corporation that has paid for my education ever since I became an orphan and was taken into its care. I know nothing of my life before the Corporation took me in, and everything I am is a result of its care and protection.

I am a product of a century which started at the height of class-conscious imperialism and ended with a society so reduced to totalitarian commonness that in my final years at college the saying 'mediocrity rises' proliferated. I am an example of a system which encourages ordinariness, a product of a vast empire of companies that has now splintered off into many separate corpora-tions, each with its own autonomous control. I am one of the faceless thousands manufactured by this corporate society, with just enough education to serve my masters, and the right haircut and fashion-conscious attire to fit in with my contemporaries. The only individualism in me lurks somewhere so deep inside my desolate soul that it may never emerge to my human exterior, which was bred with the sole purpose to conform. My generation has been taught to be so in touch with the latest fashion that we have become faceless; we are victims of design. But, oddly enough, although I was taught to think of myself as a man with no face, somewhere inside my soul I sense that I might become an individ-ual, but that my individuality has not been allowed to surface yet. Indeed, the day that happens I will no longer be of any use to the Corporation: corporate ethos dictates that people with character cease to be trustworthy and are therefore a threat to the organization. And so, as I say, my name is of no importance and I trust this will remain so.

After being fostered by the Corporation as a child, I was sent to Corporate college, and after completing a course as a researcher I expected to be assigned to work of some historical importance, perhaps the decline of Conservatism and Communism in the latter part of the twentieth century. Or maybe the emergence of Wales as the leader of European industry after the great decline of the Deutschmark less than a decade after the Berlin wall came down.

After such high expectations, imagine my surprise at being summoned to Head Office on my first day as a fully fledged archives clerk to be informed by the editor-in-chief that my first assignment was to complete a history of the pop-music explosion of the mid-1960s. My share of the task was to document the life and times of one Raymond Douglas Davies, who was a composer and the lead singer of the Kinks, one of the leading beat groups of that era. I was told to deliver the manuscript by the end of the spring quarter, in time for an autumn release. As today is the first of the year this means that I have three months to complete my task.

I had studied some of Raymond Douglas Davies' work while on a short course in sixties pop culture at college, but the job neither excited nor interested me. I had no alternative but to accept, as many others were waiting in line to take my place, and my refusal would not have kept me in good standing with my superiors. But why had they picked me to document the life of someone who had emerged in post-World War Britain to form part of what was called the 'Swinging Sixties'? The prospect was daunting. The challenge nil. That night, I took a bundle of files and cassettes home and tried to absorb myself in order to get to grips with Raymond Douglas Davies. The file containing a discography and brief outline of Davies' career was small. There were also three biographies which had been written while Davies was still performing with his group. The books were full of superficial anecdotes and trite gossip, and, for the most part, showed a bias of some sort by the writer. There was very little information about the man himself; he had never been interviewed directly by any of the writers. Raymond Douglas Davies, as the books informed me he preferred to be known, was for the most part a secretive man who had kept his life to himself. There was nothing in his dossier to suggest that he had ever revealed anything of himself to the world outside of his music. He was rather like myself, in that he seemed to be a faceless individual.

I studied his photographs and absorbed many of his lyrics. I played some of his old records and liked them, even though his obviously untrained voice sounded as if he had suffered from sinus trouble, to such a degree that it conjured up the image of a man standing in front of a microphone holding his nose. I played a selection of his early hits, such as 'You Really Got Me' and 'All Day and All of the Night'. Then some ballads, which had obviously been recorded later, when his singing voice had matured. It retained that familiar melancholy style, but sounded deeper. Then one LP in particular, *The Village Green Preservation Society*, suddenly unleashed inside me memories of events that I had not yet experienced. The lyrics seemed to have a subtext to them, as if he were sending messages in code. I had not known my parents and when I was first taken in by the Corporation as an orphan after what must have been a traumatic childhood I was prescribed sleeping pills to counteract my severe nightmares. I have dutifully taken these every night since I was eleven years old. As a consequence, while I am no longer plagued by harrowing night-mares, I do not dream at all. After staying up for most of the night listening to *The Village Green Preservation Society*, I took my sleeping pills as usual and went to bed expecting the dark shroud of drug-induced sleep that always blacked out the world until the alarm clock woke me the following morning.

Instead, an astonishing thing happened: I had a dream. At first it was only a sound of a train in the distance; almost like the first commuter train at dawn as it made its way from the depot far away. In my sleep, the sound of the distant train was comforting.

Sometime in my childhood I must have lived near a railway. Then, the peace was shattered. I was in a small room and the door was locked so that I could not escape. The only light in the room came from a yellow street lamp which was almost right outside my window, on the first floor of a row of terraced houses. I heard the sound of drunken people shouting in the rooms below. I crawled over to a lamp stand, took out the bulb, switched on the light and then stuck my fingers into the bare points. The sudden surge of electricity threw me across the room, sending a numbing sensation through my entire body.

I woke up and realized that this was not a dream: it had truly happened to me as a child and only a miracle had prevented me from being killed. It must have been this incident which necessitated such powerful medication.

I went back to sleep. In another dream I heard a train in the distance again, only this time I was sleeping on a bed of hay. In my dream, I woke up and crawled out of the hay to see a bright sunlit day in the country, with early morning dew reflecting the sun into my eyes with almost blinding power. The train was the old-fashioned steam train that had disappeared almost fifty years before I was born, and yet the image was so vivid that it was as if I actually remembered seeing its round face, with a driver next to a man shovelling coal into its engine. It flashed across the countryside which was ablaze with bright sunlight reflecting off the morning dew.

Before I slept I had been listening to 'Last of the Steam-Powered Trains' on Raymond Douglas' *Village Green* album, and yet as I dreamed it was almost as if I had been experiencing someone else's dream. This came within what I knew to be my own dream, and yet I also knew that it was somebody else's recollection. Raymond Douglas' words and music had possibly imposed themselves on my subconscious.

I decided to throw away all the books and printed material and let the music tell me about him. That's when I heard something in his music that made me think of the family I had never known. I

4

thought that perhaps I had heard Raymond Douglas' voice as a child. Maybe my parents, whoever they were, had played some of his records to me before my family was dissolved. Perhaps my editor had chosen me for this precise reason. I decided to track down Raymond Douglas Davies through his songs which in a strange way provided me with a link to my own past.

The following night I took my sleeping pill as usual but again I started to dream. This time I was in a mythical world inhabited by witches and wizards. All the folk-tales of mankind appeared in the dream: legends and fairy-stories that I had never heard of were suddenly familiar to me. I remember being there; seeing the history of my ancestors and observing their small lives, which existed almost like the insects that inhabit the twilight world somewhere underneath the dark moist soil and the richly coloured leaves of autumn after they had surrendered their souls to the earth. It is a time before the Corporation took over the world; a time before continents united to become one commercial enterprise; a time when there was a country called England.

The next morning my alarm snapped me back to consciousness. It was obvious that this project would be more than just a documentation of somebody else's life. I would be discovering a great deal about my own brief history, information that had been closed to me from childhood. I was full of excitement, fear, anticipation, expectation and confusion. I was so excited that I cut my chin with my razor as I shaved. I looked at the blood trickling down into the bathroom sink and felt, for the first time in my life, that life was just beginning. My soul was beginning to emerge and come to the surface like the blood from my face.

At work later that morning, a female researcher named Julie walked past my desk and dropped an envelope into my lap. Inside was the address where Raymond Douglas was last known to be living. That afternoon I found myself standing outside a disused factory in north London. The old building had been used as a studio in

Raymond Douglas' heyday, but now it was covered in graffiti; its windows were boarded up to shut out not just the pilfering homeless underclasses but almost every other kind of humanity. Barbed wire was wrapped around an old neon sign which had the name Konk on it.

I pressed the bell marked 'office' and a robotic-sounding female shouted down the entryphone. I felt the need to disguise myself. I explained that I was a composer myself as well as being a fan, and I hoped to have an audience with Mr Davies. I was asked to stand in front of a television camera which was pointing down at me. I waited for what seemed like minutes while unseen eyes scrutinized me. The secretary then asked me several questions about Raymond Douglas' songs. I was grateful for the research I had put in prior to the visit.

'What was the name of the first record company to sign the Kinks and when did they sign them?'

I hesitated for a second; then closed my eyes and took the plunge. 'Pye Records signed the Kinks in January 1964.'

'Who was the motorbike rider in *The Village Green Preservation Society*?'

'Johnny Thunder.'

'How many albums did the Kinks record for MCA records?'

'Two studio albums, plus one live album called *The Road* that was outside the original contract.'

'Who, apart from Dave Davies, does Raymond Douglas Davies regard as the greatest rock guitarist: Eric Clapton, Jimi Hendrix or Jeff Beck?'

This took me by surprise. I made a wild guess. 'Jimi Hendrix.'

'Correct. Enter.'

The front-door entry-lock buzzed and I was in the hallway of the legendary Konk Studio. To my amazement, there was no one there to greet me. I shouted upstairs for the secretary but there was no reply. There was an uncanny dead feeling about the place, which was festooned in cobwebs and dust. It was as though I was entering the tomb of a great Egyptian king instead of a derelict factory that had once been used by the Kinks to make records. I cautiously made my way through a labyrinth of corridors until I reached a door that creaked open as I approached. As I peered around the corner of the doorway, I heard a familiar nasal voice: 'Who, what, when and why are you here, lad?' The voice was that of Raymond Douglas Davies.

I struggled to find a reply which would ingratiate myself with him. 'To study. To learn.'

'And to steal, no doubt.'

The bitterness in his voice gave it a new edge. I tried to calm a potentially heated moment. 'No, truly, sir, I have come to learn about the time in which you lived and pass on your knowledge to composers of the future.'

There was an uncomfortable silence. Then I heard Raymond Douglas sigh deeply as he spoke: 'You speak of the future. There is no time here. No future nor past.'

Raymond Douglas was sitting just beyond the only shaft of light in the space. The sound of his voice gave the impression that the place we were in was neither a room nor a hallway. The atmosphere was dense with stale air and hanging smoke, like a room where there has been a party the night before. Like all legendary figures, he did not seem as large or as small as I had imagined him to be. In the half light I could not distinguish his somewhat shrunken frame too clearly and if my calculations were correct, he must have been in his late sixties. The only feature visible in the gloom was the large black overcoat wrapped around him, which looked as though it had once belonged to him.

His voice was abrupt, curt and almost toneless, but the questions came like bullets.

'I shan't bother with your name until I decide whether it's worth knowing. Do you watch television?'

It was obvious that Raymond Douglas must have lost all sense of reality many years ago, but I was not going to let that stop me. 'Of course I watch television,' I replied.

'*The Lucille Ball Show*? No, don't tell me, let me guess. *The*

Flintstones? *Muffin the Mule*? No, I think that you're a *Woodentops* watcher – or *Bill and Ben*. That's it! *Noddy* . . . *Rupert Bear*. I loved watching the telly when I was a kid.'

I remained silent, somewhat stunned. All those programmes had vanished from the television screens long ago. He was an old man, after all. I couldn't work out his accent. He seemed well spoken, but he pushed out his vowels in a way that made him sound like a pantomime Cockney. It was as if every word had a question mark after it.

His voice remained strong. He was a powerful and sly inquisitor. 'Do you think that Eydie Gorme has nice breasts?'

My silence irritated him and he shouted. I struggled to try to remember who Eydie Gorme was. I had only a vague recollection that she had been an American pop singer in the 1950s. Raymond Douglas was not about to wait for me to remember. His impatience led to another rapid verbal assault, and his voice increased in volume as he spelled out the meaning of what he was saying: 'You know, breasts. Threepenny bits, Bristols, jugs, knockers, mammaries, bosoms. You know – tits.'

'Eydie Gorme?' I asked weakly.

I waited for the next onslaught, but his voice dropped to a lower, hushed tone. 'Nah, probably not a tits man, are you. The loveliest tits I ever imagined hung from the shoulders of Eydie Gorme. Saw her picture, I did, in the *Sunday People* when I was a boy. She – Eydie – was wearing a beautiful low-cut black dress. You could just see the crack of her tits, or knockers as they used to be called. I used to keep my thumb in the page with her photograph, and pretend to be reading the sports page when my mother walked in. When the coast was clear I used to turn back and peek at Eydie. I was too young to know what sex was, or to think bad thoughts about her breasts. I was just artistic enough to appreciate the delicious curves and what lurked beneath that black gown. Subsequently, whenever I met a woman, I measured her sexuality by the distance between her chin and the tips of her nipples. The same as I had done with that photograph of Eydie. I was only a boy when I saw the picture, but I'll never forget those beautiful, long, sweeping chests like ski slopes, similar to the Queen Mother's, bless her heart. What a pair of mams! Sit down, kid, I like you.'

'I'm not staying long.'

"Course you're not. Sit down anyway.' He kicked a chair towards me. 'There, it's got your name on it. Oh, but I didn't ask you your name, did I? Still, never mind. Be seated. Stick your little botty on the perch.'

He watched silently as I carefully sat. His voice took on a quizzical tone. 'Not a poofy type, are you? Don't answer that, I don't want to know yet.'

'Do you think I'm a poofy type?'

Raymond Douglas cracked up with raunchy laughter, as if to convince me of his own masculinity. Then he suddenly stopped. "Course not, but you never know, especially nowadays. I remember one poof in particular – his name was Vassall. I was at Art College at the time, and he was on trial because he had given secrets to some Russian who was also a poof. I am not offending you, am I? Because it's not intentional. It's just that "poof" was a popular word at the time. I always thought that Vassall was the perfect name for a poofy, subversive traitor because it sounds like Vaseline. One up the bum, no harm done, as they say in versatile circles.'

I sensed that Raymond Douglas was goading me, trying to give the impression that he was an insensitive bigot. He had failed to arouse any interest on my part on the subject of women's breasts, and so now he was attempting to penetrate my own sexuality. He ranted on.

'What's the difference between a queer and a gay? I'll tell you, one does it because it is his natural bent, as it were. There is no choice, because that is the way a queer is. The other does it because it is fashionable. When I grew up, queers did it in public toilets because they had to: there was nowhere else to go if you'd picked someone up in Muswell Hill on a Saturday night. Nowadays, because it's fashionable, gays do it in public just in case there is a photographer around.

9

'The conquest is the most important element, not the execution, because after the conquest you are in control. Then you can do anything you want with that object — because that's all they are. By then they are enjoying being conquered, being subservient. They cease to have identities: they become objects. That's when you begin to detest them.

'I believe that it is impossible to have sex with somebody you love and respect. What do you think? No, don't answer, you're too young to know. I had a girlfriend once, a prudish, school-teacher type. We were together for five years and had a reasonable sex life, but she turned into a miserable old cow who withheld sex whenever I did something she disapproved of. I mean, do me a favour. I was supposed to be this internationally acclaimed rock and roller. A sort of latter-day Byron and my bleeding live-in, God rest her soul, decided that I should be punished for the most trivial of domestic offences — not rinsing the bath out properly, leaving the top off the toothpaste or picking my nose in bed. I mean, it was a fucking outrageous way to treat a pop star and sex-symbol.

'Anyway, it was only when I left her that she actually came on extra-strong: she wanted me back. While I was living with this other woman I used to call on my former girlfriend, out of guilt, probably, just to see if she was all right. One thing would lead to another and we invariably ended up having sex of the most erotic type imaginable. On the carpet in front of the fire. By windows with the curtains open. That sort of stuff. The poor cow must have imagined all sorts of sexual activities that I might be perform-ing with my new girlfriend, and in her own sad way she was trying to top them.

'One night she was stripping off for me in front of the electric fire and, as she took off her sweater to reveal a beautiful black slip, I suddenly thought back to my childhood and that photograph of Eydie Gorme. I couldn't go on. Not because I didn't fancy my ex-girlfriend or out of loyalty to my present girlfriend, but because of that image of Eydie Gorme which had made an almost indelible, pseudo-religious impression on me. And also Eydie was married to the singer Steve Lawrence, whom I admired.

'What do you think, lad?'

I thought he was a perverted, over-lustful, degenerate sexist weirdo. 'It's interesting. Do go on,' I replied.

'No, I've said enough. Anyway, it's quite possible that I'm wrong, because over the years I've discovered I have a habit of mixing truth and fantasy. It happens to most people as they get older; it's a genetic, chemical fact. With me, well, it's always been the case. I did see a picture of Eydie Gorme when I was a kid a long time ago. As for the rest, the rest is the same combination of fact and fiction that exists in all our lives. They go together like fire and water; flesh and blood; fiction and fact. Still, that's enough. Did you bring any charts for me to look at? You know, music. You did say that you wanted to learn.'

I hesitated. Then I asked him to turn the air-conditioning up, to clear the stale smell from the room. I fumbled in my briefcase pretending to search for the manuscript paper that I knew was not there. 'Charts? I have some, but I mainly have tapes.'

I heard him fiddle with the air-conditioning and, as the smoke cleared, I could see that Raymond Douglas was sitting in the corner of a control room of an old recording studio that had once been the centre of his emotional empire. All the records he had made had been played back in this room at one time or another. The thin hissing sound of the somewhat ineffectual air-conditioning seemed to have his songs on its breath. His chair, which was on castors, enabled him to rock back and forth slowly, in and out of the light, as he spoke to me.

'Rock and roll.'

His craggy face disappeared into the shadows, then slid back into the light. This time it had a glimmer of a smile: he was immersed in his own cleverness. Overwhelmed by his self-taught, instinctive use of words to create a double meaning, he repeated the words as if it had not been obvious what he had meant the first time.

'Rock and roll. Yeah.'

He paused and looked at me as if I ought to be impressed. He pouted, and then sucked his cheeks into his mouth as he continued, with a slightly pompous air: 'I used to play in a rock and roll band and now . . .'

I knew what I was going to say was wrong but I couldn't resist the cheap shot. 'Now you're playing in a rocking chair.'

He looked hurt. Then angry. My interjection had caused a momentary interruption of his poetic flow. He stopped rocking and, after the briefest glare in my direction, he slid his chair backwards into the shadows. As we both sat in our own darkness and listened to the sound of the air-conditioning, I remembered a line from one of his old hits:

> I wish today could be tomorrow.
> The night is dark, it just brings sorrow.

His songs had celebrated sunny afternoons and sunsets at Waterloo; they were about normal British people, and had communicated ideas which in some ways had educated and engaged ordinary people more than any video or history book had done. I had the impression from his work that he was afraid of the dark, and yet the poor old bugger had obviously spent so much of his life in dimly lit recording studios under artificial light that he had learned to treat it as a friend.

The silence continued. I had started to win his confidence, and then blown it with one line. But it was clear to me that he had been taking me for a sucker, had been lying to me from the moment I walked through the door. Winding me up with stories of erotic sexual escapades with ex-girlfriends and his fascination with Eydie Gorme.

I began to think that it had been a bad idea to come for this meeting. I hadn't realized until now that in another time Raymond Douglas would have been something of a hero to me. I had never wanted to meet any of my heroes before, because I had always felt that they would never live up to their work.

Anyway, why was he making himself so accessible to me? This

was uncharacteristic of what little I knew about the man. And the silence was beginning to make me feel uneasy. The sound of the castors on his chair was the only indication I had that he was sliding around the room. I knew he was there somewhere, but I couldn't see him clearly. I just knew that his eyes were looking right inside me. Suddenly his voice boomed through the massive loudspeaker which was built into one side of the wall: 'Two . . . two . . . testing one, two, three.'

He leaned forward again, an evil grin on his face. This time, speaking through a microphone which he was holding in his hand, his voice had a cynical curve to it which made him sound like a bingo caller. 'Welcome and good evening, or should I say good day, or did it ever really matter a damn to anyone in this Godless establishment? Did you know, we even work on Sundays in here?'

'I didn't. But I could have guessed . . . If this were a truly Godless place, I suppose you would work Sundays.'

My voice sounded small and detached, like it belonged to somebody else. His boomed out even though he spoke only in a whisper.

'Godless, says you. Yes, I always suspected that it was. Tell me, boy, are you with the Corporation?'

The volume rose in a crescendo until the word 'Corporation' resonated through my skull.

I decided to play safe. 'I thought we both were.'

'Why did you think that?'

'Well, isn't that why we're both here?'

'I'll ask the questions for the time being, if you don't mind, lad. Now, I will ask you plainly: have you been sent by the Corporation?'

I answered, not knowing nor caring about truth, meaning or motive. I opened my mouth and words came out that were not connected to anything I was thinking: 'I truly do not know why I am here or indeed whether or not the Corporation has sent me. However, if you feel for some reason that it should be so, then I will agree that it could be a possibility that the Corporation has

13

sent me, although I am sure you will agree that on occasions, these directives are non-specific. In all honesty, I do not know.'

The abject stupidity of my answer brought forth such a bellow of laughter through the microphone that it started to whistle with feedback. He put the microphone to one side and spoke in his normal voice, but in a tone that indicated he had finally uncovered the truth.

'I think that you have been sent, and you're here to help me do the re-mix of my past. If that is the truth it is also the case that we have met before.'

By now I was afraid of him. His intimidating, bullying manner had started to terrify and appal me.

'I don't recall having had the pleasure,' I replied.

'Of course you don't know now, but soon you'll realize that you have indeed met me once before. Let me introduce myself. I am Raymond Douglas Davies, Raymond Douglas to my friends. As there are none of those left and I despise formality, you can call me R.D. Or, if that is too much for you to remember, you can simply refer to me as you and I will refer to you as me. I trust I am sufficiently clear on this matter, which I refuse to discuss any further.'

I had an uneasy feeling about this. It was as if he had some mysterious power that could watch my thoughts and then manipulate what I would say. I also had the feeling that his authoritative attitude was put on – it was some sort of defence mechanism. The room became silent again and I looked up at the small shaft of light which came through the roof. Outside, it was probably a perfect crisp winter's day. In here, there was hardly any light at all. I was just thinking about how to move the conversation on to the subject that had brought me here in the first place when Raymond Douglas suddenly answered my question without even allowing me the courtesy of asking it for myself. He had anticipated my request and moved on, as if pushing a fast-forward button on a video. I had an uneasy feeling that it had all been well rehearsed. Raymond Douglas, or R.D. as I was now obliged to call him, sat

back and positioned himself under a small shaft of light as he
began to speak. It was obvious that he was an old ham, and the
shaft of light added a touch of theatre to the occasion. R.D. took a
deep breath and began to speak like a classical actor; his tone,
however, was pious and patronizing.

'My name is Raymond Douglas Davies, and I would like to
tell you about my life, because I feel that it is the only way I
can possibly be of help to you. I have lived so long and yet I
know so little about the world and its strange ways. I have
learned very little from my mistakes, and my achievements
are fading into my clouded and confused past. If you listen to
me, you may learn something about yourself.

I do believe that, for the most part, all men (and women)
are born equal. That is to say, we are all as purple and
confused as one another when we come of the old black
tunnel of hope. I can't speak for anybody else, but I definitely
had a feeling of hope as I emerged from that dark, slithery
world.

You see, being born is easy. It's what happens to us once we
get outside that makes me wonder why on earth did God put
us and our mothers through all the screaming and squelching
in order that we should survive through this bloody torment.
What a stupid predicament to be in. I am convinced that I was
born to prove a point. As I was born, I felt like saying to my
parents, 'Yes, it is possible to have a son, Mr and Mrs, and I
do sincerely hope that I have made you both very happy.
Now, would you please have me adopted before I start to
have any real affection for you, because having been where
I've just been, it's obvious that one day I am going to be
taken away from you. Or should I say, that we are going to
be separated forever? And, that being the case, I would like to
say thank you and good-night now, to prevent any
unnecessary pain to you both when one of us departs this
world.'

I have only a faint recollection of what happened before I was born, but I do know that I entered this world with a clean sheet. I was supposed to be innocent and new-born, but because I was so fresh in this world and so close to the last I felt that I knew more than all those grown-up people around me. As the doctor pulled me out and held me up, I saw faces staring with wonder. Some even had tears in their eyes.

It is as if I am there now. I see a line of pretty young women who look at me in astonishment. Their heads bow down as I am passed around them. One of them looks at the tiny piece of flesh hanging between my legs and giggles. A tall man, obviously my father, kneels by the bed and starts to weep. This confirms my early suspicions that although, as I have said, it is my belief that all men are created equal, I have been born into special circumstances. I am not merely the seventh child of a seventh child, born at midnight on the day of the summer equinox in the year that brought a World War to an end. Outside in the street the All Clear siren mingles with the distant sound of church bells ringing in a glorious cavalcade as an entire nation celebrates. I have been born a king.'

2

'The early days in my little kingdom were full of splendour.
The flowers of summer had reached full bloom. The birds
sang in orchestrated harmony and echoed my own
contentment: I was spoiled and mollycoddled to an excessive
but wondrous degree, totally befitting the arrival of the first
son in a family of girls. Attractive girls, I might add, who
innocently played with me while I took every opportunity to
look up their skirts. Life was simply perfection. Even as a
child I was a dirty old man. Between meals I sat in my pram
and gazed up at the green, tree-lined street and never had to
lift a finger; my every whim was catered for by my adoring,
doting mother. I was rarely unhappy and, because I was given
everything I needed, there was no reason for me to cry. When I
did, it was at night, when it got dark. For some reason I
thought I might have to disappear again into that dark tunnel,
and I had visions of dark red blood, and I heard my mother's
agonized cries. In those moments the only way my mother and
sisters could pacify me was by playing records on our old
wind-up gramophone. They would put on all the records in the
house, everything from 'Temptation' sung by Perry Como to
'Cocktails for Two' by Spike Jones. Even then I would nod
off only when somebody forgot to take off the record. The
sound of the needle rocking back and forth, in and out on the
spiral, put me to sleep. Ah yes, happy days.'

It was no surprise to me that R.D. had enjoyed his infancy. It
came across in his songs.

The air-conditioning had started to clear the room, but there
was still a dark cloud of smoke floating above us.

R.D.'s face changed. When I say changed, it could have been only an eyebrow raised or a rounded smile turning into a curve of disapproval, but it had giant if subtle nuances. I mean, this was only a small look, but in less than the blink of an eye it had moved me to another world. It was as if a giant magnifying glass had been put up to his face and made it a thousand times larger: the tiniest emotion seemed like an earthquake.

R.D. became totally silent at this point. I could hardly hear him breathing. A small dark cloud, which had been hovering between us, took on a new shape. It rose slightly, then adjusted itself with a small motion. If it had eyes, it would have looked straight at me, inviting me over for a heavy discussion. I declined inwardly. It turned, almost smiling, as if to say, 'You, another day.' It moved in the direction of Raymond Douglas and placed itself over his head. Then, with almost erotic submissiveness, it surrendered itself and settled gently over his face, until it covered his entire head. The cloud was just a cloud, but it seemed to translate into an inner voice, both a message and a warning: 'He is mine.'

I was struck by a panic attack. I tried to shout but no sound came out. My heart beat hard and a searing pain shot across my chest. I thumped my chest with a rapid panic: a 'Come out! Come out!' motion. Eventually, a sound came forth: 'Speak. Say something. Don't die. Speak.'

'Sunlight. Trees. A woman's voice. A child in a pram. Me. Eyes look up. Sunlight.'

His voice became my voice, but it sounded like a small child's, a high-pitched and terrified monotone, like he was scrambling out a desperate message with his dying breath. Each word had a full stop, but there were whole pages between them.

'Sunlight.

Trees.

Woman's face.

A child in a pram.

Me.

Sunlight.'

This time it wasn't his voice. It was mine. Suddenly I was inside him, speaking his thoughts, seeing the world through his eyes, observing with his vision. My hand reached down to my crotch and I scratched myself. This was not a habit of mine, but it was obviously something R.D. had done over the years. Perhaps I would get used to it. I was in no position to argue at this point.

It was strange, but I had actually started to enjoy the uneasy pleasure of being inside him. I tried to breathe normally, but my chest was not functioning with its usual efficiency. My joints did not feel as supple as before and I suddenly felt these dull patches under my skin, as if my blood was not flowing properly. I was just getting used to this new experience when I realized that he, or in my present circumstance, I, was beginning to turn into yet another person. The dark cloud hovered closer and began to engulf me. Then darkness and a flash of light. At first I thought that a lightbulb had blown, but then I felt as if I had been electrocuted. My body shook and I started to scream like an animal in pain, caught in a deadly trap. Such a hideous yell that when I covered my ears with my hands, the sound already inside my skull echoed around until it oscillated into feedback. The words became a string that was being stretched to breaking point. Tense. Strangled. Longer with each shriek. Sunlight. My sister. She is so young. Stop the car! My sister. She is so young.

The sound became so intense that I started to shout in order to cancel out his voice. To no avail. His voice took over mine and they became one, in perfect synchronization, until my persona had completely surrendered to his will. I began to see the sounds as pictures: clear, high-definition, 70-millimetre Technicolor Sensurround images; some moving, some static, all from another man's past but all instantly recognizable to me. This time as I screamed for him I saw the images clearly. Sun, trees, woman's face, a child, me, my sister, she is so young.

'I saw the sun, trees and a woman, a child, which was me, all from a summer's day long ago. Again, these people seemed like strangers to me and yet I knew every one of them. Then the sky became dark and I found myself being thrown to the gutter. A car's headlights almost blinded me as I fell and rolled into its path. As the car ran over me, I found myself luckily placed in the centre, between the two sets of wheels. I felt the powerful engine as it roared inches away from my face, and was just marvelling at my escape when a piece of machinery struck my right arm and sent a dull thud down my side. The pain soon spread down my entire body. Then, as the car passed overhead, I felt a piece of metal tearing out my arm as it lifted my tiny body and dragged me along the road after it.

My inner movie cut to the tranquillity of the street. Sun. Trees. Woman. Me. Pram. I looked up at the woman, and as she smiled I saw what she was seeing. Down the tree-lined suburban street, I zoomed to my sister Peg: a beautiful sixteen-year-old with long blonde hair flowing across her face, and kissable red lips. Then down to the straight, padded shoulders on her post-war dress, beautiful breasts, slim waist and withered arm, a grotesque deformity poised claw-like and clutched beneath her right breast.

Peg of my heart; I'll take you home again, Kathleen. My poor sister, she is so young; all that was missing was the hump.

I admired the way Peg carried her disfigurement. Perhaps it was because she was confident about the rest of her looks, for she was indeed the most beautiful girl I had ever seen. Although her crippled arm was always apparent, even though she tried to conceal it, she was continually surrounded by good-looking young men eager to spend everything they had to wine, dine and win her favour.

This all happened before I was born and yet I was somehow born with her suffering smouldering inside me.

Another image. This time Peg was changing the nappy on a baby. I was confused, because although the baby was undeniably Peggy's, the infant with the beautifully chubby bottom was as black as the ace of spades, with tight black curly hair. Was this a witch's curse? Did black baby girls come as part of a package deal with a withered arm? I discovered that my kingdom was part of a larger empire that had colonies full of people whose skin came in various shades from brown to black. Peg had taken up with one of these black men who had come to my kingdom to find work, and, as a result, had become pregnant. Even though in England in the 1950s it was almost unheard of for a white family to bring up a black child, Peg decided to have the baby and take the inevitable consequences, which included ostracism by some 'friends' and neighbours. The father had fled back to Africa, but little black Jackie grew into a beautiful but strong-willed child, which was fortunate for her as she was to encounter hardships and prejudice as a result of being one of the first black children in the neighbourhood. Jackie could handle it though. She had the voodoo. Peg had a record by Billy Eckstine, a black American singer with a Jewish sounding name. The song was 'That Old Black Magic'. For a while my mother would not allow the record to be played in the house, because it reminded her of the man who dishonoured my sister, but sometimes when she was not there one of my sisters would put it on the gramophone and the house would throb with sexy and subversive lyrics.

Listening to that song, knowing my sister's circumstances, was my first insight into how a song could draw attention to the trials and tribulations of ordinary people.

For all I knew, my new niece Jackie could have been on this earth as a direct result of a pop song. Like Peggy, Jackie would survive. She had to. She grew, frizzy-haired and beautiful. The only black kid on the street.'

Suddenly my experience came to an abrupt end. I was not sure how or why I had experienced such a personal remembrance of another person, but I had. Raymond Douglas stopped talking and looked over towards the light. As his head turned, I saw the first thing that confirmed his identity to me: a long, thin scar running down the right side of his neck. I was just about to ask him where he got it when he pushed up a fader on the console in front of him and a sound resembling a sonic boom shook the whole room. Again, as if inside him, I experienced a jolting sensation, as if I were being thrown across time itself. I flinched, and as my eyelids flicked open and closed like the shutter in the camera, an image appeared on a screen in front of me and I saw myself running across another room. This time I found myself in the kitchen of R.D.'s mother. The adults tried to grab me but even as a four-year-old I was difficult to catch. Soon I had escaped from the main house and was running into the dark garden. R.D.'s voice became mine once again:

'What motivated this sudden burst for freedom? I don't know. It was either fear of something in the house or simple, blatant exhibitionism, an attempt to grab the spotlight from my newly born brother. The feeling of exhilaration as I dodged past the final outstretched adult hand was still with me as I fell. It was, for a split second, a truly magical feeling, like a sky-diver, fully horizontal, arms outstretched into the starry night. Then real stars as my face came to rest on a jagged rock. My nose and mouth seemed to disintegrate on impact. The next thing I remember is my Auntie Dollie holding me in her arms. I was crying, but my mouth was full of blood, broken teeth and snot, some of which had gone down my throat. My last images of this dramatic little scene were Auntie Dollie's finely chiselled face as she tried to pacify me, then, my infant brother lying in his pram, abandoned by the rest of the family who were trying to mop up my blood. This was my first victory over my newly arrived adversary sleeping in the cot by the kitchen table. All the pain I was suffering was inconsequential. I was once again the centre of attention.

After this triumph came a series of dentists picking and

chipping at my broken teeth. Countless injections of novocaine into my gums in a run-down surgery above a bicycle shop in the Holloway Road. There was no way of knowing how my second teeth would grow in, and the dentists said it would be best to defer any further treatment until they started to appear. My sinuses were damaged, and the doctors felt that they should also be left for nature to cure. As a result of that momentary lapse into exhibitionism I spent my early childhood waiting for signs of abnormality to show.'

As R.D. paused, I looked at my notepad. Everything had been written down in such detail that it was as if I had experienced it myself. R.D. looked exhausted.

'That's enough for one day. Now I must take my leave. Piss off, lad.'

I collected my belongings and left Raymond Douglas alone in his sad little control room.

That night I received a telephone call from Julie, the researcher from my office. She was full of questions about the interview. I was too ashamed to say that apart from a few sordid and somewhat dubious reminiscences about girlfriends and theories on homosexuality, I had in fact been able to scratch no deeper than most of the reports in the newspaper clippings that were in my briefcase. There was no way I was going to reveal my occasional jaunts into R.D.'s subconscious. She would have thought I was mad. Julie was professional enough not to pursue the issue and, after suggesting that I take her to dinner later that week, she wished me good luck and hung up.

I thought of seeing Julie on a purely social basis. We had met several times over coffee in the work canteen, but I had never had the confidence to ask her out. Now suddenly, out of the blue, I found myself being invited out by her. Julie was about 5 feet 6 inches tall; there was something about the way her long blonde hair framed her face that gave the impression she was more beautiful than she actually was. She was three years older than me and at twenty-two seemed to me to have experienced a great deal of life.

I took my sleeping pill and went to bed feeling that I had accomplished two great feats in one day: locating and starting my interviews with R.D., and being asked out by Julie. I closed my eyes and wondered what it would be like to kiss Julie on the lips, then to make love to her with the curtains open as R.D. had described making love to his old girlfriend. I felt the blood start to pump gently into my groin, but was too drowsy to take advantage of my erection. Then I thought of the dark cloud that had covered R.D.'s face. That must have been some cheap magician's trick he had picked up on tour. He had a reputation for theatrical pyrotechnics, after all.

Then I thought of Julie again and imagined her naked in bed next to me. As my head took that familiar chemical plunge into the depths of slumber my final thought was that even though I had just met him, R.D. had already started to corrupt me.

As I went under, for the first time I was grateful for the sleeping pills that prevented any form of dream world. Even so, just before I awoke I saw an image of a frightened crippled child being led into a building by a cruel nurse wearing a uniform so starched it emphasized her lack of emotion. I saw the child's parents following behind. The hospital was Victorian and the shabby, freezing-cold halls stank of urine and disinfectant and echoed with the cries of sick infants. The two parents sat quietly while the nurse held up the child's mutilated arm. The doctor looked on with sadistic pleasure as the child cried out with pain. The mother wept as the doctor informed her that the child's arm had to come off to prevent infection. The child's screams echoed around the cold, unsympathetic corridors as the doctor took out a large hacksaw to begin the amputation. The parents struggled with the doctor and eventually freed the child and ran out of the hospital.

I heard myself shouting: 'Peggy. My sister. She is so young.'

I woke up in a cold sweat. I had experienced somebody else's past'.

The following morning I walked towards R.D.'s studio like a zombie in a trance, but I had been taking sleeping pills for so long that I took their numbing effect for granted. On the other hand, Raymond Douglas was buzzing with energy. He picked up where he had left off the story of his childhood the day before.

'To be abnormal in my kingdom was a pitiless existence, for in the world of children there is no compassion for freakishness of any kind.

For example there was a man whom I used to see walking around the streets in the suburb of north London where I grew up. A little figure with his head bowed, his sad face forced to look at the ground by a crooked humped back that followed him as he shuffled along like an embarrassed hanger-on, trying to keep up with the world. Some children used to laugh as he walked by. Others were too afraid of him to laugh. He was not an ugly person, but to young and perfectly formed bodies, this wretched little soul was the ugliest creature on God's earth.

Imperfection is something children do not think about unless they are imperfect themselves. It is easy to ridicule the afflicted. They have no rights. Their thoughts and feelings are of no importance to an uncaring world. Pity is easy, but it is difficult to care. Like Peg. He knew his place, only his was lower because he was part of the legion of the world's cripples. Banished to the back row of society with the other outcasts; to learn the ways of the half-wits and child molesters. The sexual deviants, wife-beaters and other lepers. The cripple, if he wishes to function in the world, must accept this role without question. Stand in the back of the class with the other dunces and eat humble pie with the unemployed and the unemployable. As I was the centre of my own little world, I could not entertain the thought of being imperfect in any way. But as I watched the hump-backed man hobble down the high street, I said a silent prayer for myself, because something inside told me that I, the king, was at one with this unfortunate individual. At the age of ten I had been hurt in a soccer match, which resulted in severe pain in my lower back. My mother had taken me to the local doctor for a consultation. As I walked over to his desk I heard him ask about my family medical history, and whether my back problem might be hereditary. Then the doctor approached me, my mother cowered into a corner with her head bowed, and I stood still as the doctor walked around me. I played a guessing game: which part of me would he prod first? Dr Aubrey stood behind me and remained silent apart from the sound of his slow, asthmatic breaths. I stared at a large photograph of soldiers standing in a field during the Boer war where the doctor had served as a young man. Dr Aubrey had framed it and hung it on the wall. I felt his cold hands gently prodding my lower back, and I immediately thought of the hunchback, and how my world would be shattered if I was forced to trudge the streets with a hump on my back, like the little man. Surely kings cannot be cripples? I was contemplating my abdication speech when I remembered that Richard III had a hump, and even Ivan the Terrible was supposed to have had a bad back. The doctor's thumb pressed each vertebra as he worked his way up my spine. As he pressed he muttered the occasional words: 'Play soccer? Swim-lumbar-Harley-Street-specialist-X-rays.'

Before the doctor touched me I had been perfectly normal. I knew that if he had not pointed out the problem, then perhaps it would have gone away. Instead here I was, coming to terms with the fact that I was a cripple. As I left the surgery, Dr Aubrey looked at me over his bifocals and smiled, which made him look like Winston Churchill. He said to my mother, who was leading me out of the consulting room, 'Mrs Davies, that boy of yours will become a preacher. Believe me. I can not only tell a man's ailment, but also his occupation in his face and by the manner he walks into the room. Mark my words, that boy will become a preacher.'

A preacher, I thought. Perhaps, but still a cripple.

I started to think about how to cope with my deformity when it finally became visible to the world. Would I wake up one morning to discover a large lump on my shoulder? Would a magic walking stick arrive in the post and turn me into an instant cripple? Perhaps Harley Street would be the place where they would suddenly give me the hump. I was due to see a specialist; perhaps such debilitating growths had to be administered by a specialist. The old hunchback continued to walk around north London, as busy and self-contained as ever. I began to study him so that I could develop his techniques. Perhaps there would be side benefits, such as priority seating at football matches and on buses. I had often seen cripples get preferential treatment; pushed to the front of queues and so on. I decided that it would be far better if I were confined to a wheelchair, then there would be no 'ifs' and 'buts' about my disability. A plain, common-place hunchback looked almost normal compared to a wheelchair case, and the latter generated much more pity. If I was to be a freak, I would go all the way.

Now that I was resigned to my fate I found myself walking home more upright and confident. Each day I looked in the mirror to see if anything had appeared. Each day, to my disappointment, there was only pain, and no visible evidence. How annoying that I should be in pain and the world should see no evidence of what I had to endure. The whole situation was beginning to irritate me so much that I decided to take the matter into my own hands and accept that I was a cripple on the inside, so that I would be psychologically ready to accept the deformity when it eventually surfaced. I wanted physical evidence. A sign. Something for the world to see. An X-ray. But even an X-ray showed only the bones, the physical inside. The soul was not visible. The soul. The one part of a person that cannot be seen. Or touched.'

Raymond Douglas suddenly stopped talking. There followed a long silence, almost as if his brain had frozen over solid, leaving him in mid-sentence. For a moment I thought that because as a child of the sixties he may have done too much acid. It is well known that former addicts exhibit similar symptoms: they start on one subject, then, after a minute or so, move on to an event which occurred at a totally different time in their life. We had started at pre-birth; gone straight on to when he was four years old; and now we had suddenly jumped ahead to when he was ten. And all the while that black cloud still hovered. I knew that it was only a matter of time before it descended on one of us.

I said brightly, to lighten the atmosphere, 'How about a nice cup of tea?'

I knew he liked tea. His references to it over the years had elevated it to a level with bread and wine at Holy Communion. He had compared tea to the finest wine, had promoted it to the extent that its powers of healing rivalled that of any witch's brew. But the black cloud had descended again:

'Tea?' he answered weakly. 'I would, but the water's not fit to boil. There's no water for it.'

I tried to sound optimistic, but only succeeded in sounding like a nurse: 'Since the water is boiled up, it will taste grand.'

'No, the water has too much lead. And the tea bags are made in a factory. Nobody drinks real leaves anymore.' R.D. was starting to sound, and look, pathetic and old. But I knew it was a ruse. 'Well, I'm going to have a cup. You can have some if you like.'

What was I doing? Was I playing into his hands? I went to a little kitchen down the corridor, found some tea bags and brewed up some strong tea. Fortunately, there was an old Brown Betty teapot, which would add authenticity to the occasion.

I arrived back in the control room to find R.D. sitting in exactly the same position as when I had left. According to what I had read, this was one of his standard ploys: he deluded his companions into believing him to be so feeble that they would indulge his slightest whim. Then he would snap back, full of energy, and with a barrage of devastating vitriolic comments. It was at moments like these that he was at his most dangerous. He was more than just temperamental. He was a total energy vampire. Exhausting to be with, and yet with such mystique that it was impossible to leave: if his mood changed all the energy would come pouring back.

I sat down opposite him and set down two mugs. One of them was a souvenir made to commemorate the Coronation of Queen Elizabeth II. I diligently obeyed the ritual of the tea-making ceremony, knowing full well that any slip on my part would bring about the severest of reprimands before the final rejection and eventual dismissal. I poured the hot tea into the mugs, then added just enough milk to bring it to a rich, watery brown. I knew it was important to ensure that the milk was added while the tea was still moving around in a whirlpool. This would guarantee that the milk blended with the tea in a natural flow, rather than with the aid of a spoon. That would have been vulgar, according to Raymond Douglas' book. A slip in etiquette. Spoons are only used as a last resort. As he moved forward into the light, I noticed his eyebrow raised at my compliance with his tradition. I even detected a faint glimmer of approval in his eyes, and a slight pout of his lips. The old queen liked me. I was in.

He wrapped his hands around the Coronation mug and told me how, as a child, he had been allowed to watch Queen Elizabeth's Coronation on his sister's old black-and-white television.

'What a beautiful day it was, the coronation. A day off from school, flags waving from every house. Coronation. The word just epitomizes empire, Commonwealth, good winning over evil. The Queen's Coronation was very erotic: a country standing to attention like a mass erection. I possibly had the first hard-on of my life on Coronation day. It had something to do with all these old men in heavy cloaks, paying homage to this young, beautiful woman at Westminster Abbey. The sexiest part was when they surrounded the throne with screens so that the world could not see what was going on. Even good old Richard Dimbleby, who was doing the television commentary, spoke in a whisper, as if he was not supposed to be there. To me the whole idea of millions watching something forbidden and hidden from them struck me as being rather special. Historians may well prove me wrong, but the times one thirty or quarter past three spring to mind as being those of ultimate erotic anointment. I remember those times most vividly. The rest is just horses hooves clumping down Whitehall and little Union Jacks being waved by featureless blurs. Boring stuff on the black-and-white nine-inch TV screen.'

R.D. held the mug in his two hands, staring down into it. Once the tea had cooled to the right temperature, he slowly lifted it to his lips and took a long sip. It seemed to revive him, and even made him look younger. It also gave him strength enough to put up that formidable barrier between us. Before we were completely separated by this emotional wall, I decided to lunge in with my next question. But before I had the chance to speak, he answered:

'It is difficult to explain the way creative vampires work. There is no blood involved, no cloves of garlic nor crucifixes. It is hard to explain except through a fairy-story. Do you believe in fairy-stories?'

He did not wait for a reply.

'Then I will begin. Once upon a time there was a room in a house called the Front Room. It was so named because it was at the front of the house, by the street. It was reserved for special occasions: Christmas parties, wedding receptions, birthdays, christenings and funerals all took place in the front room. Important visitors were always shown into it. It was also the official sickroom when there was an illness serious enough to call a doctor to the house. The sick person was moved down from one of the upstairs bedrooms to the front room. Guests slept there. People laughed, cried there. My sisters courted their boyfriends in there. Every special time and occasion was celebrated in the front room. The first time that I, Raymond Douglas, saw David Russell, my baby brother, was in the front room just after he had been born. I was ushered in by a careful relative and told to remain silent. I peered around the bedpost and saw my mother holding this purple-faced, newly born brother in her arms.

I remember that first shock of being presented with a rival brother, but I learned to treat this person as a companion rather than an interloper. A few years later we played cowboys and Indians in the front room. From behind the armchairs that served as rocks in the American Wild West, I emerged as a cowboy after being attacked by an Apache Indian, invariably played by my long-suffering brother. I fell from the settee on to the floor and lay dead until my vicious murderer came to scalp me. As David Russell quietly came close to me with a rubber knife in his hand, ready to scalp his seemingly unconscious brother, I sprang to life and smashed him across the side of the face with the wooden handle of my toy shotgun. Tears flowed and I hid behind the full-length curtains by the front-room window while David Russell tearfully ran to Mum in the kitchen.

David Russell and I had become companions, but I had not completely forgiven my brother for invading my turf. And although Mum punished me for such violent behaviour, I knew that my sentence was always half as severe as it should have been, because I was the first boy in a family of girls.

However, I did not entirely escape punishment. I was punished by my own conscience. As I slept at night I had a recurring dream. My brother and I were playing on the edge of a cliff. David Russell slipped over the edge and I grabbed him as he fell. There we would stay, one brother literally holding the other's life in his hands. As the dream turned into a nightmare, I felt my sibling's hand slip from my grasp, and the pathetic cries from my falling brother caused me to wake, shouting and sweating. As I looked over at my brother sleeping peacefully in the next bed, I knew that I would always have to protect this interloper, even though I could never quite forgive him for spoiling my solitary but idyllic existence.

Later, the front room became the place where we learned to play music on the old family upright piano our parents had bought from Berry and Co. in the Holloway Road.

Our older sisters played all of their be-bop records on the radiogram in the bay by the window of the front room. Then, as the sisters grew, they put on records by Johnny Ray, Perry Como, Jo Stafford, Les Paul and Mary Ford, Kay Starr, Hank Williams, Slim Whitman, and did the latest dances with their most recent boyfriends. Everything from the tango to the creep, the smooch to boogie-woogie, jive to early rock and roll: Bill Haley and the Comets, Elvis and Little Richard, the Ted Heath Band, Chris Barber and Lonnie Donegan.

Later we brothers brought home records of our own early guitar heroes: Chet Atkins, Chuck Berry, Duane Eddy, James Burton (who played the solos on Ricky Nelson's records), Leadbelly, Big Bill Broonzy, Charlie Christian, Tal Farlow, Johnny and the Hurricanes, Les Paul again. All of them played on the radiogram in the front room. When we had our first rehearsals, they all took place in the front room. Sometimes, the neighbours from next door complained and on several occasions even called in the police.

Once David brought home a little 8-watt valve amplifier that he got in a secondhand shop. It became known as 'the green amp'. The green amp amplified our guitars at our early performances in local pubs, when both of us were barely teenagers. Later, with a friend from Coldfall estate, Pete Quaife, we played at a ballroom in Muswell Hill, all of us plugging into the green amp. The green box was not powerful enough for all three of us, the crowd couldn't hear, and the derisive boos and howls from the teddy boys and spivs at the Atheneum Ballroom, forced the manager to administer the 'theatrical hook', dragging us offstage while we were still playing 'Ghost Riders in the Sky'. The group was dragged off, but the green amp, attached by the umbilical cord of our guitars, continued to perform. Eventually even the green amp followed and departed the stage. (It was eventually to be replaced by a Watkins dominator, an amplifier of more volume, but less character.)

Back in the front room, partly out of the desire to sound as distorted as the fuzzy guitar on Memphis Tennessee and partly out of frustration with Mum and Dad's radiogram, which by now, due to excessive volume, had blown a valve, David took some of Mum's knitting needles and stuck them into the speakers of the little green amp. He christened it the fart box.

It's hard to describe that old front room. It had a magical quality. I felt that in some strange way God was always there, judging and giving guidance where necessary. I went to a Church School, but the closest I felt to God and religion was not in St James's Church, but in the front room.

It's equally hard to describe one's work. The motives behind it, the reasons and circumstances. So difficult now.

At school, particularly when I was ten or eleven, I was suffocated by the amount of normality that I was subjected to. I knew how to count, and yet they, the teachers, pushed all these complex forms of mathematics down my throat. I could read, but I wasn't allowed to read what I wanted. I was force-fed the school syllabus, and all because it was deemed to be the standard. The norm. I was not particularly bright in the sense that I could only absorb information that interested me. Anything else either put me to sleep or made me physically ill. And some old bastard had decided that children should be judged at the age of eleven so that they could be segregated for the rest of their lives. No consideration was given for talents outside the limited range required by the examining board. That would have enabled the normal thinkers to go to normal schools that would have sent them on to average universities where they would have received adequate diplomas before returning to normal society. Instead the misfits were destined to become factory fodder, farm workers or manual workers like my father, with no incentive to achieve or realize their potential. The segregation had nothing to do with intelligence. It was more where you lived, how active your parents were in the parent–teacher association, how you spoke, what you wanted to be, how you fitted in, how often you went to church.

I sat at my desk on the day of my Eleven Plus exam and looked at my paper. I felt that it was more than my intelligence that was being tested. It was my whole being, my philosophy, my feelings for the world, my family, my dreams, hopes and habits were all to be put up for grading by the Greater London Examining Board. I had to decide either to play the game their way, and succeed or fail according to their rules, or take my own route. I decided to settle my own fate. I signed my name at the top of the paper, and did nothing more for the rest of the exam. The room was silent, apart from the anxious scratching of pencils, and yet inside my head was a triumphant explosion, like the opening cannon shot of war. I had made my first statement to the world. But it was also like watching opportunity float away on a piece of paper down the river. It would damage me, but at the same time it was a victory. For the first time in my life I realized that it would be a battle between me and them.'

R.D.'s description of the Eleven Plus saddened me. My classless society had come too late for him. Wanting to know more about his schooling I asked if he had had a problem with numbers, but this only served to move him to another series of remembrances.

'Numbers and calculations, subtractions, divisions into the particles thereof. Thirteen. Seventh child added to a seventh child should logically equal fourteen, but in my case it was unlucky thirteen. Why is it two lucky numbers can add up to an unlucky one?

34

She stood by the door, my sister Rene. The eldest of my six
sisters. She was thirty years old and it was my thirteenth
birthday. Outside the window of my parents' house in London
N2, it was the day before midsummer. The sun was shining
but it put a hard glow around everything it touched. The trees
cast a cool shadow across the front door where Rene was
standing. She walked in and looked into the front room,
where I was sitting. Half in the room, half out. Dressed in her
smart topcoat, with her immaculate, permed fair hair covered
by a little hat. She looked so old.

Rene had married a Canadian soldier called Bob, who was
based in London at the end of the Second World War. Bob
was half American Indian and was given to bouts of heavy
drinking back in Oshawa, where they had gone to live. As a
result, Bob and Rene's marriage had fallen on to hard times.
Mum often received letters full of horror stories about
drinking, fighting and physical abuse. I was young and
unconcerned with who was right and who was wrong, but I
learned to anticipate the air of doom that descended on the
household every time those dreaded blue airmail letters arrived
from Canada.

Long before, when Rene was just a teenager herself, Dr
Aubrey had diagnosed a rheumatic heart. 'The child will not
live past thirty,' the doctor had whispered to my mother as
my unsuspecting sister left after the examination, but Rene
went on to dispel any doubts about her health and became a
fine athlete and artist. She was well on the way to becoming
an art teacher when she was swept off her feet by Bob just
after the war. They married and emigrated to Canada.

It was Rene who, when she came back to visit us, brought
the first Elvis Presley records I ever heard. 'Hound Dog',
'Don't be Cruel' and 'Heartbreak Hotel' were soon blasting
away all the syrupy big-band ballads, and it was Rene who,
while describing Elvis' performance on the *Ed Sullivan Show*,
first used the word 'sexy' to me. 'When that guy's hips

moved, the hairs on my back stood up so stiff I felt like a porcupine.' It was Rene who had held me up when I was born and shown my sisters my 'little pee-pee' and it was Rene, on an earlier visit to England, who first noticed the sadness in me. One night she crawled into my bed so that I would not be afraid of the dark and had promised to stay there until the sadness went away.

Now, on the last day of her life, she spoke softly and clearly to me, her sharp Canadian accent still dominant over her north London drone. Every word seemed to be uttered with breathless care.

'Thirteen, it's Rayday. A teenager. Do you know that today is your first day for growing up?'

Rene was on heavy medication, and because of this she sometimes spoke on different levels to the rest of us. This was nothing unusual. As she stood half in, half out of the front room, she proudly held out my birthday present: a brand new Spanish guitar.

'Now you can learn all those songs you hear on the gramophone and play them on your own guitar.'

'What about you,' I asked. 'Will you play them with me?'

I picked up the guitar and tuned it as best I could. Rene sat at the piano. She started to play a familiar show tune from *Oklahoma!* which suited her vamping piano style. It was typical 'play by ear', which nearly everybody in the family could emulate at the get-togethers at Christmas, weddings and any other excuse Dad could find for a party. The piano sounded a little out of tune and gave the high notes a screeching quality. I tried to accompany Rene, and she slowed down so that I could slot in with my limited technique. She finished and stared at the piano.

'That was good.'

She took a deep breath and got up from the piano. Then she walked over and gave me a kiss on the forehead.

'Don't be sad, Ray, and there's no reason to look so

unhappy. Practise your guitar and make sure they give that old piano a tune up.'

She walked out to the front gate where my mum had been standing for a while. I stood by the window but couldn't quite hear what was said. It was an exchange that seemed too private for anyone to hear. Very little was actually said, it was more like a slow-motion silent movie, but delicately acted, and with no need for subtitles. After a few minutes Rene walked up the road to the bus stop. Mum stood and stared up the suburban road long after Rene had disappeared. The image of my mother standing at the gate was still in my head when I heard of Rene's death the following morning. Rene had been ordered to stay in bed by the doctor. She had been told that if she had another attack, it would be fatal. Rene, who had always loved to dance, had made her mind up to go to a ballroom in the West End. It was my birthday and she had bought me a guitar, played the family piano for the last time and gone to the Lyceum Ballroom, where she had collapsed and died while the orchestra played a song from *Oklahoma!*

After Rene's funeral my mother called her husband all the foul names she could string together. Made all the accusations a woman in her situation usually makes. The poor man just sat in his chair and allowed my mother to slap his face. He could only say that for all his obvious faults, he loved his wife. It was then that I swore never to love anyone in a way that would hurt other people. I soon learned that getting hurt is part of being in love. I had seen Rene's husband drunk a lot, and violent. I saw my dad drunk a lot. I've been drunk a lot. I've been violent. Perhaps people are violent with the ones they love because there is a wound in them. A fragment of emotional shrapnel lodged in their hearts from the battleground of romance. It's not just like that corny old song, you always hurt the one you love. They hit the one they love and then they wail like a wounded animal, as if they were the one injured. Perhaps love twists itself inside out and sees itself distorted in a mirror. Then despises the reflection and wants to destroy itself.

We all have our own personal Satan, like we all have our own God. When he sees our love twisted, the little red man in all of us turns and smiles because he has become all-powerful. Truth becomes deceit, innocence turns to guilt.

At the drunken wake which followed Rene's funeral, and for many Christmases afterwards, I would cringe in fear and embarrassment as my family sang 'Goodnight Irene' and 'You Always Hurt the One You Love'. Even as a thirteen-year-old I could not bear to see adults reduced to this cheap show of emotion. On reflection, perhaps I was as moved as they were, but I forced myself to be ashamed because I could not tolerate love and grief being treated in such an ordinary way. They were singing popular pub songs to externalize their feelings of loss; I wanted to hear angels singing unearthly chords of unimaginable beauty. But all I heard was that pitiful singsong full of tears, beer and cigarette breath. An Auntie kissed me and spilled her Babycham. My father took a swig of beer as he slid down the wall and spilled the rest on the carpet. My mother sliced another sandwich and shouted who wanted mustard. Another Auntie's false teeth fell out as she hit the top note in the chorus of 'You Always Hurt the One You Love'. My sister was dead, her body turned into ashes and the only song they could sing was this. Perhaps this was all they had.

Throughout my childhood those songs we sang at family parties reflected our joys and tragedies: our romantic inhibitions unlocked by Mario Lanza singing a popular love ballad, our fears and anxieties calmed by a George Formby ditty; passions were aroused by songs made popular by Bing Crosby and the Andrews Sisters, Vera Lynn spoke for our lost love in 'We'll Meet Again'; Cab Calloway gave my father Fred a chance to step out for an imaginary rendezvous with 'Minnie the Moocher', while Nat King Cole soothed and calmed a troubled heart. Everyone in the family had their own theme song. Slim Whitman sang 'Rosie Marie' and 'Indian Love Call' for my eldest sister Rosie and her husband Arthur. Mum drooled over a record called 'St Teresa of the Roses' by somebody called Malcolm Vaughn, a sort of syrupy, opera-style ballad. Soon the family became hip to the more up-to-date pop songs (apart from Dad, who remained loyal to 'Minnie the Moocher'). We went through our performances in ritualistic sequence. Dave and I acted as DJs until it was time for us to pick our guitars and perform our party piece. Eventually it was Dad's turn, and he would stagger over to the piano and belt out a song. He was often so drunk that he would not so much sing the words as assume the attitude of the lyrics so that an impression of what they meant came across. Then he would trip over the carpet during his hoochie-coochie dance routine, thus bringing his performance to a premature end. He always went down a storm with the audience, even though we had seen it many times before. Then it was time for Mum's finale. Tears flowed from her eyes as she sang along to 'St Teresa of the Roses', and Dave added to her misery by turning the volume up full. Because of a distorted speaker, poor Malcolm Vaughn, who was quite an accomplished tenor, ended up sounding like Louis Armstrong.

The only part of Rene left that I could identify with were the Elvis Presley records and the guitar she had given me. I felt that if these were to remain a fixture in my world, then I would have to withdraw emotionally, leaving my body to live another existence.'

3

To help classify my disease

Raymond Douglas turned towards the control panel in the studio, pushed up a fader and 'Fancy', from his LP *Face to Face*, started playing. He clearly thought the lyrics to the song were appropriate to this particular phase of his life.

> Fancy, if you believe in what I believe in
> Then we will be the same. Always.
> No one can penetrate me.
> They only see what's in their own fancy. Always.

I thought these words were non-specific, and this just confused me further, although that may have been R.D.'s aim. Even so, I sat and listened. The song did have a whimsical charm. R.D. sensed the way I was feeling and, after turning the volume down, he began to speak over the music. I prepared myself for another of his maniacal rants: an inner darkness that he was inventing for my own rapidly increasing confusion and his pleasure. I was completely unprepared for what came next.

'I gradually withdrew from the real world. I sustained a severe kicking on my shins during a soccer match when I forgot to wear shin pads. The bruises went down, but I tried to toughen up my resistance to any further injuries by tapping away at my legs with a hammer I had found in my father's tool shed. The blue marks faded to yellow and I returned to the tool shed and tapped away again, until the blood came to the surface. I told my parents I had been hurt playing football, but one day my mother found me with the hammer. I said that I wanted to see what pain looked like instead of just feeling it. Thinking back now, it was, apart from being a reckless and

40

stupid act, a horrible attempt to manipulate my parents' emotions. My mother took me to see Dr Aubrey. He said that the bruises would soon heal, but after hearing me talk about my dissatisfaction with the world he realized something was troubling me deeply, and it was clear to him I needed special help.

It was obvious to all concerned that I had not been my usual self since Rene had died. People commented on how glum I looked. I rarely smiled, never laughed, and when I did manage to lift my eyes from the floor, I stared at people as if they didn't exist. This later became known as my silent period, and it culminated in my Uncle Frank referring to me as 'the miserable little bleeder with the long face'. Once Uncle Sonny, who worked on the railway, sat down and drew me a picture of a train. For some reason this made me laugh. Uncle Son was a kind man who couldn't draw to save his life, but his efforts both amused and touched me. But apart from this rare moment, my presence alone resulted in the most festive party turning solemn simply by my sitting in the corner looking downcast. A dark cloud appeared before me more and more frequently, and 'the miserable bleeder' was becoming a liability to family and friends alike. I was not the same happy child who in earlier years had stopped the show at family gatherings with my stirring rendition of 'Temptation'. My back ache had turned into a face ache, and when I told people about the pain they shrugged it off – because they couldn't see it.

Mum and Dad were referred to a counsellor in Crouch End who, being too overworked, had given me a brief interview which concluded with me being given some square pegs to fit into round holes. That was the extent of my evaluation.

Only my mother waited outside. She listened attentively as the child therapist reassured her that I was not going to be put into a straitjacket. Dad was too busy to come along. He had nothing particularly pressing to do, but the poor old boy couldn't face the possibility that his eldest son might be slightly odd. So he dismissed the whole thing as a load of balls. He could see nothing wrong with me. After all, I might have become a Spurs supporter, which to an Arsenal devotee like my dad meant automatic incarceration in the local asylum.

I had been brought up an Arsenal supporter like my father before me, but I had a secret admiration for Bobby Charlton, Duncan Edwards and the whole Manchester United team – the Busby Babes. However, the greatest captain in the land at this time was Danny Blanchflower, of the dreaded Tottenham Hotspurs, Arsenal's historic deadly rivals. Spurs' away kit was sometimes all-white, the same as the mighty Real Madrid wore. The Spanish champions were the greatest club side in the world. Dad wouldn't have minded me wearing a white polo-necked shirt if I were going to Jack Straw's Castle on Hampstead Heath to be around all the woofters, but if it meant I supported Tottenham, that would have been the final humiliation. He would probably have put me in Colney Hatch – the home for the emotionally disturbed.

But I still followed Arsenal as avidly as before, and every Saturday at five o'clock I ran to the paper shop to get the *Evening News* so that Dad could check his pools results. So in Dad's eyes there was nothing strange about me whatsoever. Mum, on the other hand, studied me while I rocked to and fro restlessly every time the television was on. She saw me cry for no apparent reason when I read the newspapers. (This happened even when Arsenal won.) She watched me stutter and try to drag out words when talking to schoolmates and relatives.

My 'problem' was discussed in the same shameful whispers as that of the 'queers' who hung around the toilets at the Quadrant bus terminal at the top of Muswell Hill. The same as the black couple from Kentish Town whose son smoked drugged cigarettes. The same as the middle-aged man with such an enormous penis that his wife was not able to satisfy him. (He was discovered by the milkman in the act of making love to a cow at the back of the Express Dairy next to the Ritz Cinema at the top of Muswell Hill.)

I had joined the ranks of these so-called weirdos, and even though it made me unsuitable for the conventional world, this uniqueness gave me a certain status among peers and adults alike. People spoke to me as if I were from another galaxy and did not fully understand the strange beings from Planet Earth. Kind and thoughtful relatives offered me extra pieces of cake and continually reassured me that everything would be all right. According to one frustrated teacher at William Grimshaw secondary modern, there must definitely be something wrong with me, because I felt so normal. It was just that my perception of the real world had changed. My loneliness was complete, and any comfort received from the outside was superficial only, because inside the safe world of my own invention, my soul could not be touched. And even though I was never told what was wrong with me, it didn't seem relevant. What mattered was that I was not like 'them', whoever 'they' were. Life had become a reproduction: it was not the real thing.

My parents were referred to a special children's clinic for educational therapy in Pembridge Villas, Notting Hill Gate. My unwillingness to communicate with others had given the assessors the idea that I was backward and could only communicate with Planet North 10 via a therapist.

Miss Blair was my counsellor at Pembridge Villas. She asked me to draw pictures. For some reason I always drew a lone figure carrying a small bag heading down a long stretch of road towards distant mountains.

'You've never seen real mountains, have you?' she asked.

'Only in my dreams,' I replied.

'What are your dreams?'

I remembered many of my dreams, but said I would not answer her. She had once told me some of her dreams, and indicated that she could help me solve my problems by interpreting mine. I told her my guitar would fulfil all my dreams for me. My sister Rene had said so. Miss Blair asked me how the guitar was going to achieve this, and I explained how versatile the guitar was; how it was my ambition to have an orchestra of guitars to interpret my dreams for me because my thoughts could not be put into words. Miss Blair sat back in her chair and studied me. She said that the guitar was not versatile enough to do this, but she would be interested to hear what ideas I had. It was almost as if she was daring me to communicate with her, but I would not be drawn so easily.

Miss Blair and I often sat and studied one another in silence. She was in her mid to late thirties. Dark hair hung over her shoulders in an unkempt sort of way. I was not sure then whether she was attractive or not, but as an adult I am sure she would have intrigued me. Perhaps I would even make a pass at her now.

We sat and played word association games. Sometimes she got a medicine ball and threw it at me just when I was responding to a word. Eventually I got wise to this and started to say nothing at all. She became frustrated and threatened to give me a short, sharp shock, to put me in a group where there were children with real mental disorders. Still I said nothing. One day, after a long silence, she jumped up and shouted that she had left an egg boiling on the stove and she had to go home to prevent a fire. I never saw her again. The next day I saw the principal, a wizened old lady, who said that there were many boys with my problem. I asked what my problem was, but the old lady just smiled and patted my hand. She never told me what was wrong. They never do, because they don't really know. Perhaps I was simply suffering from terminal normality.

The result of my twice-weekly visits to Pembridge Villas meant that I fell behind with my normal studies. This made me even more of a stranger to my schoolmates. I had a strange double identity: an average schoolboy one day, and a troubled misfit the next. Some catching up was easier than others. For example, I had no problems with sports and art. Even English studies were just within my grasp. Maths, a subject which did not come naturally to me, soon became totally beyond my comprehension.

My natural talent at art was encouraged by my art teacher, Mr Bond, who gave me extra tuition after school. This presented yet another problem to my friends, who were sports fanatics. Anyone carrying a paintbrush who was not an interior decorator was clearly a homosexual. Splashing around in a muddy bathtub with naked men at Finchley FC was one thing – it was manly and normal, even if some of the older men sometimes came out of the tub with hard-ons – but art lessons outside school hours implied that there was something unnatural going on. Once my mother arrived at around five o'clock, long after the other students had left, to find Mr Bond standing over me while I tried to mix colours. She ranted on and on in no uncertain terms: 'You have no bloody right to keep my boy behind after hours!' I explained that Mr Bond was merely trying to push me towards an A level certificate; there was no other motive. The following day Mr Bond, after complimenting me on my work, whispered that he thought my mother was 'a woman of outstanding character'.

I never asked my mother why she had interrupted what was clearly an innocent attempt on my teacher's part to push me through an exam, particularly as my school absences were making it perfectly clear that I would not stand an earthly chance of passing anything else.

At the same time, I had kept up my sports. The sports master, Mr Wardle, had seen me win a few races. When it came to representing the school in the relay, three runners and I were chosen: Griffin and Ebberson were both members of athletics clubs, and had special training; Stacey was another very fast runner. When we came to practise, Mr Wardle announced that Griffin would lead off, Stacey would run second, the tall, elegant Ebberson would be third, and, to my surprise, I was to be the anchor man. He said that he hadn't picked me to run the final leg because I was the fastest, but because he felt that if I was in front when I received the baton I would let no one pass me. Maybe he saw the hunger inside me. Whatever his motives, he knew I would not let him down.

On the day of the race we won convincingly, beating the best from all over the district. I was particularly proud as both my parents were there to cheer me on, and it was even more gratifying as they rarely attended events together any more.

Our team was just celebrating the victory when one of the other teams made an appeal, and the judges ordered the race re-run. We had won so convincingly – a full ten yards ahead of the next team – that out of bravado we decided to run dressed in our tracksuits, both as a protest at the judges' decision and to underline our confidence in our abilities.

The starter's gun went off a second time. I took up my position and soon felt the thumping of the on-coming runners. I quickly checked my red spikes to see if all the mud was cleaned off, and then heard, 'Run! Go now!' Quick flashes of colours from the shirts of the other runners, which I had not seen in the first race, indicated that we might not be in the lead and so I went. I thought of my parents; that they were there, how proud they were; then about the stupid tracksuit I was wearing, and what a complete prat I would look if we lost. I could see the finishing tape clearly; victory was in our grasp again. Then my foot hit a slight bump on the track. A dull pain went up my spine and down my legs. Somehow I kept running. A pain went through my chest and squeezed the muscles there. My body was telling me to stop but I kept running, and we finished first for the second time that day. The pain made it impossible to bend down and untie my shoelaces, so I pretended I was so proud of our victory that I wanted to wear my running gear for the rest of the day.

I concealed my injury well enough to be picked for the soccer team that winter, and to bowl in the cricket team the following summer.

The day before my A level painting exam I was practising my leg spin in the prefect's room, throwing an imaginary ball to another boy, who I thought held an imaginary bat. However this time the boy swung around brandishing a brand new Stuart Surridge cricket bat, and, as he was only feet from me, my right index finger crashed down on the end of the willow bat just as he was attempting an imaginary cover drive. I stared at the finger, which had been dislocated at the second joint, and for a moment it looked comical as it dangled back to front on the end of my hand. It was only when I realized what had happened that I fainted.

The following day I took the art exam with the first finger of my painting hand held rigid in a splint. Mr Bond came in to the room. He said nothing, but I knew he was furious with me. Afterwards he looked at my work and commented that while I would be able to run like a greyhound for a few years, my art would sustain me for the rest of my life – if I allowed it to.'

R.D. stopped talking and cleared a cough by thumping his chest a few times. He looked up at the small beam of reflected light. He grunted disapprovingly, then sighed.

'What's it like out there? Is the air still like soup?'

'It is,' I replied.

'I predicted this,' he muttered, 'in my *Preservation* Trilogy. Did you study it at school?'

I didn't have the heart to tell him that it was considered a minor subject.

'Of course,' I said.

'Classics, I suppose,' he growled.

The syllabus had hardly mentioned the Kinks.

I also couldn't let him realize how I knew so much about him, so I pretended my introduction to his work came as a result of finding a whole pile of gramophone records in my father's attic, alongside an assortment of *Penthouse* magazines and *Roy of the Rover* comics. R.D. didn't know I had not known my parents. I was becoming as cagey as the person I was interviewing. I was supposed to be the one doing the interrogation, but R.D. seemed to have such an insight into my character it was as if he had known me when I was young.

I continued, feeling embarrassed about what came out of my mouth: 'My father was a disciple as well as being a great admirer of your work, sir. He was a student and a fan.'

'A fan?'

'He saw you perform when there were live concerts.'

R.D. saw through my pitiful subterfuge. 'Don't patronize me, lad. You talk about so-called live concerts as if they died out centuries ago. Great Scott, lad, we're only talking about a decade or two! Anyway, nothing has really changed. There must still be illegal gatherings at so-called live entertainments.'

R.D. obviously wanted to comment on the state of modern pop music, but it was completely over my head. He suddenly changed the subject. 'Society hasn't changed that much. You call the children of the empire your brothers, but believe me there is still a social pecking order. A higher echelon still runs the country from a position of privilege. The only thing that has changed since I was your age is that then we were conned into believing that there was a future full of equal opportunities, when the class system broke down. Now everyone has reverted to type.

'The age of indifference parodied us on television and forced us to accept ourselves as stereotypes, to be manipulated by the corporations into being reduced to mere commodities. To see a product, buy it, then become it. That's when I decided I would never become part of that system. That's when I withdrew from public life.'

'But you continued to write in isolation.'

This brought forth a bellow which nearly shattered my eardrums.

'I have always written in isolation, you stupid little bastard!'

'Even in the sixties?' I answered politely. What a boring old fart the man was!

'Even in the sixties. I was never fooled by the "swinging sixties".'

'Why didn't you say something about society then, when you had the opportunity to be heard by millions?'

'I did for a while. Then I realized that I would have to stand with other so-called celebrities and turn my concern into a show-biz spectacular. I chose to be an outsider. These were concerts for the starving, charity records for the bereaved, sing in harmony for disaster and national mourning. It was fine for a while, until every catastrophe became a cue for some do-gooder entertainment figure to start a crusade for a worthy cause simply to prolong a career.'

I felt that R.D. genuinely believed what he was saying, even though he sounded bitter. I mentioned some of his work, and how humorous it was.

'They, the critics, would say "wry wit, sarcastic humour, tongue in cheek". All that sort of crap. I'm bitter. I always have been, and I've learned to accept it and be proud of it. The secret is to lighten the bitterness with a little humour.'

I could not believe this was Raymond Douglas Davies speaking, the man who had grown up in what was referred to as the era of optimism. He just sat there, bitter and sad, still writing letters and songs of protest about society, which had begun to treat him with disrespect and suspicion. I needed to get away from this topic and back to his schooldays. Even though he had told me most of the story, I felt something was missing.

I had heard his *Schoolboys in Disgrace* album from the mid-1970s. In it the headmaster, symbol of the establishment, sends his dis-graced schoolboy down the road to ruin after he has been humili-ated in front of the school, punished for a crime he didn't commit. Later, when the schoolboy resorts to crime to survive, the same establishment that put him on the downward spiral in the first place comes back to punish him in adulthood. This theme had been carried on into the *Preservation* section of the Trilogy, when the disgraced boy returns as the evil dictator Mr Flash. After a military coup the rebel armies, financed by the superpowers, invade, and Mr Flash is overthrown by his old schoolboy enemy, Mr Black. Again the establishment returns to haunt him.

It was clear to me that this theme had been important throughout Raymond Douglas' life, and in order to draw him out I told him about my own unhappy childhood, and my attempts to find an answer to the nightmares that had haunted me. How the Corporation had taken me in, educated me and even gave me employment.

I apologized to him for lying about the parents I had never known, but I explained that that was how I had imagined them to be. I was prepared for him to throw me out. I was starting to make my way to the door when the strangest thing happened. He stood up and walked straight into the beam of light. I saw his eyes for the first time; they were full of emotion.

'You poor kid. I think I understand. I would like to help you, if you will allow me. I have never really helped anybody in my life, and you seem as troubled as I was at your age. Perhaps this is my opportunity.

'How old are you? No – let me guess. You soon know when the person is the same age. You have experienced many of the same events, gone down the same road, fallen in love with the same movies, books and music. Without realizing it, we have paralleled each other's lives. It is nothing to do with the way we speak, the topic of conversation, or even how old we look. I am often amazed to discover how varied in age my contemporaries look, and how diverse their range of occupations are. You can spend years with a person and think that you have a bond with them: personal jokes, little knowing habits and gestures. Then, all of a sudden, somebody else arrives and the two of them start talking in front of you as if you never existed. They are not cutting you out deliberately, it's just that they have that magic connection because they're from the same generation.

'I feel no gap between you and me, although I'm old enough to be your father, or your grandfather, even. I somehow think that you are capable of grasping my whole theory about society, and that the *Preservation* Trilogy has obviously had a profound effect on you. I am touched that my writing has inspired you so. You have grasped that my music has never been for young people alone, because we are all young and old at the same time.'

R.D. sat me down in his chair. I felt honoured, but tired at the same time, and I was desperate to get home. Unfortunately, Raymond Douglas had a different idea. He obviously felt that he could at last confide in me.

'During my time at school in Pembridge Villas, it had been decided that it would be in everybody's interest if I moved out of my parents' house and stayed in Highgate with my eldest sister, Rosie, and her husband Arthur.

Arthur's brother Stuart had been a fighter pilot; he had died in the Second World War. Arthur kept a picture of him on the living-room wall, with poppies decorating the frame. Stuart, like Arthur, was handsome in the true 1950s matinée-idol tradition. It was as if they both had a sort of diffusion around their features. They both looked like film stars, which is probably why Rosie fell for Arthur. That and the uniform. The only uncomfortable part of Arthur was his tendency towards bitterness. His father had been a strict disciplinarian, and Arthur often told us how he and his brother were made to chew their food forty-two times before swallowing, a tradition Arthur tried to pass on to his son Terry and me. However, I was in a rather odd position, in that I was actually Arthur's brother-in-law, even though he was old enough to be my father. While my unfortunate nephew Terry had to eat his meal with his father silently counting, I could swallow my meat and potatoes whole. My rebellious eating habits often led to days of stomach pain and bouts of chronic constipation.

Terry and I slept in an upstairs room in Rosie's house in

Highgate Hill. I was so happy there that I found sleep to be a
terrible inconvenience. The world seemed too wonderful to
actually 'die' for all those hours. My life in Yeatman Road
was a mixture of the beautiful and the tragic. I watched Terry
while he slept, and I gazed in wonder as his beautiful half-
open mouth drew air in and out, emitting the faintest whistle
as his lungs blew it back into the universe. I admired his
perfect features, soft olive skin, silky chestnut eyebrows poised
just beneath a proud, long forehead; then a chopped, parted
fringe which unfortunately often resembled that of Adolf
Hitler.

By now my bowel problems had spread to the unfortunate
Terry who, encouraged by me, ate masses of chocolates and
starch-filled cakes in order to redress the imbalance caused by
Arthur's traditional table manners. Thus another rebellion was
born. Not against Arthur, because in a strange way I
understood him. My fear or dread was that one day I would
feel as unhappy and as unfulfilled as he did. His search for
another life seemed to me to be as futile as my wish to break
the four-minute mile or climb Mount Everest.

At that time Arthur's whole life seemed to be one of
overwhelming frustration and unhappiness. His brother Stuart
had, in many respects, done everything that Arthur had hoped
to do himself. Stuart had even died for his country. Arthur
had survived and he must have cringed as successive
governments squandered what was left of what Arthur's
generation called the 'Empire'. The world Stuart had died to
protect had turned its back on Arthur, making him seem a
tormented, empty person.

Poor Arthur was so tense, unrelaxed and so reliably
pessimistic, and yet Rosie loved him. Terry both feared and
loved him, as I did. It was difficult to understand then, but in
Arthur we saw our futures. As he walked out of the house
dressed in his waterproof mackintosh and his correctly
buttoned jacket, Arthur was a signpost to my own life and,

for a while, my muse. So were Terry and Rosie, eventually. With all of them I treasured the moments of merriment and optimism, on the occasions when Arthur forgot his all-consuming sadness.

On a late Sunday afternoon in winter I decided that I had to move further, fly the nest and visit the big bad world of the city. I walked across to St James's Church, which looks down above north London. I caught the 134 bus and sat upstairs, looking down as the bus took me into the West End. I got off at Leicester Square and walked through the narrow streets of Soho. This was my first solo venture – at the age of fifteen – into the dark, seedy world of sleaze.

I didn't realize it at the time, but that bus journey was my entrée into my adult life. I was on the road for the first time on a red 134 London Transport bus. Before this journey the bounds of my musical world had been marked out by watching Rodgers and Hammerstein musicals; listening to Country and Western music on the radio; hearing my sisters' be-bop records and early rock and roll; and family gatherings around the piano, singing popular hits of the time, and hits of my parents' youth, music-hall songs. This time I was out by myself, experiencing a new world, a dark world of neon lights and nightclubs, cafés, street-walkers, small-time underworld crime characters. I spoke to no one, I just walked and observed. My walks around Soho made some impression on my subconscious, and even began to influence the way I played the guitar. My attitudes towards the world changed at this impressionable age. Experience changes the way you think about chords and the notes you play. You bend the notes differently: I decided that I was an adult and I would leave school as soon as I could. I secured a job in the layout department of an engineering magazine in Rosebery Avenue, Holborn. I soon discovered that even though I had my own office, I was really nothing more than a glorified office boy. My lunch-breaks were usually spent walking around the Gray's

Inn Road, looking for a cheap restaurant where I could get a meal in exchange for the luncheon vouchers provided by my employers. I could have stayed and had lunch in the printing shop with the other workers, but they were all militant unionists, and spent their time playing cards and complaining about the firm, discussing how they could bring about the next confrontation with the management.

There was an old balding man who wore blue overalls and never did anything but play cards. They called him 'bastard', because that's all he ever called anybody else. He used to pick his nose a lot, and fart. Sometimes, when the supervisor came to check up, he pretended to clean the printing presses, but as soon as the super left, Bastard whispered under his breath, 'Bastard.' I suppose he was my introduction to the down-tools school of trade unionism. Bastard totally perverted the meaning of the word 'union', and the way he and his cronies took the piss out of me for working in my tea-break started to depress me. It got to the stage where I pretended not to work so that they wouldn't give me a hard time.

Every Thursday I went to the design and layout office in Threadneedle Street. The reason I had taken the job in the first place was to do some design and the advertisement in the *Evening Standard* had particularly mentioned 'opportunities for artistic youth'. Well, this was my chance to show that I was indeed youthful and very artistic. To my disappointment, I spent most of my time making tea. On the odd occasion when I was allowed to prove myself as an artist, the head of the department gave me lavatory paper to sketch on, so that if the work was sub-standard, they could always use the paper in the toilet. Even for an early school-leaver, I did not consider this experience was stretching my talents as a designer.

I left the magazine and, after a series of equally dead-end jobs, I decided that at fifteen I was still young enough to go back to school.

The brief period away from school had left me considerably
behind the others, but I still kept up with all my sporting
activities. This time I entered the district school boxing
championships. I won my preliminary bouts, but in the final I
was unfortunate to find myself matched against Ronnie Brooks
from Stroud Green. I was a reasonable boxer, but young
Brooks was the reigning school boxing champion of Great
Britain. I was undeterred, and took extra lessons in the art of
counter-punching from my brother-in-law Joe, who had been
a fighter of some repute in his day. I hyped myself up into
thinking that I might win, but sadly, on the night of the fight,
Brooks tore through my defences, and though I managed to
land several hard blows to his already battered face, the referee
intervened to prevent what little brain I had from being
spilled all over the floor. My head ached for days afterwards,
and I had nightmares about those flashing white lights that
had appeared every time Ronnie had hit me. I began to
associate those flashing lights with defeat, and I was determined
to avoid defeat in the future. I felt like a leader but I was not a
winner yet. But it was the sort of luck I had – I couldn't just
fight anybody. It had to be the schools champion of Great
Britain and Northern Ireland.'

R.D.'s account of his continual fight against injuries, combined
with his need to achieve a victory of some description, resounded
inside me, bringing fresh concerns about my own confused adoles-
cence. But I was beginning to treat most of what R.D. said with
cautious scepticism; particularly the shin-tapping incident.

I did understand his somewhat distorted reasoning for wanting
to see pain on the outside as well as just feeling it inside. Nevertheless, I was not sure whether to believe him or not. It was obvious
that he felt he had been wounded by the world, but was he
covering up the real cause for this period of emotional imbalance?

That night I tried to read some old clippings to find a clue of
some sort; I even browsed through the other biographies about the

Kinks, but in the end I threw them aside and went back to the music. I played *Lola Versus Powerman* and *The Money-go-round*. Also 'Wish I Could Fly Like Superman', an American hit from the early 1980s. It was clear that R.D. was at war with some altar ego whom he felt was trying to suppress him all his life and, as well as conducting his normal life, he was at the same time having an inner struggle with this mysterious dark figure who was always looming in his subconscious, looking for an opportunity to knock him from his pedestal. There was a track on *Lola* called 'The Contender'. The lyrics alluded to life being like a boxing match. R.D.'s inner life was both like a battlefield and a bizarre pantomime at the same time. I somehow managed to appreciate the way he felt, even though he was trying to baffle me whenever possible. At times he really was funny – a cross between an old queen and a vaudeville clown.

That night my dreams were vivid and terrifying. I was on an operating table being tormented by a large dark figure. I was flat on my back and could see a reflection of a person, probably me. Every time the dark figure tore pieces of skin from my body, I could see the helpless reflection cry out with pain, but because I was numb I could not respond in the same way. The more I resisted, the more the reflection cried out in agony. Even though I tried to scream, knowing that was the only way to stop pain being inflicted on him, it was impossible for me to make a sound. It was as if I were the equivalent of R.D.'s inner pain, and the reflection in the mirror was what must have been going on inside him. As I woke, I felt a pain shoot up the side of my face. I crawled across the room and looked in the mirror. I saw that I had a cut lip and a bruise on my cheek.

When I arrived at his studio later that day, I continued to ask R.D. about his schooldays: I felt I was on to something. I was hoping he would let it slip out because, even though his childhood had been unhappy, he could not resist talking about it. He picked up where he had left off.

'For some reason the four houses at William Grimshaw secondary modern were all named after scientists, inventors and a writer: Stephenson, Faraday, Kipling and, lastly, my own house, Harvey. At the last house meeting of my secondary-school career I was, surprisingly, voted in as both house and sports captain. This was, according to Mr Lill, my housemaster and maths teacher, a unique honour. He made a short congratulatory speech, saying that he hoped that my new obligations would not interfere with my chronic absenteeism and out-of-school activities. The laughter soon turned to applause and cheers. As it subsided, I assured him that I could find time for both.

It was only when I ran on to the soccer pitch as the new captain of Harvey that I realized it was possibly a put-up job. While most of the members of Harvey were capable scholars, the sporting element consisted mainly of fatties and hideously unathletic stick-insects. It was difficult to muster eleven boys who could walk properly, let alone form a soccer team.

And then, while captaining Harvey house against Faraday, my leadership abilities received a further blow when I was almost reduced to a hobbling cripple. I went up for a high ball which came over from a corner kick and was immediately pushed to the ground by two large Faraday defenders. As I fell, my lower back struck the base of a goalpost, which in those days was square. The pain numbed my entire system as my old injury was aggravated, which resulted in me being carried from the field. I was determined not to let the team down, however, and I scrambled to my feet and managed to finish the game.

The pain in my back lasted for weeks, but I was afraid to tell anyone in case it meant I would have to give up my position as house captain. Eventually, though, I had to see a doctor. I soon found myself sitting outside the specialist's room at the Middlesex Hospital, dressed only in a flimsy gown tied behind me, waiting while the specialist showed my

X-rays to his students. I was both the centre of attention and
the side-show. The door opened and I was summoned into a
large hall full of young students and doctors. I was asked by
the specialist to touch my toes. When I found this difficult he
stood squarely in front of me, took hold of my shoulders, then
asked me to bend from side to side as far as I could. I was
obviously in pain.

He asked whether I enjoyed sports. I announced proudly
for all to hear that I hoped one day to play for England. The
specialist walked over, smiling as he spoke, 'You'll never be
able to play sports again, my lad. Just look after your health
and be thankful you can still walk. If you'd been in a car
crash, it would have been called a broken back.' When I asked
what had caused my sudden disability, he merely waved his
hand and said I had a bad back. Bad back? I had just been told
by this pompous old toad I was a cripple!

As soon as the pain of my immediate injury made it
possible for me to look convincing on the field, I persevered
with my sporting endeavours. One thing was certain; where I
could, whenever I could, I needed to win.'

At this point I broke in and interrupted R.D. 'Why was winning
so important to you? Your music gives me the impression that you
were not in competition with anyone else – that's what gives it its
uniqueness.'

R.D. nodded. 'I was younger, and I was inspired by the chase,
the conquest. Good against evil. It helped me through my own
difficult childhood, where I needed a role model to help me
through my insecurities. In order to guard my self-confidence and
keep some self-esteem I had to win at something.'

He drew back, and returned to the facts.

'My next big race was against Griffin, whom I had run the relay
race with earlier. I was going to have to pull off something
spectacular in order to beat him. I had watched the 1960

summer Olympics on television as Herb Elliott smashed the
1,500 metre record. Because I was a sprinter, my attention was
also drawn to the 100-metre dash and a German runner called
Armin Hary. I had watched Armin Hary 'beat the gun' –
basically, an incredible reflex action to the sound of the starter's
gun. He appeared to stand almost upright on his blocks waiting
for the start. All the other athletes had a traditional slow rise
for the first six or seven strides, but Hary was up and running
before them. I was encouraged by this, as the slow rise was
difficult for me with my back problems. I badgered my
parents to buy me a pair of white lightweight Adidas spikes,
the same as Hary wore. That summer, with my white spikes
and faster, more upright start, I defeated Griffin in both the
100 and 220 yard sprints. In the longer race I felt him catching
up to me in the final few yards and I threw myself at the tape
to win by a few feet.

Dave ran over and said what a great victory it was. He
knew how important it was for me to leave school a winner.
Griffin came over and shook my hand, and as he spoke I
realized that the poor fellow had the most debilitating stutter.

There were two more sporting events before I left school,
the first the district inter-school sports, which included
grammar schools, as well as secondary moderns. These meets
were always extremely competitive, as grammar-school kids
were considered superior in every way: they were the bright
ones who had passed the Eleven Plus exams. I was established
as champion in both 100 and 220 yards, but I nearly lost the
220 before I ever ran it. A friend told me that another school
had a runner named Brander who was half a second faster
than me. The thought came into my head: 'I may not win
this!'

The following day I watched Brander as he limbered up
and got down into the classic crouch start. I settled into my
normal upright start position, then at the last minute decided
maybe I should assume the classic crouch position. As the

starter shouted 'Get set' I lowered myself, wanting to run in the most orthodox manner possible. As soon as the pistol went, I realized this was a grave mistake. A shooting pain went across my back, but I forced myself on. I watched Brander tear away in the outside lane. He seemed miles away. But once I was upright it was obvious that I had beaten myself by breaking my own individual style. As we entered the final fifty I started to catch him, and finished just a stride behind him. He shook hands with me with a tremendous look of relief on his face. He had obviously heard about me, and for all I know someone had told him I was half a second faster than him. In any event, I had mentally brought about my own defeat; I had tried to be orthodox, just like everybody else.

By the time we had won the 4 x 100 relay, the pain in my back was so extreme that once again I could not bend down to take off my spikes. A girl whom I had a slight crush on at the time but had never dared to speak to came over and asked if I needed help. As she untied my laces, she looked up and whispered that, even though my face was not up to much, the girls had voted me the boy with the best arse in the school.'

'What was the girl's name?' I inquired.

R.D. scratched his chin and looked up at the skylight. 'Julie,' he said, 'Julie Finkle.'

I laughed out loud. 'Julie Finkle. That must be a joke name. Nobody was ever called Julie Finkle. Not in Muswell Hill, anyway.'

R.D. looked over at me, spread out his arms and shrugged his shoulders, like a spiv trying to sell a stolen car. 'I kid you not, old son. Trust me. It was Julie Finkle.'

R.D. leaned back and continued his tale.

'Two days before I left school for good, there was one last meet. I wanted revenge. I used my normal starting stance – and I also had the knowledge that I was the boy with the 'best arse' in the school. With my small female fan club, I won the 100 and the 200 yard dash. Then the meeting was to be decided by the 4 × 110 yard relay. Plaistow Grammar, our rivals, had a fine team, but as I was handed the baton I could already see the kids spilling on to the track near the finishing line. Mr Wardle's assessment had been astute: once I was in front no one could catch me.

I breasted the tape and threw the baton in the air. Mr Lill, the maths teacher, tried to bring me down to earth by pointing out that if I had given the same commitment to my academic work, I would have gone to a grammar school and been running for the other side. I replied that if I had gone to a grammar school, possibly I would not have had such a will to win.'

The will to win. The phrase kept going through my head as I walked home after another day with R.D. I was wasted, but the sound of R.D.'s voice talking about the will to win echoed in my head. And that mystery girl, Julie whatever her name was. Could she have been the Julie in 'Waterloo Sunset'? It's often said that first love can have the most impact on a person's life.

I started to think about my own life. About sex, even. About the researcher at the office with that name, Julie.

I phoned her and got her answering-machine. Her voice sounded husky and dark, in total contrast to the way she looked. I telephoned several times just to receive the message before leaving a message of my own: 'I want to know everything about the *Preservation* albums. See all the clippings and reviews. Find out about a school for disturbed children in Pembridge Villas, Westbourne Grove. Look up the records at the old Middlesex Hospital and track down X-rays of R.D.'s back. I'd like anything at all you can find out about a girl called Julie Finkle.'

I sat in a hot bath. Afterwards I put on *Face to Face* and listened to 'Fancy'. I took a pill. Went to bed. I slept, but did not dream.

The next day I stopped off at my office to see the editor-in-chief, but he was out. His secretary, a large blonde Amazon of a woman with a thick Australian accent, told me that my project had been pushed forward and the Corporation wanted me to hand in my work at the end of every week. Damn. I hadn't actually started to put any of the pieces together yet, and already I was being hassled.

I arrived at my rendezvous with Raymond Douglas to find him more perky than usual. The old chap was evidently enjoying the collaboration so much that he had even put some of his life on cassette for me to play while he went to make the tea.

I pressed the start button and found that he had resumed where he had left off the night before.

I had been living at Rosie and Arthur's house in Highgate, where Rosie had an old Grundig tape-recorder, and it was on that tape-recorder that my earliest attempts at song-writing were documented. There was an instrumental called 'So Tired', written in finger-picking Country-Western style, which conjured up southern plantation songs with images of black slaves toiling away in the cotton fields. There was also a two-chord shuffle with the same phrase repeating over and over. This turned out to be my first stab at writing 'You Really Got Me'.

Later on, back at my parents' house, I sat down in the front room one day and started to write a song on the old upright. I thumped out these crude fifths with my left hand, and Little Richard-style eighth note chops with my right. I thought of a melody to go with the phrase I'd come up with at Rosie's house: 'Yeah, you really got me going, you got me so I don't know what I'm doing.'

Then I called Dave in from the kitchen where he was having dinner with the rest of the family, and he picked up his guitar and plugged into the green amp. He started playing along with the riff I was punching out with my left hand. As the amp warmed up I heard that wonderful distorted sound. It was a perfect representation of my anger, and yet beautiful at the same time.

As I taught Dave the song some of our sisters came in to listen. Peg sat on the settee next to her daughter Jackie, Mum hovered by the door, half afraid the neighbours would call the police again. When we got through the song for the first time, our small audience applauded.

I had written 'You Really Got Me', and it had happened in the front room because all important things happened there. All the family parties and singsongs had contributed in some mysterious way. It was as if the idea had been in the air.

I took the entrance exam at Hornsey Art College and passed with no difficulty. It was simple enough to get a grant from the local education authority, mainly because my father had been ill, and unemployed for a while. Partly because I had talent. Partly because working-class kids were now being given a chance to prove themselves.

I went to college and became absorbed in the social life there. This consisted of parties, pubs, dances and excursions to museums and art galleries, on the pretext of furthering our artistic studies. These days out were usually spent in cafeterias and pubs, trying to chat up girls and being given the cold shoulder. On nights off, I trained twice a week at the local soccer club, where I played as an outside right. On weekends I took a course at a theatre school and covered all the basics, including improvisation, fencing and what can only be described as mind projection.

I was told by my tutor to stand at the top of Crouch End Hill and project my mind down to the bottom by the traffic lights and focus on some unsuspecting passer-by in order to 'will' the subject to turn around. I tried for a couple of days and eventually somebody responded. I am not sure whether or not it was because his will had submitted to mine or whether he had his own reasons for turning. Perhaps he wanted to see if that nutter was still at the top of the hill. What mattered was that I believed that I had done it. I had only been with the theatre company for a brief time, and yet I had already grasped the fundamentals of acting. Fundamentally, I couldn't.

By this time my sister Peg had married an Irishman named Mike Picker. He had come over to England, joined the British Army and fought in Korea. But because he was from the Republic, he was considered by my parents to be a foreigner, and was treated with suspicion. Mike gave me access to learning about the technique of guitar playing. He also introduced me to classical guitar music through jam sessions at his small flat in Muswell Hill. Mike and I listened to records, usually Buddy Holly and early pop and blues. He concentrated on the guitar solos and I imitated the vocals, which Mike then recorded. Mike and I were fond of Country players like Merle Haggard and Chet Atkins. Hank Williams became my favourite combination of singing and playing. His songs had a crying quality to them that seemed to sum up some of my own darker doubts about the world. I had never experienced what it was like to have a 'Cheating Heart', but I was certainly a 'Lonesome Cowboy'.

Mike, who as a guitarist was far superior to me, went to classical guitar lessons with Louis Gallo, a teacher in Finsbury Park. What was learned there was then passed on to me by Mike, who played with me the duets he had been taught by Gallo. This hand-me-down style of learning was probably the best way for me to be taught. At school I had always rejected any direct tuition. I improvised: my method of spelling sometimes led to rather inventive variations on the English language. The same applied to music. If I didn't know how to play a certain phrase, or I didn't understand the way it was written, I invented my own way of performing so that I could fudge my way through the piece. This was not considered acceptable in the days when 'real' musicians sat down in front of a sheet of music and played exactly what was written. I had attempted piano lessons some years earlier, with a local retired army major who had taught my sister Gwen. He said that I had piano player's hands. Unfortunately, the major passed away after only a few lessons, so Mike took over, and my player's hands gave me a fast finger-picking style.

I went back home and sang duets with my brother Dave. We played Hank Williams' records and tried to learn the harmonies. We didn't know – or care – that they were simple two-part harmonies, we just wanted to get the emotion in Hank's passionate performance across.

One Saturday afternoon I was waiting for Mike to come back from work so that I could have another guitar lesson. It was a beautiful, sunny, crisp summer day. Peg and Mike's flat was in the attic, so I could see out over the semis and their gardens. It was then I had my first taste of anything resembling a sexual encounter. A woman was sunbathing naked on her roof. She must have known that people could see her, but she didn't seem to care. It wasn't that she was naked, it wasn't that she was beautiful, it was the fact that she obviously didn't care. That was the first time I was even remotely 'turned on', and it was not by what I had seen, but rather by what I felt due to a complete lack of inhibition on the woman's part. From that day on I tried to organize my lessons with Mike so that I could coordinate them with my rooftop goddess. And when the weather was fine, sure enough, she was there.

After a while, she realized I was there, glimpsing her from the little attic window. She knew that I could see her – that was even more thrilling to me. And in some way my musical activities became more sensual as a result. My little guitar exercises became infused with eroticism. The book I was working on was by Ferdinando Carulli, and his music, combined with the vision of my bare beauty, turned the exercises into something I'd never before encountered. Music had suddenly taken on an extra meaning for me. Subsequently, when Mike and I imitated a Buddy Holly song – for example,

'Every Day', 'Rave On', 'Oh Boy' — I sang not just to imitate the record, but to my secret audience. In my mind, I was singing to that woman across the rooftops.'

The tape came to an abrupt halt just as I was getting interested in
R.D.'s revelations about his early sex life. The door opened and the
old rocker walked into the room carrying two mugs of piping hot tea.

'I hope the tape was to your satisfaction,' he said in a slightly
evil way.

'It was quite interesting.'

'Crap, really. I was just filling you in with some basic fodder.'

'No, really, it was very interesting.' I was becoming a good liar.

'You're not a very good liar, son. Still, never mind. You'll
improve with experience. I did.'

I tried to change the subject. I was not going to let him think
that he had the ability to tell when I was lying or not.

'What about Peg's illegitimate daughter? Where did she live?'

'With my mother and father. Poor Jackie. She was a pretty
kid, but she had to put up with all those jibes from the
kids at school. Even the other kids in our family called her
Blackie-Jackie. Her cousins Phil and Irene used to mock her
openly about her colour, and asked in all innocence if her
father lived in the jungle. Mum would scold them and give
Jackie a big hug, but it was obvious that the child was
deeply hurt. I think it was hard enough for Mike to be
accepted, being Irish and all that. To expect him to take in
Peg's illegitimate black daughter was too much. You forget
that this was the late fifties. There were very few black
families in north London. Mike tried to accept Jackie, but
he and Peg fought a lot, and then the subject of black men
often came up. One of the first songs I wrote was a little
ditty to sing to Jackie whenever she felt sad.

67

One day I arrived for my guitar session with Mike to discover that Peg had decided to leave him. She couldn't carry all her belongings because of her bad arm, so I had to help her carry her suitcase up Muswell Hill towards Mum's house. Tears were pouring down Peg's face. She suddenly stopped dead in her tracks and looked at her arm.

'Raymond, I'm a cripple.' It was as if she had only just realized the fact. 'Mike. I can't leave him.'

We immediately turned around and headed straight back to the flat where Mike was waiting. It wasn't until she was without Mike that Peg realized that she had a crippled arm. You see, loving someone and the knowledge that you are loved in return makes you forget all the faults and hang-ups you might have about yourself. Anyway, I was happy because it meant that I could resume my guitar lessons with Mike. And savour the shabby rooftop decadence of the nudist of Onslow Gardens, N10.

I was sitting in Peg and Mike's living room watching television one night, and a programme came on which showed clips of films from all over the world. The show was introduced by a film-maker called John Grierson, who had apparently invented the term 'documentary'. I saw a film clip of the black folksinger Bill Broonzy playing in a jazz club. There was also a clip from *The Seven Samurai* by Akira Kurosawa, and another from a documentary by Robert Flaherty called *Men of Aran*. Suddenly I was not just being entertained, I was being educated and artistically motivated by the images I saw on the screen.

The following week I took an afternoon off and got on a bus which took me to the Classic Cinema at Hendon Central, where *The Seven Samurai* was showing. I was stunned by everything: the photography, the acting, the story, the heroism. The whole film was such a complete work of art that it rivalled any picture I had seen by Rembrandt or Van Gogh.

Its power stirred emotions in me which even rivalled the
feeling I had when I stood on the north bank at Highbury
with my father and saw Arsenal score a goal. These samurai
heroes were as real to me as Roger Byrne, Duncan Edwards
and Bobby Charlton of Manchester United. As inspiring as
Herb Elliott or Armin Hary. The film led me on to discover
other film-makers: Polanski, Truffaut, Fellini and Bergman. Bill
Broonzy became my new musical hero.

This was a different kind of art to the one I was being
taught at school. The next project I embarked on was a study of
the Russian film-maker, Eisenstein. My notebooks were full
of thumbnail sketches of faces and camera angles in the style
of Eisenstein rather than studies in the style of John Bratby,
Mondrian or Piero della Francesca. This annoyed many of
my tutors and caused a certain amount of derision from other
pupils, except one film buff by the name of Paul O'Dell. He
accompanied me to art-house cinemas, in Oxford Street and
Soho, and we also started making little 8-millimetre features
together. Paul, or Poddle as I called him, had to be the director,
because he owned the camera and could afford the film stock.
I helped work out directorial moves and contributed to
storylines, but my role was as collaborator and occasional
actor, but it was still worth while; we were actually putting
images that came from our own imagination on to film.
Anything else at art school seemed dull in comparison.'

Raymond Douglas was sitting bolt upright as he told me about his
love of film. I broke in and asked R.D. what he thought about art
and the attitudes of the other pupils at college with him in the
early sixties. This turned out to be a big mistake. The pantomime
Cockney took the stage. Overture and beginners, please. The
house lights dimmed and the performance began. I imagined a
pub-style piano to accompany R.D.'s monologue.

'Artists, whatever their abilities, for the most part, are

unreliable, randy buggers. That's what I remember from art
school, anyway. And they are for the most part tit men.
Particularly if they are drinkists. They pillage ideas from the
world. They seduce unfortunate souls into becoming matter
with which to mould their corrupt talent on to a canvas, into
a play or a book, or into a song. Show me a great artist and I
will show you a conveyor-belt of deceit, seduction and
debauchery in the quest of the so-called perfect artistic item.
Artists are mean, perverse and wretched examples of humanity
and yet, as one gazes in awe-struck humility at the Sistine
Chapel, it is easy to forget the self-righteous hypocrisy and
religious deception which commissioned it and enabled the
artist to turn his poor unsuspecting muse into a work of, for
and in the name of almighty God.

And I understand that Bach heave-hoed his missus with
such regularity that an abundance of little Bachs were
unleashed upon an unsuspecting planet that was already
'fugued out' by Johann's over-active left hand. Ah, but what
bass notes . . .

So, there was I, Raymond Douglas, the seventh child of a
seventh child discovering that art for art's sake was not up my
street. Film, my next love to sport, was rapidly taking over as a
genuine creative option, but access to film study was somewhat
restricted at Hornsey. Then there was music. Song-writing not
only gave me an emotional outlet but might even be a means of
earning a living. There was just one thing missing: how did a
wretched art student living off a Middlesex grant in a suburb of
north London find himself a fucking muse? I adored soccer,
music and art. But somehow they all got confused. If my
creativity had to rely on a winged messenger carrying divine
inspiration to me across the mighty universe to my house in
north London, he would have found my loyalties so muddled
up that he would have probably had me playing outside-right
for Manchester United carrying a sketch pad and a set of oil
paints.

The main problem was that I was not content to create just for myself. I had to do it for somebody. An audience. A Julie Finkle. I could draw my family and friends and turn them into characters that were not their own. Change their names and put different clothes on them. This was easy. But what and where and how would these people figure in music? Songs until now had been an outlet for my own confused sexuality and confinement in the society in which I lived. These songs were a hobby, a way of passing the time, and yet the songs appeared as if they were a lightning-rod from the Gods, yes, Gods, the entities that floated around in the universe, gave life to animals and created the planet Earth. Sent the spark of humanity down the slopes of Mount Sinai to Moses and gave him the Ten Commandments. The God who made thunder and earthquakes, and made mortals cringe in fear. The Gods that would take as well as give, being merciless as well as kind. I, who at first was born a king, then became a humble working man, had seen through the inconsequential role-playing of the world and the unfortunate misplacement of my existence, this light of hope, and it shone beyond my earthly presence. This wonderful, merciful light was lifting, albeit momentarily, the dark cloud which constantly surrounded me. It had, in an instant, transformed me. I had tried to paint after Michelangelo, Modigliani, John Bratby and Cézanne, but now I was writing a song, and it was from my own experience, my own enlightenment. It was a bad, bad ballad, but it was totally my invention. It was fucking brilliantly bad and all my own work. I had found my muse. Inside. And now all I had to do was to create a monster for myself. I, who was born a king, was not cut out to be a tea-boy or messenger. I laughed when my mother showed me an advertisement for a sign-writer in the *Evening Standard*. From now on, I would be writing my own signs. That night, I saw the stars for the first time and wrote poems and lyrics until the cold morning air made my lips freeze.

The gods had pulled away a veil and exposed their universe, and my stationary body moved through the galaxy faster than Yuri Gagarin.'

The imaginary honky-tonk piano accompaniment ended suddenly with a gigantic Wagnerian chord. Raymond Douglas stopped talking and moved over to the control panel by the studio console. He hit a switch and the television came on to one of the monitors that were set in the wall. He flicked from channel to channel like a child playing a video game.

'When did you first realize that you were not born to be a king?'

There was a momentary pause. Then R.D. smiled and turned the video on as he spoke.

'I finally realized I was not a king the night my dad came home and said that he was out of a job. This happened while I was at art college, and it had a profound effect on me. I had gone to get my grant, and for some reason I had to go to the local labour exchange for some papers. As I left the dole office I saw my father walking away from the building. He had probably been there to collect his unemployment money. I never told him that I had seen him there. Never talked about the incident.'

R.D. started singing in a quiet but deliberate tone, 'Get back, get back, get right back in the line . . . Do you know that song? Obviously not. I suppose memory can distort things after a while. My dad, for example. I have no real specific memories of him, I just have visions of him enjoying himself at parties, getting drunk, doing a soft-shoe shuffle or jumping around like a crazy chicken, like a black man. Although I do remember him in a hospital bed once, nobody told me what was really wrong with him. I think he must have had what was in those days called a coronary. He recovered, and led a normal, active life as far as I know. Another memory is of seeing him on his allotment. He was tending his garden, which he rented from the council. We had a long garden at home, Dad had a greenhouse there, and it was always full of tomatoes and flowers, but he needed this allotment, because it was away from the house, I suppose. He talked to me a lot there, confided in me. I think he was a crazy old guy, but in a charming way. He confided in his flowers. All these things are like clear, clean, technicolour images. But going back. It was the image of seeing him leave the social-security office that really stayed in my mind. You must know "Get Back in the Line". Well, it was inspired by my dad.'

'Did you ever think that you should have had more training for what you're doing?'

'Oh, do leave it out, my dear boy. Shit, no! What do you think I am? If I'd gone to college to learn music and finish my education I would have just been another expert. What I did, what I *do*, is unique to me. I don't need no fucking training. Sod that. I did try learning the piano again, learning about music, when I was in my late twenties. I went to this piano teacher in North Finchley. She taught me wonderful things about music I had never even considered, but I found that the more I learned, the less of my instinctive self was in my music. It was other people's invention, what other people had written, other rules.

'Anyway, looking back like this is really irritating. It's difficult to recall every incident in my life in chronological order. The best way to work myself out, is in those flashes and memories that come up during the songs, like a collision between the past and the future. Anyway, I can't sit down and write songs. I could never tell you how to write a song, I just don't know where it comes from. It comes from a combination of wanting, fear, hope, feelings – nothing particular. I don't know. Who gives a shit, anyway? I'm getting tired. I want to get out of this. Have you heard enough yet? I want to go.'

'Where are you going to go?' I asked.

Raymond Douglas looked taken aback for a moment, then put on a false grin as he answered:

'Wherever I bloody well want. I want to go to a party. No. Do you know where I'd like to go? Back to the art school dance. Pull a nice tart, get pissed and go for a bunk-up. Now, those were the days. I remember sitting on the bus travelling down from Muswell Hill to Hornsey Art College with some other students, who were all talking about the Cuban missile crisis. There was a rumour that the call-up was coming back and we would all be enlisted in the army. That didn't appeal to me much, particularly as I was about to start looking for my first set of gigs.

The dance at Hornsey Art College always had a good band headlining. That year it was going to be the Alexis Korner Blues Band which at the time was setting the standard for would-be R and B bands. I was one of the first to arrive so that I could approach them for work, but Alexis didn't turn up until the last half of the second set. Even without him the band sounded great. Graham Bond was superb and a pre-Rolling Stone, Charlie Watts, was on good form. When Alexis made his star's entrance, wearing a cool leather jacket, tight corduroy trousers and cowboy boots, the band seemed to take on a new life. He was the definitive bandleader in the same way Duke Ellington and Count Basie were.

After the gig, I plucked up my courage and went to speak to the man himself while he was packing away his guitar. I explained that I was a guitar player who wanted to get a gig in a blues band, and Alexis nodded and listened and after a while gave me a number to ring the following week. When I called the number, Alexis answered and told me to go to meet a man called Giorgio who ran a club near Piccadilly called the Scene Club. I was astounded to discover that Giorgio was expecting me; he took me to a quiet corner of the club to talk to me. His voice was low and although he spoke in a whisper, I could hear every word he said; he must have acquired the technique from spending most of his life in nightclubs. I couldn't work out whether Giorgio Gomelski spoke as if he was German, Russian, Greek or French; his accent sounded like he had lived in a lot of different places. He told me to bring my guitar down the following Friday so that I could sit in on an audition with the Dave Hunt Band. He was looking for a young guitar player and if I was any good at all I could land myself a regular gig. The following Friday I arrived with my guitar and my hair combed *à la* Tal Farlow. Nobody told me what to play so I just followed the tenor player's riffs. I managed to finish without making too many fluffs and Dave Hunt offered me the gig.

During the interval Hunt offered to take me to the pub. I may have been naïve, but I was not so green as to refuse a drink when the bandleader paid, but there was a support act playing with us called the Rolling Stones and I wanted to stay. When I told Dave Hunt that I wanted to wait and see the Stones' set, he looked at me and said the Stones were nothing more than a glorified skiffle group. It may have been skiffle to Dave Hunt, but there was energy coming from the stage and they had the audience jumping around.

As the Stones started playing 'Roll Over Beethoven' Hunt led me to a pub at the corner of Archer Street where all the out-of-work jazzers picked up any gigs that were going. The pub stank of another age, another music, but my thoughts strayed back across the street where the Rolling Stones were playing to an audience that was turned on to the excitement of the rhythm, rather than standing back with the aloof cool jazz audiences. I found myself playing three nights a week with Dave Hunt's Band, which was a combination of mainstream jazz and big-band-style blues players. The musicians were older and I learned a great deal from them. Dave Hunt himself was a trombone player and took the occasional vocal lead on songs like 'The Night Time is the Right Time'. The real lead singer and star attraction was a West Indian guy called Hamilton King. Hamilton was an accomplished harmonica player, and when he sang he turned a quite ordinary bunch of musicians into a group of wild voodoo men. He had large, bloodshot eyes that reminded me of a Mau Mau witch-doctor. The saxophone player was Lol Coxhil. Lol was the coolest looking of all the band. His slightly balding hair was tightly cropped and he wore an immaculate dark Italian-cut suit, which I suspected was actually hand-made. Lol could dovetail his riffs into whatever I was playing, and he made me sound better than I really was.

The Dave Hunt–Hamilton King Band was good, but it was obvious that its music was too purist to go any further than the club gigs we already had. When we had a night off we hung around the pubs in Soho to see if there were any other gigs going.

One night Charlie Watts said he was considering leaving Alexis Korner's band to join the Rolling Stones. I told him I thought they were really an exciting group, but Charlie had reservations because he was more into jazz and blues and it was obvious that the Stones wanted to make pop records and become as well known as the Beatles. Dave Hunt had described the Stones as a skiffle group simply because they just had a rhythm section with no conventional lead instrument, like a sax or trombone. To me, they sounded just like my favourite Chuck Berry records – the way a modern R and B group should sound. With the exception of Lol, the players in Dave's band were playing R and B because it was the current fad and they could get work from it. I felt that the Stones were actually turning the Chuck Berry–Muddy Waters standards they were playing into their own music.

The deal I had with Giorgio included 2s. 6d. for my tube fare, and in order not to squander my meagre earnings I got a lift to Soho from Rosie and Arthur before Arthur went on the night shift. Then I would walk back to Highgate at three in the morning when the gig was over. Next morning, I would crawl out of bed just having had enough rest before going to art school. Rosie, my surrogate mother at the time, was appalled by some of the dives I entered once I was deposited on the pavement, but she knew I was happy to be playing, and possibly she was secretly relieved to have me out of her hair for a few hours.

One of the gigs on the weekday run was in a subterranean pit in Gerrard Street, that in days to come would be turned into a pinball arcade. At the time there was a low-life bar-cum-coffee shop upstairs, where local pimps sat and discussed trade. Downstairs, where we played, was the club, a dark pit of a place that hardly ever got more than thirty people in it at a time. The stage, such as it was, was a little raised platform in the corner of the room, and it was so small that the whole band couldn't fit on it. On these occasions we became known as the Hamilton King Band. Our music become more ska and had a more ethnic blues and Caribbean flavour to it.

Our second set was at eleven-thirty, and was usually attended by some of the pimps, who entertained business associates with their working women. Sometimes the women came in alone, to put their 'feet up'. One particular lady named Miriam often came and sat with me when I was on a break. She listened to me talk about my trivial suburban normality as well as my dreams and ambitions. I could explain my problems to her, knowing that there was no way that she would ever tell anybody about them.

One night she came in alone and asked me to dance with her. We danced to a slow record called 'Honky Tonk' by Bill Doggett, or maybe it was something by Jimmy Reed. She held me tight and danced with her eyes closed. There were just two or three blue and red lights in the basement. When we danced towards these lights I could see that Miriam's mascara had run, as if she had been crying. She had always seemed so grown-up and matter-of-fact about the world. I had always felt that she was in control and nothing could affect her. That night I saw how sad she must have been all that time. She took me over to a part of the room that was dark and empty. The band were on a break and so everybody was upstairs. For a while, the whole place seemed to be ours.

She whispered something to me about me always playing for her, and how when I spoke to her it reminded her of the dreams she had once had, and that now she would do something for me. Then I felt her hands against my skin as she slid them under my shirt to feel my backside. She kissed me on the side of the face with such gentleness and assurance that somehow I could not resist, because I could feel nothing forced in what she was doing. Clumsily I tried to explain that I only had 2s. 6d. on me. I expected her to push me away, to shout at me for being so cheap, but instead she just grabbed me harder and kissed me on the mouth. Any tenseness in my body soon dissolved away. She was indeed a total professional. Her whole body felt relaxed, the complete opposite to any other ladies I had encountered. As she left, she kissed me once more on the cheek and this time she felt like an auntie.

She kissed me goodbye, walked up the stairs and back onto the street. I watched her thin, muscular calves flex into tight balls as her toes squeezed against the tip of her high-heels. I walked to the bottom of the stairs and saw her fully lit by the neon above. She stopped to fix her make-up in a shop window, then lit a cigarette. For the first time I noticed her black, shoulder-length hair and her bright red overcoat. As she walked away and out of sight, her face changed and took on a hard edge to it. She soon disappeared into the crowded street.

The girls from my own world seemed shallow somehow, and never had the same attraction for me after the mysterious woman who called herself Miriam. The girls at art college were either too rich and spoiled, or poor, talented and waiting to get knocked up so that they could be looked after by some man for the rest of their lives. I started to get impatient with the prick-teasers, and disgusted by the inexperienced ravers. In a perverse way, the less I cared for them, the more they went out of the way to ask me out.

I became a challenge, but by this time I was becoming disenchanted with the art-school racket, and was fast losing

interest in its pretentious airs and graces and self-satisfied
opinions on colour, dimension and perspective. Art school had
been taken over by the graphic arts and commerce. Perhaps I
was foolish not to know that it had never been any other way.
All the artists I truly admired had died poor, and now their
pictures were owned by the rich and famous. And the fake
socialism of student life was beginning to appal me. It was
such a charade. While women like Miriam were lying on their
backs or kneeling down in front of strangers to scrape a living,
the students were smoking dope and drinking beer, quoting
Karl Marx and complaining about the plight of the poor
artist. My sketches became full of empty motorways with lost
people walking around the perimeter. Human beings
scrambled around unable to find a place to live in a concrete
post-war world of high-rise dwellings and second-rate luxury,
pretend silk and fake fur. There were no expressions on the
faces of the people in my pictures because my people, the
people that I cared about, were being given the arse-end of the
universe. The war was over, but the system had remained the
same. Art was supposed to hold a mirror up to the world.
Now the government was telling the schools to show society
a pretty picture of itself. Pop art was emerging. Bright colours
and crazy angles. Pretty pretty and petty. In the bistros of
Belgravia and Chelsea the bright young things were partying
as if a dazzling upper-class new age was about to emerge. The
working class was still in its place in the coal mines of
Yorkshire, Wales and the north. The mill towns were still
employing cloth-capped workers who lived in terraced back-
to-backs next to these dark Satanic mills, and although there
was still a certain amount of poverty, the artist L. S. Lowry
was attaining a fashionable following for his colourful paintings
of matchstick men in these northern working-class towns. The
toffs and debutantes of Kensington and Knightsbridge were
beginning to acknowledge that something was changing, and
instead of suffering the same fate as their aristocratic forefathers

in the French Revolution, they decided to join the fray. The wine flowed freely in the exclusive clubs, only this time the well-to-do were going with the flow.

At the Scene Club in Soho audiences were beginning to dwindle so much that during solos members of the Dave Hunt Band would take it in turns to go into the audience in order to applaud. One night as Lol and I sat on a break, the DJ in the club put on 'Da-Doo-Ron-Ron' by the Crystals. Lol and I sat against the wall staring at the empty club. As the record played at maximum volume, I watched Lol finger the notes of the song on his saxophone as if to play along. I was amazed to see that he was attempting to play every instrumental line on the record except the melody. He started playing a part of the song and then, once he had learned it, he seemed to immediately lose interest in it and move on to another phrase. It came to the sax solo on the record. That famous dry, fat solo that was being heard on every jukebox around the world. Instead of copying it note for note the way I would have done, Lol fitted his own subtle harmonics around it and turned it into an avant-garde jazz solo. It was purely instinctive. He didn't even know he was doing it. During the next record, which was 'Madness' by Prince Buster, Lol leaned over and suggested that I form my own group and play simple music that young people could relate to. He said it in such a way that it had a hidden code in the words. The word 'young' made me think that he was happy just learning to master his own instrument, playing in clubs like the one we were in. I had wanted to form a group with Lol, to find an audience for what he wanted to play, but it seemed that Lol didn't need it, Lol's audience was in his head. I, on the other hand, needed a different experience, because I was coming into the music from another curve. I had been listening for the melody but this particular melody had not interested him enough to want to play it.

Lol missed a couple of gigs after that. Someone in the band

said it was because Lol, who came from Aylesbury, had been delayed because of the Great Train Robbery (which had taken place there at about that time). Somebody else said that they had heard that he had gone to play in Denmark, which still had an audience for jazz. Somebody else said that he had thrown away his immaculate Italian suit from Austins of Piccadilly, grown his hair long and was last seen playing solo on the street outside Tottenham Court Road tube station dressed as a beatnik. Although it was most unlikely, I preferred to believe this. He was cool enough to carry that off.

For a while whenever I heard the sound of a busker playing the saxophone in the underground, I followed the sound, but I always came to a dead end. The source was always lost in an echo and I ended up walking in the wrong direction until the sound was gone. After a while, I stopped looking.'

5

Here come the people in grey

Raymond Douglas fell silent and moved over to the control panel by the studio console. As he stood up, I could see under that large overcoat that he was still in good physical shape for his age and larger in stature than he sounded on record. He flicked a switch and the television came onto one of the monitors that were set in the wall. R.D. watched the television, absorbed in a gangster film. He looked over at me, saw that I too was watching, interested, and immediately turned off the video.

'I'm tired now, son, so do me a favour and bugger off.'

I tried my luck one more time. I needed to know about his early career. This time I seemed to have caught his attention, and he picked up again.

'My brother Dave had started his own group with an old school friend called Pete Quaife. David Russell Gordon Davies had transformed himself into a totally cool-looking fourteen-year-old with a thin, wire-like body. He was always an agile little hard nut, but a bright kid at school. His exploits with the girls from the local convent school were turning him into a local legend and, on top of all this, his guitar playing had improved beyond my wildest expectations. My playing had developed into a slow, soulful and slightly contrived style handed down to me by the blues-playing jazzers, whereas Dave had what can only be described as a jack-in-the-box technique, full of crazy staccato phrases which perfectly mirrored his more aggressive speech pattern. I decided to leave Dave Hunt's Blues Band to join up with Dave and Pete. My last gig with Hunt was at the Richmond Jazz Club. It had originally been the Rolling Stones' regular gig but they had signed a record contract and were on their way to success. We had inherited some of their regular audience, and so the gig was well attended. During the break between our two sets, somebody asked me if their friend could borrow my guitar. I said I had no objection, provided this person could actually play. What followed was an exhibition of such complete blues-guitar technique that it left me almost in tears. The 'fill in' guitarist was Davey Graham, who was already a legend to all blues fans, both for his playing and his gypsy lifestyle. He, apart from Broonzy, was the greatest blues guitarist I ever saw, and he turned my imitation Gretsch guitar, which was still being paid for on the hire-purchase, into a tool of absolute beauty. He made sounds that are impossible to explain. It was deeper than soul music, and left my nerves numb with envy. After he finished playing, he thanked me and disappeared into the bar, and I swear that I felt the strings of my guitar still ringing with the sounds he made with it.

After our second set, I told Dave Hunt that I was leaving his band. He started to show desperation rather than rage, and said that the band needed me and everybody liked me and that there were some prestige gigs coming up. That he might be able to pay more money, that the band needed somebody young. He didn't seem to understand that this was exactly why I was leaving: I was young and wanted to make my own music. That last gig taught me two things. The first was that I would never be the greatest blues player in Britain because that was Davey Graham. The second was that if you want to go, don't just threaten to – go. I did. I walked out of the club and, as Dave Hunt's band played 'Night Train', I was gone.

Pete Quaife and Dave had formed a group with John Start, a gangling blond drummer who went to their school. We rehearsed in John's father's garage, and played several local youth clubs and school dances. Another group doing the rounds at the same time was the Moontrekkers. This band had some heavy investment from one of the band's parents, who was in the motor trade. Their lead singer was another former pupil of the William Grimshaw School, Rod Stewart. Rod, who was without doubt the Elvis Presley of Muswell Hill, played the Saturday-night spot at the local youth club, and Dave and Pete's group played the Thursday-night spot. I came into Dave and Pete's group as more experienced and accomplished at playing to a slightly older and sophisticated club audience, but Dave's abrasive guitar playing had improved so much that he had assumed the mantle of lead guitarist. Although he hadn't played in a band, he had toured the clubs as a punter along with a clarinet-jazz fanatic called Lew Lewis. Lew, whose dad ran the Victoria Arms pub in Highgate, was a big jazz fan and allowed us to rehearse in the pub's cellar, as long as we did at least one jazz standard. This was no problem because at nearly every gig we had ever played there had been requests for the obligatory 'Twelfth Street Rag' or 'When the Saints Go Marching In'. These songs passed as jazz at wedding receptions and gigs at old people's homes. Kenny Ball and his Jazzmen had already topped the charts in Britain and America and Acker Bilk's success in the charts meant that no proper cover group was worth its salt unless it could bash out 'Petit Fleur' and 'Midnight in Moscow' on request.

Art school was beginning to frustrate me more, especially as my work, which was generally up to standard, was being assessed for a new diploma which had been brought in to replace the old Fine Art syllabus. The new word for the new age was graphics. Commercial artists were to be encouraged more than out-and-out painters who, according to the Middlesex Education Authority, would end up starving in an attic somewhere and living on the dole. The new attitude in all art colleges was directed at earning a living and making money. This did not include people like myself who saw art as a form of self-expression.

The swinging sixties had arrived. Outside my narrow, self-centred world, there was a style revolution in progress, and it seemed that all the smart students at the college were rushing headlong into it. People were talking about a place called Carnaby Street, where a young designer called John Steven was re-dressing the fashion-conscious. Tab collars and Chelsea boots were in and beatniks, who had been until now the hippest of the hip, were starting to put their long pullovers into mothballs or giving them back to their grandads. A few years earlier John Osborne had written *Look Back in Anger*, and the 'angry young men' who had already started a revolution in the theatre were starting to emerge as standard-bearers of a new wave of British cinema. Alan Sillitoe had written *Saturday Night and Sunday Morning*, and Dave bought the book and lent it to me. David Bailey was taking photographs of Jean Shrimpton, and Mary Quant had become the world's trendiest designer. Christine Keeler embarrassed and disgraced an entire government and, in doing so, showed ordinary people that the so-called ruling classes could be as morally vulnerable as the rest of us. People with northern accents were suddenly appearing on television and radio and they were being taken seriously. Overnight it was fashionable to be working class and at art college. I remember an aristocratic debutante rushing into the cafeteria to announce triumphantly that she had discovered that a distant relative had actually been a labourer on a building site in Croydon. None of this was affecting me, because I felt that I had always been what all these silly, confused trendies were trying to become. I was already working class, and therefore not required to change. Pete Quaife's girlfriend Nicola confirmed this on the way to a rehearsal as she explained why she thought that the group would succeed.

'It's because you all look and sound like . . . now,' she said.

Without thinking about image and style, we four musically confused youths from Muswell Hill found ourselves, through no fault of our own, to be in fashion.

Meanwhile my sketchbook was full of drawings of the M1 motorway tearing through the little rows of streets and playing fields of north London. In the pictures a sad, anonymous figure always appeared somewhere in the distance as proof that some living form was defiant enough to exist. I was that lonely figure standing by the motorway. I had drawn myself into my own work and it was becoming so personal that I stopped showing it to my teachers. My real world had become confused with the images in my head. It was obvious that I needed to work or at least communicate with other people to stop myself going completely over the edge. What I demanded from my drawing was too complicated for me to understand, and the people who were supposed to teach me were either unprepared, unwilling or, as it was not part of the syllabus, uncaring. It was all too deep and too horrifying to confront, and yet the images revealed the truth to me with such undeniable clarity. In order that I would not become that faceless 'no man' I drew in my pictures, I would have to define my own rules, invent my own method of communication. In fact, totally re-invent myself. A dark cloud appeared as I fell into a deep empty cavern where people with dead souls sat on street corners. I saw corpses driving cars. Decaying bodies standing around in pubs ordering pints of bitter. I started to live inside myself once more.

My on-and-off art-school career was going from bad to worse. Paul O'Dell and I formed a college film society. I eventually plucked up the courage to confront the college principal and suggest that, as the whole school syllabus was being revised, the education authority should set up a full-time film department. The principal promptly showed me the door, after pointing out to me that I had only got into the college on the strength of my talent, and talent alone would not be sufficient to survive under the new regime. I took this to be a subtle enough hint that I would soon have my grant taken away and would be out on my ear. This served only to whet my appetite for music even more, and after a

brief spell in the theatre department at Croydon Art School, I
found myself looking for a future playing in a group.

Pete Quaife had found us a new drummer called Mickey
Willet, because John Start's father had decided that John should
go into the family jewellery business. Mr Start had kindly
financed the purchase of some matching pullovers and shirts
for us to use as stage wear. We had bought the clothes from
Marks and Spencer in Wood Green. Mr Start, being a good
businessman, kept a strict tally of how much he had invested
in the group. Just before his son departed, Mr Start appeared
on my mother's doorstep like a tallyman collecting the weekly
subs. Somehow Mum paid him off, but not before a
considerable amount of haggling took place. This was not the
first time we had received a visit from somebody demanding
payment for hire-purchase or overdue rent, and Mum had this
sort of situation down to a fine art. She simply raised her
voice to such a level that passers-by would stop and listen to
the argument, embarrassing the tallyman to such an extent that
they would have to leave. On this occasion it got to the
stage where it seemed as if it were Mr Start who owed my
mother the money. Finally he took some money on account
and escaped.

Mickey Willet was quite a bit older than the rest of us.
Although he was a smooth-looking character, Pete's girlfriend
Nicola said that he spoiled the look of the group. We were
all rough and far from ready for stardom. Mickey Willet
looked and sounded as though he had seen it all.

Then something came up that sounded like a wonderful
opportunity for us to earn some extra money; perhaps to
invest in some new equipment and stage clothes. Willet and
Pete had met a couple of society types in a pub. Their
names were Grenville Collins and Robert Wace and they
were looking for some young musicians to serve as a backing
group for Wace, who was to be managed by Grenville.
Some lucrative society dances were on offer, as well as several

debutante balls. The button-up casual sweaters from Marks and Spencer, courtesy of Mr Start, were wearing a little thin at the elbows and beginning to smell somewhat, and, as Mr Start was still demanding the remainder of the money he had advanced to purchase them, we decided to give them all back to him rather than start our careers carrying a bad debt and smelly sweaters. Grenville advanced us some money and we went to Carnaby Street and bought pink tab-collar shirts and dark blue corduroy trousers from John Steven.

The only difficulty I had with the new set-up was that, apart from being upper-class public schoolboys, both Robert and Grenville were both at least six feet five inches tall. We could dig it, the society debs would dig it, but would the kids at the local youth club be turned on by a six-foot five-inch stockbroker in a pinstripe suit singing 'I Like It' by Gerry and the Pacemakers and 'Rave On' by Buddy Holly? Would they understand him when he sang 'Twist and Shout' with a plum in his mouth? Grenville was certain Robert's singing would be well received and, as he was in the managerial role, we assumed everything would be in order.

Suddenly our rehearsals were attended by society toffs from Belgravia, drinking champagne and cheering with delight every time Robert took a vocal. He finished each song to rapturous applause from his friends. We were amazed at how well Robert was going down, and this was only the rehearsal. Grenville convinced us that when we finally appeared in public, Robert would have the showbusiness world at his feet and the top agents and record companies would be banging down the door in order to sign us.

Grenville did not lie about the gigs, the first of which was at the Guildhall in the City. Others followed, at the Dorchester and at a large country mansion in Sussex. The society gigs themselves were a triumph for Robert and Grenville. Bobby had visited the showbiz tailor Dougie Millings and had a blue serge suit made for the engagements. He had also had his two

front teeth capped especially for his debut. The champagne
flowed, the caviare was eaten and Bobby Wace was the toast of
Belgravia. It was also remarked that the 'scruffy little backing
group', which was being fed in the kitchens while Bobby and
Grenville cruised the ballroom, was also quite enjoyable. It
seems that we had arrived. In Sloane Square at least.

The trail of triumph continued throughout the debutante
season of 1963, and while the world of politics was being
shaken to the core in the aftermath of the Profumo affair,
Robert Wace's singing career was blossoming. Grenville had
taken to the role of manager with such confidence that he
decided to accept an engagement at a working-class youth
club in the East End of London.

At the beginning of our set the audience danced and
applauded as we thumped through our own versions of Bo
Diddley and Slim Harpo numbers. Then, as Robert strolled
on to the stage, grabbed the microphone and started to sing,
the audience gradually went into a coma. Their jaws dropped.
They watched in stunned silence as Robert went through the
same motions as he had at the Guildhall or Casanova Club.
After a while, a little Cockney mod girl in the audience
started to snigger. This spread to her friends until the whole
front row started to laugh and sing along and we thought that
Robert had won the audience over. If Robert had been
a clown or a bandmaster at community singing, this would
have been considered a success, but after two or three songs it
became obvious to all that Robert should not have been up
there in the first place. His confidence shaken, he faltered. His
charm had carried him through at the deb dances and society
parties where he had been with his peers, but it didn't work in
east London. Robert, a gentleman to the last, accepted the
mistake with good grace, left the stage, allowing Dave and
our road manager Jonah to finish singing the remaining songs.

This experience must have given Robert stage fright because
at a subsequent performance at a club in Mayfair he hesitated

in front of his friends, on what was his home turf. He must have had too much champagne before the show, because he started singing so horribly out of tune that Grenville was seen sitting at one of the tables with his head in his hands crying out to himself, 'Sing no more, Robert, sing no more!' Robert bowed to his audience, and, after pausing to ponder a career that might have been, smiled gallantly at his few loyal admirers, then did precisely as Grenville suggested. Robert left the stage and sang no more.

It was obvious to Robert and Grenville that their scruffy little back-up group had something going for it, in that it could hold an audience. It was therefore decided that Robert and Grenville would form a management company called Boscobel Productions, a name taken from Boscobel Place, where Robert's father lived, and from then on they would be our managers.

According to Nicola, Mickey Willet was a fantastic drummer but still didn't look right, and after a few disagreements with the management, he decided to leave the group. He could not see the humour in Grenville's superior manner and Robert's extravagant behaviour in the way the rest of us could. On one occasion Robert's Mini was stuck in a traffic jam in Clapham on the way to a gig. Grenville stood on top of the car directing traffic while the rest of us huddled in the back. When confronted by a policeman Grenville explained that Robert was on his way to Buckingham Palace, but he had inadvertently taken a wrong turn. The confused policeman looked at Robert, who silently exuded aristocratic calm in the driver's seat. In a matter of moments a path through the traffic had been cleared. Not content with this, we asked for the policeman's name and address so that Robert could recommend the Queen to give the constable an award for gallantry. Mickey Willet, being a responsible adult, might probably have been offended by this, but the rest of us thought that Robert was suitably rebellious. Our replacement drummer was a northerner called Johnny Green. He was very handsome, and resembled a 1950s film matinée idol; but Nicola didn't like the way he parted his hair.

At this time we had started making a film with John Cowan, a prominent fashion photographer. The group (minus Green) assembled at Cowan's studio near Hyde Park every Saturday morning and embarked on a day's shooting around London. It was all fairly silly stuff, mainly inspired by Richard Lester's work with the Beatles. Cowan used to dream up bizarre antics for us to act out while he pointed the camera. One such antic required us to drive through a car wash in an open-top Land Rover. Robert and Grenville looked on while the rest of us froze and caught colds. The only thing that made it bearable was that John Cowan was always accompanied by his attractive girlfriend, a model called Jill Kennington. The way she swaggered around in his oversized sweaters showed that they must have been very much in love, but even so she gave the impression that there was at least a spiritual involvement with us. When we froze she gave us hot tea, and that was certainly worth shivering for. She had a habit of wrapping her hands around the mug of tea before she gave it to you which turned the act of drinking tea into a sensuous forbidden affair. Poor John Cowan. On this occasion, his camera was pointed in the wrong direction. The real movie was happening when he had his back turned.

It helped us to see the rushes of ourselves, because we could see our natural habits and develop them further. Dave developed a silly walk. I developed a pompous pout. Quaife acquired cigarette etiquette which I christened the Mayfair Droop: a lit cigarette was held between the first and second finger, the elbow rested on the other arm, which was wrapped around the chest; the wrist of the hand holding the cigarette was then relaxed and extended downward, enabling the cigarette to be waved around with contempt in faces of non-smokers. It also helped if the shoulders were hunched slightly, to show conclusively that the Mayfair Droop had no regard whatsoever for environment, personal health or body posture.

For some reason the film never got finished and John Cowan went away on a photographic assignment. Unfortunately, he took Jill Kennington with him. All I had was that personal little 'inner' movie which my eyes shot between Jill Kennington and myself. Shot in extreme close-up on a very long lens.

By now, we were building up quite a following around some of the youth clubs in Muswell Hill. On 23 November 1963 we were booked to play at the Moravian Hall in Muswell Hill. The day before, I was visiting my sister Gwen in her cottage near my parents' house. We were sitting in the kitchen having tea when a news flash came on the television that President Kennedy had been killed while visiting Dallas, Texas. As I walked the three miles up to Highgate where Rosie lived, I wondered what sort of country could allow such a thing to happen. All of my recent musical influences had come from that far-off place and yet this news had made me feel that I would never want to go there. By the time I reached Rosie and Arthur's house, I had picked up the news that somebody had been arrested for shooting the president. I was convinced that there was going to be a World War and that atomic bombs would start dropping on north London at any moment and annihilate us all. To my relief Muswell Hill and the rest of the world was still there when we played the Moravian Hall the following night, but the taste of violence and the black-and-white television images from Dallas would not leave me.

Robert and Grenville were anxious that we should sign a long-term contract with them; they felt that we had a genuine chance of becoming successful. My parents had to countersign on our behalf because Dave and I were still underage. Even though my parents liked Robert and Grenville, they were concerned about our signing anything. Mum and Dad had recently

signed numerous hire-purchase agreements in order for us to
buy some guitars and, as a rule, they had an aversion to
documents of any kind. But after being told that her boys
might be on the London Palladium by the following
Christmas, my mother countersigned the Boscobel contract.
That is the one time in my life I wish I had seen a lawyer,
because then all the legal implications would have been pointed
out to me.

The first big break came when we were engaged to play at
a Chinese restaurant, called the China Garden, on the Edgware
Road. It was at a New Year's Eve party and there was an
agent called Arthur Howes there. He was responsible for
booking all the major package tours at the time and would be
a valuable contact for us. Howes sat back in his booth, attired
in traditional Chinese regalia, surrounded by other agents and
hangers-on in business-suits. Howes declared that he loved the
band. He immediately asked Robert and Grenville to meet
him in his Soho office later that week to discuss terms. So,
now we had managers and we had an agent. We had even
been offered a spot on the Dave Clark Five tour later that
spring. All we needed now was to get a recording contract, so
that we could have a single to coincide with the tour.

Meanwhile, Johnny Green had decided that being in a pop
group was not what he had in mind for himself, and he left.
Boscobel Productions immediately put an advertisement in
Melody Maker and booked the upstairs room at the Camden
Head pub for auditions. Grenville assembled us and spoke like
a commander giving his subordinates the day's battle-plan:

'His name is Mick Avory and he comes from East Molesey
in Surrey. He has played in skiffle groups and learned to play
the drums while in the boy scouts. He says he played in a
group with Mick Jagger before he joined the Rolling Stones.
He has a day job delivering pink paraffin.'

Avory spoke in a deep south London accent as he struggled
into the room carrying his own drums. Dave and Pete, who

were standing on the little rehearsal platform in the corner of the room, were both dressed in plastic capes, tight black trousers and Cuban heels. Quaife, who had by now been groomed by some of the more camp hairdressers in Carnaby Street, quietly suggested that Avory looked like 'a beautiful butch beast'. Unfortunately, Avory both heard this and took it seriously.

'I've got a girlfriend,' Avory said in his deep, flat drone. Quaife continued the wind-up. 'So've I, love. Don't mean to say that we all don't bend from time to time.'

Dave joined in and started laughing and coughing in a high-pitched, feminine voice. I jumped in: 'Put your drums down there, dear, and don't mark the floor, I've been on my knees scrubbing it all afternoon!'

Avory did not see any humour in the situation. We introduced ourselves to him in a limp-wristed way and continued to camp it up until we started playing. Then it was all heavy blues and rock and roll. Nicola nodded her head up and down to the rhythm. After two or three songs we were all smiles, and a team. Nicola took the rest of us to one side and said that Avory looked right, even if he bit his tongue and hardly moved his body while he played. She also thought that he resembled Rock Hudson and would attract some girl fans.

When the rehearsal was over, Dave, Pete and I all reverted to talking in high-pitched voices. Avory thought he was on safer ground by directing his conversation towards Robert and Grenville. He was concerned about being in a group who wore plastic capes and leather caps and asked if we were sexual deviants. I was never clear whether he considered this to be a good or a bad thing.

'Tell me, will I have to dress up like them?' Avory inquired.

'Undoubtedly so,' replied Grenville, as he cocked his eyebrow and put on a stern face to accompany the Mayfair Droop.

Robert joined in as if Avory wasn't there. 'He'll also have to grow his hair, what?'

Avory mumbled half to himself as he started to pack up his drum kit, 'I'll 'ave to think about it and ask my girlfriend if it's all right. I'll let you know in a few days.' He stopped at the door as he left. 'I enjoyed playing with you. The music, I mean.'

'The feeling's mutual, love,' Quaife pouted back and held out his hand as if he expected Avory to kiss it. Avory groaned and, after shaking hands with all of us, slowly backed out of the room.

After he had left, Grenville told us that Avory had been to have his hair cut short before the audition so that he would impress everyone. When he turned up and discovered that we all had hair down to our shoulders, he thought he wouldn't get the gig.

As I watched Avory pack his drums away into his little pink-paraffin delivery van, I thought how sad he looked, and hoped that he would join the group because in many ways he was a little like I was before I had joined a band: all lost and looking for some friends to play with.

Within a few days Avory had become a member of the group. This time we were convinced that we had found someone who would be there on a permanent basis.

Robert and Grenville were impressed by the success of the Beatles' manager, Brian Epstein, but they didn't have his experience in record shops, and in many ways they were out of their depth when it came to doing business with ordinary people. They could deal with high-powered upper-class hustlers, but they had some difficulty making the kind of social adjustments necessary to deal with ordinary plebs. Robert and Grenville had knocked on nearly every door in Denmark Street's Tin Pan Alley and had promptly been shown the door by all the publishers and record companies.

But finally they managed to persuade Brian Epstein to come down to the Camden Head pub to watch us rehearse.

We were astonished to find ourselves performing in front of
the manager of the Beatles. As we went through our tiny
repertoire of blues and cover songs, Epstein looked at us all
individually, like a man trying to spot a quality racehorse at
an auction. The audition came to an end. Epstein displayed a
keen interest but said that he would have to consider the
political ramifications of having yet another four-piece group
on his roster. We took this to be a pass but we were thrilled
that he had actually expressed some interest in us in the first
place. Pete asked Epstein if he would like to go down to the
pub for a pint of lager but Epstein looked at his watch and
asked Robert to give him a lift into the West End, where he
suddenly remembered he had an urgent meeting. Robert and
Grenville grasped the opportunity of taking the Beatles' manager
home and rushed off downstairs with him, leaving us to pack
our gear away. Five minutes later Grenville reappeared at the
top of the stairs. His face red and sweating with humiliation,
he rushed over to the window to look down into the street.

'Good God, this is so embarrassing. Robert's mini won't start
and we can't get a taxi. You've all got to come down and help.'

We peered out the window to see Epstein the showbiz
supremo as he slipped in the mud trying to give Robert's car
a push. Robert was trying to rev up the engine and leaned out
of the car as he called back to Epstein, 'Just a little harder, old
boy, I think the engine started to tick over just then.'

It was a cold winter's night, but Epstein was sweating
underneath his cashmere overcoat.

Eventually we all gave a hand and Robert's car started. As
we watched Robert drive away in his minivan with Grenville
and Brian Epstein huddled in the back, we assumed that even
if there had been a slight possibility that the Beatles' manager
was interested in us, the chance had been blown by the fact
that he had been seen in such humiliating circumstances. We
observed our manager looking out of the window as he sped
off. There was a faint smile on his face, but it failed to cover

up the fact that he had ruined Epstein's cashmere overcoat, dented his ego and probably ruined Robert and Grenville's chance of signing us to Epstein's empire.

Next it was decided that we should meet another contact, called Larry Page, who had advised Robert and Grenville on how to go about putting all the necessary pieces into place in order to obtain a record contract. Page had been a singer in the early days of British pop, along with Tommy Steele and Cliff Richard and the Shadows. Larry also had connections with a publisher called Eddie Kassner, and all these connections would, according to Grenville, help secure us a deal with a record company.

Page was tall, but not quite as tall as Wace and Collins. He had fair to blond hair and his face was framed by a pair of thick black-rimmed spectacles, which gave him the look of a cartoon character. He had been known as 'the teenage rage' when he'd been a singer (and was renowned for having dyed his hair blue on occasions!). He spoke in a west London accent that had been softened by a showbiz transatlantic twang. Larry Page had seen quite a few songwriters come and go during his time in the music business. He had been a singer at the Two Eyes Café in the 1950s, and, although he was not a musician himself, he had an instinct for anything that sounded vaguely commercial. He sensed that I could write songs and encouraged me to do so. Despite the fact that he was older than we were, he came from a similar background; once we got past his self-protective showbiz veneer, he was a down-to-earth guy, and we felt we could trust him. But it was obvious that Robert and Grenville had nothing in common with Larry Page, nor he with them. They were simply a means to an end for each other, and that was that. But what end and by whose means? Larry had the wheeler-dealer, street-wise expertise to find his way into meetings with record companies, and Robert and Grenville had the society contacts to get that person into any club in Mayfair. Our music made everybody associated with the group feel classless, but that feeling disappeared as soon as the music stopped. Robert and Grenville regarded Larry as a necessary evil, he was no better or worse than anybody else they'd met in the music business. If they could have retained the camaraderie they all had whenever the group was playing, they could have conquered the world together.

Larry knew an American record producer with the unlikely name of Shel Talmy and, as I had already expressed my admiration for American producers such as Phil Spector, Larry thought Shel would fit the bill. It was arranged for us to meet in a pub next to the Royal Court Theatre in Sloane Square. Shel and I talked about songs and sounds and other groups and overall we made a good impression on one another. It was decided that Shel would take us for auditions at record companies with the view to getting us a record contract.

Soon we were up for an audition at Decca records, but after hearing us play three or four cover songs, they showed us the door. Back at Larry Page's office in Denmark Street, an emergency meeting was held. Larry was not bothered unduly that Dick Rowe at Decca had turned the group down: Dick Rowe had also turned the Beatles down, 'So what did he know?' But Larry was concerned about music-biz insiders' perception of Robert and Grenville. In Larry's opinion 'There was no way that any self-respecting record-company executive would put his balls on the line for a group managed by an upper-class double act like Robert and Grenville.' According to Larry, they had started at one end of Denmark Street and worked their way down until somebody took some interest.

Robert and Grenville visited me at Rosie's house. They suggested that Page should be brought in as part of the 'team', in order to help secure a recording contract for the group. Yet Grenville and Robert talked about Page as if he were a faceless soldier on the front line of battle, one who was ultimately expendable. That was their manner, the way they were brought up; I, on the other hand, felt more ambivalent.

In the group when there was a disagreement we either talked
about it or fought about it, but we always directly confronted
one another. Perhaps it was different with businessmen?'

R.D. stopped talking. His head dipped down. This was a bad sign.
An ominous cloak of self-pity started to engulf him like an
overwhelming drug. The atmosphere was dark and full of doom,
and it was obvious that his downward spiral was in full flow.
Then, without warning, his head snapped back and he shouted, 'I
suppose you think I'm a useless, self-centred soul?'

'Not at all,' I lied unconvincingly.

'I'll let you into a secret as well. Nobody knows this.' R. D. got
up and slowly made his way under the control desk. His old bones
creaked and he struggled for breath as he reached underneath to the
patchbay. He cursed as he stretched deep behind the filth. The
years of neglect were all too apparent. Eventually he dragged out a
pile of old exercise books tied up with some string and brown
paper. R. D. pushed them towards me.

'Read 'em and tell me what you think. I've never asked anybody
else before.'

I suppose I should have appeared more grateful. Perhaps he
should have been less magnanimous. My predicament was an
awkward one. Suddenly this crazy old guy, renowned for his
secrecy and maniacal sense of privacy, was giving me the personal
memoirs of his life wrapped in dusty brown paper.

'It's all there. Most of it. The dreams and the disappointments.
The achievements and the failures.'

I unwrapped the brown paper, and discovered an assortment of
exercise books, smart leather diaries and scraps of paper. They
resembled him in many ways: some expensively bound, others
cheap and cherished, old and dusty.

'There seems to be no order to it. How can I possibly unravel
this?' I pleaded.

He did not answer, and even though I could not see his face I
could sense that he was smiling.

'Then put it in order for me. Edit it together, like an LP. No, more like a long song.'

As I opened the first exercise book, I heard him press a rewind button and the master tape went into reverse. We were both entering another time and space. I was surprised to see that the old diary was quite concise – it almost had some style. I handed it over to R.D. who began to read out loud.

'Our first official recording session took place at Pye Recording
Studios at Marble Arch in January 1964. Although I had
written a few songs for the group, Shel, Larry and Arthur
Howes had decided between them that we should record the
old Little Richard song, 'Long Tall Sally'. This was a song
that the Beatles had put into their stage act for their European
tour and our management thought that it would make an
excellent first release. Pye Records had agreed to release the
record on their label, and we paid all our own recording costs.
We also recorded three other songs which I had previously
demoed: 'You Do Something', 'You Still Want Me' and 'I
Took My Baby Home'. We had also made demos of other
songs I had written, 'I Believed You' and 'You Really Got
Me'. Page had said that the record company would not go for
'You Really Got Me'. On a previous occasion when I had
played the demo in his office, Page had even stopped the tape
before it got to the end of the song. The general consensus
was that it was either 'too bluesy' or 'not pop enough'. We
were starting to put the song into the stage act, but everybody
thought that it was too risky to record it.

As Avory had not joined us at this point, it was decided we
would use a session drummer called Bobby Graham. I had
heard his playing on other records and was bowled over by
his style and power, which was very reminiscent of Dave
Clark's drumming on all of his hits. Graham added a tidiness
and a dimension to our sound, which had usually been
dependent on the distorted fuzziness of Dave and me playing too
loud through amplifiers that were not equipped for the volume.

As we were tuning up in the studio Dave played a chord

which started to feed back through the amplifier. This caused the chord to oscillate between the pick-up on his guitar and the Vox AC 30-amp that Dave was plugged into. On top of the Vox was the little green amp that Dave had started using to get the fuzziness into the sound. The engineer, who was placing a microphone in front of Dave's speaker, jumped backwards. Dave smiled and played an even louder chord. This time, instead of a low melodic whine, the feedback had a piercing whistle that made the engineer put his hands over his ears. Dave held the screeching guitar aloft to maximize the feedback. The engineer screamed and ran out of the building into the street and, as far as we know, he never returned.

Eventually Dave was persuaded to turn down his amp and we got on with the recording. The instrumental back tracks were recorded first and then it was time to put on the vocals. When we played back the songs at the end of the session, Dave and I were both amazed at how Shel Talmy had managed to smooth out all the rough edges in the track and make the songs sound very polished and professional. I was astonished at how good we sounded even though it didn't sound like us at all.

'Long Tall Sally' was to be our first single, with 'I Took My Baby Home' on the B-side. Pye Records had offered us a contract to release three singles with an option in their favour to renew. Robert and Grenville took a percentage as Boscobel Productions and passed on a payment to Larry's company. Shel Talmy was to produce the singles and Arthur Howes was set as our agent. All we needed now was the record to be a hit and we would all be destined for success.

'Long Tall Sally' was to be released in a few weeks, and we still needed a name for the group. While we had been playing the deb dances with Robert, we had been called the Boll Weevils, after a song by Bo Diddley. I always thought that this sounded a little too twee. Later we called ourselves the Ravens, but Robert thought this sounded too suburban.

One evening, we were having a drink in a pub with Larry
Page and somebody commented on the fake-leather capes
Dave and Pete were wearing. Someone else said that we were
wearing kinky boots, similar to those worn by Honor
Blackman in *The Avengers*. Larry overheard someone call us
'kinks' and concluded that, because of the kinky clothes we
wore, and the fact that the new drummer looked a little like a
police identikit version of a pervert, we might as well call
ourselves the Kinks. We looked at one another in an
unimpressed sort of way, said no more, finished our drinks
and left. A few days later Larry showed us the mock-up of the
artwork for the advertisement for the single and there we
were: the Kinks. I hated it, but Larry's eyes were glowing
with excitement.

'*Kinks*. It's short – five letters. You'll be bottom of the bill,
so you need something that will stand out.'

'But people will think that we're all weird!'

'Well, that might not be such a bad thing. I can see it. The
curiosity value will be incredible. That's the gimmick. You'll
all dress in leather with whips and riding boots. Very kinky.'

Larry was walking around the room, in full flow. Dave and
Pete were excited but not taking the whole thing seriously.
Larry continued enthusiastically:

'Then we'll have some shots done of you wearing the
leather gear. Whips and leather. We'll put the pictures in the
trades. They'll love it. But you've got to get the new stage
gear made. Lots of buckles and leather straps.'

I went along with it. I knew that we could change the
name when the record flopped, so I didn't care. Larry was the
only member of our management team with showbiz
experience and so it was considered that he knew best. I hated
the name, but what did I know? I hated my own name even
more, but I had been walking around with that all my life, so
who was I to complain?

Several weeks later, we, the Kinks, found ourselves in John

Steven's boutique in Carnaby Street having the final fitting
for our new stage gear, a mixture of Thames-green, skin-tight
Robin Hood with *Avengers*-style leather trimmings. An
amalgam of 'period' B-movie costumes and S and M. Like
our first record, the gear was devised on a whim and hastily
thrown together in order to cash in on a fad and meet a
deadline. The only difference was that our record, at least,
sounded finished, whereas our clothes looked as though the tailor
had forgotten to sew the material together before delivering.

Then there was the problem of my teeth. To be precise, the
gap between my two front teeth which appeared in
photographs as a black space whenever I smiled. This
particularly worried Larry, who, as a singer himself in the
early days of pop music and skiffle, knew that singers had to
have flawless looks, clear complexions and, most of all, rows
of bright white sparkling teeth. I was the lead singer on the
single and I had all three faults. Two could be overcome by
large quantities of make-up, but the last and fatal flaw, namely
the gap between my two front teeth, could not be easily
overcome.

At least Larry was to the point. 'They'll never let you on
the box with railings like that, cock. I've fixed you up an
appointment with a dentist. He'll sort you out.'

I sat quietly while the dentist looked at my teeth with
disapproval. Then he became confident.

'We've sorted out many big stars with worse problems than
this. This will take no time at all.'

I felt immediately reassured, and not such a freak after all.
Then I heard the sound of a drill being started. It was a sound
that brought back memories of my endless visits to the dentist
as a child. It was all too obvious that this was not going to be
as simple or as temporary as I had been led to believe. When I
asked what was going to be done, the dentist casually explained
that he was going to cut away my existing two front teeth
and replace them with caps. He assured me that it would be

permanent and make me look more acceptable. I immediately jumped out of the chair. After frantic telephone calls to Larry and Grenville, we agreed to compromise and put temporary caps over my existing teeth for the television show. If I was comfortable with them, the dentist would do a more permanent job at a later date. And so I made my first appearance on *Ready Steady Go!* with the largest front teeth since Bugs Bunny.

A cameraman was heard to say to his director, 'You want the singer in close-up. You mean the one with the goofy teeth?'

We did our spot on *Ready Steady Go!* After the song the interviewer, Michael Aldred, spoke to Dave and made some bitchy remark comparing us with the Rolling Stones. Dave gave a reply full of innocent wit, and a delightful smile at the camera, and it was all over. My only contribution, apart from miming the song, was to stand bolt upright in the background and smile my new smile as Dave did his interview. Cathy McGowan, the show's female presenter, struck up a conversation with Pete after the show and they seemed to have a lot in common. The producer, Vicky Wickham, a large strapping lass, was tremendously enthusiastic about the Kinks; she seemed more than satisfied with our performance. Although I was the lead singer of the group, it was Dave with his long flowing hair and Pete with his gift of the gab who really grabbed centre stage after the show.

Outside the studios my niece Jackie and some of her friends, who had already formed a fan club, were waiting to mob us as we emerged. Robert and Grenville had also arranged a photographer to be on hand to take pictures of the event. We were surprised to see that a picture appeared in the *New Musical Express* the following week. The television exposure gave the single a tremendous boost and it entered the *Melody Maker* chart the following week at Number 42.

Someone in the family had taken a picture of us as we were

miming the song on television. Pete Quaife insisted on wearing his stage gear for days afterwards, even though it was impractical for normal everyday activities, such as sitting down. Fame and fortune seemed to be waiting around the corner for us, as if they were only two stops on the 102 bus. In the week after our television debut the Arthur Howes Agency was busily filling our diary with engagements up and down the country. Photographic sessions and interviews followed, and that single chart entry at Number 42, although a small first step, made us all feel that we were walking on air.

The following week, the record had dropped away out of sight and there was even a rumour that somebody had bought the record into the chart for that single week. If such rumours were true, we were in no mood to believe them. As far as we were concerned, the name the Kinks was on the map and we had, albeit in a modest way, made our first little dent in the world of pop music.

The first ever official Kinks gig took place at the Town Hall, Oxford, on a cold night in February 1964. The opening act was an R and B group from London called the Downliner Sect. Both groups were playing Bo Diddley songs, and so it was a night notable for the sound of maracas, which echoed around the half-empty hall. This gave the impression that somebody was shaking a giant pepper pot.

A series of gigs followed, and we started travelling to small clubs up and down the country. The Kinks were billed as having appeared on *Ready Steady Go!* and would sing their chart-smashing hit, 'Long Tall Sally'. They were assorted gigs with strange-sounding names like Club Noriek, the Jungfrau, Mr Smith's, the Goldhawk Social Club, Klooks Kleek and the Ram Jam. We were billed as R and B, but our pop-sounding record was not treated seriously by the blues snobs, who, because we had appeared on television and made a single, all of a sudden decided that we had sold out. We were starting to attract an audience of fans outside of our normal circle of friends and relatives, and I was surprised to see that they were a pretty snazzy-looking bunch, even though they were predominantly mods.

Just after we had taken Mick Avory on as drummer, I was asked by Larry Page to write a song for another group he was producing. He played the tape of my song and immediately asked me to sign a contract for it. Later I found myself standing in a crowded underground train on the Northern line, clutching the agreement for a song called 'I've Got That Feeling'. It was the height of the evening rush hour, and sweaty commuters were being thrown around by the erratic motion of the train. Office workers going back to the suburbs from the city. Back to homes, evening meals, cocoa, families, television. I hadn't bothered to read the small print of the contract. Surely that was irrelevant. What mattered was that my song had been accepted by the publishers and I was a 'songwriter' All I knew and cared was that the song had my name as composer next to the title. I vaguely remembered seeing 'For the payment of one penny', and '50 per cent to the composer-writer'. That meant I was to receive 50 per cent of every record and performance, whatever the figure was. Later that night my mother looked at both me and the contract with suspicion, almost as if I had done something illegal to get it. In fact the publisher's signature was already stamped on to the bottom of the standard one-page agreement. Eddie Kassner probably didn't even know that I had written the song.

The song was to be recorded by an all-girl trio called the Orchids, and produced by Larry for Decca Records, who had previously turned down the Kinks, and so the fact that my song was recorded for that label added a little sugar to what had been a bitter pill. There was no actual money involved yet. That would come later, when the record became a success. My work was done. All I had to do was turn up at the session and brood in the corner, like the average moody young genius songwriter. In my dreams, I

imagined the musicians looking over for a nod of approval
from me at the end of the take. Then I expected everyone
would applaud and carry me out of the studio to the strains of
'For He's a Jolly Good Fellow'. I had no idea that the musicians
would all be session men. Unlike my group, who would have
willingly recorded for nothing, these musicians were
professionals doing a session as part of a job. The realities of
the situation were far from my mind. In my dreams, the song
had already reached Number 1 and had been voted song of
the year by the critics. Frank Sinatra had chosen it for his next
film. What next? An Oscar nomination? A Nobel Prize
perhaps? Now I realize it was just a lousy little pop song, but
in my imagination it was the greatest piece of art yet created
by man. What an innocent fool I was. But as I looked around
the subway train the ordinariness of the commuters crushed
together around it was as though I was already free.

The weekend before the Orchids recorded 'I've Got That
Feeling', the Kinks had some gigs up north. But not ordinary
gigs, because we would be playing in the heart of 'Beatlemania'
at the Cavern Club in Liverpool. The club, which was
responsible for discovering the Beatles, was the centre of the
world of the Merseybeat, and we, an untogether group of
pretenders from London, would be trying to encroach on
their territory. In February 1964 the Beatles were at their most
popular in Liverpool, and the northern groups had a monopoly
on the charts, with a few exceptions like the Rolling Stones
and Cliff Richard and the Shadows. Bob Wooler was the
manager of the Cavern and he had booked us in for one of the
lunch-time beat sessions. His approval was vital to our future.
If he liked us and we went down well, the word would spread
to other promoters around the country who would book us
on the strength of this gig. If we failed to impress, then we
might as well throw our instruments into the River Mersey,
because if you couldn't break the Liverpool scene, there was
no future anywhere else. But more than anything else, we

were to be paid £25 for the gig. If they paid it here, they would pay it anywhere.

We drove up to Liverpool in a converted ambulance, which Robert and Grenville had purchased for £200. My brother-in-law Brian had left his job as a test-flight engineer at Handley Page Aircraft to become our tour manager. He had met my sister Gwen at the Atheneum Ballroom in Muswell Hill. He had watched her week after week as she danced with one boyfriend after another, but he was terrified of asking her for a date in case she refused. When eventually he plucked up the courage, the romance escalated, and after a brief courtship Gwen and Brian decided to get married. Soon they realized that Gwen had become pregnant, which brought the wedding forward, and after the briefest of engagements, Brian and Gwen walked down the aisle at St James's Church, Muswell Hill. By the time he became our tour manager he and Gwen had brought three delightful daughters into the world.

Our arrival at Lime Street, Liverpool, was on a bright, winter's morning. The air was crisp and the sun, which cast large shadows across the cobbled streets up to the station, was as bright with enthusiasm as we were. We were tired, dirty, uncomfortable and excited as hell to be there. Brian suggested that we freshen up in the public toilets in the station and get changed in the ambulance, as he was not sure what the backstage conditions were like at the Cavern. This gig would be in front of the most hard-to-please audiences in the country, well known for their down-to-earth honesty, which at times bordered on cruelty. A real 'Scouse' has the ability to ask you a question with an exclamation mark at the same time. When a Liverpudlian tells you that you look like crap, you'd better believe it. Anywhere else, a criticism is received as an opinion which may or may not be right. In Liverpool if they say you stink, you go to the bathroom and wash.

After we had washed and brushed ourselves up, we found ourselves setting up on stage at the Cavern Club. The

lunchtime audience was already in, and watched stern-faced as
we carried on our equipment and began to organize ourselves.
Waiting for their judgement, we were like condemned men
erecting our own gallows while gawping masses awaited our
execution. Fortunately, like an execution, it came and went
quickly and nobody felt a thing. Unlike the condemned, we
hung around afterwards and mingled with the crowd to see
how we had gone down. By all accounts Wooler thought we
had done well, and said to Brian that he would book us again.
A local girl called Diane said that we were quite original. Her
girlfriend had also been impressed by us and they were both
coming to see us play later that night at a ballroom on top of
a desolate hill top just outside Liverpool, . In fact they were so
impressed that they decided to bring a few more girlfriends
and travel up with us in the back of the ambulance.

The gig was in the middle of the moorland on the top of a
windy hill. Diane had said that a female beat group, called the
Liverbirds, were opening the show for us. We would both be
playing two forty-five-minute sets, and even though the
Liverbirds were alternating with us, the Kinks' name was
bigger on the poster, by virtue of the fact that we had been
advertised as being on *Ready Steady Go!* Diane and her friends
were concerned that we would leave Liverpool with a good
impression. She seemed to know everything. All the sights
were pointed out to us. All the necking with her girlfriends in
the back of the ambulance was polite and well organized. The
girls sucked Polo mints to keep their breath smelling fresh,
and also not to give away where their mouths had been. And
as I watched the Liverbirds' singer with the bouffoned hair
belt out 'Anyone Who Had a Heart', it struck me that these
Scousers had a most wonderful warm sense of humour all
their own. They celebrated human failings instead of trying to
cover up the faults. They were absolutely unimpressed by the
rest of the world and by what people thought of them. They
were honest, proud, emotional, scruffy and soulful. Nowhere

else could have produced the Beatles. Lennon and McCartney would write great songs as long as they had the heartbeat of Liverpool behind them. For once I was not ashamed of being ordinary, and when I felt sorry for myself I thought of these no-nonsense, northern people, shut my mouth and sucked on a Polo. There were no dark clouds over my head when I was in Liverpool.

We were tired but confident as we started our long drive back to London. Brian, partly because he was an intrepid adventurer, and partly to save money on Bed and Breakfasts, had decided to face the cold night and return to London straight after the show. The band sat at the back of the ambulance, and Jonah, our next-door neighbour and equipment boy, sat in the front with my nephew Terry, who was talking to Brian to keep him awake. As we fell asleep one by one, Brian started to reminisce about his days in the RAF, when he had been stationed in Hong Kong. 'The greatest days of my life,' he said nostalgically, 'until now. This is nearly as exciting.' Brian was an optimist. A true Kinks believer and fan. To Brian, the group was like a little army on manoeuvres. Our battleground was the motorway.

On the drive down the motorway, Brian's conversation moved back from the RAF to the present. He was looking forward to getting home, and kept referring to Gwen: 'Gwen would have liked this, Gwen would have enjoyed that, Gwen will laugh when I tell her about this and that.' Suddenly there was a crunch, a pop and a dull thud. Then the ambulance shook and choked. Brian pulled over, and after an inspection of the underside of the vehicle declared that the 'big end's gone'. I didn't know what big ends were, and even after subsequent detailed explanations by Brian, to this day I'm none the wiser. Brian's bubbly humour descended into pitiful concern as he delicately persuaded and coaxed the ailing ambulance down the motorway at ten miles an hour. By the time we arrived back home, Brian's eyes were like organ stops – out on the end

of stalks. Dark rings under his eyes. White, pallid face. He was
still mumbling to himself: 'The big ends, it was the big ends.'

We had stopped listening 250 miles before. We had returned
triumphant, even if our chariot was somewhat disabled and
our driver reduced to a quivering wreck. The road had
certainly given Brian a new outlook on the world. In the
RAF there was always someone else to give orders in a state
of emergency. What seemed to hit Brian more than the big ends
was the fact that we were truly on our own. No one would help
us except the Automobile Association. We couldn't send an
SOS for ground- or air-support because there was nobody
else fighting our war with us. And yet there was something
else in Brian's eyes: a realization that touring on the road meant
freedom. As long as we got to the gig on time and played on
time, the world was ours. This was an excitement we all felt.
That's what pulled us together and turned us into a group.

Despite our success at the Cavern we went into the Dave
Clark tour a little under-prepared and disorganized. The Kinks
were being paid £250 a week and that was like a steady job.
But out of that we had to pay commission of 40 per cent to
assorted managers and agents as well as our own bed and
breakfast, which meant that there was hardly any money left
for us. But we were keen and ready for the big time which
we thought was just around the corner, so the fact that we
were making no money didn't bother us.

Although we travelled on the same coach as the other acts,
it was every man for himself when we reached the theatre.
(Brian had been left at home to cut down the overheads.)
When we arrived in a town the stars, Dave Clark and the
Hollies, were dropped off at their hotels. Then we drove to
the theatre to unload the gear. All the other bands had road
managers on board to lift the equipment off the bus and
assemble it but the Kinks had neither the finances nor
the space allocated on the bus for any extra bodies. So we

hauled our own amps onstage and set up ourselves.
After that came the task of finding the cheapest Bed and
Breakfast to stay in. Once this was done, we rushed back to
the theatre just in time for the show.

Package shows usually performed twice daily in each town,
and had six bands on the tour playing sets lasting between
fifteen and thirty minutes, depending on their popularity and
fame at the time. The opening act on this tour was a group
from Liverpool called the Mojos. The Kinks were on second,
by virtue of our one television appearance and our record
having reached 42. Mark Wynter, a solo singer in the
traditional heart-throb mould, was on next with his backing
group, and the Hollies, riding high after hits such as 'Stay' and
'Just One Look', closed the first half. After the interval Mark
Wynter's back-up band played a few more songs, then the
comedian who acted as master of ceremonies told some jokes
while the stage was quickly re-set. Then the Dave Clark Five
performed. After a short break to let the first house out, we
set up again and repeated the show for the second audience.

We thought that we had done enough at the opening
concert at the Coventry Theatre to earn some praise in the
press, but we were to have a double disappointment the
following week, when not only did our record drop out of
the charts but an article in the *New Musical Express* by Richard
'the Beast' Green gave us the worst review of the whole show.
The only song that earned any praise at all was 'You Really
Got Me'.

On the stage of the De Montfort Hall, Leicester, the
following day, the tour manager, Malcolm Cooke, added to
our shame when he announced in front of the whole touring
company that the Kinks were to be moved to the opening
spot in the show and that the Mojos, whose recording
'Everything's Alright' was now entering the charts, were to
go on after us. We had suddenly gone from being the blue-
eyed boys to being the whipping boys. Everybody on the

tour felt it their duty to advise and criticize, and the more they told us what a shambles we were, the worse we performed. Before the tour we had wanted to put in some blues songs, like Howlin' Wolf's 'Smokestack Lightning' and Slim Harpo's 'Got Love if You Want It', but we were told that this was a pop-music tour and all the songs either had to be in the charts or at least covered by another chart-topping group. We had already started playing 'You Really Got Me', and even though nobody knew the song, it seemed to go down well. But opening the show meant that we would have to cut our act from five songs to four, and so 'You Really Got Me' was thrown out and replaced by something more familiar to the audience.

At first, we took our relegation to heart and played with our heads down, but after a few nights Dave started to jump around again and a few girls in the audience started to scream. I was still depressed and humiliated, and as a result my raving was restricted to shaking my head and arms and shimmying on the spot: I refused to move my feet from the ground. I had decided that I was to be totally professional and do this tour just for the money. All £20 a week of it.

After the show, while the other bands went off to their hotels, we would stay to pack our equipment back on to the bus. This was the one time we actually scored over the other groups because we got to talk to the fans that had stayed behind, waiting backstage. We were given a lot of encouragement from fans of the other bands. If our show was not a hit with the press, we made up for it by doing our own PR after the show. Quaife was particularly at home doing this, so much so that on many occasions he converted Hollies and Dave Clark fans into Kinks fans as well.

As the tour travelled from town to town, Avory began to come out of his shell. He kept everyone amused with stories of working on a building site with a gang of Yugoslav refugees. Another of his stories concerned an early sexual experience with a Scout master in East Molesey who persuaded him that in order to be a good scout he had to massage a certain part of the Scout master's anatomy every day while swearing the oath of allegiance to the Scout troop. It was only on reading the life story of Lord Baden-Powell that he discovered to his relief that the stroking of Scout masters' private parts was not essential when taking the pledge.

Quaife was becoming more outrageously showbiz by the day. His thick stage make-up was never washed off after the show, and the collar of his stage shirt became caked with Max Factor. However Pete was the band's best ambassador when it came to negotiating space for us to change backstage, and his powers of persuasion over Malcolm Cooke, the tour manager, often saved us from changing in the nearest public lavatory. Pete finally reached the conclusion that it was more expedient to stay in his stage gear all the time, eliminating the need to change at all. He had the ability to make it seem as though he was continually pursued by admiring fans. If Number 42 in the charts was to be the pinnacle of our achievement, then Pete Quaife was going to make sure the world remembered him for it for as long as possible.

Even though Dave was still barely seventeen, he was fast becoming known as the resident raver of the tour: staying up later, getting drunk more, getting into trouble more and sleeping less than anybody else on the tour. The Kinks may have been the least known and the worst act on stage, but we had affectionately been taken on as the tour mascots by some of the other bands.

The tour bus became a friendlier place once everybody assumed their position according to their chart status. Eric Haydock, the Hollies' bass player, had taken the Kinks under his wing, and was constantly advising me to trade in my imitation blond Gretsch guitar for a Fender Telecaster. Eric was a friendly, chubby-faced Lancastrian with an accent straight out of *Coronation Street*, and he made a point of calling us by our full Christian names: 'Raymond this, David that, Peter should and Michael should never do this or that'.

All Eric's references to the Dave Clark Five were not so complimentary. Dave Clark was a quiet north Londoner who had become amazingly successful, not so much because of his musicianship but because he had a shrewd head for business. He also had an astonishingly dark suntan for a musician touring England in the depths of winter, and his stage act was somehow presented with a kind of contrived machismo that proved to be timeless in the sense that it was both decades ahead and behind its time. The Dave Clark Five were definitely a product, and it was probably for this reason that Eric had taken such a negative response to their act. They were also Number One in the charts with 'Bits and Pieces', to which they insisted on doing a military-style goose-step every time they performed it on stage.

There was so much equipment and so many cables connected to their equipment that on several occasions the whole power supply would blow up, causing an embarrassing delay while the long-suffering electrician repaired the fault. After a while Dave Clark and his four chums started to suspect that it was sabotage, and one night after a show in Southampton Clark stopped the coach on the way back to London to hold an official inquiry. He threatened that when the saboteur was eventually caught, the offender would be summoned to his quarters where 'a punishment of the severest nature' would be implemented. Graham Nash of the Hollies wondered if the sun-tanned drummer was showing signs of cracking. Mick Avory asked if Clark had been a boy scout, and, if so, offered to help administer the punishment. Dave Davies swigged his beer and gave a V-sign, and Eric Haydock looked innocent and said nothing.

Halfway through the tour, Pye Records released the second single from our first recording session, 'You Still Want Me'. The message came via Malcolm Cooke that our management wanted us to put the song in the stage act, which we reluctantly did. We breathed a sigh of relief a few weeks later when the record was officially written off as a flop. Although it was a sweet enough pop song with a good beat, the only thing worse than its eventual failure was the possibility of it being such a big hit that we would be forced to perform it every night for the rest of our careers. Even so, we were disappointed that we had not got into the charts, and we had seen enough of the music business to know that unless we made a hit record, and soon, we would be on our first and last major package tour.

The Kinks were still considered the sloppiest group on the tour and messages were reaching us that even our biggest supporter, Arthur Howes, was thinking of replacing us. Our act needed help. Enter Hal Carter.

The Kinks had set up at the Bedford Granada ready for the performance. I had stayed behind so that I could wash my hair in a sink backstage. It was almost impossible to get hot water backstage in those days, but the Bedford Granada was one of the better equipped theatres on the circuit. I was just starting to wash the lather out of my hair when a voice – a hard Liverpudlian twang with a hint of an American drawl – floated across to me:

'Are the Kinks here?'

I remembered a line from an old John Wayne movie:

'Who wants to know?'

'Hal Carter, that's who. I've been sent by Arthur Howes to work on your stage act, which, I understand, is in desperate need of attention.'

Hal stood in the doorway of the dressing room, his head was cocked over to one side, similar to the classic shots of James Dean in *Giant*. That's where the similarity ended. Hal had a little turned-up nose which seemed to lift his whole face with it. This included the top lip, which exposed his protruding front teeth and gave his mouth a cocky sneer. This produced

an angry punk image, similar to early Elvis Presley or Cliff
Richard, and was probably acquired by Hal after many hours
in front of a mirror. The only problem was that Hal didn't
look like Elvis or even Cliff. He looked like Hal. Also, Hal
was slightly cross-eyed, which made a mockery of the look of
inner turmoil and menace he was trying to project. I could
sympathize to a certain extent because his crossed eyes had
exactly the same effect on his image as the gap in my two
front teeth had on mine. It made us both look a little
vulnerable and, to less sensitive people, stupid. Hal tore into
me verbally; without pity.

'I wasn't aware you were in the group. I thought you were
a roadie, the way you were washing your hair in the sink.'

His eyes squinted as if he were about to reach for a gun. His
voice dropped to a whisper, the Scouse 'R's rolling through
the veneer of acquired Americana. My eyes zoomed into close-
up of his face as he spoke.

'You are one of the brothers, aren't you? Well, dry your
hair. Let's get the group on stage and work on this act.'

Hal made me smile, and somehow gave me confidence. If
our stage act was half as good as Hal's real life performance,
then the Kinks were assured of stardom. Even if only in 'B'
movies.

After watching our act for the first time, Hal came silently
into our dressing room. He walked up to us all individually,
and stared each of us out for a second, similar to the way a
prize-fighter stalks his opponent before a boxing match. Then
he stood and watched as we packed up our few belongings.
Avory stood behind Hal and mimicked him, striking a similar
moody pose; he pushed up the end of his nose with a finger
and crossed his eyes. The rest of us tried our best to carry on
without sniggering, but eventually Dave burst out laughing.
Hal's eyes grew larger and went slightly more cross-eyed as he
spoke in a calm but rapid, contemptuous monotone:

'You were rubbish tonight, lads. I'm here to improve your

act by the time we reach London. And if it has not improved significantly by then, you are off the tour and back on the street. So I want you all onstage tomorrow afternoon for a rehearsal as soon as you've loaded the equipment.'

During the next few days Carter put us through a series of vigorous rehearsals. He told us where to stand, how to behave and what to play, shouting out corrections to us from the auditorium while we ran through our songs:

'Quaife, stop posing. Ray, let's see some sign of life. Dave, let's see you rave on your own. Avory . . . it doesn't matter, forget it.'

He suggested that we cut some of our blues songs and put in some conventional pop hits of the day.

'That song, "You Really Got Me", is all right, put it back in . . . Cut out that "Smokestack Lightning" number. You're not doing yourselves or anybody else any favours by playing that . . . Change this . . . Try that . . . And try not to cover your eyes with your hands every time the spotlight comes on your face . . . you're supposed to be professionals.'

On one occasion, Hal was giving us a particularly harsh criticism when he was interrupted by Graham Nash of the Hollies. Graham said Hal should let us be a blues group if that was what we wanted to be, and not try to turn us into a cabaret act. After Graham finished, Hal resumed his tirade, adding that it was he, Hal Carter, who was responsible for the success of most of the pop groups in the country, and that even the Hollies had been indirectly influenced by some of Hal's innovations. We were not in a position to argue or question his claims. Our act was beginning to go down slightly better, and we assumed that it was because of Hal. Even so, Carter was not going to let us think we had improved.

Hal assumed that, as I was supposed to be the songwriter of the group, I was the person with the most influence over the other members. In thinking this way, Hal had missed the most important thing we had going for us: *nobody* had a say over what we did or didn't do. Everything was a group decision at that time. If we weren't a group, it would be a solo act. I had been a solo act from the day I was born, and it was very lonely at times. Playing with other musicians taught me that it was easier playing with other people than it was on my own. The writing part was lonely enough. It was almost a relief when I heard the group play something that I'd written. Proof that I wasn't going mad. Our first two singles had been flops, and, although I felt mainly to blame for the situation we found ourselves in, I didn't feel that desperate because we had that one song, 'You Really Got Me', which nearly always got a good reaction.

But somehow the spark wasn't quite there. I think it had something to do with the way we were being projected . Hal deduced that the song was right, but there was something in our stage presence which failed to communicate to the audience. They applauded every night, but there was always a darkness between us and them. We did not feel as one with them. Hal had done a good job on our stage act, but that's all it was . . . an act.

It was decided that we needed to smarten ourselves up by purchasing some new stage clothes. Robert took us to Berman and Nathan, the theatrical costumiers. During the tour we had started to get a reputation as Dickensian-type characters. Avory was called Bill Sikes; Dave was the Artful Dodger, I was Smike from *Nicholas Nickleby* and Quaife insisted on being Pip from *Great Expectations*, even though his manner suggested that he was more like Mr Micawber. We tried on what we thought were clothes from the Victorian era, but Monty Berman explained that they were in fact hunting jackets. He matched the red hunting jackets with white frilly shirts from another period in history, put us in black riding trousers and Chelsea boots, and lo and behold, we looked like us.

Our first concert with the new red hunting jackets was at the Gaumont Theatre in Bournemouth. We were standing

behind the curtain ready to open the show as usual when
Graham Nash and Allan Clarke of the Hollies were seen
staring at us from the wings. Graham came up to me and,
after scrutinizing my new stage gear closely, announced that,
in his opinion, our new gear was fab. 'Now you look like the
Kinks.'

The new clothes were an instant hit, and although we
were still the opening act with two flop singles behind us,
our spirits were high and we were optimistic about our
future.'

Raymond Douglas paused, as if he wanted this particular event in
his life to last as long as possible. Then he did one of his instant turn-
arounds. From being an optimistic old timer reliving his youth, he
became a confused old man.

'It's only life, anyway. What can I tell you? I can't possibly
explain it all to you. Most of what would mean a lot to me
would probably bore you. I could tell you every intimate
moment, and describe it all in the most grandiose manner, using
an eloquence far beyond most people's capabilities, but still I
would never capture that single moment of magnificence, when
an original thought is born, and you know that nobody else has
ever seen the world in quite the same way. We had our own
identity. That knowledge. That millisecond, my dear boy, is a
lifetime. Now turn off that bloody tape machine. I'm knackered.'

There was a silence. I turned off my tape recorder and tried to
rest my eyes. We had been talking for some time and I hadn't
realized it. I yawned and began to nod off. Soon I was asleep,
drifting in R.D.'s memoryland.

7

Mixed up with a floosie

I heard a distant sound of an audience applauding. R.D. appeared like a magician as he moved into the light and spoke down a microphone. His eyes looked mad, his voice was full of menace.

'And now I give you my life. Would you like my life, or are the rights already acquired?'

I shot back in my seat. Had he been deceiving me all along? Perhaps it was something that he had slipped into my tea when I wasn't looking. After all, R.D. had been around in the hippy era and hippies were fond of sprinkling substances into other people's food. That was my only possible explanation. How else could he make me believe that I was experiencing his past in my body?

Raymond Douglas smiled and disappeared from view. I found myself transported to another time. His time. My reality had suddenly turned into R.D.'s experience. As I drift out and into the light, the spotlight, I try to get up but I am trapped. There is the sound of an audience coming through the speakers, and the room closes in. The audience comes closer and closer. Then I become Raymond Douglas and I am on stage in his place. The audience is cheering, teenage girls are screaming and I am bowing to their applause. Where am I? The audience seems like it is from another time: girls in miniskirts and bouffant hairstyles smiling at me. It's noisy, so noisy . . . so much noise and adrenaline. I look at the band. There they are: Dave, Mick and Pete, all smiling at each other. They all look so young. They've obviously played something very exciting, because the audience is continuing to stand and applaud. I actually feel like I am alive and living in this place, with this audience. Is this my reality? Was it my past looking forward? Or is it the future looking back? Am I alive now? If this is my present? What a fantastic place to be. I am on a stage, in the spotlight, and everybody loves me. Just like Raymond Douglas must have felt at his family party, I am the centre of attraction. In the front row of the audience is a sexy-looking brunette, licking her lips as she stares at my groin. I shout out to a bouncer at the front of the stage: 'Where am I?'

The bouncer shouts back: 'The Pier Ballroom, Southsea.'

Why am I here, of all places? Why has he chosen to bring me here? The Pier Ballroom must have been magnificent in its heyday when the big bands came to play. Now it is a relic from another time, on its way out, along with the music halls and the end-of-the-pier variety shows. The Kinks have just played the last chords of 'You Really Got Me'. Why isn't it a more prestigious setting? The Blackpool Opera House, when the Kinks opened for the Beatles, would surely have been more appropriate, or even one of those famous *Ready Steady Go!* programmes. I would have loved to have met Cathy McGowan when she was young.

Now I am in the world of Then, sitting backstage after the show waiting for the crowd to leave so that we can go to the front and pack up our equipment. I look up and see Dave laughing and joking with Mick and Pete. They accept me as R.D without question. A pretty girl with red hair and a Mary Quant miniskirt runs into the dressing room and starts to hug Dave. He immediately puts his hand up her skirt and gives her a french kiss. Moments later I find myself in the room next door with the girl with dark hair who was standing in the front row. She is kissing me all over and is starting to undo the zipper of my hipster trousers.

The question, 'Why Southsea?', is still on my lips as I feel the brunette slide down on to her knees and kiss my groin. As I close my eyes, I feel the girl's wet tongue swallow me up like a vacuum cleaner. My whole body seems to be drained down into that one area of sublime wetness and suction. I feel the brunette's hair, which had been stiffened with lacquer, as her head rolls from side to side at my waist. I smell her lipstick and face make-up as it begins to rub off on my body.

The whole room starts to revolve when suddenly I hear the voice of Raymond Douglas boom down into my ear like the master of ceremonies: 'Why Southsea lad? Because this was as good as it got.'

I find myself caught in the nowhere land of present and past, no-going-back. My body is about to explode with pleasure. I try to ignore R.D. but he keeps shouting in my ear.

'Enjoying it, lad? Because this was great. Tonight, for the first time, you discovered something precious, vital to your existence. This was the thing that saved me and will save you from yourself. Tonight, as well as having the best blow-job of your life, you discovered your audience.'

By now his angry voice is almost shattering my eardrums, but the brunette is in full flow and my body is hers. Raymond Douglas turns up the volume and continues mercilessly; like a television evangelist.

'Tonight you and your audience recognized each other, and that long – so long – lonely battle was nearly over for you both. The Gods had answered your prayers, and the confusion and gloom which had been yours since before puberty had finally been swept aside. Hallelujah!'

By now I am groaning uncontrollably. My head is banging against the door and the brunette is heaving back and forth, still with her head attached to my penis, her mouth slurping like a giant suction-pump. Still Raymond Douglas is shouting down the microphone. Even louder. The brunette growls. I make noises like a wild animal caught in a trap. Raymond Douglas shouts like a mad preacher.

'Now you can conquer the world. Now . . . now . . . *now!*'

I find myself shouting with him. Suddenly the room turns dark and the brunette disappears.

Blackness.

I open my eyes.

I am back in the studio with Raymoond Douglas. He looks frozen in time, in the same position as when I first saw him.

I felt somewhat embarrassed. It was the same feeling I had when I discovered that two people had to make love in order for me to be born; and it left me with the same feeling of guilt. What made me feel more uncomfortable was that Raymond Douglas seemed to have manipulated the whole incident to prove a point. I was not sure how he had achieved this, I had given up trying to rationalize the absurdity of the situation long ago, but through it all I felt that something special was at the end of this experience. This strange old man was not just telling me about his life, he was making me experience it for myself, the same way he had done with his songs. He made people think that he was singing for them, and his experience was also theirs. Perhaps Raymond Douglas was opening doors in my memories that I had forced myself to close long ago. I was trying to regain my composure when R.D. started at me again.

'The audience had not just been applauding and cheering, it was not just screams of excited teenage girls, it was a genuine appreciation of something new and something different. I felt uniqueness: we had our sound, and it was, to us and to our audience, totally original.'

I felt happy for Raymond Douglas, and honoured that he had shared that experience with me – even if I had been embarrassed by the incident with the brunette.

I wandered home aimlessly. The experience had indeed opened a door into myself. Why was I going through this experience? I only wanted to do my job, after all. They had given me what had seemed a relatively simple project, but now I was caught up in R.D.'s world and I was not doing my job properly.

At home the phone rang. I waited for the answering machine to click on so that I could screen the call. Paranoia was suddenly inside me. I heard my own voice say, 'I'm not in at the moment. Please leave your name, number and the time of your call.' It was Julie from the office. I picked up the telephone and she immediately fired off questions.

'Where have you been? What have you been doing? How is the work going? When will I see you?'

There seemed to be an underlying series of questions beneath the obvious ones. Suddenly she had become an inquisitor. It made me uncomfortable.

'I can't see you tonight, I'm very tired, very confused,' I explained.

'What are you confused about?'

'I can't tell you right now. I don't want to speak over the phone.'

'Are you afraid that we're being bugged?' She laughed.

'Yes,' I said, 'bugged. I really feel I'm being followed and scrutinized. Every move I make is being monitored in some way.'

'You're paranoid,' she said.

'Perhaps, perhaps I am. Yes, paranoid.'

'You must have the work completed soon, you know that.'

'I know that,' I replied. 'I can do my job. Don't worry about it. The book will be finished on time.'

I put the phone down without even saying goodbye. I realized that Julie could have been planted by the Corporation. Damn.

I thought of R.D.'s Julie Finkle and I felt as though I wanted to set off to find her. All R.D.'s clues were in my memory now. I promised myself that I would search and I would find her.

I went to bed. Before I could reach for my sleeping pills, I drifted off. I dreamt. The dream was like the present; as if it was the only thing that existed. My only reality.

Dave Davies and I were in the van outside a ballroom somewhere up north. We were shouting abuse at each other. Brian and Mick Avory tried to stop the fight but we were determined to destroy each other. We punched, scratched, spat and clawed. Skin started to come from our faces as our nails tore away flesh until blood was exposed. Dave bit my cheek. I kneed him in the groin.

Then I was in the back garden with my father. He looked at me and smiled as he held up a headless chicken. He threw the body down and the chicken attempted to run around without its head. Back in the van, there was blood. My head smashed against the side of the van. Some skin came away from my elbow as I retaliated and smashed Dave in the face.

Then, we were on stage singing 'You Really Got Me' as we were in the flashback to Southsea, only this time there was blood streaming down our faces. As the song reached a climax, I saw the van outside, with its doors open. There was blood, our blood, and chicken feathers smeared all over the inside, as if there had been some strange, ritualistic sacrifice. I woke up sweating, and after I took a long shower, I went to the bathroom mirror to see whether or not I still had skin on my face. I was relieved to see that it was intact. I took two sleeping pills and went back to bed.

The following day I decided to try to see Julie before going to meet R.D., but as I turned the corner I saw my boss talking to another executive outside the Corporation building. I called Julie's office but there was no reply. I rang my extension to leave a message in case she should call me, and was amazed when it was engaged. I panicked and slammed down the phone. As I ran back to the Corporation building a limousine pulled up outside and my boss got in. The limousine drove straight in my direction, as if the driver was following me. Although I was still slightly hung-over from the sleeping pills, I remembered Julie saying that she thought I was becoming paranoid. To escape detection, I ran through the back streets of what was left of the old city and as soon as I was in the clear I jumped on a commuter car and made my way to Raymond Douglas Davies. As I turned the corner to approach the studio, I saw the same limousine pass by. I ducked into a small alleyway at the side of the building and watched the limo as it slowly cruised past. I strained to look inside, but the windows were tinted. This was a poor part of the city and it was obvious that there was not an abundance of limousines in the area. It was all too much to be a coincidence. When the coast was clear I ran towards the front door and pressed the entrance buzzer. R.D.'s voice immediately came down the intercom:

'It's OK. The door's open. You're late.'

I wondered why the door was open. Had my boss been in to see R.D.? Was I being set up by the Corporation? Was R.D. being blackmailed? As I entered the room where he was sitting, I suddenly had this dreadful suspicion that R.D. might even *be* the head of the Corporation. I looked at him sitting there: a pathetic old man. He was already pouring me out a mug of tea. As I sat down he leaned over and smiled in a benign way and pushed his Coronation mug in my direction as he spoke.

'This is for you, my friend.'

'You actually consider me to be a friend?'

'Don't question friendship. Friends are a rare commodity. Now, shall we start or perhaps you'd like to finish your tea first?'

As I drank my tea Raymond Douglas told me what he thought were vital snippets of information about himself. Who various tour managers were, the truth about different incidents at concerts – the usual facts and figures from an era gone by. I somehow got the feeling that he was trying to bore me deliberately, so that I would go away and leave him in his own private little world. He appeared to be happy in his own anonymity, but just the same I felt he needed to talk.

My mind was on other things. I kept thinking about that brunette backstage at the Pier Ballroom in Southsea, and I started to get the most peculiar feeling that I wanted to see her again. An absurd desire, particularly as she had only appeared to me as part of a remembrance on the part of Raymond Douglas. I decided to take the plunge.

'Who was the brunette?' I asked. 'Was she, you know, *the* Girl? The one you sang about in your song?'

Raymond Douglas looked over at me with a mischievous grin on his face.

'*The* girl?' he inquired. 'You mean the one who was giving you a blow-job? Oh no, she's not *the* Girl. But she was part of *the* Girl.'

His vagueness was his one consistency. I pressed for an answer just the same.

'Were there many, then?'

As he stroked away at his long chin which was beginning to show some stubble, I could see his keen eyes straining to recapture a distant memory. Again, I had forgotten that I was talking to a really old man whose lust for the pleasures of the flesh should have diminished long ago. He paused, and then a smile slowly opened the entire bottom third of his face. He had suddenly flashed on a recollection. But knowing Raymond Douglas, it was probably going to be a pack of lies.

'The passage of time eliminates some of the more intimate details of one's existence. The routine trivia like passing water and shitting and the amount of food and alcohol consumed in the course of daily survival. Sure, there were girls. Lots of 'em. It's inevitable. I'm not a woman-in-every-port man, but as the trips around the country became more frequent it was obvious that acquaintances and friends would be picked up along the way. That's what building up a following of fans is all about. For example, when we played Stoke, there was a brunette called Cindy. She was sort of the local Elizabeth Taylor, and wore black suspenders and underwear especially for me. I took a special pride in Cindy. When I first met her I could see her potential, and each time we played Stoke or anywhere in that area I suggested that she either do something with her hair or make-up. Time after time I returned to find her looking more beautiful. After about five or six visits she looked so beautiful and had such fine dress sense that she had two or three local lads after her. I felt like I had turned this pretty but ordinary girl into a complete goddess. The last time I saw her she was walking across a zebra crossing on the way to meet her boyfriend in Hanley. I felt a deep pride, like Frankenstein must have felt when his monster first stood up and walked round the room. Cindy was now so beautiful she didn't need me anymore. I wonder how many kids she had?

Yes, Cindy was a part of *the* Girl, as you put it. Part of Julie Finkle, even. But not the whole.

Manchester, or should I say the Greater Manchester area,

encompassing Stockport and Altringham, meant the
formidable Wendy. Not such an obvious beauty. A rough
type, even. But big-hearted and with her hair always neatly
lacquered and back combed. She was probably only eighteen
or nineteen, but her hairstyle made her look thirty. Wendy
was a devoted follower and could always be relied on. During
the concert she was always in the front row, then, towards the
end of the show, she drifted to the side exit and came
backstage. I always found northern girls – that is, born and
bred northern girls – to be straightforward, no-nonsense
creatures, and Wendy was no exception.

Her one obsession was that she insisted on jerking me off as
soon as the gig was over. It could have been in the nearest
bathroom for all it mattered to her. She just felt that it had to
be as soon as possible after coming off stage. She said that it
made her feel part of the energy that I had communicated to
the audience. She wanted to be part of the performance
somehow, and to her this was the final number. Sometimes
she would take me out back into the car-park and hide behind
the nearest clump of bushes so that she could watch the fans
leaving while she was making me come. After a while I
realized that she must have done the same with other bands
who came to the vicinity. And as I came she turned
me in a certain direction, to see how far it went. Perhaps she
was comparing me with somebody else in another group.
Wendy must have been some sort of factory worker or maybe
a window-cleaner, because her hands were always dry and
chapped, like they had been in boiling-hot water all day, or
scrubbing floors. I always had a sore dick for days afterwards.

I didn't feel like I was cheating on anybody. There wasn't
anybody. In fact I considered it to be part of the job at the
time. Perhaps if I hadn't, I would have been branded a queer.
And anyway, with the possible exception of Cindy, I knew
that all the girls would perform the same function for the next
band that appeared.'

★

R.D. shook his head. 'That Cindy, what a girl!'

In a way I understood R.D.'s attitude towards this period in his life. Even so, without seeming like a prude, I was a little shocked by these yarns. Something inside me wondered if R.D. was weaving fact together with fantasy. He was, after all, supposed to be a great story-teller: that is one of the functions of a songwriter.

8

Girl

I was in no mood to be taken in by R.D.'s tacky attempt to side-track me with sordid stories of his encounters with groupies. I pushed harder for an answer to the question which had started to become my obsession.

'There must have been somebody special; some girl who wasn't a groupie.'

R.D. sat back in his chair and gently scratched his stubbly cheek as he contemplated the last glimmer of daylight before it faded through the narrow skylight. He knew that I hoped he was about to give me an incredible scoop, and I knew that he was going to string me along as long as he could.

'A girl. Hmm.'

He was stalling.

'You mean a girl who was special don't you. Well, they were all special at the time. A girl, OK. Yeah. There was a girl called Pamela who I fell in love with on my first day at primary school. My mother had held my hand and walked me into the classroom and stayed with me as long as she was allowed, until the head teacher said that it was time for the parents to leave. Needless to say, to coin a phrase, I cried buckets of tears, as did many of the other little children. The few who didn't cry laughed at the others. Pamela laughed at me at first, but when she realized that my sorrow was genuine, she came over to my desk and did her best to console me. She had pigtails, smelled of sherbet and looked like a miniature version of Debbie Reynolds. We were both five years old . . . I'll never forget that first day.

St James's Church of England primary school had a village

atmosphere and traditional values were religiously upheld.
During country dancing I discovered that I had a crush on a
partner called Carole Wilson, whose father, I recall, owned
and ran the local bicycle-repair shop. Carole and I danced the
Durham reel, and as we held each other and danced, I caught
a whiff of disinfectant on her breath. Probably she had had to
gargle after blowing up all those inner tubes at her Dad's
shop. Whatever it was, the perfume was alluring.

After her there were numerous crushes and fancies. But I
suppose my first experience at being truly hung up on a girl
was when I was at art college. She was in the Fine Arts
department with me, but in another group. Judy was tall, thin
and had straight dark-brown hair trimmed around her jawline
to frame her extremely angular features. She always had heavy
eye make-up on, and her face was powdered so white that she
resembled a Japanese geisha girl. She always wore a single-
breasted black leather jacket, a black skirt cut above her knees,
black leather boots and carried a black handbag. Everything
was black, as I recall. Juliette Greco had made quite an impact
on the girls at art college in those days. Judy was a beanpole of
a girl and possibly a little taller than I.

She lived on the other side of Highgate to Rosie, near West
Hill, and she often let me walk her home. If I had been able to
afford a motor bike, I think that she might have taken a liking to
me, but as it was I was your average nerdy art student who
desperately needed somebody feminine to reassure me that I was
a male. We hung out together and even kissed and groped on
occasions, but for the most part we were a fatal combination.
Judy in her black clothes. Me with my bleak outlook. I don't
recall whether or not I got to what Americans call 'first base' with
her. I must have felt something for her, though, because she had
the ability to make me very unhappy, a sure sign of love. When I
was on the Dave Clark tour I phoned her up and invited her to
one of the London dates, and she actually said that she wished I
would drop dead. I must have made quite an impression.

Then after I left Hornsey Art College, I did a spot in
the theatre department, at Croydon Art School. I met a
student called Margie, who had a small round face and large,
almond-shaped eyes. Margie and I spent most of our time
getting drunk on rough cider, and we ended up arguing about
everything. She often slapped me around for what seemed to
be no reason at the time, and then walked away as if nothing
had happened.

The one thing all these girls had in common was that as far
as I was concerned they all remained virgins. I did not think
of having a sexual encounter with any of them. It wasn't
until . . .'

'The brunette backstage at Southsea?'

'What about the brunette backstage at Southsea?'

'What about her?'

'She was definitely not a virgin, if that's what you mean.'

'Was she *the* girl? And was she always so uninhibited?'

'She was rude, if that's what you mean. I suppose you could say
that. She had no morals, but in a way, she had an honest streak to
her that I hadn't really encountered in other girlfriends at that
time. She was no prude. That was one of her qualities. She was
very straightforward and honest about her intentions, and she
probably was considered vulgar to straight people. Even though
people can sometimes perpetrate the most outrageous acts, there
might be an element of truthful humanity in what they're doing. I
found it liberating in a strange way – sort of clean filth.'

'Clean filth?' I asked.

R.D. took a swig of his tea before continuing.

'I have never fully understood the meaning of the word
filth, in its true sense. When I was at school the teachers
brainwashed me about the concepts of beauty and correct-
ness: for some reason, beauty was packaged with morality,
beauty passed exams. Filth was something that should be

washed off your hands. But I soon learned that beauty sometimes contains a certain amount of imperfection. Things were certainly not perfect in my life, and I was not perfect. I remember being in bed after a gig watching this beautiful brunette rolling her head around all over my body. Anita was a very experienced seventeen-year-old. Tall, lean and supple, and with a talent for doing extraordinary things with her mouth. I think that 90 per cent of the time I spent with Anita was spent looking down at the top of her head. It was definitely a man–woman relationship, and Anita was a stickler for jungle manners. A voodoo baby with small hard breasts and short black hair. I had met her in Soho but she came from the West Country, and, when she was romantic, her accent would twang better than a sweet blues guitar. Bed was very basic: 'You Tarzan, me Anita.' Then she licked her way up to my neck and stopped with her tongue still out, rigid. 'Where did you get that scar?' Then she kissed me under the jaw. Anita said that my scar was so large close up, yet on stage you couldn't see it at all, even from the front row. I asked her if my scar was ugly, but she explained that scars are only ugly when you try to hide them. She taught me not to be ashamed of my scars. Outside or inside. She talked a lot in bed, a real motormouth, and the only way I could stop her was to pat her lightly on the top of the head. This was our sophisticated communication system, the patent of which is still pending. Anita then slowly disappeared back down under the sheets. She taught me that even for a budding songwriter words are not everything. Actions speak volumes, and, in situations like this, Anita rarely spoke.

She had recently broken up with someone in a famous band. I asked her which one, but she would never say. I narrowed it down to two groups, both from Manchester, but she wouldn't say whether it was the lead singer or guitar player. As they had both been Number 1 in the charts, a beginner like me considered that I had scored quite high on the points ratings.

I knew that my life with Anita would be a learning
experience.

Anita made me believe in myself and would often give me
pointers after a stage performance. In a strange way, she was
teaching me both on stage and in bed. I knew that I was not
as good as she made out, but she really did try to coach me as
best she could. The best way to describe Anita was to imagine
you were playing for Arsenal in the Cup and she was in the North
Bank with the supporters, cheering you on. That cheer would
give you an extra couple of yards' speed. She was like that;
she gave me adrenaline, made me feel talented and sexy and
when she came it was as if I had scored a goal in the Cup
Final. To me her mouth exposed all the rawness of life, all the
beauty and ugliness of the world. Unholy and, at the same
time, righteous. And when she made me come, all the
grotesque shame that I felt would be softened by her gentle
West Country voice: 'It's all right, my darling. It's what people
are made of.'

Each night I played with more confidence because of her. I
actually felt that I had something more to offer the audience
than just a good rhythm-guitar sound.

Anita moved into a little attic flat in Chalk Farm with
another girl, called Doris, who knew even more groups than
Anita. I often stayed with Anita when I came back to London
and was amazed by the amount of celebrities who filed in and
out of the flat. It wasn't a knocking shop. It was just that
people wanted to be there. Stars of stage and screen, you
could even say. Familiar faces trying not to be recognized. It
was easy for me, in that I was not famous and had nothing to
hide. A certain drummer from one of the most popular
groups of the day sat outside Doris's flat with me one afternoon
and confessed that he envied me: I, a comparative nobody,
lived the way I wanted. I could float in and out of relationships
without ending up on the front page of the *News of the World*.
I was somewhat taken aback that this man envied me, of all

people, particularly as I had bought so many of his group's records when I was at school.

By the time the Dave Clark tour had finished, the Kinks had built quite a strong following around the country, and we started doing some small ballroom and club dates. Sometimes I took Anita on tour when we played out of town. She rode with me in the back of the van behind the equipment, where she huddled under a blanket and resumed my education in stagecraft.

The day Rosie, Arthur and Terry left to emigrate to Australia, I took Anita up to a northern sea resort where we were playing a gig that night.

I freaked out a little after the show. I had a few drinks too many, and as Anita and I were walking along the beach in the moonlight, I suddenly started screaming. A part of my family had left, possibly forever. Once the emotion started to come out, I found that it had snowballed into an uncontrollable frenzy. I blamed it on the moon, the drink and my sister emigrating to Australia. Anita blamed it on the fact that my records had flopped, that I was getting a bad break from society, and my overwhelming fear of failure, plus my complete and utter insecurity and lack of confidence in myself. After I had finished shouting abuse at the sea and the moon and anybody else who would listen, I collapsed in a heap on the sandy beach and wept like a pathetic child. Anita told me in no uncertain terms that if I was as unhappy with my lot from life as I said I was, I should emigrate to Australia with my sister. Then I could fester in my own bitterness over there instead of staying on to fight the so-called system with my music. Anita wasn't just good at doing things with her body, she had a head on her shoulders, and she could see through my sadness right to the truth. Perhaps the other 'girls', as you call them, could see the same thing, but they either despised what they saw or they couldn't cope with it – my sadness was so overwhelming. Anita walked back to the Bed and Breakfast

alone, and I stayed on the beach for a while longer. I thought
about what she had said, and realized that my only chance to
get even was to make a hit record. My desire for success was
stronger and even more important than the music itself. I
looked into the sea and saw myself again. I looked the same as
when I had drawn myself as one of those faceless people on a
cold, suburban street corner. I knew that I wanted to become
successful and hated myself for it.

Our first single flopped. Our second single had received some
attention. Briefly. And then it vanished apart for a few copies
bought by proud relatives. Cynical *aficionados* described Kinks
fans as 'mourners at a wake'. Our moment had gone before it
had fully been. Pete Quaife, our bass guitarist, would probably
start looking in the Situations Vacant section of the *Evening
News* for a commercial artist's job. Dave and I were fighting.
Dave and Mick Avory had started fighting. The promoters up
north came backstage after gigs and gave us advice on how to
improve our act. The speeches were almost identical.

'They've all been here.' They would say, as if they knew
various celebrities on a first-name basis, 'Ringo said to me . . .'
'Cliff and the Shadows were so grateful for the gig . . .' 'Billy,
that is, Billy Fury, is such a professional . . .'

Waiting for the local impresario was like waiting to meet
the Pope, only the Pope would probably have been more
down-to-earth.

'Now, lads, listen to what I say and you could earn
yourselves some decent brass.' They all had a different solution.
Variations on a theme. 'Stick in a ballad', 'You're too loud',
'Turn up the vocal', 'Play softer'. They all had good intentions,
no doubt, but they were condescending to the point of vomit.
My aim was to be so good that the buggers would be left
speechless. But I was still a novice. They would say their bit
and leave as they came. Unwanted, yet full of self-importance.

Mine was the first generation not to be called up for
National Service. Some of the promoters thought we looked

effeminate; others were convinced we were pansies. Avory said that some of us probably were. Especially with a name like the Kinks. Dave said that listening to those well-meaning know-alls reminded him of the teachers at school. Dave had particular cause to feel resentment, as he had been expelled from school for making it with one of the girls who went to a convent near Hampstead Heath. His was a story of sad consequence. There was Dave, banging away behind a clump of bushes on Hampstead Heath during the lunch-break, when up walked his headmaster, who, by some strange twist of mystic fate, had decided to go for his lunchtime constitutional on the Heath. I suppose Dave saw that headmaster in all authority figures, including the promoters' faces when they hinted that we would never be as famous as Gerry and the Pacemakers, or the Searchers. Mick Avory must have thought of the foreman on the building site where he worked after leaving school. Quaife was the only one of us who didn't seem frustrated by the nightly lecture. Perhaps Pete agreed with what was said. For all we knew, he was probably going for a job interview the next time we were in London, or, worse still, he might join another group.

No criticisms, however, could match the dressing-downs we received from Hal Carter, who had stayed on as our tour manager after the Dave Clark tour had finished. Hal had been around. This could not be denied. He had been in at the beginning of it all. Hal had worked with and been on first name terms with star names like Billy Fury, Shane Fenton, Larry Parnes and Val Parnell. He also claimed to have a lady friend in every town, and although this was often the case, we thought that he would inevitably blow his credibility with an overblown showbiz chat-up. But the chat-up always worked. Then he tormented us for days as he withheld the details of his conquest. But on a daily basis he refused to help carry equipment, stating emphatically that he was only there to work on our stage act which was, to be fair, pretty bad.

The truth was that we had no stage act. Acting was
for actors, but Hal became obsessed with turning us into
artists like Billy Fury, Cliff Richard or Adam Faith. Even
though Anita had been doing a Herculean job on my self-
confidence, there was no way I could pass as a matinée idol
with my spotty face and adenoidal speaking voice. Dave was the
prettiest, so Hal made Dave dive down on his knees, legs
open, for the girls to get an eyeful. Hal thought Mick Avory
was best left at the back beating his drum – that's when,
according to Hal, he wasn't beating his hampton. Quaife was
made to complement Dave's gyrations with the occasional
twirl and pouting lip. I was meant to sing and try to be
invisible.

When Hal lost his temper his transatlantic drawl snapped
back into his original Scouse accent, bawling a 'waste of time',
and 'last', which I later found out was Liverpudlian for the
worst. Even after a relatively good gig Hal stormed into the
dressing-room to bawl us out:

'You thought you were good tonight, I suppose!'

'No, Hal, honest.'

'No, you can't fool me. I definitely saw a smile on your
face. Well, while you're feeling so happy with yourself, lend
us a fiver. Go on. While you're on cloud nine, give me a sub.
I'm doing this lousy job for nought as it is.'

'You know I would if I could, Hal, but I'm skint myself.'

'Oh yeah, tight ass, that's you, Davies. Well, if you ever
make it I must remember not to touch you for a loan. Still,
there's not much chance of that, judging by tonight's
performance. Dave was the only one doing it right tonight.
Quaife was posing, Avory was dreaming of the next wank
and you spent all your time looking at Anita. Dave was
the only one doin' it. The poor bleeder was raving on his
own.'

'Give us a break, Hal, we were all working our bollocks
off,' protested Mick.

Hal's eyes became more crossed and cocky, sensing a perfect wind-up.

'Bollocks is right, Mick. It was.' Hal moved in and stuck his turned-up nose right in Mick's face. 'A load of kack.'

Mick sat motionless, staring Hal out. Then Hal turned on Quaife.

'One day you're all going to surprise me and rave together on cue. Ray was standing like a spastic, and Dave was the only one raving, on his bloody own.'

At this point Dave stood on a chair by the dressing-room window, vodka in one hand, the other holding himself so he could aim while he urinated out the window. He slowly turned around to Hal as he said, 'That's because . . . I'm a raver.'

Hal rolled his eyes. 'Very nice. Charming. Why can't you piss in a beer glass like a normal person?'

A girl's voice giggled outside the window. 'Is that you, Dave?'

'That's right, darlin'. Hey, Hal, you mean to tell me Billy Fury pisses in a beer glass?'

The sound of Fury's name taken in vain made Hal explode. 'Billy is an artist. He doesn't piss anywhere except in the toilet, which is just about where your future is.'

Dave turned and urinated over Hal's boots.

'Oh, I apologize, Hal. Please forgive me for mentioning Billy Fury in the same sentence as "piss", but while we're on the subject, why don't you piss off?'

'All right, I will, but where will you be without me?' Hal wiped his boot with a towel and looked at me. 'Ray, I want you to come to my room tonight to talk about new material for the act. Mick, leave the hampton alone for the night and Dave, I'm going to write to your mother and report your behaviour to her. You're laughing now, but she'll clip you round the ear when you get home. Oh, and Quaife, you've got too much make-up on tonight, or is that left over from last

night? You know that big white sink at the top of the B. and
B.? Well, it's called a bath. I want to see you in it.'

'Yes, sir. Does Billy Fury bathe every day, sir?'

'Fury is a consummate artist, and don't you forget it! He is
immaculate at all times! In all the years I worked with him, I
can never remember him going to the toilet or bathroom!
Now, if you don't mind, I have to pay my respects to our
employer for the evening and then organize our B. and B.'

Hal left in the company of our landlady, who on this
occasion was a middle-aged divorcée with two inches of
make-up on her face and large, sagging boobs. She was
apparently the proprietor of a raving bed-and-breakfast and
would often organize parties for the groups Hal brought
to town. I imagined that once Hal and the landlady arrived at
the B and B they would probably retire to her private quarters,
discuss the old days when Hal was Billy Fury's roadie, then
after a couple of Dubonnets Hal would be expected to get his
leg over for old times' sake. But if Billy Fury was indeed a
great artist and Hal had learned anything from him, he would
have taken one look at the landlady's face and felt obliged to
put a paper bag over the unfortunate woman's head before
doing the business. I tried to put such sordid thoughts out of
my mind; I wanted to imagine them sitting in comfy chairs
having a quiet chat about the virtues of Fury's heart-pounding
ballads and his consummate stage presence. But the knowledge
that this particular landlady was attracted by most of
the young men who frequented her establishment led
me to believe that the evening would inevitably end with
a bang.

I followed Hal and the landlady down the little passageway
from our dressing room, and all he could talk about to the old
boiler was our show and how great he thought we were. I
even heard Hal say that he believed we would be successful
one day. I think Hal really knew that 'You Really Got Me'
was going to be the song that would do it for us.

Hal, despite his showbiz bravado, genuinely tried to turn the group into something. We had definite shortcomings, but if nothing else Hal started to give us confidence in ourselves. Before he arrived to advise us, I had decided that Mick should attempt to play as loud and dynamically as Bobby Elliot of the Hollies. On some occasions we got onstage early and I went out front while Avory slammed away on the drum kit. I shouted, 'Louder! Louder!' Mick slammed the drums as hard as he could, but I was not satisfied. I was upset that we had been demoted to opening the Dave Clark tour, and I was taking my frustrations out on poor Avory, whose hands were often bleeding at the end of rehearsals, from the sheer force of hitting the drum. As he walked away, covered in sweat, I was grateful the snare drum had been the recipient of the violence, and not my face. Avory had big hands and could throw a punch. At the same time, I knew I had a sound in my head, and I was not hearing it onstage. I tried hard – too hard. Sometimes I was a little bit obsessed, I suppose . . .'

Suddenly, and without any warning, R.D. stopped talking and slumped down into his chair for a short snooze. I had no idea what to do. Was R.D. exhausted? After all, all this had happened so long ago. Or was he trying some sort of trick?

As I watched him sleep I thought about the questions I wanted to ask him, particularly about the sixties and what it was like to grow up at such an exciting time. It is true that it was not only the man himself who interested me, but how he achieved what he did. The man himself could seem so ordinary. When Raymond Douglas hit the big time, he went for the complete antithesis of stardom and headed straight for the most ordinary lifestyle imaginable. He got married, moved into a bedsit in Muswell Hill and pushed his newly born daughter around in a pram. Could it have been true? Raymond Douglas – the man who wrote 'You Really Got Me' and 'All Day and All of the Night', two songs which many thought broke the rules of pop music and smashed through the barriers of the establishment to create a new order and in many ways redefine the word rock – actually derived pleasure from pushing a pram around Muswell Hill. Later he was even depicted in the book *Rock Dreams* doing so. Why, I wondered. Could it be that he just wanted to prove that he was a normal guy, even though he was supposedly rich and famous. Maybe he revelled in his ordinariness, at the same time turning on the fame when ever he felt insecure.

This was all conjecture on my part. But, as many interviewers had learned to their cost, questions about his private life traditionally raised his anger. He had started the yarn about the tragic ex-girlfriend as soon as I had met him, but it was obvious that he had been winding me up. In any event, it could not have been true. It's a sure sign that people want to avoid a subject when they volunteer information about it. It's a psychological game they play, to make the questioner think that the ground has been covered already. People who spin fantastic yarns do so because they are probably too insecure to let their true personalities surface, and Raymond Douglas did not seem to be an exception to this rule.

Now he was sleeping, I found myself being rational and clear-headed, but when he was awake he was such a overwhelmingly confusing personality that it was impossible for me to think straight. Perhaps it was the dark, stuffy control-room we were in. It was his nerve centre, and all the gadgets lying around were geared to enhance communication. Digital sampling devices had been flashing on and off as he had been speaking, tapes were running. The whole place was literally wired for sound, so why not feel a little intimidated and exposed?

There were empty beer cans lying around the room, and so I tiptoed out and headed for the nearest off-licence, to buy some fresh stout for when R.D. woke up. As I walked around the run-down neighbourhood he chose to live and work in, I thought, OK, Muswell Hill was where he grew up, and it was understand-able that because he married when he was still a teenager, he had chosen to live near to his roots in order to feel more secure. There was nothing really wrong with that. But I was not convinced. I wondered why he never moved to a fashionable area like St John's Wood, Weybridge or Chelsea. Surely he could not have been worried about losing touch with his working-class roots? Perhaps success was too much to cope with and marriage made him want to be ordinary. Is that what marriage does to people? Do they stop being rebels overnight? Why didn't he stay with that girl Anita? She seemed much more of a kindred soul. Good music, bright ideas and a brilliant sex life. Why change that? Perhaps he had been lying to me after all. He could be so convincing at times. R.D. dangled the truth in front of me like fishbait on the end of a hook. Then, once he knew I was ready to take the bait, he snatched it away from me. He led me down any avenue his evasive old mind decided to travel. He took me along dark corridors occasionally opening a door into a brightly lit room, only to turn out the light again once he felt his power slipping. It was like being held captive in his head. What must it have been like for him? He had lived this way all of his life.

On the way to my off-licence I passed rows of derelict buildings that must have been bristling with English family life in their Victorian heyday. Now they had become almost like a third-world community. Different nationalities bringing their own culture to every household. Graffiti-covered walls giving a hint of colour to the suburban greyness. It was almost poetic justice for someone who wrote about the old Empire to choose to spend his time in a community that mainly consisted of immigrants.

R.D. had found a disused factory and initially turned it into what he regarded as his own creative hospice, a refuge for musicians to create without pressures. These were good intentions, but, like most men of noble ideals, he saw his dream fall victim of the economic realities of the time. Now he was a prisoner, incarcerated in his factory of ideas and creative dreams.

By the time I got back to the studio, R.D. had woken up. I found him sitting bolt upright in his chair as usual. It was as if he only came to life when he was in my presence. I opened a can of stout and passed it over to him. I felt more in control of the situation and asked him to continue. R.D. willingly obliged.

'Where was I? Love . . . Girls . . . Oh, yeah. We had recorded 'You Really Got Me' on our original demo reel, but the song was not considered to be pop enough for a market that demanded the word love in every other line. But it was the only original song we had that could compete with all the cover songs we were playing.

I had built on the words that had just seemed to pop out of my head as I wrote the song in my parents' front room. I always liked the idea of making a record which was repetitive, like an African tribal chant. That's the secret of all great dance music: it's tribal. People fall into it naturally because they knew the dance before they were born. Anyway, I loved to see the kids dance at Kinks gigs and I wanted to write something that they would jump around to. Dave had more or less exclusively taken over the lead-guitar playing, while I took most of the lead vocals and played rhythm. Dave's stabbing style made even a ballad seem rough when compared to more accomplished pop bands in the charts at the time, like Billy J. Kramer and the Dakotas, the Merseybeats, the Shadows and even the Beatles, whose rugged edges had already been filed down by their producer, George Martin. The Rolling Stones had had some success with a Chuck Berry song called 'Come On', and a cover of the Beatles' 'I Wanna Be Your Man'. Even though Mick Jagger's voice was rough, the rest of the band sounded clean compared to their live performances, so I wanted the next Kinks record to sound as if we had recorded it live.

Eventually during that summer Pye Records relented and begrudgingly let us into the studio to make the record. Shel Talmy insisted that we use session drummer Bobby Graham. Even though Mick had been with the band for several months, Shel had decided Graham would get the drum sound he

wanted much quicker than Mick and as we were paying for
the studio ourselves, we didn't want to waste time. Graham
was one of the busiest session drummers on the scene. He had
been the 'ghost' drummer on many pop hits. Mick would be
on the session, but only playing tambourine.

Hal Carter had eventually left after a disagreement with our
management and so we had been reunited with my brother-
in-law Brian. Even though Hal was no longer with the group,
he popped into the studio before the session and gave me one
more piece of advice:

'You know at the beginning of the song, when you start
singing? Well, I don't know whether you're singing to a girl
or a bloke. I've always thought you were a bit limp-wristed
and suspect, but I never imagined you singing the song to a
geezer, even though I have had my suspicions about you and
Quaife. So put all my doubts to rest and start the song by
singing to somebody – Jane, Carol, Sue, bint, tart – even
just plain 'Girl'. Whatever you do, you have to make it
personal.'

I took Hal's advice about personalizing the song but decided
against starting with 'tart'. I opted for 'girl' at the beginning
of the opening line. 'Girl' instead of 'Yeah' meant a lot to me,
but no one in the studio seemed to notice the difference.

I knew as soon as I heard the playback at the end of the
session that the recording wasn't right. There was echo on
everything and my voice sounded distorted. The curse of
Malcolm Vaughn, played on my mother's radiogram, had
finally come back to haunt us.

I took the acetate to Larry Page and tried to explain how
I thought the record could be improved, but he flatly
refused to hear my argument. Then I played it to Robert and
Grenville, and got a similar response. At the time Dave had a
girlfriend called Linda who put my feelings into words when
she said that it didn't make her want to drop her knickers. I
tried to explain to Shel that I would probably never write

another song like it and that this was our last opportunity to make a great record, but he also refused to listen. He said that the producer's word was final. I threatened to leave the band and never have anything to do with the music business again, but nobody took any notice. Hal Carter pointed out that after two flop singles we were lucky to even have the opportunity of making another record, let alone re-recording the thing. Grenville really didn't know what the fuss was about; in any event, he did not profess to be an expert in recording technology. Robert Wace broached the subject with Monty Presky at Pye, but a cry of outrage greeted the suggestion. I feared that the debutante season would soon be under way and Robert might be considering a return to the stage and my temperamental outburst, along with 'You Really Got Me', would be forgotten after a few weeks.

In despair I met Anita in the Gioconda Café at the end of Denmark Street. I just sat with my head in my hands, worrying what would happen if this version of 'You Really Got Me' came out. Anita had been in the studio when we had made our original demo. She had been like a good-luck charm on that session, dancing away in the corner of the studio while Dave played his guitar solo. Now she and I were not together anymore, she had moved in with somebody who I suspected could provide that long-term relationship that she had told me she had always wanted. She had only agreed to have a coffee with me for old times' sake, but as soon as she saw how unhappy I was she said she would have a word with Larry if I thought it would be any help. I thanked her but remained despondent.

Later that day as Pete and I walked to his house on Coldfall Estate, I wondered if he would ever move from the street where he was born. If this record was not a success, Pete might as well go back to work in the commercial-art studio where he had had been the year before. Knowing Pete, I'm sure he would have found another device to take him out of the ordinary, but he must have suspected that this was our final opportunity to make good as a group. Quaife could not see what the problem was with the record. I tried to explain that it didn't sound the way it did live; particularly after the crowd's reaction at Southsea. Pete agreed that it was special that night, but the difference was not enough to risk being thrown off the record label. We turned the corner and headed towards Pete's parents' house in Steeds Road, N10, and I had an image of Pete walking the same route when he was sixty. It made my stomach tighten up with anger.

The next day I found myself alone in Larry Page's office in Denmark Street. Larry looked at me from across his desk and after a long pause said that he might have a solution to our problem. Kassner Music had not yet given a mechanical licence to Pye to release the record and, even though it was a long shot with the risk of possible legal action, it might be enough to make Pye put back the release date. That would give us time to re-record the song.

Larry put the wheels in motion straight away. According to Grenville, Pye Records had threatened to throw us off the label when he heard that we had not granted them mechanical rights, especially as that put us in breach of the watertight contract they had with us. Pye considered legal action at this point, but decided not to sue for damages as there was no money to pay them with in any event. The best solution would be to let us re-record the song as long as we paid for the session ourselves.

We were booked in IBC Studios, which were located in a basement in Portland Place. The recording personnel were the same, but this time they knew that we wanted to make the record sound the way we played it live.

Again Bobby Graham played the drums and Mick was on tambourine. I played rhythm guitar, Dave played the lead and Arthur Greenslade was on piano. This enabled us to build a wall of sound which would be complete without having to do overdubs, which would have necessitated copying from one tape to another, losing a generation of sound quality. It also meant that we would not waste any valuable studio time. The studio personnel regarded the re-recording as an indulgence. There was a lot of clock-watching and even Bobby Graham, who was one of life's more supportive session men, glanced at his watch when I asked Shel if we could do another take. Shel, slumped in his chair, looked down at me from the glass booth, gave a giant sigh down the intercom and reluctantly agreed. I was being treated like a spoiled child and being allowed to have my way until the clock ticked over to the last second of the three-hour session. Then they could throw us back on to the street along with all the other aspiring pop stars who would then go nowhere. This was take two and it had to be right. If I had asked for another take, I'm convinced that Shel and the engineer would have left the building.

When Dave played the opening chords, Bobby Graham forgot the complicated introduction he had planned and just thumped one beat on the snare drum with as much power as he could muster, as if to say, 'OK, wimp, take that!' For the next three minutes he was one of us. We managed to keep an R and B feel to it, even though we were making a pop record.

Now it was Dave's solo. The moment had to be right. I shouted to give him encouragement and spoiled his concentration momentarily. He looked over at me with a dazed expression, as if he had done something wrong. His mouth relaxed and his jaw opened, and for a split second he seemed to stop playing. I thought that I had blown it for all of us, but then Dave's eyes squinted as his face broke into that arrogant sideways smile that I had learned to love and hate over the years. The little runt hadn't even heard me shout. We had just thought of looking at each other at the same crucial moment. He gritted his teeth and sneered at me before turning away to play his solo.

After the back track was recorded, Robert came into the studio and paid the two session men their fee. I watched Bobby counting his money. It was one of those embarrassing and yet necessary moments in the life of a studio musician; the point where the artist finishes and the hired hand takes over. Arthur Greenslade was another old-time session musician, but even he showed some interest when they played the backing track over the studio speakers. Graham smiled and started packing up his kit so that he would be out of the way by the time we did the vocals. He knew that we had done something special.

Then all I had to do was the vocal. I remembered the first day I had thumped out those chords on my parents' piano. I was as alone as I had been then. I thought about Hal telling me to communicate and how dreadful my vocal had sounded on the first recording, so I made a conscious effort to make my voice sound pure and I sang the words as clearly as the music would allow. I suddenly remembered all those family singsongs around the piano, with my dad getting drunk and my sisters dancing with their boyfriends. I pictured Rene watching them. Then time jumbled together and I was performing on stage in front of an audience. Those thumping chords started playing down my headphones and in the first row of my imaginary audience I saw a girl. Every emotion I had was focused on that one image, and nobody could deny me this moment. I had invented myself and somebody to sing for. At last I was happy with something I was doing. I was so elated that I started laughing when it was time for me to sing my first line. Even this did not affect what was happening. I was like a gambler on a winning streak. I couldn't lose. As the song moved into the first key shift it was as though I felt completely alive for the first time. I wanted the song to go on forever.

As Brian drove us along Portland Place after the session, he said the record would be Number 1. We all shouted abuse at him but nobody was really arguing with what he said. The van went quiet after that. As we drove past Regent's Park into Camden Town, I looked at the people on the street and wondered how many of them had lived lives which had been unfulfilled. All their disappointments and unrealized ambitions. I looked around at the group and thought how much I loved them. Then I thought just how marvellous the experience had been and how lucky I was just to have got this far, to have one of my wishes come true. Now I wanted to communicate to all those people just how possible it was to take that first step. The record was still in my head and I was still the character in the song. I had just been born.'

Leaving insecurity behind me

'Back in Muswell Hill, Dave's girlfriend gave the new version of 'You Really Got Me' her seal of approval, which indicated to me that her knickers must have undoubtedly 'dropped' as soon as Dave played it for her on her Dansette record player. The whole band was pleased with the result, as was the management team.

Robert Wace had met a certain Lady Cowley, an ex-model who had married into high society and 'Tiger', as she was known, often turned up at concerts in some of the seediest clubs, dressed to the nines and acting like an eccentric member of the royal family. These were heady times for Robert, who had at last found a friend with a suitable pedigree with whom to share his slightly buffoonish playboy lifestyle. When he wasn't turning up on my mother's doorstep at two in the morning, demanding slices of bread and dripping for himself and Tiger, he was party-hopping in Belgravia. But from the moment we finished making the record, everybody in our little operation started moving with a new purpose. It was not that we were just pleased with ourselves, we genuinely thought that we had produced something that sounded different from anything else that was around, and yet was commercial at the same time. It was like the world was waiting for it to come out, even if no one had heard it yet.

We played a few more dates up north and by now the M1 motorway had almost joined the M6, making it possible to reach Manchester in a little over three hours. This time I stayed on to visit a girlfriend in Rawtenstall, an old mill town outside of Burnley. While there was no heavy romantic attachment there, I was fascinated by her elegant, tall figure and incredible hair dyed pale blue and piled on top of her head, forming an amazingly large beehive. I had met her at our concert the night before and wanted to know if she would wear her outrageous hair-style to work at the mill the next day. We went back to her little terraced house by a stream that ran past the bottom of the garden. There I was treated with the finest northern hospitality, and I reciprocated by staying on my best southern behaviour. She didn't go to work the next day, but instead travelled with me on the bus to Manchester. It was a sunny day and so we walked around the streets and parks surrounding the Manchester bus-station while I waited for the coach to London. We lay on a grass verge and she told me about all the things she wanted. Nothing vastly mind-boggling or different, but they were hers. I was trying my best to listen, but my eyes were still focused on that outrageous beehive as it sat on top of her head, adding a ridiculous touch to what was otherwise a very romantic and sensitive moment. She told me her dreams and then kissed me with a kiss that tasted a little like tin. I put this down to the fresh spring water she drank in Rawtenstall, and pondered for a moment that it may have been the water that turned her hair blue. She asked me to stay; I said I would come back; but although I did play Manchester again, I never saw the elegant Lancashire lass with the amazing blue beehive.

During the next few weeks, I went to visit as many old friends as I could find. I even tracked down a few old flames from college, including Margie, my art-school friend from Croydon. I was not sure why I was doing all this, but I knew that I was uneasy about many things. Margie and I had always had a turbulent relationship, and she was not averse to slapping me for no reason, or making mind-boggling comments during a mundane conversation. I sat on a park bench with Margie and spoke romantically. I told her that I felt something was happening inside me which I did not understand, like a flower that was beginning to grow in my stomach. It had already taken root and it felt as though buds were beginning to form on the ends of thin branches, gradually spreading up to my chest. Margie looked over at me with a sad look on her face and told me that I probably had cancer.

After this disappointment I found myself back with Anita. Her new relationship was not going as planned and so I stayed with her in her flat in Chalk Farm. One night I went to sleep but woke to find Anita looking out the window. She called me names and said that I could never love anyone. She soon started to put conditions on our relationship, conditions I neither understood nor cared about. We were so happy as we were, why change that? She stood at the window and cried, I have never understood why. The band had made a fabulous record and, whatever happened next, we all knew that it would give us our best shot. So why was she crying? I knew that she had been seeing other boys, and so it wasn't that she would be lonely. Her sobbing was starting to make me feel guilty and I told her to stop. I understand people crying together, then they can both understand what the grief is, but there was something so desperately lonely about her that night, and could not understand how I could be contributing to her sorrow. Perhaps she did not understand it herself. Earlier in our relationship Anita had taken purple hearts and other mild forms of speed to keep herself going. She had fallen for some musician and a long-term relationship was beckoning, and so she was desperately trying to get her life together and clean up her act. I realize now that she may have been going through mild depression.

She accused me of being self-centred and selfish. In her opinion I was only happy as long as my record sounded like a hit. I couldn't understand this uncharacteristic outburst. Anita was usually so in control, more mature and streetwise than I was, and yet she was sobbing like a rejected child. This was all so different from the confident person who had taught me so much about myself only months earlier. She had always known what I wanted, but now she despised me for taking the opportunity once it was within my grasp.

That night I watched her sleep. I stayed awake while the morning light sculpted shadows around her cheekbones. I kissed her gently as she slept. She half woke up and snuggled against me, but as soon as she was alert enough to realize who I was she pushed me aside.

Once again Arthur Howes had used his influence to get us booked to play on two highly prestigious Beatles shows, the first of which was at the Bournemouth Winter Garden. The Kinks were to go on in the second half of the show, in the most unenviable position, just before the Beatles. To get us on the show, Arthur had probably thrown down the gauntlet to Brian Epstein, saying that the Kinks were the only group brazen enough to play the spot.

Our single was to be released later that week and there was already quite a buzz going around about it. We also had our own little following of fans who we knew would travel to support us. In the circumstances we needed all the support we could get, as Beatles' audiences were renowned for screaming for the Fab Four while other groups tried to perform. The only way for these groups to attract attention was to play a Beatles song and, as most groups had at least one in their repertoire, all the groups in the opening half of the show seemed to oblige, much to the delight of the Beatles' fanatics.

During the interval we were putting the final pieces of our stage gear into place as a photographer set up lights at the side of the stage so that he could take a quick snap of John, Paul, Ringo and George as they breezed into the backstage entrance. The stage manager had just given us the two-minute warning to start our set when we heard screams from the direction of the stage door. Some of the crew and other hangers-on rushed across the stage and nearly knocked me over as I tried to tune up my guitar. A flash bulb popped where the photographer had been standing, then there was the sound of raised northern accents and slow, deep, drawling voices getting laughter from obvious, banal comments – the sign of true celebrity. A nervous electricity immediately went through the building. The Beatles had arrived on the premises.

The stage manager delayed the start of the second half while the Beatles finished the photo shoot, then, when it was over, the audience screamed as the house lights dimmed for the start of the second half. We waited nervously behind the curtain as the master of ceremonies went out to warm up the crowd. We were hoping that there might be a slight warm-up for the Kinks, but instead the audience was informed by the MC that the Beatles had arrived and would be on stage very soon. Just to make us feel completely at ease, we then saw John Lennon and Paul McCartney (or 'Pull My Cock Off', as Avory had re-christened him) standing in the wings watching us tune up. They were already dressed in their famous collarless Beatle suits, ready to go on, and I was amazed at how similar they looked to their wax replicas which had recently been added to the collection at Madame Tussaud's. Lennon walked up to me and stared over at my guitar, on its stand next to my amplifier. He put his hand up to his cheek and looked over the instrument as if it were a rare antique. Without asking permission, he touched the tone control, while I looked on in astonishment. I suppose that I should have felt privileged to have one of the Beatles take the trouble to make a comment about us or our instruments, but in the circumstances I felt as though I had been violated.

'Is this yours?'

'Once my mum has paid off the hire-purchase.' I thought that this working-class comment would impress him, but he was unmoved.

Then, as Lennon's arm raised to brush a little bit of dandruff from the shoulder of my red hunting jacket, he paused to take a peep at the audience through the curtains.

'Excuse me,' I said nervously. 'It's our turn. You're on after us.'

Lennon gave a stern look down his magnificent long nose, while his mouth broke into a broad grin.

'With the Beatles, laddie, nobody gets a turn. You're just there to keep the crowd occupied until we go on.'

As he left the stage he threw out a parting comment: 'Well, lads, if you get stuck and run out of songs to play, we'll lend you some of ours.'

I wanted to shout that we didn't know any of theirs, but the lights had dimmed and the curtain had started to open. An imaginary bell sounded for round one. We were on.

For the first few minutes the predictable happened: the audience were chanting for 'John, Paul, George, Ringo.' The sound of their voices was like swift punches to the head and every time the blow connected, there was a flash of white light. I remembered back to when I was at school and had fought Ronnie Brooks, the schoolboy boxing champion of Great Britain. Every time he had hit me, a white light had flashed before me. The trainer in my corner had told me to go down as soon as I was hurt. I had been hurt but had refused to obey. Later that year I beat him in the hundred-yard dash, and he told me that even when he punched me out of the ring, he thought that there was something about me that was a winner. It had to do with stubbornness, and willingness to get hurt in the cause of victory.

Well, as the Kinks played their opening song, the sound of 'We want the Beatles' hit me harder than any of Ronnie's punches. This time though, the referee would not stop the fight. We were supposed to play Slim Harpo's 'Got Love if You Want It' next but instead I shouted to the others to play 'You Really Got Me'. Dave turned up his amplifier, which caused it to feed back slightly, and the high-pitched frequency cut right through the screams of the Beatles' fans. For a moment the audience was silent. As soon as Dave played the opening chords, they were with us. It was as if we had taken the first round off the Beatles. As John Lennon and Brian Epstein watched from the wings, I felt like shouting in my best Liverpudlian accent, 'This is not one of yours. It's one of ours!'

Later I watched the Beatles play from the wings and actually heard some fans screaming 'We want the Kinks.' John Lennon shouted something back down the microphone before the next song, just to show that he was still in charge out there. Ringo played with superb, soulful aggression, which made me realize why – apart from their catalogue of songs and their world fame – they had such a hard core of followers. Also, it was easier to assess their true capabilities from the side of the stage, without the benefit of conventional, 'front on' television-camera angles. From this angle it was obvious that they had once been a fine rock group. It was not their fault they were having to live out the roles the public had cast them in. I could also see the slight disagreements and 'niggles' appearing among them. The crowd was screaming so loudly between the songs that I couldn't catch the remarks the group were shouting to each other, but it was clear that while the world was shouting their praises, these particularly public moments were the only time the Fab Four could actually communicate with each other. Interviewers could not hear, managers could not intervene, the stage was the only place where they could be brutally honest with one another. The Beatles were at their peak, but the rifts between them were clearly discernible.

For the second Beatles show the following week, Epstein decided that to give the show a better overall balance, somebody else should go on before the Fab Four. The Kinks were to close the first half. Word was already out that we had stolen so much of the limelight the week before that it had been decided that a 'less aggressive' group take our spot. The group chosen to fill this thankless role was a band from

Shepherd's Bush called the High Numbers. The unfortunate Brian Epstein could not know that he had replaced one set of upstarts with another. The High Numbers were later to change their name to the Who.

At the time, the Kinks were opening their act with a Bo Diddley song called 'Cadillac'. As the curtains opened the rest of the Kinks played a frantic rhythm, and then I rushed on from the wings. As I prepared for my dramatic entrance, Paul McCartney, who was hiding behind a curtain, suddenly emerged and grabbed hold of me, preventing me from making my entrance and leaving the rest of the Kinks playing with no lead singer.

'I suppose you are the star,' he shouted.

'I suppose I am,' I replied.

Then he let me go and I ran on to the stage. It was obvious that the Kinks were beginning to find their audience and had earned a little respect from the greatest pop group in the world.

Thank Your Lucky Stars was a popular television show which had a review segment where three members of the public would be asked to vote on the week's new releases. One girl, Janice, had become a regular, and her catch phrase, 'I'll give it five' (the highest mark), had been picked up as a slogan by almost the entire nation. The sound of 'I'll give it five' spoken in a thick Birmingham accent was an indication that something was destined for success.

Brian Matthew, the host of the show, had been the first person to mention the name the Kinks on television, and he was therefore regarded by us as a supporter of the band. Really he had only given us a casual mention. He was commenting on some of the strange names being chosen for groups at the time and in his opinion the Kinks was the strangest sounding. (Patrick Doncaster, the *Daily Mirror*'s pop critic, had also written about us somewhat negatively, saying that while the Kinks was probably a name that grabbed the attention, the group might find it hard to live with later on. We were in no position to worry about the effect the name would have on us, we were only concerned that people noticed us at all.)

The three records chosen for the panel to review included the latest release by the Dave Clark Five, and while we expected a fair reaction, we never dreamed that the record of the week would be anything other than Dave Clark's follow-up to 'Bits and Pieces'. The records were played and the panel made their comments. It was Janice 'Oil geeve it foive' who really raved about 'You Really Got Me'. And then the Kinks record was voted record of the week. This was unimaginable success.

Now the rest of my family was starting to take more interest in the group's progress; my mother had started to get inquiries from distant relatives. Cousins started to emerge from all parts of the country, and Dad often found himself inundated with free drinks from his cronies at the pub.

The record came out the following week, and we had been re-booked on *Ready Steady Go!* The appearance would more or less guarantee some sort of chart action, even though we were not expecting a high entry. Tuesday was chart day and the buzz of expectancy went around the house every time the telephone rang. Finally Grenville telephoned and I was summoned to speak to him. I was informed that we had gone straight into the Top 30, and we were to go on *Ready Steady Go!* again the following week to play two songs live. This was a sure sign that the record was going to be Top 5. A few weeks earlier the Animals had been recalled in the same way, and 'House of the Rising Sun' had immediately gone to Number 1 in the charts. We didn't even give a thought to the fact that though we had become quite an exciting live act, we were generally unpredictable, and therefore a bad risk on live television. We had had a BBC radio audition earlier that year and failed it. The fact that our record was being played on the BBC pop radio shows was an indication that they now might consider us less of a risk. So we felt more confident in ourselves, especially as the daily record sales came in.

The small venues we were playing around the country were all beginning to sell out and extra bouncers were having to be called in by the promoters to hold back the growing legion of screaming girls. I discovered that even a slight glance at a girl in the front row would cause her to roll her eyes and scream with ecstasy. We found ourselves having to find secret entrances to the village halls and ballrooms we were playing to prevent ourselves being mobbed by fans. My brother-in-law Brian had difficulty coping with the newly added role of road manager–cum–security man. A few weeks before Dave and I had been two young in-laws who played in a group and were prone to fighting in the back of the van. Now it was like we were being pursued by the entire population, and treated like items of rare china, wrapped in cotton wool after every performance in case we might break before the next showing.

On the few nights a week when we were not working, we found it difficult to leave the house without being pursued through the streets by adoring followers. We began to develop a series of new rules to life, centring on knowing secret departures, recognizing prearranged knocks on the door and coded messages of arrival. In a matter of days, we had been transformed into celebrities. Our moves were monitored by our admirers and all of our needs catered for by our management and other interested parties. The imaginary hump on my back, which had been with me since my childhood, started to disappear from my consciousness. Even though the shyness that had always accompanied me never quite went away, it was replaced by a strange, naïve over-confidence that only naturally shy people who have been thrust into similar situations can relate to. In short, I was emotionally totally out of my depth. Our success increased every day and I felt like a long jumper who woke up every morning to break his own world record. Everywhere we went, 'You Really Got Me' was being played on the radio.

The group and our assorted managers assembled in Arthur Howes' office to hear the news that Pye Records wanted us to record an LP. Jimmy O'Day, who worked in Arthur Howes' office, came over to congratulate Shel Talmy and asked me how many songs I would be contributing to the album. I surprised everyone by saying that I expected to have only five or six songs ready. This was unusual simply because since the Beatles' *Please, Please Me* album, every group that wrote was expected to write everything on each album. But Shel said that he had already started looking for songs for us to cover. Pye wanted the album as soon as possible and the first session was booked for the following week. As Shel walked me through Soho from Howes' office in Frith Street, he said, 'Enjoy walking down the street anonymously, because pretty soon you'll be recognized everywhere you go.'

Just over six months earlier, we had appeared on *Ready Steady Go!* as newcomers with not much hope of making more than the bottom regions of the charts. Now we were headlining the show and I even felt confident enough to go on television exposing the gap between my two front teeth. I had developed a technique of singing with my top lip stiffened in order to expose 'the gap' as little as possible. We decided to play Slim Harpo's 'Got Love If You Want It' first, with 'You Really Got Me' as our second song. The show was no more than a blur, partly due to the fact that I had downed a couple of stiff whisky-macs to fend off pre-show nerves. Directly afterwards we were driven to a concert in south London, and then, to finish a triumphant day, Robert's girlfriend Tiger threw a party in our honour at her house in Mayfair.

During the concert I recognized Margie, my college friend, and asked her along to the party. All through the show she stared at me in that strangely hypnotic way that suggested she may have been taken all the publicity surrounding the Kinks a little too seriously. But I had forgotten how unpredictable she could be. At the party she started talking to Avory and calmly announced that she wanted to rescue me from my own devices so that the world would not deprive me of my true destiny. At art school it was common for people to live and speak in metaphors and communicate by means of their own invention (such conversations often followed a long pub crawl). Avory, however, was a solid chap from East Molesey, which is situated firmly on planet Earth, and he immediately wrote Margie off as a nutter. 'Come down from up there, Mick Avory,' Margie said in an ethereal whisper. Avory just sighed and looked over in the direction of two dollybirds. Afterwards, Margie followed me back to Grenville's flat in Lennox Gardens, where we all consumed even more brandy and champagne. By now Margie was telling everybody to 'come down from up there', particularly me, but I was already 'up there', and so drunk that I was in no condition to argue with her.

She begged Grenville not to change me as a person, and Grenville raised an eyebrow and promised on his word as a gentleman. Then he disappeared into another room and Margie became slightly deranged. This resulted in a scuffle during which I found myself flat on my back in a helpless drunken state. Margie was on top of me with her legs pinning down my arms, her hands pressed firmly around my throat. At first I tried to laugh it off, but I soon realized that Margie was in fact trying to throttle me. She was only a tiny creature but had found sufficient strength to overcome me. The last thing I remember before passing out was Grenville shouting at Margie to let go of me, while Margie's eyes glared into mine with a look of the possessed.

I awoke the following morning on the same spot on the floor. Grenville was already up and about. I tried to speak but could only croak: a combination of over-indulgence followed by what some might call strangulation. When I looked in the mirror I saw that Margie's fingers had left two large red marks on my neck.

'Where's Margie?' I asked. I was concerned for her.

Grenville strutted across the room looking polished, with his morning ablutions already completed, while I shuffled around trying to avoid the smell of my own breath. Grenville was so immaculate with his pin–striped suit and smartly slicked-back public-school hair that I imagined that instead of getting undressed for bed like other mortals, he simply got into the wardrobe and dangled from a coat-hanger all night.

'Oh, the girl.' He casually mused. 'What do you expect me to say? What else could I possibly do in the circumstances?'

I walked over to the window and felt both hung-over and ashamed. I saw Margie sitting in the gutter outside with her head down. All the time I had known her she had been a virgin, and if what Grenville had just said was true, he must have taken that away from her. Perhaps in her own bizarre way Margie was doing her best to ensure that I would cling to whatever innocence I had left. It was as though she was trying to prevent the world taking away my moral virginity. As it turned out, she was too late. I felt as though I had already become a whore.

Grenville called a doctor and it was decided that I should not sing for a few days. As I left the flat Margie was still sitting on the steps outside, but I didn't speak to her as I walked past. I was ashamed that I had not fulfilled the wishes she had for us both. And I think I disliked myself a little more.

A few months earlier I had met a girl in Sheffield, where the Kinks were playing. Rasa, the daughter of Lithuanian refugees, had skipped off from her convent school in Bradford and hitched to Sheffield to see us play at the Esquire Club. She was pretty, blonde, and had fine Slavic features. Her almond-shaped eyes gave her face almost an Asian quality, and her green eyes darted about busily as she took in the performance. After the show she arranged a meeting with us through Hal Carter.

As we talked, she found that some of the things I said unlocked a little of the restlessness in her. She was also an understanding listener. We gave her a lift to the railway station and, as she got out of the van, I kissed her hand in a gallant gesture. The others whistled and made insulting noises, but Rasa curtsied politely and left. We had exchanged addresses and a few days later I received a letter from her about arriving back at her parents' house in the early morning light, listening to the dawn chorus. Very innocent stuff.

A week after the party at Tiger's I had fully recovered from Margie's throttling. We played on a television show in Bristol and I met a singer from Bradford named Kiki Dee. Kiki knew Rasa who happened to be in London at that time. I telephoned a number given to me by Kiki and arranged to meet Rasa at Tottenham Court Road tube station. Although the station was packed with Thursday-night shoppers, I saw Rasa's long blonde hair through the crowds of commuters that packed the entrance to the underground. She had her back to the crowds as she pretended to study a map of the London underground system on the wall. I walked up behind her and paused for a moment before letting her know I was there. Her hair, which was almost white in places, hung down her back over her three-quarter-length brown suede coat. I seemed to know everything I needed to know about her at that moment and actually considered walking away. It was almost as if this could have been the beginning and end right there, which would result in a perfect relationship full of thoughts of what might have been. As I hesitated, she turned around and saw me, as if she had eyes in the back of her head.

We walked around Soho and, after a meal at Leon's Chinese restaurant in Wardour Street, we walked down to the Thames Embankment, then crossed the river to sit by Waterloo Bridge. She told me that she had come down to stay in Willesden with her sister, but that she was going back to Bradford soon. I took her home to her sister and everything felt fine inside me. It was not just that I had started to like myself a little more. The flower that I had felt growing inside my chest was not the cancer Margie had diagnosed but the beginning of something not as deadly but frightening just the same.'

Suddenly R.D. hesitated, then stopped. He clenched his fist and thumped it against his chest.

'The obsession starts. That's bad. Margie was wrong about the cancer, but in some respects she could have been right. Love like that is something beautiful, but, like cancer, it's almost better to have it cut out before it can do any damage. Love spreads to the entire body. It eventually takes over your entire soul. You make wrong decisions. Do senseless things. Become irrational. I saw other girls walking down the street; in parks; fans even; and yet somehow they all looked like Rasa. Damn stupid fool. Yeah, You Really Got Me now. Let's watch a movie. Hey, how about Charlie Varrick?'

R.D. was trying to get away from the subject of his first wife. He put on the Charlie Varrick video but I kept pumping him for answers.

'Was Rasa *the* Girl?'

R.D. pretended not to hear while he watched Joe Don Baker, playing a character working for the Mob, beat up Varrick's sidekick, played by Andy Robinson.

'I love this scene. Sheer force. God, that punk really got what was coming to him. No! I often thought about it, but Rasa was not *the* Girl.'

R.D. switched videos as quickly as he changed the subject. After Joe Don Baker had dispatched the unfortunate Andy Robinson, R.D. stuck in a video of *The Third Man* starring Orson Welles, the familiar scene where Welles walks from the shadows and makes his first appearance as the haunting Harry Lime theme starts to play.

'Maybe it was the music from this movie that made me fall in love with Rasa. It reminded me of refugees; post-war deprivation and all that. The chick in this movie is also a complete goddess. Almond eyes, long flowing hair and that accent. Man!

'Rasa was like her. She was born in Germany as her family fled Lithuania, and then she spent the first few years of her life in a displaced-persons camp in Hull. Finally they moved to Bradford. I suppose I fell for the whole refugee story like a complete sap, but even so, she seemed a great kid. I had never met anyone quite like her.'

'How would you rate her?' I asked.

'Rate?' R.D. bellowed. 'A five. A definite five out of five.'

I found myself becoming gradually engrossed by the wonderful old black-and-white movie. R.D. saw that I was interested in something other than him and decided that it was time to go on with his story.

Top of the Pops 10

'The group had just headlined a Sunday-night concert at the Torquay Theatre and our record was at Number 2 in the charts. We had originally been booked by the promoter as a back-up to two girl singers, performing somewhat predictably as the Other Two, but since our chart success the very shrewd promoter had decided to elevate us to headliners and close the show as well as using us as a backing group for the girl duo. This somewhat odd situation could have easily been avoided by hiring another group to play behind the Other Two. But as that would have necessitated paying an extra fee, the promoter decided that in order to fulfil our contract, we would play behind a gauze drape to conceal our identities while the girls stomped through their songs. Then during the interval we could slip into our red hunting jackets and be transformed into the stars of the show. This would have worked but for Tony Marsh, the compère of the show, who let it slip to the audience that the blurred figures behind the net curtain were special mystery guests.

Marsh had built up a reputation for himself by standing in the wings and dropping his trousers, exposing his balls to the artists onstage. As well as this, he was well known for his incredible sexual capers in Bed and Breakfasts and hotels up and down the country. Tales of his exploits as a formidable drinkist and raconteur were legendary in the music biz and Arthur Howes often travelled to a show not so much because of the artists performing but because he knew that Tony Marsh would be the compère. Arthur was the typical 'Mr Entertainment', and he believed that everyone should play his own particular role in the great music hall of life. He addressed us in a quiet, deep, calculating Cockney accent, as if he was parting with a secret every time he spoke: 'You see, boys, I love performers, and Tony Marsh is a performer, on and off stage.'

Arthur then pointed to Terry McGrath, his booking agent, who was propped up in a corner of the dressing room, downing whisky and water. McGrath was small and red-faced. He wore a trilby hat that made him look like a racecourse tout rather than a theatrical agent. On one occasion, the Kinks arrived at a gig to find McGrath in the promoter's office doing the financial settlement. McGrath had obviously been overwhelmed by the shrewd promoter's hospitality and had apparently had 'one too many'. As the Kinks walked past Terry, he looked up at his artists and inquired 'Who are these people?' But we needn't have worried. Terry may have had a tipple or two and forgotten the name of his act, but when it came to the financial settlement he was always on the ball for us. Arthur spoke as if McGrath was not there. 'Terry drinks a lot, as we all well know. But Terry is a grafter and as long as he grafts, he stays regardless of the drink; if Terry doesn't graft, he goes. Terry knows that, don't you, Terry?' Terry only half responded to the sound of his name.

Arthur then moved across to Dave, who was quietly strumming his guitar. 'Now David here is a raver. No question about it. I know where I stand with Dave the Rave. That's what I expect and I'm happy because as long as Dave raves, I know that I won't be disappointed. I've come down to see the Kinks and Tony Marsh and I expect to see ravers and performers who won't disappoint me. There, boys. The secret of success. Don't disappoint the punters.'

That night was no exception and Arthur was not disappointed. Marsh had not only created complete havoc for the unfortunate Other Two by blowing our cover to the audience, he also insisted on drinking a toast to the Kinks backstage after the show. There was nothing wrong with this except that local dignitaries, including several middle-aged lady councillors, were present and Tony's balls were protruding effortlessly through the unzipped trousers of his dinner suit. As the embarrassed entourage headed for the nearest exit, the slightly cross-eyed compère was heard to inquire innocently whether it was something that he had said that had offended anyone?

Grenville ushered us out of the theatre, past the waiting fans, to catch the night train back to London. We had a concert at the Streatham Ice Rink the following night, but the main reason for us being in London so soon was that 'You Really Got Me' might go to Number 1, and Brian Somerville, our press agent, wanted us to be available for the interviews that were bound to crop up. Grenville's qualities of leadership were starting to shine as he bribed a ticket-collector into finding us all seats in the third-class compartment of a train that was already full. He later bribed the same ticket-collector into upgrading himself into first class, leaving the rest of us freezing in the rear carriages. By the time we reached London we all had colds except for Grenville, who strutted along the platform to the nearest black cab. He roared straight off to his office, leaving the rest of us sniffling in line at the cab rank.

My mother had dreaded the sound of the telephone ringing ever since she had received the call telling her that my sister Rene had died. Telegrams were worse. Only the very best or the very worst news was carried in a telegram. When my Auntie Dolly's husband was 'missing in action' during the Second World War, she must have received the news by telegram. That day, however, I received my first ever telegram. It informed me that our record had reached Number 1 in the charts.

I had gone straight to bed after the train journey, but almost as soon as the telegram arrived there was another knock at the front door and there was Grenville, with a large, chauffeur-driven Daimler to take us to the West End for interviews and photographs. As the car drove us through Trafalgar Square, we stopped at a zebra crossing to let some pedestrians across. One of them was John Cowan, who six months earlier had started making that film with us. I wound down the window and shouted, 'John, our record has just gone to Number 1.'

Cowan looked in the car and gave a deep sigh. 'I should have finished that bloody film.'

We drove off, leaving him pondering his lost opportunity.

The rest of the day was a complete whirl. Interviews, photographs, handshakes, pats on the back and smiling faces.

That evening we played Streatham Ice Rink. The ice had been covered with boards, and a stage erected at one end, but the place was so full of people that the ice melted, which meant we had to cut our concert short. Nobody seemed to care, and as far as I know nobody complained. There was only one song that everybody wanted to hear that night, and I think we played 'You Really Got Me' twice.

As we left the backstage area for the upstairs bar, my dad came towards me with a group of people. He was wearing a dashing blue suit and his hair had been smarmed down with Brylcreem specially for the occasion. I thought he was going to shake hands with me, but instead he put his arms around me and kissed me on the cheek. Then, as I tried to think of something appropriate to say, someone plonked a camera in my face and a flash bulb went off. I just said something inane like, 'I'm sorry it wasn't football or cricket or something. Sorry it had to be this.' Dad laughed and said that he was proud of me. I truly cannot remember anything else after that moment. Perhaps the world should have stopped turning there and then. Everything should have ended.

The next day we all met in Arthur Howes' office to read the newspaper stories about ourselves and listen to Arthur's plans for tours. For once Grenville, Robert and Larry were all in the same room together with us and the barriers and petty squabbles were forgotten. Everybody was genuinely delighted. Arthur Howes opened yet another bottle of champagne and declared, 'Well, boys, just goes to show what a bit of teamwork can do.' Nobody argued. We felt like a complete team. Perhaps I was the one who had written the song, but the success belonged to every one of us. The others had probably experienced personal moments similar to the one I had with my dad. I hadn't played for a famous football or cricket team, but I was playing in a winning team of sorts and now nobody could stop us.

The first recording dates for the album were pretty wild events, with various guest musicians calling in to see Shel in the control room. To watch the latest 'hot' band recording and hanging out, just in case there was something going down that was worth knowing about. To see if there was some secret that would change people's lives. The obvious focus of attention was Dave's little green amp plugged into a Vox AC30. It had been responsible for the unique sound on 'You Really Got Me'.

All the tracks were put down with the same recording team as the single. We recorded songs by Chuck Berry, Slim Harpo and Bo Diddley, and a song I had just written called 'Stop Your Sobbing'. With the exception of 'Sobbing', Bobby Graham played drums on all the tracks and a songwriter called Perry Ford played piano in place of Arthur Greenslade. The only time a few outside session men came into the studio was when we recorded 'Bald-Headed Woman', a song which Shel's own company had published and which credited Shel as composer. The group was a little insecure with the song and so Shel invited John Lord to play Hammond organ and Jimmy Page twelve-string rhythm guitar in an attempt to add some professionalism to the performance and guarantee the song a place on the album (and some songwriting royalties for Shel). The same crowd stayed around while we put down back tracks to 'Long Tall Shorty' and 'Lover not a Fighter' and everybody went home happy.

Rasa had come to a few of the sessions and had contributed some backing vocals. She sang the same vocal line as Dave but hers was an octave higher. The two of them together sounded like one animal, half male, half female. Shel liked the sound and encouraged her to come to the sessions whenever we did back-up vocals. I wasn't opposed to this as Rasa and I were seeing each other regularly by now.

Larry Page and his girlfriend Lee took Rasa and me out to dinner and then dropped us off in a place called Isleworth. We ended up in a house that belonged to somebody who was a friend of Rasa's elder sister. Even though Rasa had been given the key to the house, we both felt that we were entering the house illegally. It was rather like the story of the three bears. 'Who's been sleeping in my bed?' said the Daddy Bear. The next morning the sun shone through the bedroom window and woke me up. I had to be at Pye Studios by ten o'clock to start a recording session and I had no idea how long it would take to get there.

As we rode into central London on the underground I started to think of something to record at the upcoming session. We had more or less exhausted our supply of cover songs, and I was definitely not going to sing another Shel Talmy composition, so I toyed with a melody I had composed as a guitar instrumental years before, at Rosie's house. When I got to the studio I showed the chords to Dave and Pete and we ran through the song. While we put down the back track I called out the chords to them through the microphone and sang some impromptu lyrics to give some idea of the melody. I had intended to make up angry and passionate lyrics similar to 'You Really Got Me', but somehow this gentle melody started happening in my head and the words 'It's your life and you can do what you want' came out instead. It was as if my own guilty conscience was supplying lyrics for me.

Everybody in the studio liked the rhythm track and they were very excited about hearing the lyric. I said that I had a sore throat and asked if I could do the vocal the next day. Everybody believed me but in fact there was nothing wrong with me at all. I just didn't have the lyrics to the song completed yet. When we started work the following morning I asked everyone to put the backing vocals on first, making the excuse that I wanted to sing along with them. As Dave, Rasa, Pete and myself sang our 'oohs' and 'ahs' I was still trying to think of something for the lead vocal. I thought back to some poems I had written the previous year in a small exercise book. There was one about being tired of waiting for success to happen. When it eventually came time for me to sing my part, I sang the first words that came into my head. Afterwards, when we played back the song in the control room, Shel turned and said that I had written another Number 1 song, but we should leave it off the album so that we could release a more up-tempo record to follow 'You Really Got Me'.

Even though I was pleased about the record, the whole song had somehow managed to make me feel depressed, because I felt that I had not been in control of what I was doing. In the course of less than twelve hours I had both written and recorded a Number 1 song in Marble Arch and helped produce a new human being in Isleworth. I should have felt elated, but instead something inside me protested, something which had always resisted normality and all the ensuing traps and restrictions that accompanied this condition.'

Raymond Douglas stopped and looked down at the empty can of Guinness that was lying on the console. There was no need to ask him why he had suddenly come to a halt. I could see that he was scouring through his past in order to figure out exactly where everything had started to go wrong for him, and I thought how ungrateful he seemed for his success, particularly as he had wanted success so desperately. Maybe he had ended up with the wrong girl, maybe not. One thing was for sure, Raymond Douglas had certainly started out with the wrong music publisher. To add to this first error, little refugee Rasa, whether she knew it or not, had a creation happening inside her that neither Raymond Douglas nor she had any control over whatsoever. No publisher on earth could stop this creation coming out.

'At the end of that week, Rasa had to go up north to start the winter term at St Joseph's Roman Catholic girls' school in Bradford.

The Kinks were doing dates up and down the country, pursued everywhere by screaming fans. There were dates in the Lake District arranged by a promoter who was aptly named Terry Blood, and for the first time we found ourselves playing Scotland. After one of the concerts we were invited back to a castle by an eccentric Scottish laird who insisted that we stay the night to sample his twenty-five-year-old malt whisky. Dave was later found swinging on the chandelier dressed in full armour and brandishing a sword while the laird looked on in fear for the family treasures. I sat outside and thought of a lyric for a song that I was writing for Dave to sing called 'Come On Now'.

The next date was at the Barrowlands Ballroom in Glasgow. The concert had sold out faster than any other and, fearing a riot, the promoters had built a giant stairway from the dressing rooms, located at the back of the hall, to the stage at the opposite end. We had to walk over the audience like circus performers on a tightrope, and we reached the stage to find that nearly all our shoes had been pulled off by the fans as we crossed. This was almost a typical occurrence at the concerts during this period. After each show Brian Longstaff and Ray Lovegrove (our new assistant roadie) repaired torn shirts and trousers that had been ripped from our bodies as we performed. This was becoming a daily ritual. Brian joked that he should be paid extra as he was acting as seamstress as well as road manager.

After the Scottish segment of the tour, we played a small club in Halifax and I was reunited with Rasa. Backstage after the concert, she announced that she was pregnant. I did my best to make her feel happy about this, but in the car on the drive back to London afterwards, I felt a deep shiver of fear in the pit of my stomach. Rasa's sister had supplied the house; Larry Page had driven us to it. No, it was just paranoia. I thought of the terrible scenes at home a few years before when Dave had put a schoolgirl in the family way, but now it would be even worse: the newspapers were following us around everywhere looking for juicy stories to print. I thought of all those times when I had slept with Anita and nothing like this had happened. Maybe the best policy was to say and do nothing. For the time being. Perhaps it would all go away.

Eddie Kassner asked me to his office. Kassner was short and so stocky in stature that he was almost square-shaped.

'Raymond,' he said. '"You Really Got Me" has been to the top and is starting to do very well for us all over the world. Soon it will be released in America and we anticipate that it will be just as successful over there. Now' – and this was like an order – 'Now we need a follow up single immediately.'

Kassner opened a door to a little reception room with an upright piano against the wall. He spoke in his Austrian-refugee accent that bore a strong resemblance to Peter Sellers' in *Dr Strangelove*.

A few days earlier, Eddie had taken Rasa and me to dinner and told us about his hard life during the War. His tragic tale had made an immense impact on me and as I sat down at the piano stool I still had Eddie's life story echoing around my head. Eddie had told us how he had started publishing songs in Austria before the Nazis came and put him and his family in Auschwitz. He was the only member of his family to survive. When he came to London, he and his wife were so poor that their baby had to have a cardboard box for a cradle. Even so, Eddie dreamed of building a music publishing empire.

By now Kassner had me sitting at the piano and he was standing next to me with his hand firmly on my shoulder. I started to play the chords to a song I had been writing called 'All Day and All of the Night'. Suddenly, another door opened and to my surprise I saw Anita standing there. She looked as attractive as ever, with her black hair now down to shoulder length. There was no plausible explanation of why Anita happened to be there unless Kassner and possibly Larry Page had asked her to come along for old times' sake. It was certainly not my idea, I hadn't seen her since the night I left her crying in her flat in Chalk Farm. I wanted to speak to her but now Kassner was in full flow, speaking loudly above my stabbing piano chords. It was as if I were providing a melodramatic accompaniment to the silent movie of Eddie's life.

'In order to provide food for my wife and child I sold sheet music in the streets by day and worked as a waiter in the evenings. Then I would go to Covent Garden market and pick up vegetables that had fallen off of the backs of delivery trucks into the gutter. Eventually I managed to get Vera Lynn to sing one of the songs I published, and she recorded it and put it on the B-side of a record that went to Number 1.'

I was still thumping out the chords of 'All Day' on the piano and although Kassner was back in the past, he still managed to acknowledge the occasional lyric that I shouted through his maniacal rantings.

'Yes, Raymond. Good. I like it. Then I managed to obtain the world publishing rights to "Rock Around the Clock" by Bill Haley. It was then that the Kassner Empire was formed.' Anita came and sat next to me and for a moment there was the same loving look on her face as when we had first met. She leant into me and kissed me on the cheek. I slipped into another key on the piano and sang,

'The only time I feel all right is by your side.
Girl, I want to be with you all of the time.
All day and all of the night.'

Anita whispered 'I love you' in my ear and left the room.
There was no way I would be allowed to pursue her: my exit
from the piano was firmly blocked by Kassner. 'Raymond, I
definitely feel that if you give me this song I will make it such
a hit that it will put you up there with the immortal ones:
George Gershwin, Cole Porter, Ivor Novello.' I wondered
why Kassner had not put Chuck Berry and Lennon and
McCartney in with the immortal ones, but I quickly concluded
that in Kassner's view the only good songwriter was a dead
one. This didn't much matter to me at the time, as I was more
interested in the whereabouts of Anita, who had disappeared
as mysteriously as she had appeared. Kassner took me back
into his office and lit a cigar in celebration of his prodigies'
latest composition.

I walked over to the window and looked down at the
street, hoping to catch a glimpse of Anita, but she was long
gone. There were plenty of tall slim girls with thick mascara
round their eyes and black shoulder-length hair. They all
had the look, but somehow it seemed superficial: it would
change as soon as the next look came along. Anita had the
spirit of the time inside her, and whereas the times were
having a profound effect on me, somehow it was impossible
to have a similar effect any sort of change in her. I felt
Kassner's hand on my shoulder, but this time the publisher's
voice was more restrained:

'Raymond, I will make you wealthy beyond your wildest
imagining, but first we must sort out your management
situation.'

I looked back over my shoulder to see Larry at the
doorway:

'Eddie's right. This just isn't their world. It's a joke; it's a miracle that you've managed to get this far. If it hadn't been for Eddie and me, you and the group would be out on the street now, instead of coming off a Number 1 single. Eddie is about to make you an offer so generous that you will find it difficult to believe.'

Kassner butted in before Larry had a chance to continue: 'Forty pounds.'

I was confused: 'Forty pounds?'

Larry reiterated: 'Forty pounds – a week.'

Kassner's eyes glinted at the sound of money. 'Forty pounds a week, *for life*.'

'If, and only if, you sign all of your songs over to Kassner Music,' Larry continued.

I understood Larry's desires: fame, money, success – recognition. These were all normal to me. But as I looked over at Eddie Kassner, past those thick, horn-rimmed spectacles, there was a completely empty look in his eyes. It was a look of a man who had been exposed to extreme suffering and whose soul had been punished to the point where all feelings for the rest of humanity had been squeezed out of him. No amount of money, no matter how great the Kassner empire might become, could take away that look of emptiness in those dark soulless eyes, which still carried the horrific scars from the wounds that had been inflicted in the concentration camps during the Second World War. It was as if part of Kassner's soul had perished and what was left was trying to grab all that it could from the world in a desperate attempt to replace what had been taken from him. Eddie Kassner's eyes displayed no sign of pity, or even cruelty for that matter. It was a look that defied every emotion which could be felt on this planet. It was an expression I had never seen before, a look from hell, and it sent a chilling sensation of fear down my back. This aside, I almost pitied him as he repeated:

'Forty pounds. It's a lot of money, Raymond, my boy.

Then your songs will be mine until fifty years after you are dead. And I understand that this girlfriend of yours, this Rasa, is a refugee like myself. Talk to her, she will understand what wonderful good fortune you have discovered.'

The very idea that someone like Kassner had any information about my private life made me feel a little paranoid. The fact that Kassner and Page were offering to buy my ideas for eternity was bad enough, but to know that my most intimate affairs were being discussed by these people made me feel sick in the stomach. I left the office, not commenting on the offer, and walked around Soho looking for Anita and the sense of freedom that she had represented to me. It was getting colder and it would only be a matter of time before some fan recognized me. Shel had been right when he had predicted that the success of 'You Really Got Me' ensured that I would no longer be able to walk around the streets. The cover of anonymity had been blown. Soon I went back to the comfort and warmth of Rasa's sister's flat in Willesden, to have tea and biscuits while waiting for the days to go by before announcing the news of her pregnancy to the world.

Back in the less mundane world of pop music, the Kinks were considered the hottest property of the year. We flew up to Glasgow to appear as special guests on the Billy J. Kramer package show. We performed before Kramer and as we sang the audience rioted, and ripped up the seats, causing the theatre management to call the police to restore order so that the rest of the show could proceed.

As we left the theatre, a confused Billy J. Kramer looked at the carnage that had been left behind. I had apologized, but Kramer was still speechless. He was a very successful artist in the true Billy Fury tradition, and although he had been part of the whole Merseybeat explosion, he had never been present at an exhibition of this type of mayhem. These were more than

just adoring fans. There was an atmosphere of violence that
had been stirred up by the Kinks. During the show Dave had
been dragged from the stage by fans and sustained a cut on his
hand. He had proudly displayed his bloodstained shirt and
held his bloody fist aloft as he walked out of the theatre past
Kramer, but Billy J. seemed too dumbfounded to comment.
We had to fly straight back to London and more police were
required to protect us at Glasgow airport, where we strutted
through the terminal still dressed in our red hunting jackets.
By the time the aeroplane took off, Billy J. must have been
singing 'Little Children', knowing that the 'little children' he
was performing to had just ripped the Glasgow Theatre to
shreds.

Whenever I had a chance I travelled back to Bradford
after each performance to stay at Rasa's parents' house. This
often meant getting the night train after a concert, or
cadging a lift from a programme-seller who lived in nearby
Leeds.

We were star guests on the Gerry and the Pacemakers
tour, along with Gene Pitney and Marianne Faithfull. The
fact that we performed before the end of the concert gave
me the chance to make a quick getaway before the majority
of fans could assemble at the stage door.

One night Judith Simons, a columnist from the *Daily
Express*, appeared after the show. Simons said that there had
been a report in the Bradford *Telegraph and Argus* of marriage
banns being read out in church giving notice of the upcoming
wedding between me and Rasa in St Joseph's Roman Catholic
church in Bradford. The next day there were reports in most
of the daily newspapers that 'a Kink' was to be married to a
Bradford schoolgirl. Rasa's parents had proudly announced
the engagement of their daughter in the *Telegraph and Argus*
and a date for the wedding had been set.

When I told the rest of the group that I was to be
married, they just looked at me in a sympathetic way that

suggested I had decided to commit suicide some time in the near future and had asked them to attend. They tried not to comment too much about it after that. The truth was that we were all too busy to think about the fact that was about to sign away yet another part of my freedom, but as long as it didn't affect my flow of songwriting, they seemed not to mind too much. My parents on the other hand were obviously concerned that I was too young.

The management team called a crisis meeting and Brian Somerville appeared at the next concert with both Grenville and Robert in attendance. After a brief discussion Somerville expressed his irritation at not being consulted over the matter beforehand, it was decided that the damage had been done and that everyone should make the most of the publicity. I had always been a publicity-shy individual but was now trapped into having my most personal laundry aired in public. Fans in the front row at concerts started holding up banners with 'Don't Do It, Ray' written in bold colours. The most vigorous opposition came from fans, particularly young women, who stopped me in the street to say that I was wasting my life. On the other hand, the older women who worked at the Blue Boar café on the M1 motorway put me in their protective care. They often interrupted me when I tried to strike up conversations with anyone from the opposite sex. Again I was confronted by the horrific realization that my personal life was under a microscope. Whenever a reporter asked about my upcoming marriage, I simply walked out of the room. This angered Brian Somerville, who was used to artists who cooperated with the press. He could not see why I should be any different.

In Bradford, the *Telegraph and Argus* reported that Rasa had been accused of theft by a jealous friend and was to be taken to court. As a result she was asked to leave the Catholic secondary school where she was a pupil. I went up to Bradford to see if I could be of some assistance and found Rasa's mother

on her knees praying for forgiveness in front of photographs
of John F. Kennedy and the Pope. Rasa's father said that soon
Rasa would be my responsibility, and unless I provided the
best possible legal counsel, it would not be the daughter of
Lithuanian immigrants in the dock, but the future wife of
Raymond Douglas Davies, the lead singer of the Kinks. In
any case, that would be the story the newspapers would print,
because the date of the trial was put back until after the
wedding.

After a concert in Shrewsbury Robert Wace arrived with a
telegram saying that Rasa had been taken to an emergency
ward in Bradford suffering from an internal bleeding. Robert
drove me through a blizzard to the hospital immediately after
the concert so that I could visit Rasa.

Bradford Infirmary was nearly as cold inside as the freezing
snow was outside, and I found Rasa propped up at the end of
a large draughty ward. She had taken a job at Baird's radio on
the assembly line and had collapsed and nearly had a
miscarriage. She started to cry as she told me that it had been
necessary to tell her parents that she was pregnant. Robert
took me to a hotel for breakfast and a stiff brandy and
reprimanded me in a concerned but good-humoured way for
making a complete mess of my private life. For the first time
Robert seemed more of a friend than a manager. He concluded
his lecture by saying that if he had been allowed to manage
my personal as well as my professional life, he would have
considered me much too immature to enter, let alone develop
a personal relationship. According to Robert, marriage was
for adults. 'You should have listened to your mother, old boy.
She would have set you right.'

He was right. I should have listened to my mother. But it's
easy to say that now, years after the event. Those were not the
times for listening to advice from elders. We were very young
and impulsive. Perhaps in my case it was more to do with my
insecurity. None of the other guys in the group was listening

to his parents' advice. Even Robert and Grenville were involved in the pop business against the better judgement of their respective families. It was all right to manage a pop group as 'a bit of a lark', but to give up a career at the stock exchange because of it was going a little too far for someone from the professional classes. Once, in a bar somewhere in the City, Grenville had been snarled at by a former associate at the firm where he had previously worked, and the same indignant gentleman had even uttered the word 'traitor' as Grenville left the premises. Grenville was brave, bold and young like the rest of us, and didn't give a hoot.

We were in Manchester rehearsing 'All Day and All of the Night' for *Top of the Pops*. I had just met my favourite Motown group, Martha and the Vandellas, who were on the show performing 'Dancing in the Street'. I particularly liked Martha because she had a gap between her front teeth which was even larger than mine, and she wasn't at all inhibited by it. As they mimed their song in rehearsal, I stood and watched their manager take a picture. I was astonished to see an image of Martha come out of the camera almost instantaneously – I had just seen my first Polaroid photo.

After the rehearsal I sat with Grenville and explained that people had been telling me I had a bad publishing deal, and that I had received no writing royalties yet and when the royalties did eventually arrive, it was not clear who would receive them. Grenville said it was because there was a clause in the contract that allowed the managers to take 30 per cent of my income . When I asked why, his only answer was 'Because it's in the contract.' 'Then why not take it out?' I asked. Grenville looked pale and for once his eyebrows dropped. 'We can certainly try,' he admitted. Many people in the music business considered Robert and Grenville were upstarts whose lack of experience had resulted in us signing a contract with Pye Records that would haunt us for years to come. However they were also gentlemen, and had no

intention of upsetting an artist who would obviously make
them a considerable amount of money, and so they agreed not
to commission my songwriting. To this day I prefer to think
it was because they felt it was the gentlemanly thing to do.

Dave was certainly not listening to his parents' advice. He
was enjoying the life of a pop star to the hilt. All-night parties
with Brian Jones of the Rolling Stones; late nights at clubs in
St James's; an endless stream of girlfriends up and down the
United Kingdom; plus countless run-ins with various
representatives of local constabularies as anxious parents
reported daughters missing for the night. Dave had taken up
photography and developed his own negatives in a makeshift
darkroom at our parents' house in Fortis Green. While there
was absolutely nothing wrong with this in itself, Mum had
inadvertently come across some sordid black-and-white prints
of young ladies in various stages of undress. This caused
uproar, and after all sorts of ructions and threats of disciplinary
action the darkroom reverted to being a pantry. Mick had
frequented the same clubs as Dave, but he usually ended up
in the early hours of the morning at bars that were hang-
outs for drag queens and various members of their
entourages. This was far from the protected lifestyle of his
parents' home in Molesey, but perhaps Mick felt more
at home in these establishments since his encounter with that
Scout master. Mick was 'straight', but because he was so
obviously male, old queens were attracted to him like bees
to honey.

The recording of 'All Day and All of the Night' was a
frantic affair, with the Kinks arriving in London late at night
from a gig up north to record the song the following morning
at Pye Studios, where the first album had been recorded. Only
three hours of studio time had been booked, and the track had
to be completed by one o'clock so that the group could drive
straight back up north for another concert that night. We still
attracted a large amount of curiosity when we worked in the

studio. On this occasion a session singer called Johnny B. Goode asked if he could help out with the backing vocals. He was a friend of the group and Talmy had no objection to him joining the session to add to the slightly heavier sound we had in mind. He thought that the extra falsetto would compensate because Rasa was not there. Perry Ford played piano and Bobby Graham was again playing the drums, with Mick Avory playing tambourine. The back track was put down very quickly in the same manner as 'You Really Got Me', and the guitar solo was again played live by Dave.

When we went upstairs to hear the playback in the tiny control room, we found it crowded with onlookers and assorted musicians. Among then was Jimmy Page, who cringed as it came to Dave's guitar solo. Perhaps Page was put out about not being asked to play on the track, and we were slightly embarrassed by the amount of jealousy shown by such an eminent guitarist. Perhaps it was because he thought Dave's solo inferior to anything he could have played, but Dave had not only invented a sound, but also had every right to play whatever solo he felt fitted the track. Bobby Graham had also shown some displeasure because I had requested a certain drum fill to be played before the second and third verses.

It was a drum fill I had heard on an old Buddy Holly record called 'It's So Easy' and it had always been my ambition to have it played on a Kinks recording. It was a simple enough request, but it had obviously annoyed the session drummer so much that he had played the fill with such splendid venom that it took on an entirely new sound of its own. But rumours started that the Kinks were getting big-headed and their egos needed clipping.

'All Day and All of the Night' had been released and was moving up the charts just as rapidly as our first single. Everyone assumed that it would end up in the Number 1 position, but there was talk that the Beatles were bringing out a new single, and it was obvious that the Beatles would go straight to Number 1.

The new tour with Gerry and the Pacemakers, Gene Pitney and Marianne Faithfull was becoming a series of what were referred to as nightly rave ups, particularly at the hotels afterwards. On one occasion a night porter refused to serve Dave and Gerry Marsden with another round of light ale and Dave grabbed an axe from the wall and proceeded to chop up the front desk of the hotel. Marsden tried to deter Dave but eventually was roped in as an accomplice. Another night Dave called Brian Longstaff to his room to help stop the blood flowing from his penis, which had been torn during an over-zealous sexual romp with a local girl. This was the era of Dave's fascination with musketeers and cavaliers. On this occasion the unfortunate girl had been seen running down the corridors of the hotel dressed only in Dave's thigh-length leather boots while Dave followed her brandishing a duelling sabre. By this time everyone in the tour party considered this a normal occurrence and nobody took any notice. But when Dave appeared with a towel wrapped around his bleeding groin, everybody started to panic. Dave was rushed to hospital where he was given a blood transfusion and the ripped foreskin was attended to. The girl insisted on staying behind at the hotel to receive her 'groupie' dues, and received her rights from a willing member of the stage crew.

There were also rumours of a relationship between Marianne Faithfull and a leading member of the touring company. These both intrigued and infuriated Gerry Marsden, and he sent the tour manager on night-time sorties over the rooftops of the hotel to peek through bedroom windows in order to verify his suspicions. One night the tour manager disappeared and we concluded that Marianne must have been alone on this particular night and invited the tour manager into her boudoir. Marianne flatly denied these allegations the next day. On another occasion the entire hotel was woken at three in the morning by the sound of crashing as somebody fell from a fire escape on to a pile of dustbins. In the morning Marianne denied that anyone had been in her room. Even the tour manager was reluctant to confirm his involvement in the affair. Gerry and I decided to hold our own investigation into the matter and questioned everybody on the tour. Gene Pitney was far too respectable to climb fire escapes, and so was eliminated from our inquiries. We were not in possession of sufficient evidence to actually confront any suspect, save for a pair of soiled ladies' knickers which were found by the fire escape, but this alone was not conclusive. After several days we let the matter rest. The only members of the tour party who were not questioned about the matter were Gerry and me.

I sustained an ankle injury in a fall after climbing over the garden wall of Rasa's parents' house. I was taken to Bradford Infirmary for an X-ray on a suspected fractured shin, but was relieved to discover that it was only a sprain. Even this presented me with difficulties during the concerts. I would sing 'Girl, you really got me now' while hobbling around the stage with a walking stick. No one in the tour party had the investigative powers to put any evidence together concerning the falling man except for Gerry, who for days afterwards would sing 'All Day and All of the Night' every time he passed me backstage. However we decided to put the case to rest and the identity of the man on the fire escape remains a mystery to this day.'

11

**Me and my baby's gonna get on a train
that's gonna take us away**

R.D. got up from his chair and started pacing around the dark
room, chewing on a cigar butt that must have been five years
old. He was clearly excited by what he had told me and the
memories it had brought back to him. I nearly threw up as R.D.
actually lit up the old cigar while humming 'All Day and All of
the Night'. Then he did a little jig as he took the first puff, but
he immediately started coughing and spluttering.

'Fucking cigars' he muttered. 'Waste of money. Capitalism,
communism – don't mean nothing. You know what Fidel Castro
and Winston Churchill had in common? They both smoked
Montecristo cigars. Hypocrites. Left, right – don't mean nothing.'

R.D. paused and he looked pale. His exertions had taken their
toll. He began to speak fast and he started to hyperventilate. Now
he could barely talk at all.

'This is making me very uneasy. I think something bad is going
to happen. I've got a pain in my chest. I've nearly died two or
three times in my life. I don't want to die now. Thinking about
those times makes my gut roll over. Do you think it could be
karma? Like maybe I made a pact with the devil or something?
Like that day I drew myself on the street when I was at college.
Have you ever been on the underground late at night when all of a
sudden you see a drunk who's just been beaten up, and you see
another man who looks afraid, and then you go into an empty
carriage and some evil dude comes and sits next to you and you're
the only two people in the carriage? And outside, as the train
leaves the station, you hear a woman screaming. Isn't that some
kind of indication that something bad's happening? That's the way
I feel now. I have to stop. Let's have a cup of tea.'

It was also common knowledge that R.D. was known as a

hypochondriac. I tried not to snigger as I went into the kitchen. I took great care to see that the tea was up to standard, so that he would be inspired and go on. I need not have worried. Raymond Douglas was in a talkative mood. He had obviously decided to confront issues which he had always managed to avoid in the past. He sipped the tea. He smiled. He liked it. He continued.

'It was decided to have a Lithuanian wedding in Bradford, with all the trappings of traditional matrimonial etiquette. The Kinks were still on tour with Gene Pitney and Gerry and the Pacemakers, and I was to drive up to Bradford after the last concert of the tour, at the Oxford New Theatre, in time for the wedding the next day. During the final show fans were screaming at me 'not to do it'. Wherever I turned there seemed to be somebody with advice of one sort or another. The only people who said nothing were the group themselves. For the most part, we never made comments about each other's private lives, but had they commented, I'm sure they would have offered their best wishes and that would have been that.

I left the band in the dressing room after the show and drove up to Bradford with the tour manager and stayed overnight in a local hotel. There was a nagging thought in my head that something immensely important was going to happen, but it was only part of a series of events happening to me that were completely out of my control: life seemed to be in control of me. In the morning I switched on the radio in my hotel room to hear Brian Matthew, the friendly BBC DJ, offer me his congratulations on my big day. I went to the toilet and threw up. It was strange to think that Brian Matthew had announced most of the important events in my short life as a pop singer, and here he was again to remind me that I had an appointment to keep at St Joseph's Church later that day. I looked at the bedside clock and realized that I had overslept and was already late for the big engagement.

Brian Somerville was waiting for me in the hotel bar. He clearly sensed a certain amount of nervousness, because he bought me a large brandy. He then stuck a carnation in the buttonhole of my newly made blue pin-striped suit and whispered in my ear that he had two one-way tickets to South America in his pocket, in case I changed my mind. While I am certain to this day that he was serious and did actually have the tickets in his pocket, I have never been completely certain as to who would have been travelling with me. If I had consented to leave my career and other obligations behind, would I have found myself flying to South America with Brian Somerville?

The outside of the church was surrounded by screaming fans and well-wishers, but eventually the police managed to drag me through the crowd. Miraculously every part of my brand-new suit was still intact. I burst into the foyer of the church straight into a row of surprised bridesmaids, all dressed in Lithuanian national costume.

If I had any doubts as to where I was, the stern-faced bridesmaids soon made me realize that I was in the right place, even though they glared at me as if I should not have been there. I was inclined to agree with them, but, before I could make my way to the nearest exit, I found myself being pushed up the aisle of the church by none other than Brian Somerville, smiling mischievously. 'No running out now, old boy,' he said. 'Unless of course you're ready to come over to the other side.' I gave the beaming publicist a confused look: if I wanted to escape, which would be the worse fate? In any event, both sides of the church were full.

The wedding got under way and vanished into the echo of the vast Catholic interior. This cavernous place had married and buried better men than me, and as the priest spoke, words from his previous sentences returned from the back of the church and turned the event into a strange mixture of past and present. It was like birth, marriage and confession all in one. It was like an echo I had never heard before, and it turned this into an event of tremendous importance.

I turned to look at the pretty bride standing next to me and wished her all the luck in the world. I felt as if I was not a part of this ceremony. I was strangely detached. Back in the aisle of the church, I heard the sound of a scuffle and turned to see Brian extracting the film from a reporter's camera and exposing it to a shaft of daylight. I was relieved to see that some conscientious professionals were still doing their jobs.

Later, back at the home of the Didzpetris family, the wedding breakfast was in full swing. For some strange reason the English-speaking people were in self-imposed segregation at a large table in one room and the Lithuanian- and Polish-speaking contingent were in another. In the world of politics, this would have created an international incident, but in the infinitely more perilous world of matrimony, it was put to one side so that the injured parties could bear grudges in the years to come. Totally frazzled, Mrs Didzpetris had made the mistake of seating the best man, my brother Dave, next to the Catholic priest. Dave continually called him 'Holy Joe', while the priest tried to retain an air of dignified, pious calm. His faith was surely tested during Dave's speech, when he referred to the bridesmaids as 'crumpet', and Rasa's sister as a 'nice bit of stuff'.

The priest's credibility disintegrated somewhat when he was discovered taking photographs during the soup course with a camera that looked as if it had been supplied by the KGB. Only the most traditional English upbringing prevented Brian from snatching the cleric's camera and ejecting the holy man from the dining room. Mrs Didzpetris, upon hearing of this outrage, dropped a handful of plates on the floor. Fortunately, this helped break up the tense atmosphere caused by the seating arrangements. Londoners and Lithuanians alike scrambled on the floor to help the mother of the bride.

After a series of emotional farewells in both English and Lithuanian, Rasa and her new husband went to Bradford

airport with Robert, Grenville and Brian where we all boarded
a plane to London. The flight was turbulent, and while I was
concerned for Rasa because of her 'condition', Wace threw
up politely in the sick bag conveniently placed on his seat.
From London Rasa and I were to catch a train down to the
West Country for a few days' honeymoon in Exeter. For
what seemed the first time ever, Rasa and I were legally
alone.

On the train I watched her sleep in the small compartment
and wondered what life would have in store for us both. I
thought about Brian's offer to fly me to South America and
considered whether I would have been any happier there. I
stood at the window and watched the stations fly past in the
night. I thought about what life would be like if I were
continually on tour, travelling the length and breadth of
Britain. I had got what I wanted, but now I was in a trap that
demanded permanence.

It was a long cold journey to Exeter, and when we arrived
at the hotel the night porter gave us both a cup of hot
chocolate in the lobby before showing us to the bridal suite.
We must have looked cold and confused. During the next few
days, Rasa and I hardly spoke, let alone slept together. We
just walked around the streets of Exeter killing time until we
could go back to London.

It wasn't until the taxi turned the corner of the street where
I had grown up that the fact that I was going to have to
become a responsible adult sent a shock wave through my
body. An overwhelming surge of fear raced through my
system as the realization that I, Raymond Douglas, the most
insecure of the insecure, had now become sole protector and
provider, responsible for the security and well-being of another
soul. I looked at my wife sitting next to me in the taxi. She
must have had the same fear inside her, but then she was a
refugee and perhaps to her being in the situation she was in
made her feel totally secure. On top of all of this, Rasa was

carrying a child inside her and, unless I had been completely
misled, this as yet unformed and anonymous entity was part
of me.

After the initial shock I quickly found a bed-sit in Muswell
Hill and, while I was emotionally unprepared for marriage, I
did my best to make my wife as comfortable as possible. But
our first LP was topping the charts and I was due to go back
on tour. When I wasn't riding up and down the country
doing dates, my life revolved around writing songs to keep up
with the demand. As my supply of material had already been
exhausted by our first album, I used every spare moment to
prepare ideas for new songs. The bed-sit was at the top of a
large house and, while the open-plan conversion was at times
a little draughty, the light came bursting into the living room
early in the morning and made both of us feel optimistic
about our situation.

Rasa was experiencing daily physiological changes that come
with motherhood. Her underwear was stretching to the point
where it would no longer fit her, her body starting to swell as
her hormones began to reorganize and change. Both of us
were confused, happy and afraid, all at once. We were both
having to produce at the same time, but while I could put my
guitar down whenever I chose, Rasa was always accompanied
by this other creation, and it was getting bigger and more
noticeable every day. I watched her as she slept, and wondered
how it could all be happening. Then I went into the living
room and wrote some song lyrics. I was not completely aware
of what I was writing, and there was no poetic flow of any
description, I was just using songs as a sort of therapy. I
couldn't very well write songs about being an expectant father,
but the events in my life were linked in some way to my
songs. Anyone who says that creativity comes from divine
inspiration is certainly wrong, particularly in my case. I wasn't
writing songs for my wife, unborn child, God or country, I
was writing to stay sane.

I had in the back of my mind that Arthur Howes had mentioned that there had been an offer for us to tour Australia early in the new year, and while I was overjoyed at the possibility of being reunited with my sister Rosie, I was concerned that Rasa would not be able to make the journey. But I knew that Rasa would have company: some of my sisters lived in the neighbourhood, and although my mother had been opposed to the wedding she promised to have a spare bed ready for Rasa whenever she needed it. And Rasa'a sister Dalia had moved to Hampstead, and was always visiting us.

In the last few weeks before Christmas, I started sketching Rasa asleep in bed. My insomnia was so bad that most of my work was being done at night, which was the time I always dreaded the most. A strange thing occurred: the image that I was creating on paper looked totally different to my sleeping wife, and more like the sad face of my friend Margie, last seen sitting in the gutter outside Grenville's flat. I suddenly realized that there was a similarity between the two. The same delicate features, large eyes and shoulder-length hair. The horrible thought that I could have possibly married the wrong person struck me. Perhaps this was just a rebound romance. Perhaps I had needed to find somebody prepared to put up with me, and the only difference between the two of them was that Rasa told me what I wanted to hear. But I wanted to believe that this marriage was meant to be, so I tore up the drawings and tried to forget Margie as quickly as she had probably forgotten me. I even stopped drawing, because I realized that drawing was too truthful. I could tell lies in my little songs because in many ways my style had been my own invention and my subconscious was allowed to work through me and yet somehow bypass the listener: I could keep the secrets of my motivation completely to myself. The strange thing was that my songs were being heard all over the world by millions of people and yet nobody really knew what these songs were really about. On the other hand, my artwork had always been more specific and all my subliminal thoughts were displayed in my pictures. There seemed to be something more subversive about writing songs. The fact that they were part of popular culture, considered vulgar, appealed to me after the pretentious allusions of art school. There was something dishonest about the way we were being told to paint: it was an education in style rather than painting or craftmanship.

As I sat with my pregnant wife in our attic flat in Muswell Hill, I found it odd that I was supposed to be this rebellious pop singer, running away from hoards of screaming fans during the day, being thrown out of hotels by irate porters at night, causing dismay and havoc in hitherto happy suburban homes as rebellious teenagers turned 'You Really Got Me' full up on their Dansette record players, before disappearing to see the Kinks play in the local dance hall, leaving their parents sitting at home worrying whether their children would return the same as they had left: sane, ordinary, sober, with virginity still intact. Mr and Mrs Mum and Dad could relate to the Beatles because they had been on at the London Palladium and played in front of the Queen. Pop stars were meant to be good-looking and respectful to adults, in the style of Cliff Richard. Even the Rolling Stones had been sanctioned by the entertainment world and officially endorsed by the media as the acceptable face of revolution. The Stones talked about it, the Beatles wrote about it, but for two months at the end of 1964, many people thought that the Kinks might actually bring it about.

There was a hint of danger every time we went to play a venue. Police were outside waiting to be called in to stop the show, hoping to arrest one of us for inciting a riot or, better still, drink and drugs. Stories of punch-ups and backstage brawls were daily occurrences, and while groups such as the Animals got banned from hotels and P. J. Proby, the American singer, was barred from a chain of theatres for allegedly

exposing himself on stage, the press somehow accepted this
as part of the young being young. But every time the Kinks
were involved in a scuffle, it was reported with a tinge of
hatred attached to it. These Kinks were a danger to everyone, young and old. Journalists hinted that we had been
lucky to get so far, but that luck would soon run out and
we would find ourselves back in the gutter where we, in
their opinion, belonged. This caused some concern, particularly
to Somerville. He had brilliantly masterminded the Beatles'
publicity in the early days, and had made a reputation for
himself as a career-builder. Although on the surface he seemed
satisfied with the coverage we were getting, there was a hint
of professional embarrassment attached to anything concerning the Kinks. Pop music was supposed to entertain the
youngsters while the adult world continued to make the
decisions that would screw up everybody's lives. Pop was
meant to reflect the culture, not to *become* the culture. The
Kinks seemed to cross a danger-line. They invaded the very
structure of a corrupt and yet self-satisfied and precious
society. Other established stars such as the Beatles and the
Stones moved to big houses and drove Rolls-Royces
because that was the way the game was played. This was
understood and accepted by the conventional world. The
Kinks, on the other hand, didn't seem to know what to do
with their success; it looked as though we were not going to
buy into that traditional concept of successful human
existence.

While I was in my bed-sit attic, trying to come to terms
with imminent parenthood, the world outside was waiting for
the fuse attached to the Kinks' career to run out and for
everything to explode in our faces. I comforted my wife and
discussed what to name our baby while outside the world said
we were on course for annihilation. It was two weeks before
Christmas and my world was both beautiful and frightening.
It was the total living experience.

Christmas saw the Kinks at almost the peak of their initial success. We appeared on two television shows on New Year's Eve. First, we did *Beat Club* for the BBC, and then we were rushed across London to perform on *Ready Steady Go!* for independent television. We went on just before midnight to perform. I remember miming to 'All Day and All of the Night' when suddenly I saw Mick Jagger standing in the front row of the audience. I had seen Jagger perform at Hornsey Art College with the Rolling Stones, then in the club where I had been playing with the Dave Hunt Band. Now the roles were reversed. Jagger stood in front of me, not glaring exactly, but looking into my eyes, trying to work out what I was doing right. This concerned me, because everybody else was dancing and Mick Jagger, one of the most incredibly natural movers, just stood there. I was disappointed that I didn't see him dancing while I sang 'All Day and All of the Night'. That would have made my year complete, but perhaps he suspected that and decided to stand bolt upright throughout the song. After the show Dave, Rasa and I went back to Mum and Dad's house. They were still having the same old singsongs, but now they were singing 'You Really Got Me' in a pub-style version. I have a feeling that Mick Jagger wouldn't have danced to that either. On the other hand, it may have been just his scene.

January 1965 heralded the year of the Kinks' assault on the rest of the world. The UK was more or less 'in the pocket', and now there were other worlds to conquer. We went first to Paris, to play on a television show. Brian Longstaff came along as tour manager, along with Robert Wace, who had a smattering of French in his repertoire. This allowed Grenville to keep an eye on his rapidly expanding theatrical empire, as well as another watchful eye on Larry Page. Rasa went along wearing a fantastic white fur coat, which made her look like a princess from the Steppes of ancient Russia. According to some tabloid newspaper, Rasa's mother had once been connected to Lithuanian aristocracy, and the way Rasa wore the fur coat, with her almost white flowing hair, added a touch of authenticity to this claim.

We were playing a television show in a studio that was totally unprepared for human habitation. It was a converted theatre and no provision had been made for us. I had not wanted to make the trip at all, and to outsiders I was gaining a reputation for being on a short fuse, partly due to the massive work load of songwriting and partly to my worries about Rasa's impending addition. I had a row with a French technician because the group had been waiting for French bread and cheese for six hours while the technicians got their act together. In the circumstances, I felt the urge to protest in some way, particularly as my pregnant wife was in need of food. The only insult I could muster was a combination of English and French: 'Le cunt!' To my astonishment, English-style sandwiches arrived within minutes. I remembered one of the first rules I learned during my short tenure at theatre college: 'Shout and thou shalt receive.'

Brian Longstaff was equally frustrated, because he could not get a cup of tea. In the end, he put two fingers together to form the letter T. He ended up with a cup of hot water and a tea-bag on the side. Like all British ex-servicemen, Brian felt that 'Wogs begin at Calais'. He relieved his frustration by asking the waiter to stand to attention while he put the tea-bag in his mouth and then drank the water. The demonstration definitely tested his inner mouth, if not his stiff upper lip.

After the show, the Kinks played a concert at the Paris Olympia, scene of triumphs by singers like Edith Piaf, Maurice Chevalier and Yves Montand. The concert itself was a tremendous success with the public, even though Brian Longstaff had shouted at everybody to get decent equipment for us to play with. Also, his French shorthand for tea was not working as well as it had before; a fight broke out because the stage crew had provided him with a pot of boiled milk and cold water. The Beatles had been a tremendous hit at the Olympia the previous year, and people were saying that the Kinks concert was magnificent, although we felt it was the worst show we had ever done. Rasa, who watched from the wings, was won over by the sedate but warm response shown by the Paris audience.

But the real find of the trip was the promotion man from Barclay Records, who distributed Pye Records in France. Xavier, a well-dressed, debonair playboy, took us to some of the best restaurants and nightclubs in Paris. I thought that the whole trip was worthwhile just for a night out with Xavier. I also learned an important lesson about international promotion. 'Assist them in their exploitation and thou shalt eat free.' One of the numerous clubs we visited was the Carousel Club. The establishment was managed by a wonderful woman who would wait until five in the morning, when everybody was either too drugged or drunk to care, when she would release chickens and pigs from cages, putting them on people's backs so that they could dance with live animals. It was not clear whether this was a publicity stunt or a comment on the club's clientele. If animals were not to your taste, an assortment of beautiful Parisian Mesdamoiselles descended the staircase on to the dance floor and accompanied the guests for the remainder of the evening.

The following morning we flew to Marseilles to do another television show, which turned out to be on an American aircraft carrier, based somewhere out in the Mediterranean. Mick Avory and Terry McGrath, who was along to represent the Arthur Howes agency, immediately headed for the red-light district, where they found themselves two prostitutes for the night. Terry, still wearing his racecourse tout's hat, was already too drunk and incapable to do anything but to put a complete damper on the proceedings, his whore became ill and threw up in the bath. McGrath now started throwing up himself. It must have been a complete turn-off for everybody, including Mick's whore, who ran off in terror. At least Mick avoided the possibility of contracting Gallic clap. I took the opportunity of spending an evening watching my pregnant wife take a bath in first-class splendour in the deepest bathtub France could offer, in total contrast to the tiny tub in our bed-sit in Muswell Hill.

Next morning we flew to the aircraft carrier by helicopter. Rasa was once again the centre of attention, drawing wolf-whistles and applause from the American sailors as she tottered across the deck in her high heels, miniskirt and white fur coat. This was the first time I felt any sort of jealousy. Sailors after my young wife; her five months pregnant; and me with only a guitar; two hits under my belt, and a bundle full of trouble in my trousers.

The French television crew continued making every conceivable event as difficult and complicated as possible. They were as disorganized on sea as they had been on land, only this time we had to perform in gale-force conditions. But after a while I started to think of Jacques Tati movies I had seen at art college, and my anger gave way to admiration of the bungling crew as they botched one set-up after another; we began to enjoy the splendour of French un-togetherness. Eventually, the American captain of the ship intervened to say, very politely, that they either had to complete the shoot immediately or stay on board for the rest of the trip around the stormy Mediterranean sea. Then, after the TV crew was dispatched to land, we were taken downstairs, where the service men were waiting for us to play an impromptu concert. Brian Longstaff tried to explain that we had inadequate equipment. The captain replied in a deep Texan drawl, 'You either play a couple of songs for my boys, or you don't get off this boat until we get to Egypt.' We looked at each other, then at the cigar-chewing captain, and decided to play two or three songs with what equipment was available.

The following morning we flew back to London to continue work on our second album. Three backing tracks had already been recorded at IBC Studios, one of which was a song called 'Don't Ever Change'. I watched Rasa as she walked into the studio still swaddled in her now ever-present fur coat. The sad little refugee had indeed changed into a princess. Maybe I had married the right person after all.

I guess we were all changing, although we didn't realize it at the time. We had been a bunch of kids out to prove something, and now we were caught on a treadmill which demanded success. And, being a competitive sort, I was not about to be a failure. On that same session we recorded 'Come On Now', which I had written for Dave to sing as the B-side of our next single 'Tired of Waiting for You'. I had written the song while we were on tour in Scotland the previous November, just after Rasa had told me that she might be pregnant. Had the lyric been a hidden plea, a cry for help in the subconscious of a scared, immature young man? Perhaps the song should have been addressed to its author. 'Come on now. Be a man.'

The single was due to come out the weekend before we went on our world tour, and so we had to tape *Top of the Pops*, in case the record went into the charts. We were to do *Ready Steady Go!* live on the Friday before leaving for Australia. All the best-laid plans were set. Then it was announced that Winston Churchill was seriously ill; if he died before the programme aired, there would be a black-out in mourning for the great man. Ironically we were to sing 'Tired of Waiting for You' when the world was waiting for Churchill to die. However, he didn't die that night and the show went ahead as planned.

The so-called world tour beckoned. This was, in fact, only a tour of the Far East, starting in Australia. We were touring on a package with Manfred Mann and the Honeycombs (who had had a hit with a song called 'Have I the Right?'). My mum insisted that the whole family came to the airport to see us off. This caused some amusement to Manfred Mann, a likeable but somewhat cynical South African musician. During the tour he became quite a close, if somewhat competitive, friend.

For financial reasons, none of our managers came on the tour, and even Brian Longstaff was left at home. Instead, we were accompanied by Johnny Clapson, who had been hired by Arthur Howes to oversee the whole tour. Clapson must have been an ex-entertainer. He had the elegance of Cary Grant combined with the ruthlessness of a drill sergeant in the French Foreign Legion.

I sat in the Air India 707 and waved goodbye to Rasa. I saw her standing near the runway as the aeroplane taxied out, still dressed in her new fur coat. Soon we were flying over the Steppes of Russia. Icebound. Frozen. A mean, hard place. No wonder Rasa's family had left. This seemed from all superficial appearances to be a strange wilderness with no heart. We landed at Moscow Airport briefly, to refuel, and a Russian soldier, in full regalia complete with a fur hat with a red star in the middle and a gun at his side, boarded and took our passports before we left the plane. We did not argue with this stern-faced Ruskie who probably thought Dave was a girl. The inside of the airport was like one of these old black-and-white paintings that have been hand-coloured. The make-up on the ladies' faces was too obvious; their lips too red to be believable. The airport was just a show for the outside world, to cover up what was really going on inside the country.

Next stop was one of the most unforgettable of my life: Bombay. We were checked into the hotel late at night. It was built on the beach and was supposed to be the best hotel in the city. I couldn't sleep, partly from excitement at being in a mysterious continent, but mainly because of the cockroaches and ants crawling around, so I got up and watched the sun rise on the beach. It was there that I heard the chanting of native fishermen as they carried their nets to work. It was a sound that for some indescribable reason was immediately personal to me, and was to be very influential in my songwriting. It's difficult to describe how a sound or a song gets into your soul. It just connects and stays there. This sound later formed the basis of a song called 'See My Friends'. Dave's sortie into the Indian continent was less poetic. He went for a walk on the beach, but was chased by a mad dog. It was typical of Dave's life at this time that everything he did culminated in some sort of catastrophe or disaster.

Our morning adventures over, we ate breakfast on the patio of the hotel, alongside the rich British tourists who were also staying there. The under-nourished waiters brought us bread and jam to eat, along with our correctly prepared full English breakfast and pots of tea. Tea brewed with a subtle expertise that even Brian Longstaff would have been proud of. The food was so plentiful, the sun was so hot, the waiters so thin I could hardly bring myself to eat. Afterwards, we assembled outside the hotel and got on a bus to go to the airport, driving through rat-infested streets where scantily clad children played in holes in the ground. Whole families lived in these holes in the most extreme poverty, right next to the skyscraper hotels where the tourists stayed. Children were going to the toilet in the gutter and there was filth everywhere. We left Bombay behind, hot and stinking, and flew on to Madras, which was so hot that the people could hardly move. The flies swarmed around the natives' faces but they hadn't the energy to brush them aside. India was an education in two days. The world suffers. A lot of people in the world suffer, but pop groups can fly on to other continents. As we left India I realized that compared to this level of suffering, I had been given an easy route through life.

The next stop on the journey was Singapore, where the tour party was met by so many screaming fans that the local police lost control of the situation, and shots were fired in the air to subdue the rioting. I was quickly learning that in these

poor parts of the world, human life was less precious than in
the affluent and tolerant climates. I heard a scream as a body
smashed against a pane of glass outside the airport. A young
female fan was crushed against the window only feet away
from me. I tried to reach out to her when somebody pushed
me along and put a telegram in my hand. It was from Arthur
Howes, and said that 'Tired of Waiting for You' had gone
straight in the charts at Number 11. The telegram made me
feel slighty more secure with all the turmoil around me, but at
the same time the charts in far-away Britain seemed somewhat
trivial after the deprivations I had witnessed in India. The tour
was not scheduled to play Singapore until after Australia. In
the circumstances surrounding me, I hoped it would be
cancelled altogether.

Then we arrived at Perth, and were greeted by stares from
the Australian customs men, but Johnny Clapson was as
efficient as ever and got us through without too much
inconvenience. After a brief stop-over we took an overnight
flight to Adelaide. I couldn't sleep in anticipation of being
reunited with my sister Rosie, and with my nephew Terry in
particular. I watched the daylight come up over the clouds as
we flew across Australia.

We arrived in Adelaide and were driven straight to the
Grand Hotel. I waited in my luxurious hotel suite to be
reunited with Rosie. The last time I had seen her I was outside
a semi in north London, waving goodbye as I drove off in the
back of a van with Anita. I could barely stay awake because of
jet-lag, so I ordered room service to bring sandwiches. Rosie
was amazed that not only could I put the cost of the sandwiches
on the bill, but that I could actually afford to pay for them all.
The last time she had seen me, I hardly had two pennies to
rub together. We sat and hardly spoke; this was becoming a
frequent occurrence after not seeing friends or relatives for a
long time. There's nothing to say to them. They had seen me
on television and heard me on the radio, and even though

they knew me, they had been drawn into a little of the hype
and thought that I was some sort of celebrity, which was
ridiculous, because I was in fact the same insecure person they
had known before. In any event, jet-lag prevents coherent
communication. Then Terry and Arthur walked in, and after
saying how wonderful it was to see them again, I passed out
and did not wake until late that afternoon.

The Manfred Mann group were closing the show in Australia
because 'Do Wah Diddy Diddy' had been a hit long before 'You
Really Got Me'. But it was the Kinks who created all the fuss,
more out of controversy than anything else. The rest of the
performers took advantage of the Australian summer and wore
shorts and T-shirts on stage, while we were still playing in our
thick hunting jackets in temperatures of 110°; truly suffering for
the sake of art and image.

Due to this we were completely exhausted and dehydrated
at the end of each concert. The padding in the coats was quite
sufficient for the English winter hunting season, but was
totally inappropriate for the Australian summer. We also
created some dubious publicity when, before our show in
Adelaide, we were interviewed live by a local DJ who was a
renowned pommy-basher. He was doing so much more
talking than we were that Dave found it necessary to take a
hamburger that he was eating and stuff it down the DJ's
throat while the over-verbose Antipodean was in full flow.
This caused uproar with the Australian press, who did not like
to be shown to be fools, or even being forcibly fed on live
radio. There were headlines in the local press: 'Pommy Kinks
Go Home! We Don't Need You!' But to us the only thing
that mattered was that our record had gone into the UK
charts at Number 11 and we were hot shit. The Aussie media
continued their criticism, but quite frankly we didn't give a
toss. We carried on regardless, taking up the gauntlet by
performing even better than before, by working even harder
on stage. True Brits in battle! (Albeit dehydrated ones.)

A friendly rivalry was building up between Manfred Mann's group and us, as we both had new singles out in the UK. I knew that 'Tired of Waiting for You' would be Number 1, and, even though Manfred's record had gone in somewhere like Number 12, I had heard it before I left England and somehow I knew that it would not go as high as ours. This sounds over-competitive and childish, but it was the atmosphere at the time.

After the Adelaide show Dave and I went back to Rosie and Art's detached home in the suburbs of Adelaide, and were relieved to discover that they were living in some measure of comfort; that emigrating to Australia had been worthwhile for them.

Terry said that when he met me at the hotel in Adelaide, he didn't know whether to shake hands with Dave and me or hug us. I said that if he had kissed me, I would have returned the compliment. It was Terry whom Dave and I had missed more than anybody else. He was always a caring friend; more than a nephew – a second brother to me. I told him that I secretly wished he had stayed in England to become our tour manager, but emigrating with his mother and father was more important. There had been terrible traumas before they went, but Terry had finally decided to go with his parents. We all stayed up to the early hours talking over old times. Rosie played old tapes of me rehearsing with my guitar when I had lived with her. She was shocked when I revealed that one of the little 'plink-plonk' country songs on her tape had turned out to be 'Tired of Waiting for You'. We talked and talked but it was not long before the rigor mortis of jet-lag set in once again, and Dave and I slept in the back of Arthur's car as he drove us back to our hotel.

Rosie, Terry and Arthur came to the airport to say goodbye, and as Rosie helped me with my luggage I saw Manfred sniggering. I asked Manfred why he was so cynical, and he said in his wonderfully morbid South African drawl, 'I'm not sending you up, old boy, I'm just sending up the whole scene.'

It's true, Manfred was a complete send-up. Even his music was a parody of jazz and rock 'n' roll. He had some wonderful musicians in his band: Tom McGuinness on bass, a friendly, down-to-earth person; Mike Vickers, who went on to be a competent musical arranger for TV and films; and the ecstatic, multi-talented Paul Jones, with his slightly acne-scarred face and superb, and underrated, harmonica style. Because Paul sang in a lower key, it gave him the ability to make a blues song sound like a Perry Como ballad. A fascinating technique. Perhaps deep down Manfred Mann was a blues band, but Paul Jones was definitely a 1950s matinée idol even then. But the strange combination gave them a unique sound and they were responsible for some of the finest pop singles of the early 1960s, even though the playing on their records was below the competence of the musicians. I think it was Manfred's fear of being unsuccessful that made him reduce everything he did to the lowest common denominator.

The remainder of the tour was not very eventful, except for the antics of some of the members of the tour. Without naming names, one person entertained two ladies in a Melbourne hotel room, one of whom insisted on performing with a large Alsatian dog in front of members of our crew. We were assured that both women were experienced dog-handlers. As I was unable to attend, I am unsure as to whether the Alsatian actually took part in the activities, but I find it hard to believe that the dog was there merely to watch. I also understand that chains and manacles were involved in the event.

Dave was pursued by a couple of Satanists from Brisbane who insisted on uttering strange chants as they wandered around the hotel half-naked. I'm sure Dave took all this in his stride, but as his older brother I was concerned about his welfare. I was particularly embarrassed when Rosie paid me a

surprise visit, suddenly appearing at the door of my hotel
room. She sat innocently across from me on my bed, eating
cheese sandwiches and discussing old times, inquiring about
the rest of the family back home. I, on the other hand, was
more concerned about how my more imminent family,
namely my rampaging brother, was performing along the
corridor. Rosie had caught a plane overnight to stay with us
for the day. I explained that I was in the middle of writing
some songs (one of which was called 'This Strange Effect'),
but I was obviously unable to inform her of the Satanic rites
that were being carried out down the corridor, or the Alsatian
dogs performing in another bedroom.

But as tours went this tour was pretty dull really. There
were more old queens in Australia than you would care to
imagine. I remember after a gig in a small city – Newcastle I
think it was called – there was such an absence of crumpet that
a couple of members of our tour staff dressed up in drag and
we had a party. I mean, these guys were on the surface very
butch Aussies and a decade or two older than us, but one
of them was dressed in a grass skirt and had lipstick on. He
pinned me against the wall, put his lips right close to mine and
asked if I wanted to do it with him 'All Day and All of the
Night'. I mean, Aussie woofters, forget it. Much too serious
to get emotional about. The only thing that sustained me was
the thought of those wonderfully masculine childhood cricket
heroes. It was a sad night at the hotel all round, I seem to
recall. Manfred came in and complained that Paul Jones had
been the only person who was capable of attracting a chick
who resembled something other than a kangaroo, and after a
walk around the town, Manfred had gone back to his room
and walked in on another member of his group and interrupted
the poor chap's wank.

These petty male preoccupations aside, my most enduring
memory of Australia was as I looked through the window of
the plane as we taxied down the runway at Adelaide airport. I

saw Rosie, Terry and Arthur still standing and waving at us.
They looked so complete together; such a devoted family
unit. Terry was well qualified and could have had a fine career
if he had stayed in Britain, but he had sacrificed these
opportunities to be with them. I envied them so much as they
stood there. For all Arthur's strictness and stubbornness, Terry
loved him. Several years later, while I was on another tour of
Australia, I went to visit the three of them in Adelaide. It was
a hurried visit, with just enough time to say hello before it
was time to fly back to the tour on the other side of the
continent. Arthur drove me to the airport but pulled up
outside the airport perimeter at the end of a runway. The
aeroplanes were taking off and arriving over our heads. The
whole moment was for Arthur an uncharacteristically
emotional one. He told me that he had enjoyed the LP *Arthur*,
and said that he knew that it had been partly inspired by him.
He surprised me by adding that he admired some of my songs
and, although he didn't care for loud rock music, he enjoyed
singalong-type melodies, which reminded him of home and
the family parties we used to have. I was amazed by this, as I
always thought that the family was one of the reasons Arthur
had emigrated in the first place. Perhaps his reason for leaving
England really was because he loved the old country so much
he didn't want to stay around to watch it disintegrate. It
probably wasn't the sole reason, but even if it was only part,
then the album title, *Arthur, or The Rise and Fall of the British
Empire*, was even more appropriate. I told Arthur that I felt
guilty for using him as a subject for a song, but he shrugged
off my apology, saying that he was flattered. Perhaps he knew
what I was trying to say in the lyrics, how I was attempting to
make some sense of a life that seemed even more desperate
and confused than my own. As another jet landed and taxied
to the gate, Arthur told me he was going into hospital for an
operation and, just in case, he had taken care of Rosie and
Terry with a life insurance policy. I didn't understand then,

but now it seems obvious that Arthur was telling me that he was going to die. We drove on to the terminal and he even carried my bag, walked me to the gate and saw me on to the plane. It didn't occur to me at the time, but that was the only occasion I was ever really alone with him. It seemed to me that when nobody else was around he felt relaxed enough to treat me as grown-up, equal to him. A short time later, I found myself breaking the news of Arthur's death to my parents. When he died, in the early 1970s, that image of him standing with Rosie and Terry, waving goodbye on our first tour, was still with me.

Back on that tour of 1965, the Rolling Stones were in Oz at the same time as the Kinks and Manfred Mann. There was great rivalry between the tours at the box office, because the Kinks were considered to be the new rivals to the Stones and the Beatles. During a tropical storm in Brisbane, Mick Jagger appeared at my hotel bedroom doorway, shouting abuse about Pete Quaife, whom he described as the greatest liar alive. I never fully understood what it was all about but Jagger shouted that Pete was 'a fucking liar'. I explained that all Pete's friends knew that, and it was one of the reasons we liked him. He was a liar but an obvious one, which can often be entertaining. It was also clear to anybody who had read anything about us in the press that Pete was rather romantic and, to say the least, 'over-descriptive', but he was harmless. Jagger just took a beer from our fridge and walked down the hotel corridor mumbling, 'Liar, liar.'

There was a rumour that after the tour the Kinks would go on to America to do a couple of TV appearances, but the work visas still hadn't come through. Dave, being only seventeen, had to visit the British Consul every time we reached a new country to obtain a special work permit. Each day I prayed that the American visas wouldn't come through so that we could finish the tour in Hong Kong. All the adulation the group was receiving could not detract from the fact that deep down I was missing my wife. I was turning into an over-affectionate married wimp who just wanted to get home. We left Australia and headed for Singapore, where we were due to play a concert at a gymnasium with the Manfreds. During our flight I sat next to Manfred, who told me that the Kinks had got to Number 2 in the British charts – his record had only reached Number 5 so far. He looked over at Quaife, who was sitting in the front seat boasting about our success, and in his inimitable style said that while the Kinks were Number 2 Pete Quaife was telling everybody that *he* was Number 1.

Upon arrival we were greeted at the airport by the now customary hysterical crowds and bustled into the back of taxi-cabs and taken to the Goodwood Hotel, one of the great symbols of the old Empire. On the way I was astounded to see a gigantic rat, surely a foot long, crawl to a manhole and plop down into the sewers. The smell of the sewers as we crossed the bridge towards the imperialistic splendour of this grand hotel was the most putrid I have experienced in my life. Even the infamous Blue Flame Club in the prefects' room at school had never harboured such appalling odours. On arrival at the hotel, each member of the Kinks group was given his own cottage in the grounds and there were enough helpers for each of us to have his own personal servant. It was rumoured that Noël Coward had stayed in my cottage, although I felt that Mick Avory's room would have been more fitting. I felt quite honoured, especially while having a crap on the same toilet as Noël Coward – although if he was a star of the same magnitude as Billy Fury, he probably never went to the toilet at all. By contrast to the imperial splendour of the Goodwood Hotel, the concert we played at was in a poor part of the city in a converted basketball arena, the walls of which were dripping with condensation.

After the concert, I arrived back at the hotel and was given a telegram by a waiter, informing me that 'Tired of Waiting for You' had reached Number 1 in all the British charts. I ordered a bottle of champagne and drank it with the waiter as the rest of the Kinks were out celebrating somewhere, and Manfred was nowhere to be found. The waiter couldn't speak English and I couldn't speak Malay, or whatever they speak, but I tried my best to convey the mighty significance of the event. The following morning I saw Manfred and the others at the pool, and they were very sporting and good natured in defeat. Their record had only hovered around the Top 5. I couldn't help but consider this to be a small personal victory over Manfred, although I have always felt slightly ashamed about this. But I would have been devastated if the situations had been reversed.

Next, it was on to Hong Kong, where the Kinks and Manfred were to play, this time in a large soccer stadium. It was still unclear whether we would be going on to America. Then Johnny Clapson arrived at my room with the bad news: the visas had arrived, and the Kinks would be going on to America while everybody else went home. I collapsed in a huddle in my room and ordered a crate of lagers, which I immediately proceeded to drink. As a result I never discovered Hong Kong's night-life. I just remember the whole event in a hungover haze. Even at the concert I had supported myself onstage by leaning against my amplifier. It was the first concert where I wore sunglasses – even though we performed at night.

The despair really set in when I heard the length of the flight to America. I was becoming terrified of everything, flying in particular, and when we took off I watched Dave, who was also not a good flyer, tense up and remain rigid for the rest of the trip. The fact that we were not accompanied by the other bands didn't help us very much either. I missed the comradeship and Manfred's continual niggling. A kind lady who was travelling with us gave me a Valium. This didn't help much, but instead made me more depressed. Further horrors appeared on the horizon. We were told we were flying into Vietnam, where at this time the war was escalating. As we flew into Saigon airport accompanied by four American jet-fighters, we could see fires from what must have been skirmishes in the forests below. At the airport, we were ushered into a little waiting area cordoned off from the rest of the airport, and were told to wait. For the next four or five hours we were guarded by American troops with machine guns. The whole thing had an air of disaster about it and I could not wait to get out of that doomed place, even though it meant another long flight, this time to Hawaii and then on to the west coast of America.

When the 707 eventually taxied out on to the runway of Saigon airport, my nerve was almost gone. All I needed was the not-so-reassuring voice of the pilot drawling that he was 'not completely sure which end of the runway to take the son of a bitch out on to, but guessed that he was headed in the right direction'. Some passengers laughed nervously. I for one did not appreciate the John Wayne impersonation, and anxiously looked around the aircraft for the kind lady who had supplied me with Valium. I tried not to look at Dave. I didn't want him to see how scared I was. A couple of US fighter jets screamed overhead. 'Now let's see if we can get this mother off the ground,' the pilot drawled. The John Wayne imitation added the final touch of machismo to our departure from the war zone. We took off at an angle so that the tip of the left wing scraped along the runway. John Wayne was possibly wearing a large Stetson as he whooped and hollered down the radio back to airport control, proving that he was still one of the boys: if they needed him back in the armed forces, I'm sure he'd be ready and waiting. I sat back in my seat and thought how proud I was not to be like him. How wonderful to be a cringing coward in the face of such manufactured heroism. And how stupid the John Wayne impersonator in the cockpit was; if he had truly been John Wayne, he would have had a stand-in to perform that particular stunt. How ignorant some 'real' men are.'

Raymond Douglas sat back in his chair and he disappeared into the shadows.

'I want to stop now.' His voice tapered away and he sounded very old and very young at the same time. It was obvious that I was losing him again.

'Surely you must remember your first visit to New York?' I asked in fake excitement, just to hype him up.

There was silence for a few seconds, then he sprang back to life and leaned forward into the light. It took me by surprise. His head was no more than four or five inches away from mine, and for the first time I could see his craggy old face quite clearly. His hair was incredibly white, short-cropped. He leaned in even closer and his keen blue eyes seemed to look right through me. He frowned as if he were toying with my emotions. Again he knew that I was like a fish who had taken the bait; he became the angler playing with me on the end of the line, waiting for me to tire. He smirked, mocking me.

'Oh yes, oh yes, the tits, the broads, the cunt, the excess, that's what you want. You're just a journalist, after all. I was a newly married man, what sort of a prick do you take me for? Besides I had elephantiasis, or some damned disease. I was bitten by some insect in Hong Kong and by the time I reached New York my left ankle had blown up like a balloon. This presented a problem to our promoters as we were due to appear on the *Hullabaloo* TV show, and we were supposed to do a dance routine. What a joke. At the first day's rehearsal I pleaded with the producer not to make me do it but they were adamant that when the Kinks were introduced the camera would cut from the presenter Frankie Avalon to show the four Kinks dancing.'

217

Raymond Douglas paused and sat back in his chair, grunting like a dirty old man.

'After rehearsals, Avory snuck one of the dancers on the show back to the hotel and was fucking her. Just as he was about to have an orgasm, a security guard burst into his room and pointed a gun at him. This put Avory right off his stroke.'

This made Raymond Douglas laugh so loudly that he developed a wheezing cough, and it took a few sips of cold tea for him to recover enough to continue.

'When the Kinks arrived in the Big Apple, I felt a combination of excitement and fear in the pit of my stomach. Perhaps it was the food. Whatever. It was my first time in New York and I was too terrified to leave my hotel room. Later that night Avory and some of the others went out and visited the Peppermint Lounge, accompanied by Danny Kessler, an associate of Eddie Kassner's. Kessler was a chirpy New Yorker who had helped promote Gary (son of Jerry) Lewis' group the Playboys, and was eager to show us around the clubs. The Peppermint Lounge was the new hip nightspot – it had spawned the song 'Peppermint Twist', which had been a huge hit and was soon to be followed by a film of the same name. To New Yorkers, the Peppermint Lounge was the American equivalent of the Cavern Club in Liverpool. A whole spate of clubs had spread up and down Britain, and now America was beginning to feel the full impact of Merseybeat and the UK club scene. However the Peppermint Lounge was pure Americana, and the hipsters twisted into early hours displaying full-blown 1950s short back and sides, and quiffs the same as artists like Frankie ('Got to Get Back to the Alamo') Avalon and Bobbie ('Blue Velvet') Vinton. It's no wonder that the mere sight of a Kink was guaranteed to attract a crowd, and then it was only a matter of time before police were called in to restore order. It was as if visitors from another planet had landed at Kennedy. Avory had done his best to make inroads into the local culture and break down social barriers, and he ended up with a visit to the nearest doctor to obtain a liniment to ease an attack of crabs, which were proliferating around his pubic region. The ointment became almost as essential to Mick as his drumsticks. His ritual of practising on his rubber drum mat before a performance was now accompanied by the twice daily application of ointment. No wonder he looked so miserable in those early black-and-white television videos. I was miserable because of my total fear and confused identity. Avory was miserable for entirely different reasons.'

R.D. smirked as he looked at me. 'Is that what you want to hear about, sonny boy?'

I felt slightly ashamed, but I knew that the Corporation would eat this up. I was equally aware that R.D. was constantly playing emotional chess with me, seeing how I would react.

'We conned the buggers, though, because on actual transmission of *Hullabaloo* they cut to the Kinks as rehearsed to discover me and Avory dancing cheek-to-cheek. The producer was outraged. I guess it was the first time they had ever seen guys acting like queers on American television. In a strange way I think it was that shot that started it all.'

'All what?'

'The character assassination, the plot to destroy us. To get us banned from America.' R.D.'s voice went up a pitch as he got excited. 'You see, the Kinks really did it. The Stones and the Beatles implied it, but we really carried it off and it was far too real for Americans to take.'

R.D. was beginning to annoy me with his petty attitudes towards some of his contemporaries. I felt like telling him to wise up and not be such a belligerent old bugger, but I buttoned my lip and let it go.

'And you're proud of that?' I asked instead.

His voice became bitter and aggressive.

'You see, it wasn't just the music with us, it was a way of life. We rammed it right down their throats. We weren't the smart people to hang out with. They wouldn't invite Dave Davies to open an art gallery as they would Paul McCartney because they were scared that Dave would piss over the exhibits. You don't understand, everybody keeps talking this crap about the liberated sixties and how free everybody was, but the reality was that everything still had to be done within the confines of the "adult" conservative world.'

R.D. sighed, then continued. 'Still, we did the bloody *Hullabaloo* show, and, regardless of what the entertainment industry thought about us, the Kinks reached a young audience across America. All that crap with the American Federation of Musicians started around then, and haunted us for the rest of our careers. But you can find all that out from magazines and books. I don't want to waste my time talking to you about it now.'

Raymond Douglas fumbled in his overcoat pockets and produced a small Yale key with a crumpled label attached to it with a piece of string. He held up the key in a limp manner and addressed me as if I were a servant.

'Take this and go upstairs to the attic. There's a filing cabinet there with all our old press clippings in it. I guess my brain cells are going. The time, the alcohol, the abuse, the women – I'm getting too old to remember details and you'll find all you need up there. Now piss off, I'm knackered.'

I left R.D. and cautiously made my way down the dimly lit corridor, up a labyrinth of stairways, encountering the occasional cobweb on the way. It was as if the air in the attic was tainted with perfumes and odours from another era. A rat nibbled the worn-out carpet at the top of the staircase. The door to the attic was already open and in the corner of the room I could see the grey filing cabinet. I tried to unlock it but it was soon apparent that R.D. had given me the wrong key. Raymond Douglas was indeed senile, or confused by years of litigation and questions and answers and interviews, all blending into one another like an endless interrogation. I knew he was old but I preferred to think of him as confused rather than hopelessly senile. Even though he was a bitter old man – and at times an obviously outrageous liar – I liked him.

I tugged at the top drawer of the filing cabinet and to my surprise it opened. And there were the press clippings, just as he had said. I glanced at the cuttings on the top of the pile.

The *New Musical Express* had an article that started with the headline 'Kinks return from their triumphant tour of Australia and Asia'. It said the Kinks were going straight into the studio to record their second album, already entitled *Kinda Kinks*. There was a sad little clipping from the *Daily Mirror* with a picture of Raymond Douglas' first wife Rasa and some appallingly sentimental report which said 'Kinky Ray's newly wed pregnant wife awaits her husband's return because she is "Tired Of Waiting".' In the short time I had known Raymond Douglas I was not entirely sure whether he was truthful, a liar, good or bad, but one thing I did know for certain, articles such as this threw him into a rage.

I was alone in the attic, and the building was empty apart from Raymond Douglas and the friendly rat feasting on crumbs at the top of the stairs, but I still had the feeling that somebody would burst in and attack me at any moment. Perhaps it was Raymond Douglas' way of spooking me. He had tried the eye-to-eye technique, and now he was going for a more subtle approach. Perhaps he had already psyched me out. I took the opportunity and grabbed a bundle of newspaper clippings and magazines and stuffed it in my briefcase. As I turned to leave the room I looked up to the corner near the door and saw a small red light flashing on and off. A voice boomed out through a speaker; 'Take as much as you want, they're no good to me anymore.' The rat stopped nibbling and looked up at the speaker. He knew his master's voice. 'Now make me a cup of tea the way I like it and get your arse down here, I want to talk to you, punk.'

By the time I scurried back into the control room with a Brown Betty full of tea, Raymond Douglas was ready to resume.

'Hurry up, kid, you're missing some good stuff. Ready?
Good. Sit down and shut it.
  After the tour I limped off the plane at London airport and,

before I even saw Rasa, Larry Page rushed over to announce
that we had studio time booked for the following morning.
He was anxious to hear the songs for the new album. Ha.
Anxious, my arse. It seemed to me that all the record company
wanted were the sales from the follow-up. We could have
recorded 'Three Blind Mice' for all they cared – provided it
was a hit for them. I told Larry that I had this gammy
leg but he assured me that so long as I could sing, nobody
would notice it on record. Eventually I saw Rasa. Her little
brown suede jacket was buttoned up to keep out the cold and
there was a distinct bulge in her stomach – the baby was
beginning to show. We hugged each other out of sight of
everybody else, and she whispered 'I love you' in Lithuanian.
As our little entourage left the airport an impish man wearing
a flasher's mackintosh stood holding a microphone in my
direction. He said he was from a new radio station and his
name was Kenny Everett. He wanted an exclusive interview
with me 'on my return to good old Blighty'. He was so
frantically energetic it was almost annoying, but nevertheless
he seemed keen and earnest and a thoroughly sincere Brit. But
as I spoke to him my mind was on other things, such as
getting back to my flat and making outrageously promiscuous
love to my wife. Being in America had left me somewhat
horny. Especially since as a devoted husband I had to watch
on the sidelines while Dave and Mick ran rampant.

The interview over, we drove back along the North
Circular towards home. When eventually we reached the little
attic flat the weeks of sexual frustration and desire were soon
stifled by the meek little phrase 'We don't want to hurt the
baby'. As soon as the words were uttered I knew that she was
right, but I couldn't help thinking that, bizarrely, the only
young woman in the world who wouldn't and couldn't have
sex with me was my wife. The lust that stirred deep inside my
groin, that had almost erupted with anticipation on the drive
from Heathrow to Muswell Hill, slowly subsided and withered

away into my sad underpants underneath my skintight hipster trousers. What remained of the evening was full of caressing, stroking and a newfound concern for this human being I had helped to create. However, there was also a feeling of dread, like a child who realizes that he has to share his toys with somebody else. Suddenly part of me belonged to somebody else. I felt both elated and cheated. While Rasa slept I watched her and wondered why she was there.

The next thing I can remember is limping down the stairs from No. 2 control room into Pye Studios. The release date for the record had already been set for the following month, which meant that the LP had to be completed in two weeks. And the fact that the publishers and managers wanted all the songs to be written by me made the prospect even more horrific.

I tried to think of myself as a professional. The songs we recorded were an amalgamation of all the music the band liked at the time, which was mainly Motown and more pop-orientated soul. As I sang 'You Shouldn't be Sad', Dave, Pete and Rasa sang the back-up vocals. In my head, I thought we sounded like a cross between Earl Van Dyke and Martha and the Vandellas. Unfortunately, on playback we sounded like us. We double-tracked my vocal, which was horribly out of sync with the original, and when I pleaded with Shel Talmy, who was producing this somewhat shabby epic, to let me have another try to get it more in sync, he said that we just didn't have the time to make it perfect. I knew that we were under tremendous time pressure, but I couldn't help feeling that it was Shel's revenge after I had got my own way and re-recorded 'You Really Got Me'. The whole track was a mess.

Avory had to hit a crucial snare beat, but due to a combination of jet-lag and the amount of alcohol consumed on the flight from America the night before, he missed the drum completely and what should have been a triumphant thud to herald in the second verse sounded like a whimpering click as his drum stick rapped the edge of the drum. Unlike my hard-on, which had been forced flaccid, Avory's lust for life must have been satisfied in a dingy club somewhere the night before. Or perhaps over the pages of *Penthouse* in his mother's house in East Molesey. Avory had once confided in me that some years earlier, after a similar act of over-indulgence, he had fallen asleep on his bed with his trousers and underpants around his ankles. He found when he woke in exactly the same circumstances that his mother had left some tea and biscuits on his bedside table while he was asleep.

This small anecdote aside, the whole album suffered from slovenly, callous disregard for our music. Listening to some of the mistakes made my toes curl, and will do so for the rest of my life. When I wrote 'You Shouldn't be Sad' it was intended to be a celebration of being in love and wanting to get home to my pretty wife. But due to commercial realities on the part of our record company, to get the record out in time to take advantage of what success we had, the recording was rushed and had turned the song into a joke. *Kinda Kinks* went straight into the LP charts and got to at least Number 2. It would have stayed there longer but for the good taste of our fans, who must have realized that while the songs showed promise, the record was a disaster. It was as though everyone around us was cashing in, making as much money as possible before we lost the golden touch.

The upshot of these sessions was that the release of the first single from the album, 'Everybody's Gonna be Happy', which was our tribute to the Motown bands we had worked with on various tours. It was a comparative flop compared to our last single and it only reached the lower regions of the Top 30. This created a flurry of anxiety throughout the management, publishers and other interested parties. There were murmurs that it had all come to an end and we had shot our collective wads. On the other hand the group was enjoying ever greater success at live concerts, and the B-side of the single, 'Who Will be the Next in Line?', was later flipped over to the A-side in the United States, where it became a minor hit. In some ways it could be said that this single was very successful, in that it contained two minor hits on the same disc rather than one big hit on the A-side. That's how we said we felt, but deep down we were very disappointed. People were saying 'You've lost that Kinks sound.' To this day I've no idea what they meant by that.

While we were recording *Kinda Kinks*, we were playing gigs on our days off. Driving up the M1 towards Coventry, we were listening to the BBC and heard what we first thought was a Kinks record. We turned up the volume to hear the DJ announce the new single from a band called the Who, entitled 'I Can't Explain'. We were all surprised and confused: why would a band bother to try and copy our sound? These emotions were compounded with anger when we discovered that the Who had been produced by a certain Mr Shel Talmy while we were away on tour. Then we found out that the Who had originally been called the High Numbers, and were the same band that had supported us on a few of our shows, including the Beatles' show at Bournemouth the previous year. That made Mick laugh. 'That fucking drummer's great but he's as silly as arseholes.' Dave said, 'So what if they've copped our sound, at least they're a good group.' Quaife seemed reluctant to comment at all, whereas I felt a bit pissed off at others using the sound we had fought so hard to get. But then when I thought about it, I knew I'd got my vocal sound through hearing other people sing, and everybody in the world has tried to play the guitar like Chuck Berry. So what's new?

In spring 1965 we embarked on a short Scandinavian tour. We were scheduled to play two concerts in the Tivoli Theatre in Copenhagen. The Rolling Stones had played the same venue two weeks previously, and it was anticipated that the

Kinks, who were earning a reputation for being a rowdy stage
act, would incite the teenage audience to riot. On our arrival
in Copenhagen, the promotor held a press conference in a
smart art gallery. We were treated as potential invaders,
bringing pagan, uncultured attitudes to a country renowned
for its etiquette. That is, if you didn't count the marauding
Vikings, who had pillaged and raped their way across Europe
ten centuries earlier, before they had discovered how to make
furniture. One elderly man, an intelligent, elegantly dressed
writer, pointed out that the fear shown by some of the Danish
press was based on the fact that Denmark had been occupied
by the Germans during the war, and the sight of a policeman
in uniform at a pop concert would bring back bitter memories.
I was unsure and possibly not enlightened enough to
understand what he meant until the following night. Dave
played the opening chords of 'All Day and All of the Night',
the kids rose to their feet to cheer what was already for them a
teenage rock anthem, a side door opened and a mass of police
with truncheons at the ready rushed into the auditorium. It
was a matter of seconds before a riot started, a pitched battle
between the police and the audience. The whole building
erupted. We were rushed into a small room backstage and
locked inside. We sat in stunned silence for what seemed like
hours while the fans and the police fought outside. Eventually
it was safe for us to leave, and we saw that the theatre had
been almost totally destroyed. Perhaps the Vikings had passed
this way after all. To my amazement, the only item to survive
the battle of the Tivoli theatre was a small display of records
and photographs of the country singer Jim Reeves. While all
the rock fans had been battling with authority, the sad tribute
to the late great singer had remained miraculously intact. As I
picked my way through the beautifully designed auditorium, I
made a mental note that if I ever became a Scandinavian
furniture designer and was asked to design a theatre for a rock
concert I would not use glass. A woman swore at us in Danish

and then shouted in English, 'Why can't you be good boys, like the Rolling Stones?' The next day the *Politiken* newspaper ran the headline '2000 unge i pop-tumult', and went on to say that the Kinks could possibly be responsible for Copenhagen banning rock and roll entirely.

We were informed that the following day's concert would be cancelled. Instead we were confined to our rooms at the Europa Hotel, as it was considered dangerous for us to go out into the streets, where we might provoke a riot. In the evening I heard shouts coming from the end of the corridor. Apparently out of sheer boredom and frustration at being 'grounded' Dave had consumed an entire bottle of whisky and then thrown the bottle through the window. Within seconds the lift on our floor opened, a squad of riot police ran into Dave's room and dragged him out by his hair. My first concern was that, as he had been with a girl and was only wearing his underpants, he might catch a cold. One of our road managers went to try and help Dave and was promptly beaten to the ground by the police, who were dragging Dave out of the building. We eventually discovered that he had been arrested for 'inciting a riot' at the concert the previous day and would spend the night in the cells. We were due to fly to London the next day to play at the *NME* Poll-Winner's concert, and we were told that we were going to get an award, for Best New Group. Grenville Collins tried to explain to the Danes that we had to go to play a major concert at Wembley, but in the commotion our Danish promoter had suddenly forgotten how to speak English. The only words he could come up with were that Dave would be 'slightly' beaten up and then possibly be released in the morning. Flights had to be cancelled and rearranged. By morning there was still no news of Dave. It seemed that nobody in Denmark was prepared to talk to us. Grenville phoned our publicity agent in London and explained that we might have to miss the concert. Then, out of the blue, Dave marched into the hotel accompanied by Brian Longstaff, complaining only of a 'fucking hangover'. We were marched through the airport accompanied by armed police. Everywhere we turned we saw faces sneering at us. Avory summed up the whole trip: 'Good riddance. They give you one slice of bread and call it a sandwich.'

We drove to the Empire Arena, Wembley straight from Heathrow but arrived there late. Dave bruised and battered, Grenville displaying quiet, aristocratic panic, Mick worried about his drum kit not arriving. He was reassured by Brian Longstaff that the Beatles would let us use their equipment. When I heard this I exploded: 'It took us years to get our sound, and I don't want to use their ponced-up equipment! Besides, they'll only blame us if we've changed all the controls when they go on.'

'Oh, you're not going on before them, old boy,' Wace said casually. 'You're closing the show, you're going on last, after the Rolling Stones and the Beatles.'

I continued to complain about the equipment, particularly as the show was being televised live.

'You don't understand, old boy,' explained Grenville. 'This means that, as of now, you are bigger than the Beatles.'

We sat in our dressing room and listened as the various acts played. I was still complaining about the equipment, and, naïvely, I also wanted to know if they would take our award away from us because of the bad publicity we had received in Denmark. We were all shaken by that incident and would rather not have played, award or no award. If pain-killing injections were available, I would have been first in line to receive mine.

Suddenly there was a roar from the auditorium as the Rolling Stones started playing 'This Could be the Last Time' I commented that the previous year the Stones had received the Best New Group award, and at least it was worth going on because this year it was our turn. Time passed. Avory practised on his rubber drum-pad. Our red hunting jackets had been retrieved from the chaos of the Tivoli concert, our frilly yellow shirts had been hurriedly washed and pressed. Then we heard another roar as the Beatles announced their new single and the unforgettable opening guitar phrase of 'Ticket to Ride' was played by George Harrison on his new 12-string Rickenbacker. They sounded great. By the time we went on, however, we were prepared for just a gesture of a performance. To our amazement the audience gave us as good a reception as ever.

But when we went over to receive our award, I turned to find Maurice Kinn, who was associated with the *New Musical Express*, holding four little awards. I asked him what they were. 'Runners up for Best New Group of the year.'

I shouted back to him, 'Runners up to who?'

'The Rolling Stones, of course.'

I was stunned that the Rolling Stones could be Best New Group two years running, and I stormed off the stage without accepting my award. I felt that this was a total deception, and tantamount to a slap in the face by the music business. From that day on, I re-named the *New Musical Express* The Enemy. The Kinks had refused to join the musical establishment; it was obvious to me that we would have to fight on regardless or quit. And I decided to quit.'

Raymond Douglas went into a trance-like state. His face showed all the disappointments of a lifetime. It was obvious that receiving what was for him second prize, had been a humiliation, and truthfully the whole thing sounded a little rigged, but just the same it was clear that by alienating the music-biz establishment the Kinks were doing themselves no favours. Then he suddenly dropped into this slurred, surrealistic monologue. By now I felt as though I was inside with him. I closed my eyes. I saw images, stills, slow-motion, black-and-white, of the Beatles, the Kinks, the police in Denmark, angry faces. Then, runners at the start of a race. R.D. verbalized my thought pattern.

'Running. Everybody's got two legs, right? Except those poor motherfucker cripples. My sister Peg had the use of only one arm, but people with two legs and two arms can stretch themselves physically through pain and at least give themselves a chance of winning. For some reason I found myself being forced to run in slow-motion while everybody around me was allowed to run at normal speed. When you're in control there's a chance that you can work hard enough to get in a situation where there's some possibility that you can win. But suddenly, I saw myself crossing the finishing-line first, only to be given a silver medal. The photo-finish proved conclusively that I had won. But because they, whoever "they" were, decided to disqualify me, I found myself in a situation where I had to run, to train harder, to take myself through another barrier. Something I said, or was reported reported to have said, somewhere in some half-arsed periodical may have got up some son-of-a-bitch's snout. Gimme that scrapbook!'

R.D. grabbed the book from me and skimmed through the clippings. He pointed at an article. 'It says here: "The lead singer of the Kinks says he can sing better than Frank Sinatra." I said that, yes, but not the way it was implied in the article. What I had actually said was that I could sing "You Really Got Me" better than Frank Sinatra. Here is another lie: I was quoted as saying that I thought Adolf Hitler was a "good guy". What I said was that Hitler certainly knew how to sell out a stadium. Surely that could not be misinterpreted to suggest approval of Hitler, yet misinterpreted it was. And so it's understandable that certain Jewish people in the music industry took offence. But hell, my parents had been bombed by the Germans, I had married a girl whose family had been driven from their home by the Nazis – surely it was obvious that this was a misquote. A lie? Surely if they thought about it they would realize that the statement was made by a nineteen-year-old who'd had a run of success based on giving a "screw-you" sign to the establishment. But I guess some middle-aged fat fuck always took some goddamn offence. Anyone would think that I had pissed on the Mona Lisa. Whatever I did, or imagined I did, or somebody else imagined that I did, has always awoken that little hunchbacked man inside me. All my insecurities started to come back. After the humiliation at the *NME* concert, I drove back from Wembley and the rosebud that once grew in my chest turned into a hard, bitter, prickly nettle.'

13

'That black cloud came back, and for days after the *NME*
humiliation I refused to speak to a soul, including Rasa. I sat
in the kitchen in my parents' house after refusing to go with
the rest of the band to make a television appearance in
Southampton. The official certificate, obtained by Grenville
from a doctor 'feel-good' in Belgravia, stated that Raymond
Douglas had gastroenteritis, but the reality was that I had the
shits. I was shitting myself. I was shit scared. I didn't give a
shit.

Dad asked me why I refused to go.

'Because I can't win. There's no point going if you can't
win. I can't beat them. I don't want to do any more publicity.
I don't want to pose for any more photographs. I want to get
out of this rotten business. I don't want to do it any more.'

Then, for the first time and only time my father hit me. He
was literally shaking with rage, shouting something about not
letting 'them' beat me. The sight of him standing there, tense
with anger, made me feel ashamed of myself. I was still a
product of the system that had given my parents a bad deal,
and yet I was throwing away the only weapon with which I
was able to fight back. I went to the pub for a drink with
Dad, and we plotted how we would bring about the downfall
of 'them'. There was only one problem: I had no idea who
'they' were. Neither did Dad. But after three or four pints,
neither of us gave a shit.

In real terms, the money was only just beginning to come
in. Apart from the performing-rights royalties, the Kinks were
earning good money at live concerts up and down the country.
Wace had recently acquired a Rolls-Royce Silver Cloud,

albeit secondhand. However, the chic Chelsea clubs where
Robert was a member were making discreet inquiries,
questioning whether he would be able to meet his bills in the
future. Although it was never spoken of, this was also the case
at his tailor in Savile Row. Both he and Grenville, when such
mutterings were overheard, brushed the matter of a 'flop'
single aside as a minor hiccup in our careers. As for me, I
found myself spending more and more time locked away in
my attic flat. Rasa's tummy was getting bigger, and so I was
also looking for larger accommodation. I took a modest
ground-floor flat in Midhurst Avenue, Muswell Hill, at the
rent of £7 10s. per week. All the Kinks were on a weekly
wage of £40 before tax, and so there was enough money in
the kitty to keep going.

Arthur Howes seemed to be the only person who believed
the Kinks were still the best group in the country. He took us
all for a Chinese meal to the place where he had discovered us
little more than a year earlier.

'You see, Raymond, my boy,' he said, 'what we need is
that magic Kinks sound back. Dave's chords going underneath.
Nice melody and a chorus and Bob's your uncle. You've got
the act, you've got the audience, you simply have to deliver
the goods and bingo! You're special to me, you boys.
You've got the new tour lined up and business looks like
being better than ever. Just come up with a great record.'

R.D.'s impersonation of Arthur Howes was more than convincing.
He continued talking as if still in the agent's persona.

'You see, me old fruit, I, Raymond Douglas, had suddenly
found myself having to acquire the special art of what is
described as Hackmanship: to contrive and target an audience
rather than write from an inward, subconscious flow.

The recording of 'Set Me Free' made me feel like a whore;
our managers, agents, record producers and publishers

considered it to be one of the most commercial things I had written to date. The only consolation was the recording of the B-side. 'I Need You' was also contrived to sound like the Kinks of old, but at least it gave the band the opportunity of unleashing one of the finest intros to any track we ever recorded. Just before I counted in the song, Dave hit an angry crash chord which distorted and then started oscillating into feedback through his amplifier. Bob Auger, the engineer sitting next to Shel Talmy, was visibly shaken by the aggressive sound. In the studio it was as if the chord had jumped out past the sound barrier. It was only Bob's brilliance as an engineer that managed to grab the fader on the console and pull it down so that the intro was usable. That chord more or less summed up the way the whole band felt about things at that particular time. Dave had been experimenting with feedback ever since the early rehearsals in our old front room, and often used it onstage. But this was the first time he'd used it on record.

When 'Set Me Free' entered the charts, Wace presumably ordered more suits from his tailor and put his car in for a much-needed service. Once again he felt free to run up large bills in all the fashionable clubs. Dave dressed as flamboyantly as ever, and was the darling of Carnaby Street. Mick dressed as flamboyantly as ever, and still looked like he had been given clothes that had been made for somebody else. Quaife had decided to become a fully fledged mod, and was frequently seen riding down Steeds Road council estate in his Lambretta. I, however, was not impressed by our success and remained in the flat in Midhurst Gardens. Thrift was the order of the day, as Rasa's belly by now looked as though it was about to explode.

Even though there was renewed chart success, there was a growing distrust between the band and its various managements.

There was an American tour looming that summer, and

both management factions were trying to out-do each other. Things were moving quickly, as if everybody wanted to work the Kinks while there was still a band to be worked. Perhaps their worst fears would come to pass and this was to be the last Kinks' assault as a successful band.

The package tour of spring 1965 was cursed from the beginning. Brian Longstaff was unhappy with the way he was being treated and was talking about leaving. (The Kinks were also complaining about Brian's donkey jacket, which he had been wearing since the first gigs at the Cavern.) But in many senses the group was starting to find itself among strangers. Longstaff was family, and he was leaving. That was a bad sign.

The Kinks were headlining the package tour, but we could hear whispers suggesting that this tour could be our last. There was no Hal Carter to encourage us and give us notes and corrections after each show, even though we never seemed to listen to him. The whole operation around us seemed to become very mercenary.

Dave and Mick had been quarrelling ever since Mum had arrived unannounced at the 'house of sin' that he and Mick had rented in Connaught Gardens, Muswell Hill. It had quickly become notorious for what our mother described as sex orgies. It was perhaps just a little decadent, and to be expected of two young men who found themselves in a situation where they could have almost any young girl in London. The only problem was that they tried to have them all at once. Mick's bedroom had a sign on it: 'Spunker's Squalor', and Dave's room was christened 'Whore's Hovel'. The house had become home for every teenage girl and pop fan in the district, but the non-stop party came to an abrupt end when Mum entered the premises one morning to discover a so-called orgy in progress. Before she climbed the stairs towards 'Whore's Hovel', my mother had cast some scantily clad girls into the street, like Jesus with the moneylenders.

(And there was even a rumour that after Dave and Mick moved, the new tenants had the house exorcized by a priest before they moved their furniture in.) But the hard reality was that Dave and Mick were beginning to hate one another.

All in all, this was not the ideal situation in which to embark on a tour. The inevitable punch-ups began between Dave and Mick, climaxing in the famous incident at the Capital Theatre, Cardiff, where Mick tried to slice Dave's head off with a cymbal during 'Beautiful Delilah'. Mick went into hiding for a couple of weeks. The police wanted to arrest him for grievous bodily harm with intent to kill, but fortunately Dave wouldn't press charges. For a while we thought that Mick and Dave could never work together again, and we even reached the point of rehearsing with a new drummer, Mitch Mitchell, whom we'd known from a support band called the Riot Squad. (Mitchell later went on to join Jimi Hendrix.) Finally one way or another Mick and Dave were reconciled, but everyone was walking on thin ice – and we all knew it.

Dave had been hanging around with Brian Jones of the Rolling Stones, and as a result started mixing drink and drugs. Everybody was relieved when, after several run-ins with the police and punch-ups outside clubs, he returned to live with Mum and Dad. With Dad around we had only the drink to worry about.

On 23 May I woke to find Rasa in some distress: the baby had started to arrive. An ambulance was summoned and Rasa was taken to a clinic in Muswell Hill where I was told by the matron to go home and wait by the telephone. Although the sixties were supposed to be the age of liberation, this particular clinic felt that when it came to childbirth it was better to remain in the Victorian era; Rasa, coming from a Roman Catholic background, probably felt it was a woman's right to suffer alone. As I waited in the front room of my parents' house, I started tinkering on the piano. Two hours went past and there was still no news. I had developed a tune and was now writing the words. I had just finished the lyrics to 'I Go to Sleep' when the telephone rang: Rasa had given birth to a baby girl.'

R.D. paused and put a cassette in the machine. It was 'I Go to Sleep', sung by Peggy Lee. I looked at the little pile of clippings I had taken from the attic and saw a photograph of R.D. and Rasa holding up the newborn baby. Underneath was written in R.D.'s handwriting: 'When I look up from my pillow, I dream you are there with me.' Then: 'A new life is born and an old love begins to die.'

There were random words scribbled on the cuttings: Pram. Nappies. Urine. Sleepless nights. Milk-stained brassieres. Baby doo. Loving in-laws. Proud relatives. Happy snaps. The American tour starts next week.

I showed R.D. the photograph, which made him smile. He sat up.

'It all seems like sunlight, sunlight, but from the day Louisa was born until the day we had to take off for America, it was a crazy, thoughtless time. The night before we left, the door to our apartment fell off its hinges because the frame had dry rot. There was also damp in the kitchen. I didn't want to leave them in this situation, but my dad said he would take care of them and fix up the flat while I was away. There was just enough time to kiss Louisa and Rasa goodbye and run out of the apartment, leaving them without a front door and with mushrooms growing underneath the kitchen sink. I promised that when I returned from America, I'd find us a house to live in with more space and in better shape. With mushrooms that grew in the garden rather than on the floor.'

Raymond Douglas paused.

'I find it really difficult to go on.'

'How come?'

'I didn't want to leave – I was just beginning to enjoy being a

family man, but America always reared its head like a huge serpent
and snapped me back.'

'But why don't you want to talk about America?'

'Because I know that everybody wants to know what went
on, but it was no worse than anything any other band did. All
sorts of ridiculous stories evolve when musicians get old and
fragile and their memories don't function. They imagine
horrors that weren't there and beauty that never existed. You
see, it's what the world expects. The public demands us to live
out their fantasies, but I swear that given the circumstances I
was as faithful as I could have been to my wife. And the
circumstances were that I just didn't want to be there at all.
What sort of crap do you want me to tell you? Do you want
me to say that when we got to America we stayed at this big,
swanky hotel, and there was a chick sucking my dick for a
whole day – and that I even did a telephone interview during
it? Would you think that was the truth or a lie? It doesn't
matter because you expect it. People get old and their brains
start to go. They tend to elaborate. I do know that we played
a theatre called the New York Music Center with the Dave
Clark Five again, but obviously our situation had changed
from the last time we played together. We had kids jumping
on our car wherever we went and we were locked in our
hotel rooms for our own safety – although when some redneck
came up to me on the street and said, 'Are you a Beatle or a
girl?' I just said I was a queer. After our so-called triumph in
New York we went on to Philadelphia to play a huge arena.
This time with the Supremes. I remember them singing 'Baby
Love' and thinking that it was one of Rasa's favourite tunes.
We were just a bunch of unhappy, scruffy, unprofessional
louts who shouldn't have been allowed to upstage real
professionals. But whenever we went on stage all we could
hear was the deafening roar of kids screaming. Before the
tour, it had been decided by the management that Larry Page

238

should accompany us to America. It was unclear to me how this decision was reached. Perhaps I had been too preoccupied. My new status as a family man meant I had not focused clearly on the power-games being played within the Kinks management.

In order to give himself more stature, Larry had taken to wearing an admiral's hat. I think he admired Colonel Tom Parker, who managed Elvis Presley, and must have thought that all managers should be bigger personalities than their artists. Larry didn't need a big hat. His character was large enough. Our new road manager introduced himself to us as 'Samuel Ben-Hitchcock Halevy', and he was a veteran from the days of the Shadows and Tommy Steele. Brian Longstaff had quit and with him our last contact with the original team had been severed. Because Brian was an in-law, he could always step in when Dave and I got out of control, but now everything felt dangerous and tense.

America. Guns. Seeing Kennedy killed on TV a few years before had made me think that the whole continent was full of assassins, serial-killers and Mob-style corporations. I had started playing music because it was the only way I could express myself as an individual, and yet America, the country that had always inspired that sense of freedom inside me, was somehow one of the most repressed, backward-thinking places I had ever been to. I suppose I was naïve, but I had to learn that freedom doesn't mean going west on a wagon train, with John Wayne there to see that nobody comes to harm. Freedom contains a lot of danger, and it can only be achieved after a struggle. There we were in the middle of America. Milkshakes and hamburgers. Cookies and hot dogs. The American dream, and yet I felt that the whole country was trying to cover up something that was going bad from the inside. It's strange that so many American heroes die so young. Perhaps conservative America can't face that idealism. The reality was that beneath the ice-cream-parlour image, there was a festering pool of garbage. When waitresses in restaurants said 'Have a good day', I somehow felt that they were either administering the last rites or warning me that if I fucked up, I would get shot.

I arrived at my hotel room in Philadelphia after the show to find a pretty blonde girl sitting on my bed. We talked for a while, then I asked her how old she was. Almost as I spoke, and before she could respond, there was a knock at the door.

'I'm fourteen,' she said as she smiled and fluttered her false eyelashes, patting her heavily lacquered beehive hair-do.

As I shouted 'Who's that?' I thought about the rigid laws in the States about sex with minors.

'That's probably my daddy,' she said. 'He's the local sheriff.'

Fortunately Larry – or should I say the admiral – was at hand to extricate me from what could have been a disastrous situation. Even today I can't help feeling that it was a set-up. Maybe it's my paranoia, but I felt that somebody, somewhere, was still out to get one of the Kinks.

The next day we took an early flight, then a coach, to St Louis, to Springfield, then on. I found myself in the back of a big Thunderbird with some slick-looking dude who looked like he had walked out of a Jack Kerouac novel; a punk from your typical B-movie, the one who would inevitably piss somebody off before Lee Marvin put a bullet through his brain. The punk had the first car telephone I had ever seen.

The punk turned towards me. 'Kinks? What kind of motherfucking name is that? I've got Elvis Presley's phone number. I've fucked Ann-Margret, too. I mean, she wasn't Ann-Margret. She probably just said that to get into a show – or into my pants.'

He picked up the phone and dialled a number.

'Hi, is Elvis there? Is that you, Elvis? Well, let me speak to the Colonel. Jump to it, you motherfucker, who the fuck do you think you are?'

He slammed down the phone and reached in the glove-compartment. He produced a pistol.

'These people shouldn't piss me off, 'cause when they deal with me, they treat me right, otherwise they deal with this.' He waved the pistol around menacingly before putting it down on the seat beside him. Then his mood shifted, he smiled a film-star's toothy smile and said, 'Welcome to Illinois, the home of middle America.'

When I reached my hotel room, I made sure the door was locked and I didn't leave until it was time to go onstage. I wanted to go home. I telephoned Rasa at my parents' house, but the sound of her sad little voice at the other end of the crackling line turned this occasion into a very emotional experience. I asked Sam what I should do. His reply was simple: 'Don't phone.'

'Baby Love'. Great song. Fantastic record. Sexy group. Rotten emotion.

Whoever the pistol-packing punk driver from Illinois was, he certainly had a substantial amount of rock 'n' roll taste. He had arranged for our promoter to book as our opening act a classic band from the first wave of rock music in America, the Hollywood Argyles. Their big hit had been a song called 'Alley Oop'. D'you know the song? 'Alley oop, oop, oop, oopoop'. They had this weird lead singer who looked like a Hawaiian version of James Brown and a curvaceous back-up singer who turned out to be the lead singer's wife. I knew the song but thought that the band had disappeared years before, into the backwaters of clubs and nowhere bar-gigs on the second-string circuit, lost in the heartlands of America. Singing the same hits every night. Pure bread-and-butter time.

I looked at the punk and wondered whether he was an angel, cast out of heaven for listening to the devil's music, all back-beat and thump. He certainly exuded that indefinable bullshit-like quality that epitomized the American redneck element. In other words, he scared the shit out of me and fascinated me all at once. It made me realize how close together life and death really are, and how we should appreciate the bit of life that exists in between. As the punk driver watched me watching the Hollywood Argyles, I didn't know whether his head was moving up and down in time to the rhythm of the music or whether he was counting down the moments when he could put a bullet through my head.

After the show we were taken to a cheap motel where we could rest up before leaving early in the morning for Nevada. The pistol-packing pig-nose punk driver had pissed off and, hopefully, his boss had paid Larry our fee before leaving. I was just nodding off to sleep, contemplating whether or not to phone home, when my door burst open. I was relieved to see that it was only a slightly drunk musician from one of the support groups. He was easy to recognize because he was still wearing his cabaret band suit. He was younger than the rest of the group, maybe in his late twenties. He drawled on about how much he loved the Kinks and the Beatles and how he had just missed out on the scene. Caught between generations and all that.

He asked me if he could borrow my telephone. I said that was no problem provided the telephone stayed plugged into the socket beside my bed.

'My wife will go out of her mind when she finds out that I'm in Ray Davies' bedroom.'

I didn't know quite how to respond.

He dialled a number, somewhere in Virginia, he said. His voice became raised.

'Hi, baby, guess where I am. No, I'm not with a woman, but he sure has long hair.' His voice got even louder and more staccato.

'I'm in the bedroom of the one and only Ray of the Kinks, from England. That's right. The goddamn limey Kinks and the most shit-kicking bunch of good ol' boys that you could ever meet.'

He shouted even louder, almost angrily. I was sitting on the bed with my legs apart, he was on his knees in front of me. As he shouted he lifted his arm and came down on my balls with his fist.

'I mean these guys are Reet-suckin'-Petite. And, baby, when I get home I'm gonna suck you all over. Love you, honey.'

He gently replaced the receiver. He looked up at me and stared in my eyes, I swear I could see tears. The guy had obviously been on the road for a long time, day after day on the bread-and-butter circuit. I tried to think of something kind to say because I sensed from him a feeling of genuine awe and also resentment, all combined together. I realized how lucky I was, and I swore to myself that I would never get like him: playing date after date in nowhere towns at nickel-and-dime gigs. I knew that he hadn't meant to punch me in the knackers, that it was probably a remembrance of some cheap manager somewhere who had chisled him out of stardom that had prompted the action.

I tried to lighten the load the guy was carrying by making some reference to my own home. 'I was just about to phone my missus when you walked in,' I said somewhat stupidly.

He stared at me for a few seconds, obviously only half understanding what I had said. I suspect his thoughts were with the woman who had been on the other end of the phone. Was she really his baby, or an estranged wife? He got up to leave, paused by the door and looked up at the starry sky.

'Where the hell are we? These motels all look the same. See ya, buddy.'

I never saw him again, but I will always remember him, partly because my balls hurt for two weeks afterwards. And even if Brigitte Bardot had offered her services that night I would have had to decline.

The American landscape was beginning to take on a totally

different look to the one I had experienced through movies and television. Sure there were men who talked like John Wayne and Marlon Brando. Sure there were some outrageous characters with all the movie-star trappings. But there was also an entire nation of unhappy drifters who had not been part of the American dream. Even so, the six-and-a-half-hour flight from London was culturally as if I had taken a space trip from Muswell Hill to Mars.

I wiped my feet on the mat which said 'Have a good day', as I entered the motel coffee shop for an early breakfast. I was greeted by the sight of Eddie Kassner, already sitting at the breakfast table with what must have been his kids. He stood up and hugged me.

'Raymond, my boy, I've been following you all across America.' He held me in a squeeze as tight as a vice. 'I'm not gonna let my boy get away from me. You're like my family. And here we all are together.'

He turned and gestured towards the table where his family were sitting. Before our second album had come out, Grenville and Robert had said that they were concerned about Larry and Eddie. I was just interested in making sure that I got my royalties, but our success had been so quick and tumultuous that it was only nine months since our first Number 1 – hardly time for the first royalty cheques to arrive. Eddie squeezed me again. Now, Eddie was following his 'boy' across America. I wondered why, unless he was receiving part of the commission from our live concerts. This, combined with the publishing, would have been in anybody's language, a hell of a payday. After playing the Midwest we moved on to Nevada and, in true cartoon-chase fashion, wherever we travelled, Eddie Kassner was somewhere on the horizon keeping us in his sights. It was reassuring to know he was out there.

Reno. Neon lights. Big-titted women. Big hair-dos. Nicotine-stained fingers putting quarters into slot machines, rolling a dice in the quest for that elusive big win. More of the American dream.

'We could all divorce our wives here,' Sam Levy commented. 'And they have the best prostitutes in America. Clean, professional and they never spill a drop.'

'A drop of what?'

Sam just smiled and walked on. I didn't even want to think about what he was thinking about. It turned out that Sam was right, though.

I shared a room with Dave, who wasn't drinking so much, but like me he felt a little intimidated by it all. He was eighteen years old. We had been moving so fast that we still hadn't recovered from jet-lag. I'd just nodded off to sleep when the telephone rang. I got to the receiver first and a young male voice sounded through the cracking long-distance wire.

'Hello, dear, David, it's Michael Aldred. I miss you, mate.'

Michael had been the announcer on *Ready Steady Go!* when the Kinks had first appeared singing 'Long Tall Sally'. I explained that he was speaking to the wrong person and handed the phone over to my brother, who had what must have been a half-hour conversation. I was relieved that Dave had a close friend to confide in.

Michael had become such a regular visitor to Dave and Mick's notorious house in Connaught Gardens that at one point he had almost seemed to be the in-house servant, cooking the breakfast and washing the smalls, looking through keyholes and listening at walls. The things people do in the name of friendship.

The time arrived for us to go to the gig, at a basketball arena in downtown Reno. Eddie Kassner was waiting for me in the foyer of the hotel to drive me to the concert. I mean, here I am in Reno, Nevada, and there's Eddie Kassner, my music publisher, chauffeuring me to the concert. Eddie gave one of his familiar, sinister smiles. It was so uncharacteristic, so false, almost as if he had learned to smile from a do-it-yourself help book.

'I'm here to watch my boy Raymond, so that nobody can take advantage of you.' The smile was still on his lips. It must have made it difficult to talk. 'In places like this a nice-looking kid like you can be led astray.'

I just sat there. I looked out to bright neon lights of downtown Reno and longed to be led astray out there by people who only wanted me to lose money on blackjack or roulette, but there I was in Eddie's car, and that smile was still on his face, fixed like it was under remote-control. I thought back to Eddie's description of his life during the war and deduced that after such suffering he must have struggled hard to develop a grin, let alone a smile. The doors of the car locked automatically. I was trapped. Inside and out.

The dressing-rooms at Reno looked the same as many others, but as the Kinks ran on to do their performance, we realized to our surprise that the stage was not in a basketball arena at all, but slap-bang in the middle of an ice-rink. The promoter had just plonked down a little square stage, about fifty yards away from the nearest person in the audience. In fact it was not possible to have any contact with the audience at all. The acoustics were atrocious. After two or three songs I'd had enough and I shouted for the audience to come closer to the stage, which they did as there were no bouncers around to keep them in their seats. The remainder of the concert was a riotous success, but the promoter took exception to the manner of our performance and even accused us of using bad language from the stage, which would corrupt the young and impressionable audience and incite them to riot.

We got out of Reno and went on to California, which wasn't any better. We played Sacramento supported by Sonny and Cher, a husband and wife act who had just released a single called 'I Got You, Babe'. The group literally oozed over Cher as they watched her from behind. Her long black hair hung down past her ass, which was just visible as it wiggled in a skin-tight pair of pants. Then she turned round and Mick exclaimed that both Cher and Sonny needed nose jobs. I mean, the Kinks all had fair old salmons, but according to Mick the two should have contacted a plastic surgeon. Particularly the bloke, who reminded me of Barry Fantoni, a friend from Croydon Art College. The surfer duo Jan and Dean were hanging around at this time, and they became good friends of Dave's. They were in many ways responsible for the authentic West Coast surf sound, even though the Beach Boys later claimed that music as their own.

After the Sacramento concert we found ourselves in chauffeur-driven limousines for a triumphal entry into the city of Los Angeles. The staff at the Roosevelt Hotel took one look at us and said that our reservations had not been confirmed. We were driven a little less triumphantly away in the same limousines to the Ambassador Hotel, where it was possible to purchase the status which would enable the group to have a hotel room confirmed immediately. In other words, we had to buy our way into the hotel, thereby learning an important American phrase not yet common in our native country: 'Money talks'. The question that hadn't been raised yet was whose money was talking, and, more to the point, who was spending it?

Whatever. This was America and everybody said welcome to America. Mick said they were welcome to it.

In Los Angeles, we performed on the *Shindig* show, which was the West Coast equivalent of *Hullabaloo*, and it was there that Dave and I played on a session with one of our great guitar heroes – Jimmy Burton.

James Burton had been responsible for some of the great rock 'n' roll solos of the fifties and early sixties on Ricky Nelson and Elvis Presley records, plus those of numerous other country-blues artists. His bending, twanging guitar technique was copied by Dave, Jimmy Page and many other English guitarists. He substituted the third G-string with a B-string, which was lighter gauge. It gave the guitar a special twanging quality. In many ways he was an indirect influence on the sound Dave had achieved on 'You Really Got Me'.

Shindig was one of those wild extravaganzas with whooping cheerleader-type dancers behind us as we performed our three songs: 'You Really Got Me', 'All Day and All of the Night' and 'Tired of Waiting for You'. 'Set Me Free' had also been released at this point, and we were promoting that heavily. Other performers on the show were Marianne Faithfull, Jan and Dean, Paul Revere and the Raiders and Aretha Franklin. To this day I have a vivid memory of Aretha at the end of her song hitting one of the highest notes I've ever heard from a human being. It sort of reminded me of the way Mum shouted when Dave and I did something wrong. Sonny and Cher were also riding high, and they were on the show. Cher, in particular, came to watch the Kinks. Up close, her nose didn't look bad at all. In fact she was tasty. She was concerned at how worried I looked on camera and how much I was frowning. She pushed my brow down, smoothed out my skin and said, 'You don't want to look like a forty-year-old by the time you're twenty-one.' It's ironic to look back on Cher's career and realize that she would make a successful life for herself as a young-looking forty-something.

All the songs we performed were with back-tracks, that is, with pre-recorded instruments and vocals. Because of this we had to sign a form which made us members of the AFTRA Union. The back-track was done in a studio in Hollywood with James Burton playing a supporting role of rhythm guitar to Dave's chug-chug solo on 'Long Tall Shorty'. It was truly amazing to have such a great legend playing as a sideman.

Later, after one of the rehearsals at the TV studio, I was invited by one of the female dancers to go and see the sights of Hollywood. This appealed to me, as she was not just attractive but also an outward person who recognized my shyness. She also offered her services as chauffeur in her small sports car. This girl, whose name now eludes me, took me to drive-in movies and drive-in hamburger joints, where I had the first malted milkshake of my life. Since then, malted milkshakes have become an essential part of Raymond Douglas Davies' life. On later tours, I scoured the streets after every show in search of the perfect malted. I have a top ten list of the best milkshakes in America. The number 1 slot is currently held by Binghamton, in the state of New York. As it's unlikely that I will ever tour again, this record will stand in perpetuity.

Anyway, back to my LA babe. After the tour of Hollywood she took me back to her apartment in the hills. It was not a romantic event, but obviously there was some sort of physical tension between us. Perhaps it was the way her blouse had come undone at the top, which exposed her right nipple. This was not intentional on her part, and I had seen my fair share of nipples by now. But the fact that she was not wearing a bra at all was a turn on. It must be understood that this was way before women's lib and the whole burn-the-bra thing. This girl was just fantastically naturally rude, in the most dignified, puritanical American way. She kissed me gently on the cheek as we danced. Then she put on a record and I recognized the guitar playing. I said, 'Is that James Burton?' and she said, 'Yes, that's James. He's a friend of mine.' I looked over to the corner of the room and saw a fender Stratocaster resting against a settee. Surely this dancer from *Shindig* didn't play a Strat? Shock! Horror! Had I been out for the night with my idol's girlfriend? To this day I don't know whether this was a fact, but I'd like to believe that it was. I left the girl honourably, got a taxi straight back to the Ambassador Hotel and never said anything to Mr Burton for fear of becoming an enemy for life. But I like to think that Mr Burton, being the cool dude I expected him to be, would have just smiled and told me to go home and practise my scales. I saw in him something of the old cowboy that I'd admired in all those Westerns I'd loved as a kid, and I could tell by his

guitar playing that the man was a good guy. Just the same, I
didn't want to take the chance and get caught with the gal.
Thinking back, though, I suspect she just said that to freak me
out. Of course she knew James. They worked on the same
show. And who's to say that a girl can't play a Stratocaster?
Still I wonder about it sometimes. Whatever, the evening of
milkshakes and drive-ins was a welcome break away from the
scrutiny of the record company and Eddie Kassner. By this
time I had become totally paranoid: I was suspicious because
our limousines were chauffeured by sharp-looking drivers in
black suits and dark glasses, with their hair greased back.
Echoes of Illinois, paranoia. At the Ambassador Hotel we
were given bungalows away from the main building. I decided
that this was so that we wouldn't embarrass the other patrons.

By now, I was totally wound up, and also nervous about
the upcoming concert at the Hollywood Bowl. I was
determined to confront Larry Page because I felt that the tour
had been run in a very shoddy manner. We were just thrown
on in any venue that would pay the money, and no thought
was given to the group's performance. It was not necessarily
Larry's fault, but he was the only one we were allowed to
complain to. I turned on the television to see Larry being
interviewed as the Kinks' manager and commander, the
admiral's hat still firmly in place. He looked a complete prat,
but what really annoyed me was that he was talking as if he
had invented the Kinks.

When I reached Larry's bungalow I burst in full of rage,
demanding that my wife be flown out to me. I saw Larry
standing down the end of the hallway to his room. I had just
completed the first sentence when I looked over to the bed
and saw Sam lying with his underpants down while a naked
girl licked his undercarriage. Sam liked girls to kiss his ass. He
looked like a sultan being serviced by one of his concubines.
What amazed me was that the girl never even stopped to look
up to see who the intruder was. Larry stood in an adjoining

room making a long-distance telephone call, trying to ignore Sam and the girl, who were reflected in a mirror hanging in the hall between the two rooms. I wanted Rasa flown out because I felt really insecure and threatened by the whole set-up. Larry calmed me down by saying that he had been trying to organize this, but I felt he was just stroking me in his usual manner, because he knew full well that I wouldn't walk out on a commitment.

I knew it would all boil up inside and erupt sooner or later. And it did. I think it was backstage at one of those other TV programmes where they packaged as many beat groups together as possible in order to cash in on the English invasion before the bubble burst. Fun and innocence on TV, a total meat market backstage. Some guy who said he worked for the TV company walked up and accused us of being late. Then he started making anti-British comments. Things like 'Just because the Beatles did it, every mop-topped, spotty-faced limey juvenile thinks he can come over here and make a career for himself.' He also called me 'A talentless fuck who was in the right place at the right time.' The usual schlock.

I said something about American pop music being so dull and syrupy before the British invasion. I think it was the word 'invasion' that did it. Invasion. As if nobody were allowed to invade America. The guy exploded. I think he even mentioned Pearl Harbor, then he went on to the British socialist government, and we were all nothing more than a bunch of pinkos. Then he uttered the fatal words:

'You're just a bunch of Commie wimps. When the Russians take over Britain, don't expect us to come over and save you this time. The Kinks, huh? Well, once I file my report on you guys, you'll never work in the USA again. You're gonna find out just how powerful America is, you limey bastard!'

The rest is a blur. However, I do recall being pushed and swinging a punch and being punched back. I stormed out of the building, leaving an assorted number of confused groups,

like the Zombies and Herman's Hermits, and some American
Beatle clones, looking shocked and dismayed.

I went back to my bungalow and barricaded the door with
furniture so that nobody could get in. That aggressive sod,
whoever he was, had put anger and fear inside me, even
though for once I felt proud of being British. We were not
wimps who just stood around and let people treat us like shit.
In my confused state of shock, I even imagined that the
powers-that-be, the unions, showbiz insiders, whoever, were
so pissed off that the Beatles had taken away so much earning
power from the American bands that they were looking for
any excuse to make an example of someone. They couldn't
do it with music any more, so they resorted to cheap
mob-style tactics. Suddenly I remembered the image of Lee
Harvey Oswald appearing in front of a camera saying that
he was a patsy. I decided that everybody was part of a
gigantic conspiracy. The Cosa Nostra were everywhere. Why
not? That was part of America, the same as ice-cream and
apple pie. Guns. The Wild West. What a load of fascist
bullshit.

The Kinks were distributed on Reprise Records, a company
which had been set up through Warner Brothers. We were
impressed to be on the same label as Frank Sinatra. But
Reprise was based in LA and nothing was real there. Where
were the real people, I thought as I barricaded myself inside
my bungalow. Everywhere I went I saw Eddie Kassner, Larry
Page, greaseball limo drivers, anger, fury and a gun in every
glove compartment. There was talk of union problems, law-
suits. I had just had enough. This was more than just musical
expression and all that. This was political.

Somehow the message got through to London and Grenville
arranged to have Rasa and Quaife's girlfriend Nicola flown
out as soon as possible. Everybody wanted to drain the last
drop of juice out of the Kinks while there was still enough to
go around. If this meant giving the spoiled upstarts what they

wanted for the time being, then it was a small price to pay. It was something I'd see repeated again and again: suffer an artist any indulgence in order that he performs. So, late on a hot summer's night Quaife and I found ourselves at Los Angeles airport looking for Rasa and Nicki. We were uncertain whether Nicki had made the trip since she was underage and needed her father to sign a consent form to get a passport. Nicki's parents had separated years before. Grenville had had to track down her father. He eventually was found and, according to Grenville, living in quite affluent splendour in the country. Rasa had different problems obtaining a visa to the USA. She was still a stateless person, and had to make a special application to obtain a temporary passport to leave the UK. To add to the confusion, an over-excited bureaucrat at the American Embassy had decided Rasa was a Communist because her parents had come from Lithuania, then part of the USSR, and Rasa's father had served in both the Soviet and German armies. Nobody told the Embassy that the poor old boy had no choice. However, all the formalities had been sorted out in time for the two girls to jump on a plane to New York and then change flights for LA. The first time round the airport, there was no sign of either of them. After going round once more for luck, we spotted Rasa's long blonde hair as she bent down to pick up her suitcase. Nicola was much taller and more elegant and she posed outside the terminal as if she were modelling the latest design from one of the Parisian fashion houses: Mary Quant bob-style hair, miniskirt and long slender legs.

The girls' arrival came as a great relief to our management, agency and publishers alike, as the next concert was to be at the prestigious Hollywood Bowl where we were playing with the Righteous Brothers, Sonny and Cher, the Byrds, Sam the Sham and the Pharaohs and the Beach Boys. Everyone was very aware that our performance, both on and off stage, would be closely scrutinized by the powers-that-be. Whoever they were.'

R.D. rubbed his hands together nervously. He looked over at me as if he needed my approval. I felt he was beginning to trust me enough to reveal his weaknesses.

'You see, you don't understand what it's like being thrown right in there with all these great groups. I'm not given to nostalgia, but that concert gave me such a buzz because I enjoyed the records that those other groups had made. One of those gentlemen in a dark suit and sunglasses drove Rasa and me up that impressive canyon in a limousine to the backstage of the Hollywood Bowl for the afternoon sound-check. In the distance we heard the Righteous Brothers accompanied by a full orchestra singing the opening lines to 'You've Lost That Loving Feeling'. Later that evening as we made the same journey to the concert itself, we got out of the same limo and heard a deafening roar from the crowd as the opening chords to the Byrds version of 'Mr Tambourine Man' echoed around the canyon. A priceless, vibrant moment. I think I even got a hard on of sorts.

Backstage I discovered a very different situation. It was pandemonium everywhere. The Pharaohs, without Sam the Sham, were dressed in their Arabian stage gear and arguing about some of the fuck-ups they'd made during their performance. Mick was dragged outside by one of the promotion men from Reprise Records because that was a rumour that Dean Martin, whom Mick had met in a studio a day earlier, had arrived on a motorbike in full Beverly Hills-style bikers' leather. I wanted to know if Jerry Lewis was there too, but I was disappointed to see that Dean had arrived without the other half of his old comedy team. Instead, he was accompanied by his son and a few friends who had formed a group called 'Dino, Desi and Billy'. Mike Love, the lead singer of the Beach Boys, strutted up to me, stared me out for a few seconds, made a gesture as if to say hello and then walked straight past. Dave tried to talk to another member of the Beach Boys, but for some strange reason, he received the same freeze-out I had. This could have been nerves on their part, or even professional jealousy, as we had by now earned a reputation for being somewhat rowdy, on and off stage, and we were the only Brits on the show and part of the dreaded 'invasion' to boot. Meanwhile, onstage, while Cher sang a reprise of 'I've Got You, Babe', Sonny Bono was winding up the audience by jumping in the water moat that separated the performers from the crowd. This didn't bother us too much, as by now we were accustomed to opening acts trying to upstage us. We had developed a modicum of professionalism sufficient to see us through any performance. The truth was that the Kinks revelled in rivalry and competitiveness: it just made us play harder and move more aggressively, as if a gauntlet had been thrown down by the other acts on the bill. It was similar to being a prize-fighter who had become the Champion of the World, only to discover that every small-time punk wanted to pick a fight with him. Just the same, Dave and I were particularly upset by the apparent lack of grace shown to us by the Beach Boys, because we had been genuine fans of most of their records.

After the concert we breezed past assorted celebrities that had assembled backstage. The Pharaohs, still without Sam the Sham, were strutting up and down the corridor arguing over wrong chord changes. Sonny and Cher were holding court somewhere: 'I Got You, Babe' was on the verge of becoming a huge hit all over the world. Although somewhat miffed by the lack of attention we received after our triumph at the Hollywood Bowl, something must have paid off. When Sonny and Cher later recorded an album in London, 'I Go to Sleep' was among the tracks. Before the tour I had gone to a small studio in Denmark Street and made a very rough demo of the song, which I had sent to Peggy Lee. Maybe Kassner had driven around America with it. Maybe that's why he had been smiling.

Although there were undercurrents of friction between the promoters and the Kinks management, there was never anything said directly to us. It wasn't until the next concert, at the Cow Palace Auditorium in San Francisco, that the first definitive signs appeared that all was not well. We had been billed to appear with the same package, but for some reason the promoter refused to let us perform. So as not to disappoint the Kinks fans we decided to show our faces to the audience. I muttered some words down the microphone to the effect that we wanted to play, but the promoter wouldn't let us. This resulted in the PA system being switched off and the Kinks being bustled out of the backstage entrance into waiting limousines, which took us straight to San Francisco airport.

Dave had bought a beautiful Gretsch guitar that had once been owned by George Harrison (and a photo of Dave playing it had been taken and eventually used on the cover of *Kinks Kontroversy*). At the check-in Dave put it down and looked away for a moment. When he turned back he found it had been stolen. It seemed symbolic somehow.

To this day I don't know what the hell was going down. Larry suddenly disappeared, leaving us with some Californian businessman whose name I can't recall. Even Eddie was no longer in pursuit. We flew down from Frisco to LA and stayed at a cheap motel off La Cienaga accompanied by Sam Levy and the wealthy businessman. Next morning we were hustled on to a plane to Hawaii. When we asked where Larry had gone, they brushed our inquiries aside, simply saying that he had had to go somewhere on business. I was with Rasa, and even though I was pissed at my management for walking out on us, I was overjoyed to be in her company. Her presence somehow made my feeling of betrayal seem trivial. We got off the plane at Hawaii airport and heard the sound of screaming Hawaiian teenagers – and that was when Sam and the businessman got off the plane. When the Kinks emerged there was total uproar. Sam, being no shrinking violet, walked

on ahead as a committee of Hula-Hula girls approached him.
They sang a Hawaiian song of welcome and then the leader of
the little troupe walked up to Sam, put a garland of plastic
flowers around his neck and kissed him on both cheeks.
Instead of whispering some beautiful Hawaiian welcome in his
ear, she said in an extremely American accent, 'Do you get
this kinda shit everywhere you go?' I think she ended up with
Sam. Sam obviously gave her the same kind of shit he gave
everywhere he went.

We stayed at a romantically situated hotel by Waikiki
Beach. This was long before Hawaii became truly
Americanized, and Waikiki Beach did not yet resemble Asbury
Park, New Jersey. Rasa and I hadn't been intimate since the
baby was born. I thought I would make love to her in our
hotel room overlooking the ocean. Everything seemed perfect:
the soft sound of the sea, the sun shining through a thin gauze
curtain, but Rasa turned away and there was no attempt to
reciprocate my feelings. I tried to be understanding: Louisa's
birth had been difficult and Rasa's body had been badly cut
up. It was like she had been mauled by a butcher instead of
giving birth to a child. Her stitches had hardly healed. Rasa
was eighteen years old.

There were two concerts in Hawaii, one at Pearl Harbor for
the servicemen. Surrounded as we were by what seemed to be
the entire American armed forces, I was particularly careful
not to make any comments about the Labour Government in
England and how conservative America seemed in comparison.
Then it was back to the mainland for two concerts in the
north-west. While waiting in an airport coffee shop in
Spokane, Washington, I kissed Rasa on the cheek and put my
arm around her. Moments later two armed cops arrived to
arrest me for 'public indecency'. One of the waitresses had
noticed the innocent peck on the cheek, but as she had already
taken offence at my long hair, and perhaps because we seemed
so young, she decided that my actions warranted police

intervention. Either Dave or Mick – I can't remember who – offered to drop his trousers so that the over-excited waitress could make a genuine complaint, but thanks to a timely intervention by Sam Levy we were able to leave on the designated flight.

This was virtually the end of the tour. Pete and Nicola stayed behind with Mick in LA. Rasa and I left for home. As the aeroplane took off, she squeezed my hand. I looked over to see that she was crying, but was unsure what this emotion was meant to represent. I felt for a moment that any love she had had for me had gone. Then I dismissed this, rationalizing that she was most probably relieved to be going back home to see her daughter. My fear of flying had not been cured, but the need for Valium had disappeared.

My thoughts were turning to anger because despite all the chaos and the screaming audiences that had followed us around America, I still felt uneasy about our management. The incidents involving the promoter in Nevada and California had still not been fully explained to anyone in the band. I had made further inquires about Larry, who was still missing, but the same old excuses were made by Sam. If they were taking care of business, they were doing it somewhere else and with other people. All this had turned me into a less innocent person than I had been before I arrived in America. 'Nobody abandons the Kinks,' I told Rasa as the plane took off for London.'

Raymond Douglas stopped suddenly. I watched as his face become that of a bitter old man. He sat back in his chair in the small control room and made the following declaration:

'And as for America. God bless America. The place is great. The real Americans are fine people. But the undercurrent of corruption that I experienced on my first tour there never went away.'

The old rocker leaned forward and stared me in the eyes.

'America gives. But whatever it gives, it takes back in one way or another, just like Dave's guitar at San Francisco airport. And as sure as God is my judge, in America the Corporation is controlling you and they, whoever "they" are, still want to get me. Mark my words. They do not forget.'

Raymond Douglas moved back out of the light without changing his expression. His jaw was set tight and his eyes were filled with fear. He put on his favourite video, *Charlie Varrick*. Walter Matthau was echoing Raymond Douglas' words almost verbatim. R.D. settled back into his chair and relaxed a little.

'This is only a movie, and I suppose it's not scary at all. It's meant to be a comedy. Perhaps comedy is the only way to tell the truth. But believe me, there are guys out there who are for real. I like *Charlie Varrick*. It's not a great movie like *The Seven Samurai* or *Citizen Kane*, but at least it's a bit of fantasy. You know? When Varrick beats the mob? Nice fantasy. I like to believe it's true sometimes, and that I might do it one day, but it's not like that in real life. Believe me, kid. They have got you, and once you have given them what they want once, they will keep taking until they have your soul. If you decide you don't want to give any more, they will undoubtedly dispose of you. They're not just over there. They're over here too.'

'How come they haven't disposed of you yet?' I asked.

'Because what I have frightens them.'

'And what is that?'

R.D. smiled and shook his head with dismay and disappointment.

'You know, I actually thought you were smart. Perhaps you are. Think about it. Just keep doing your job and see if I'm not right. Just keep asking questions and you might find out. You may not be as smart as I thought you were, but I still trust you.'

I asked some inconsequential questions about the remainder of the American tour, and then what happened when he returned to his beloved England.

'When I got home, you mean? That's better. Let's stick to the story. Well, I'll tell you. When I was a kid I used to run around the streets as part of my soccer training, and I passed a big white house set back from the road. When I returned to England I was amazed to find that this house was up for sale. It wasn't as grand as I had remembered it as a child. In fact, it was quite a modest-looking semi. It did, however, have some historic value. It had been built around the time of the Battle of Trafalgar and had been 'listed' by the Department of National Heritage. I looked around and immediately told the people living there that I wanted to buy it. What was more, despite an earlier offer, they wanted to sell it to me. I said I'd pay the price they were asking as long as they included the furniture. The deal was done for £9,000, but there was a minor problem. Money.'

14

They'll move me up to Muswell Hill tomorrow

R.D. leaned forward again and, watching my reactions, continued in that now familiar, fatherly tone.

'I was in the situation where I had written five major hit singles that had been successful around the world and I'd had two very successful albums, but apart from a salary of £40 a week, I had no real money. There was certainly not enough to purchase what at the time I considered to be my ideal home in Fortis Green, N2. I quizzed Robert and Grenville about money; they tried to reassure me by saying that I should be a millionaire by now. Probably I should have been; but that was neither here nor there. The unfortunate reality was that this was not reflected in my bank account.

We were all sitting in Boscobel's office just behind Carnaby Street. Grenville got up from behind his desk and declared: 'You must become a corporation. A company director. Own all the shares. We'll find you an accountant.'

'Fine,' I said.

'Then we'll have to ask your distinguished publisher if he can advance you some money.'

'But all I want is enough to buy the house!'

Grenville and Robert would hear no more. It was decided that I was fated to become a corporate entity. You see, in the old days, and I guess those could be considered the old days, a publisher signed you, let's say for the UK territory, then he did deals with the overseas publishers to promote the copyright of the song and collect royalty revenue. It was the general rule that most of the revenue from overseas territories was six to twelve months behind the UK royalties, and even the UK

261

royalties were never released by the record companies until
another six to twelve months had elapsed, so even though I
had sold substantial amounts of records, hardly any money at
all had filtered through the various account departments.
Although I didn't realize it at the time, we must have sold
between 5 and 10 million records worldwide, counting singles
as well as albums and EPs.

I was told I should take an advance of £9,000 to enable me
to purchase the property in Fortis Green and have it deducted
from my royalties when they came in. Kassner kept
mentioning that he wanted a long-term contract with me.
Until now, all my songs had been assigned to his company as
they were written and, as I understood it, that's as far as my
commitment to him went. I also assumed that Larry's
disappearance in LA had made Kassner insecure about the
position of Denmark Productions, the management company
he and Larry owned jointly, but in which he was the majority
shareholder. Being the majority shareholder meant that
Kassner was entitled not just to the publishing, but to at least
51 per cent of Denmark Productions' share of all other
earnings from the Kinks' touring and recording income.
Nice deal. It was all becoming baffling and unclear to me. I
was confused and told Robert and Grenville so. Boscobel
knew that they had to make me feel a secure and contented
artist.

Robert had been to see a solicitor, Michael Simkins, who
was known to be an expert on such intricate contractual
matters. After consulting with legal counsel, Simkins
concluded that as far as my publishing went, I was a free agent
and could sign with any publisher I wished, provided Boscobel
waived their rights and gave their consent. Simkins looked in
his late twenties, but was already an experienced music lawyer
and seasoned campaigner who had probably drafted many
such contracts himself. This time, thankfully, he was on my
side.

Years later I confronted Wace as to why he had not advised the Kinks to seek a solicitor's advice before signing the Boscobel contract, Wace said that he had thought there was 'no need'. No need? Dave was fifteen fucking years old when he signed that contract! I was eighteen and so were Quaife and Avory! No need?

It had been decided that in order to accommodate such vast revenues, if they should ever materialize, I would become a corporation. Wace's father had used a firm of accountants in the City called MacNair, Mason and Evans. Mr Wace Senior had been particularly impressed by a young chartered accountant, who according to Wace had a dazzling future ahead of him, so on his advice Robert Ransom, this new rising star, became my accountant. Although the sixties had been revolutionary in lots of ways, resulting in many class barriers being broken down, there was still a dividing line between the City, where all the 'old' money was handled by established stockbrokers and merchant bankers, and the West End, where the 'new' money was being made, mainly through the entertainment and fashion industries, the standard bearers for the new pop culture. Robert Ransom was firmly ensconced in the values of the City whereas Kassner, Page, Pye Records and possibly even Simkins were definitely regarded as West End.

It was decided that a meeting should take place between Ransom, Page and Kassner, with Robert and Grenville in attendance. Ransom sat in Kassner's office looking unimpressed, listening to the publisher explain how the money would eventually be channelled into my account. From that day forward, I entered the hallowed halls of the corporate world and was re-christened by Corporation House, Ray Davies (Limited). As Ray Davies (Limited) walked away from Denmark Street, accompanied by Mr Ransom and Robert Wace, questions were already being asked by the pin-striped advisor about Kassner's company. I watched Ransom as he strolled confidently along swinging his hefty leather briefcase, and I listened to his assessment of the financial situation. I felt fortunate indeed to be represented by such a well-respected man.

It was also obvious that I was becoming physically run down, and Rasa was involved in the awesome duties of motherhood, interspersed with bouts of post-natal depression. The management therefore decided that a short holiday would be in order, a chance for me to recharge my batteries after the arduous and controversial American trip, which had resulted in a temporary ban on the Kinks in the USA, pending an investigation by the American Federation of Musicians. It was an opportunity for me and the other members of the band to take a break. For the first time in nearly two years the group would be out of one another's company.

Rasa and I were booked into the Imperial Hotel in Torquay, a palatial remnant from the heyday of the grand seaside hotel, with palm-court orchestras, health spas, a large residents' lounge serving cucumber sandwiches, tea and crumpets, cocktails and a golf-course (just in case the beach was considered to be too vulgar). It was as if the young Davies family had been transported back to the golden Victorian age of high tea, servants and chambermaids. My young family stayed in our room for the entire week, only venturing out occasionally to walk down to the seaside promenade where, unrecognized, we could enjoy a plate of fish and chips followed by a large Knickerbocker Glory. One afternoon I was recognized by an upper-class army-officer type and cordially invited to make up a four for a round of golf the following morning. The Davies family promptly checked out of the hotel that night and took the next train back to London.

Soon after this aborted holiday, we moved into the white Regency semi, accompanied by our baby daughter, Louisa. Heaven was a cheque for £1,000 to cover the cost of an upright piano, newly fitted gas central heating, a television set and a three-piece suite. Heaven was Louisa trying to crawl on the Thames-green Wilton carpet as I played my Spanish guitar. Heaven was Louisa in a pram with Rasa pushing it up the shingled driveway. Heaven was to see Rasa smile again. Reality showed how during pregnancy and childbirth a woman loses something from her skin and hair, as if the child has drawn the energy out of her. Heaven is to see some of that coming back: breasts back to normal, if somewhat softer, waist trim, calves bulging.

And while I watched Louisa playing on the Wilton carpet, I started to write 'A Well-Respected Man'.

Although I had found a safe haven in my little semi in north London, controversy still centred around the Kinks. In particular, Mick's assault on Dave during the concert in Cardiff earlier that summer; also, rumours had got back through the musical press that the American tour had been an unhappy one, and an indefinite ban was to be imposed on the Kinks (even though the reasons were vague to say the least); and matters were made worse by the fact that Robert and Grenville's relationship with Larry Page seemed to be deteriorating. The Kinks felt uncomfortable about Page after he had mysteriously disappeared on the US tour. I had still not been forgiven for some remarks I had made in the press, and for my behaviour at the *New Musical Express* poll-winners' concert. There were yet further rumours that I had 'dried up' as a songwriter, and become a 'suburbanite'. Robert and Grenville had always known that I was somewhat suburban, but what concerned them now was that my songwriting well may have indeed run dry. Rumours abounded. Even relatives called round to the white semi and inquired whether I had 'written any songs lately?'

Robert Wace solicited the aid of the famous American songwriter Mort Shuman, thinking that Shuman would inspire me to write more songs. Shuman, along with Doc Pomus, had written many early rock and roll classics for Elvis Presley and for the Drifters, and Robert knew that I was an admirer of his work. After he had visited the Davies household, Shuman, in the manner of a Harley Street specialist crossed with Groucho Marx, gave his assessment. The genial New York songwriter's professional opinion was that 'The kid's just going through a bad patch. He just needs to loosen up and get laid. And the little wife isn't much of a help, either.'

I had formed my own impressions during the brief visit: there was a distinct feeling of animosity between Rasa and Mort. It was clear that Mort considered that I would work better if the wife and child were not around, and that a suburban house was no place for one of the newly emerging talents in rock and roll. But Mort had completely misread the situation: suburbia was and would always be a major influence in my writing.

The usual record company panic started, and a new album was called for immediately, to dispel all the rumours. *The Kinks Kontroversy* was recorded and released that autumn, and the first single, 'Till the End of the Day', with 'Where Have All the Good Times Gone' on the B-side, put the Kinks back on *Top of the Pops*.

Kontroversy, as it transpired, was an apt name for the album. I took the advice of Michael Simkins and decided to place the new songs with a different publisher. Robert and Grenville were no longer directly involved in my publishing at this stage, but none the less they attended a meeting arranged by Simkins between myself and Freddie Beinstock. Beinstock worked with Belinda Music, the publishing company that controlled and administered Elvis Presley's publishing, and Talma Motown, among many others. Simkins had done several successful publishing deals with Beinstock, and he thought he would be a suitable person to handle my publishing and who at the same time could appreciate the intricacies of the legal situation I was in. Robert and Grenville were attracted to the offices of Belinda Music because they were located in a grand building in Savile Row. Robert not only considered this a step up from the slightly tawdry surroundings of Denmark Street, but it also meant that he was in easy striking distance of his tailor, situated across the road. The building at 17 Savile Row was also used by the Alberbach family, who were art collectors and related to Freddie Beinstock. They used part of the building to exhibit their paintings. Beinstock's wife, Miriam, had helped the Ertegun brothers, Ahmet and Nesuhi, form Atlantic Records, which in the early days operated from an apartment in New York, and she was a formidable businesswoman in her own right.

The whole arrangement suited Robert and Grenville's luxurious standards. The interior of the building, particularly Freddie's office, was drenched with the trappings of the *nouvelle* aristocracy: a vast chandelier hung from the ceiling, complementing the Regency furniture and paintings by Francis Bacon alongside sketches by Picasso. Beinstock himself cut a dashing figure with his smartly tailored suit and well-groomed hair. His voice was deep American, with a very heavy European influence, which some of the impressionable secretaries who buzzed in and out of his office found quite sexy. He sounded like Henry Kissinger, and the only indication that he might have come from humble beginnings was the way he played with his cuff-links and continually adjusted his tie as he spoke. His face was long and elegant and his lower lip drooped into a good-humoured grin as he started each conversation with a joke, usually about one of his competitors. All in all I found Beinstock to be a thoroughly attractive man. My first meeting with him was also attended by Simkins. Deals were discussed, legalities were considered, conclusions were drawn and compliments were given on my songwriting abilities. The reputations of other publishers were discussed and it was concluded that Belinda Music would be the ideal publisher for me. It was also proposed by Beinstock, as part of the inducement to sign, that I should receive a slightly higher royalty than Kassner had paid, in the form of a publishing company that I would own. Beinstock sat back in his chair and pondered over a name for the new company.

'How about Davray in the United Kingdom and the rest of the world and Mondvies in the United States and Canada?'

I sat impassively as Grenville, Robert and Michael Simkins acknowledged Beinstock's witty word play on my name. All I could think about was the possibility of being not just Ray Davies Limited, but now two further identities.

At the end of the conversation, Beinstock turned to me and asked if I would like an advance. I was astonished that anybody would pay money for work that had not yet been written, and I was thoroughly embarrassed by the situation.

'How does one put a price on it?' I mused.

'How much do you think you are worth?' inquired Beinstock in a quiet, matter-of-fact way, like a doctor asking a patient the name of his next of kin before telling him he is going to have major surgery.

'I'm not sure yet, but perhaps if you allow me to take that picture.' The room fell silent as I pointed to a large painting by Francis Bacon. After a long pause Beinstock regained his composure and said that he would talk to the Aberbachs about that, as they dealt in art; he added apologetically that he only dealt with money.

Grenville and Robert were amazed that I had not asked for an advance; it was quite clear to them that I could have named almost any figure and Beinstock would have paid it. They later put it down to my 'working-class honesty'.

Concerned that the Kinks' career was on a definite wane, Pye Records came up with an idea to put out an EP with 'A Well-Respected Man' as the main track. I had already assigned the four songs on the album to Kassner Music earlier in the year, before Simkins had advised me that I was under no obligation to do so. The EP was made so quickly that nearly all the songs were recorded in the first take, with the vocal put on at the same time as the back track. This experiment proved to be a successful gamble, and the record *Kwiet Kinks* not only went to Number 1 in the EP charts, but became one of the largest selling EPs of the time. 'Well-Respected Man' was released in America, and to everybody's surprise got into the American Top 10.

Its success astonished us all, as the lyric was particularly English, and I had abandoned any attempt to Americanize my accent. Perhaps this was the effect the disastrous American tour had had on me. But what I had unwittingly done was put the Kinks into favour with the Ivy League set in America, as well as retaining the normal pop-record-buying audience. The ban imposed on us in the US gave us even more mystique to American audiences. One line in particular both gave ammunition to the critics and set up what was already becoming a loyal and varied audience: 'And he likes his fags the best'. I had naïvely meant a fag to be either slang for cigarette or, at worst, that the well-respected man had been at public school, where a fag was a boy who was designated to perform the most menial and humiliating tasks, anything from cleaning shoes to warming the toilet seat. But in America at this time, fag meant homosexual. Perhaps I had picked up the word fag during the American tour, and it had remained in my subconscious, but when I referred to fag in 'A Well-Respected Man', it was a distinct reference to the never-ending trail of dog ends from the roll-ups that my dad used to leave around the house.

As soon as news broke that I had signed a five-year deal with Belinda Music, a writ was issued by Kassner Music, claiming breach of contract on my part and inducement to cause a breach on the part of Boscobel. It was decided by my advisers and by counsel acting for all parties that until the dispute was resolved, publishing and writing royalties from the sale of any works under the Davies/Belinda deal were to

be put in escrow and administered by the law firm of
Rubenstein and Nash. In other words, I would receive no
money until the law-suit had been resolved. My only source
of income which was not affected was the performing-rights
income, which comprised royalties from radio and television
performances.

But for the moment I was enjoying life in my suburban
semi, in between tours of Germany, Holland and Belgium,
where the Kinks were particularly popular. The Dutch had
taken a liking to the more lyrical songs, such as 'A Well-
Respected Man', and pirate radio stations like Caroline and
Veronica played the Kinks material heavily. We appeared on
Ready Steady Go! on the New Year's Eve special and we
performed 'A Well-Respected Man' at one minute to
midnight. By the time we finished miming the song, it was
1966.

An age of blind, reckless innocence was coming to an end,
and an era fraught with litigation, emotional turmoil and
paranoia was about to begin. Louisa Davies was seven months
old.'

Too much on my mind

15

Raymond Douglas got up from his chair and moved over to look at the clear night sky, which was just visible through the little skylight in the ceiling of the control room. He shuffled over to the opposite side of the room and pulled out a book from under a pile of old magazines. He took a deep breath before blowing the surface dust off. Then he rubbed the remainder of the grime off with his woollen mittens. As he looked at the cover of the book he came into the light, and I could see tears of joy come into his eyes. He moved towards me, holding the book out before him.

R.D. presented me with 'Colourful Britain Diary 1966'. On the front was a photograph of an idyllic English country setting: a thatched cottage by the side of a stream. I knew that this was a gesture of good will, and possibly an attempt to rid himself of some anguish.

'Take this,' R.D. said.

I was amazed that he felt that he could trust me so much.

'Why, it is probably too personal.' I wanted to take it very badly.

'I insist. Read it and tell me what you think. I'll see you tomorrow. But – you must promise not to let anyone else see it.'

'Oh, I promise. You can be sure of that.'

I could hardly believe my good fortune. Me, on my first big assignment! This was such a coup! Later, when I got home, I opened the diary to find the inscription:

'To Ray, from Mum and Dad, Xmas 1965.' Below that, scribbled in crayon, was a telephone number: 'Klein 108 Circle 57010.' I turned the page and several sheets of Kinks venues for 1966 fell out. I turned to the page headed 'memos', and found assorted names and telephone numbers: Eric Burdon, Barry Fantoni, Bibas, Grenville Collins.

As I turned the pages I realized that most of the handwriting was not Raymond Douglas', and therefore must have been Rasa's. Small sentences with an abbreviated version of her reality: 'New Year's show on *Ready Steady Go!* Reception afterwards. Good rave show.' The next part was underlined: 'In fact the show was terrific! Party was great afterwards. Tomorrow Ray goes to Cheshire. Very good show. Got in at 3.30 a.m.' I continued to turn the pages and found more of the same. 'Tuesday, 4 January, Louisa's first tooth came through, right one on bottom gum.' '13 January, *Top of the Pops*. Number 6. Very good show. Afterwards Ray played Chesterfield where his shirt was ripped off by fans during the show. Friday, 14th. London. *Ready Steady Go!* Feel depressed. Something awful. Stayed behind for drinks and play-back.' The next entry was in red ink and in large writing; 'Ray, talking to *that girl.*'

This interested me. Also, the name Barry Fantoni was appearing quite often as a visitor to the house, among Louisa's appointments at hospitals and so-called 'rave' shows in Doncaster, Newcastle, Worthing and so on. On February 2nd the diary noted a recording session at IBC Studios and a song that I had not heard of before called 'Mr Reporter'. Underneath Raymond Douglas had written, 'Quote of the day from Shel Talmy: "I am not interested in the glory, I just want the money."'

'4 February, Louisa's injection. Notre-Dame Hall, Leicester Square. Ray left at five to go to what he described as a meeting in the office. It lasted till nine at night. Ray was so busy, even fell asleep, he couldn't even ring me, doesn't matter any more. My love just does not exist. I am truly fed up, miserable and hurt. I haven't a home, neither has Ray. Yes he has – his home is an office. In his life he hasn't any time for home life or love. Robert and Grenville just take up everything he has. "Business is business."'

On the whole Rasa's sad little scribblings seemed like the average concerns of a young wife who feels she is not seeing enough of her husband. Although the comments were abbreviated, and sometimes like those of an over-emotional schoolgirl, they seemed to reveal quite a lot about her relationship with R.D. It was also interesting for me to get a point of view from a source other than his.

I continued to read.

'7 February. Recording in morning, 10 a.m. "Dedicated Follower of Fashion" (good, no, fabulous!!), "She Got Everything" (back-track).

'10 February. Salisbury. Good show. Went straight to Pye to re-do parts of "Dedicated Follower of Fashion". Got home at 5 a.m.

'Friday, 11 February. Copenhagen.' Then the writing became minute, in capitals and underlined: 'I WISH I COULD GO SO MUCH.'

As I turned to Friday, 18 February, I realized why Barry Fantoni had figured so prominently in earlier parts of the diary: 'Ray has written a song for Barry called "Little Man in a Little Box". The recording with Barry is fabulous.' I remembered that Barry Fantoni had not only been a tutor at R.D.'s art school, but he had also become a TV personality in his own right in the mid-sixties. In 1966 he was voted TV personality of the year by *Melody Maker*.

I hurriedly turned the pages to read more of the Kinks' success on the release of 'Dedicated Follower of Fashion', but something had obviously happened at the beginning of March.

'The boys have come back from Switzerland and Ray is ill. Influenza and nervous tension.

'Tuesday, 8 March. Doctor came. Ray ill. *NME* 14. *Melody Maker* 14. *Disk Magazine, Radio London* 15.

'Wednesday, 9 March. Ray ill today. Very unsteady on feet. Seems to have got flu. Kinks go to Belgium but Ray stays in bed.'

I made a note to find out more about this. Why was R.D. so ill? What was wrong with him? He had obviously not told me everything but had given me the diary so that I could come up with my own conclusions.

'Saturday, 12 March. Ray still in bed. Will not speak or shave.

Ray's mum keeps coming up every day and bringing food for him. 10 in *Melody Maker.*

'Tuesday, 15 March. Ray very ill. Doctor came to see him. Said needed extreme rest and quiet. Ray very depressed and very ill. Many pills – sedatives and sleeping pills. Psychiatrist came (Rasa black eye). Ray nearly had nervous breakdown. Family interfering very much. Fight with Rasa. Fight with Gwen. Gwen hit Ray while he was helpless in bed. Ray nose-bleed, extremely upset. Ray's mother came over and caused a terrible scene. He had terrible argument with them.

'Thursday, 17 March. Ray went to Robert's office, punched Brian Somerville in face. Doctor came.

'Friday, 18 March. Ray is much better today, well on the way to recovery. Went for drive with Robert in country. Going to buy a house in the country. "Dedicated Follower of Fashion" Number 1 on Radio London.'

It was obvious that I was reading about the beginning of the most stressful situation so far for Raymond Douglas the rock star, and the beginnings of his rift with his wife. During this time the diary recorded many visits from Barry Fantoni and an old school friend called Jimmy Marvel, who was clearly a source of great support. Then I noticed that during April, after Ray's apparent recovery, Rasa did not accompany him so often on concert engagements. And there were various comments about Ray not telephoning. One slightly humorous extract was after Dave had to go up north with Grenville to Bradford, to defend a paternity suit: '6 May, De Montfort Hall, Leicester. Good show, Dave returned after winning the case in Bradford. Apparently the *News of the World* was bitterly upset that it had lost a front-page story.

'Friday, 13 May. Louisa went to nursery for the first time today. Ray recording 10 a.m. till 3 p.m. Recording was really fantastic. "Fancy" – absolutely great. "In Summer Time" – "Sunny Afternoon" – the most fabulous thing I have ever heard. Ray writes the most fantastic songs and gets such great sounds, it's unbelievable. Afterwards, a gig at Kent University.'

It seems that Rasa and Ray's relationship was blowing hot and cold at this point. She had a genuine respect for his songwriting, but there was still that element in her that was a fan and resented any contact Ray may or may not have had with any member of the opposite sex. During the so-called 'fallow' patch in the Kinks' career after 'Till the End of the Day', Raymond Douglas had written a sad song about a lost love entitled 'See My Friends'. I wondered why, because according to R.D. he had everything he wanted at this time. Was it about him? Or was it about other people who were not getting everything they expected? Was it about retreating from normal life and exchanging one set of friends for companions of a darker, more sinister nature?

When I arrived at the studio the next morning I immediately asked R.D. about the song.

"See My Friends". Oh, that. It went back to the time when I was in India and stood on the beach in the early morning as the fishermen came with their nets, chanting. Imagine a whole life being like a song, you have the opening, which goes into a verse, then a middle period, you bring back the verse and the chorus, have another crack at the middle, try to start the verse again, then realize that it's all over, so you usually sing one or two choruses that everybody's heard before, then it either comes to an abrupt end or you just fade out – and you've got only three minutes to do all that. In the Western world you have the opportunity to modulate and transpose. Sometimes you even get the chance to change key, without giving any clues where you are going. Those poor bastards on the beach in India had one tune and one key and contained within that was their entire life. Perhaps they knew a short cut – why bother to change key, why bother to do a fucking record deal? I bet they didn't have a publisher who wrote down every time they chanted their tune, so he could register it with the PRS, and they sure didn't get any mechanical royalties. Perhaps those fishermen were in touch with something else, and music was a way of helping them through their lives on this planet. Maybe God collects all their publishing. A couple of years later I remembered those fishermen. Somebody at the *Daily Express*, I think it was Judith Simons again, suggested that it was the first outwardly homosexual song she had ever heard. (She had obviously never heard Noël Coward sing "A Room with a View".) I just kept singing "She is gone, she is gone, and now there's nobody left, except my friends, playing across the river". Heaven knows what I meant by that. I just believe that when you need comfort, when you are in despair, any arms are welcome. It doesn't matter what sex they belong to. People place so much emphasis on gender. Love is love. Companionship, friendship are what's important. The world's obsession with the rights and wrongs of the so-called "gay culture" culminated in that screwed-up, hateful society of the late 1990s. I know there seems a lot of despair in the song, but the recording was really fun. I had this beaten up old Framus twelve-string that I'd used to record "A Well-Respected Man", and I plugged it into an amplifier. I sat close to the amplifier so that the notes I picked would cause feedback in a high frequency while I was playing. I never changed the strings until they broke. Some of them were actually rusty. Bob Auger wasn't engineering and Shel Talmy didn't know how to deal with the sound, and so he told the engineer to throw a compressor over the whole track, the audio equivalent of ironing a shirt, it spreads everything out to its maximum flatness and in doing so squashes down the essence of the sound, so that there is no meat left. I heard the playback and said to Talmy, "How the fuck am I supposed to sing over that?"

'He smiled and said, "You gotta agree, it's different." It was as if he were offering me another challenge. That was the sign of a smart producer.

'I went back into the studio and remembered those fishermen and sang in a nasal chant. I didn't think it was a deliberate attempt to sound gay or affected in any way. I was actually trying to sound like Hank Williams. But the overall effect was that the performer was definitely affected in some way.'

R.D. got up from his chair. 'Fuck this, let's go to the pub.' As he reached the door he froze on the spot.

'I forgot. I'm barred from all the pubs around here.'

'What, a harmless old boy like you, barred?'

The words had barely come out when I realized that I had offended him. R.D. scowled and slowly shuffled around the room.

'It's not my age. It's not my temper. It's the fact that the Corporation owns everything around here, even the pubs. If I speak my mind it could mean trouble for others as well as myself.'

'You really think the Corporation is that powerful?'

R.D. shook his head. 'You've a lot to learn, my boy. Anyway, you can get me some more beer later from the off-licence. Let's get back to work.'

We both sat down again and I tried to remember the thrust of the conversation. But I had lost it. R.D. took over.

'I know what this is all leading to. You see, I was so overloaded with the litigation and pressure to write that I guess my mind decided to take a vacation.'

'A breakdown?'

R.D. thought about what he had just said. Then he shook his head from side to side.

'No, it was more like a showdown. I had been angry about a lot of things that were going on and I tried to put a stop to them. I thought that I had recovered sufficiently to continue work, but I discovered that I was forgetting people's names and walking into walls. I stayed at home and started drinking heavily, until I couldn't walk at all. I couldn't sleep at night, and during the day the sun made me feel tired and afraid. Rasa called the family doctor, who had taken over after Dr Aubrey had retired. Dr Studley was much younger, but the poor man had to make a quick assessment the moment the patient walked into his surgery, because there was simply no time to deal with everyone on the NHS. The overworked GP quickly gave me the obligatory once-over: chest, heart, balls. Then he prescribed Valium and sleeping pills and told me to go to bed.

By now, with six or seven hits under my belt, I was under creative siege. I was scrutinized daily by managers to see if, like a thoroughbred racehorse, I could complete the course, clear the next hurdle. A year or so earlier, Eddie Kassner had taken out a life insurance policy on me, so that in the event of my death his royalty flow would not be affected to any great extent. This, clearly, was standard business policy. Kassner had stood with my father in the backstage bar at Fairfield Hall, Croydon, during one of my concerts, and reassured my somewhat confused parent that he guaranteed Raymond wealth beyond his wildest imagination. Was this a reference to his offer of £40 a week for life? At the time my dad was really only half listening. The one thing that mattered to my dad at that moment was that the Guinness tasted good and the backstage bar at the Fairfield Hall let you run up a tab, which I sincerely hope that Dad made Eddie pick up.

Here I was, six or seven hits later, lying semi-conscious in bed, so confused by all my ideas for songs, and so baffled by all the litigation, that my overloaded brain was experiencing a total shutdown of business. The parts of my brain that dealt with my daily functions had taken to overwhelming fits of paranoia and, as it turned out, they were totally justified. As for the rest of my brain, the parts that dealt with dreams and the subconscious, it was like the small shopkeeper who had suddenly found himself expanding, and put up a sign which read, 'Moved to larger premises'. Everything was centred on jealousy, greed, resentment, misunderstanding and a total lack of trust in everything and everybody. I think that was the way that the messages were being interpreted inside my head, rather than the real actions happening in the outside world. But I had discovered a theory, 'When in doubt, trust your paranoia, it's probably the most accurate reading of the world.' Whatever they tell you otherwise.

With 'A Dedicated Follower of Fashion' such a hit, people
started coming up to me in the street and singing the chorus
in my face: 'Oh yes he is, he is, oh yes he is,' as if to say that I
knew who I was. Unfortunately, my inner and somewhat
distorted sense of reality told me that this was not who I wanted to
be: I didn't know who I was. I didn't care that everyone loved the
song or that it was being quoted on television and in the tabloids as
a comment on the times. I saw myself on *Top of the Pops* and tried
to throw the television out of the kitchen window. In the end, I
compromised with my concerned relatives and put the television
in the gas oven. The cord was still attached to the wall and
through the glass in the oven I was still performing. 'Oh yes he is,
oh yes he is.' After that I declared I was going to bed and woke up
a week later with a moustache and beard. The moustache
drooped and made me look like a Mexican peasant. I tried to go
for a quiet walk. 'They seek him here, they seek him there.' I went
back to all my schoolboy haunts – the playing fields, the
alleyways, the broken fences – and none of it seemed to have
changed. The only difference was me.

I rushed home and got straight on the telephone to my
publicist, who was already angry at me for not behaving like a
star and, most of all, like a man. I shouted down the telephone
that I had no intention of giving the press access to my sick
bed. This anger turned to total disgust when I announced that
I wanted to give up showbiz and return to being a schoolboy.
'Oh yes he is, oh yes he is.' Somerville ranted on about letting
the side down, unprofessional, uninteresting. I responded by
farting down the telephone in true schoolboy manner, then
hung up.

I rolled up all the money I had on me into a bundle and
stuffed it in my socks. I then proceeded to run all the way
from my house in East Finchley down to Somerville's office
in Denmark Street in the West End; a distance of about six
miles. Upon seeing me burst in, Somerville took cover behind
his desk. I threw a punch and missed. He ducked, and, in

doing so, accidently banged his rather large chin on a chair.
He made a frantic telephone call to the police, saying he had
been attacked by a madman and was under siege in his office.
What followed was a Keystone-cops-style chase around the
small alleyways surrounding Denmark Street. The police
would run past a doorway and I would emerge from the same
doorway and run off in the opposite direction. I ended up in
Eddie Kassner's office, which was just a few buildings away. I
must have been insane to go in there, but there was a part of
me that genuinely wanted to make peace – I didn't want to
hate anybody. When I was ran in and gave the receptionist a
kiss it was obvious to her that I was a little emotionally
unstable. But she immediately told her boss that I was there
and I was ushered in to the 'lion's den'. Kassner hugged me as
if I was the prodigal son returning. His accountant, David
Dane, brought me a cup of tea. I said I couldn't understand
why they were doing this to me. Kassner said that equally he
couldn't understand why I had left to join Freddie Beinstock's
company. David Dane said that surely I must have known
that by signing with Belinda Music, I would instantly be in
dispute with Kassner?

I can't remember much more. The receptionist, who as I
recall was a woman in her late thirties, arrived with some tea
and biscuits and promptly placed her bottom on my lap, to
soften me up. She was a motherly type, but still very attractive,
like a continental actress from the fifties: big chest under a
clingy sweater and a waist pulled in tight by a large leather belt.
A nice bit of old. Soon, before I got into a more compromising
situation, Robert arrived like a knight in shining armour.

He was accompanied by a doctor who wrote a medical
certificate which explained my eccentric behaviour to the
police. After they were satisfied by the doctor that I was
acting under extreme stress, they allowed me to return home,
provided I remained under the doctor's care.

The doctor dropped me off at my house, and explained to

my wife and manager that I should rest as much as possible and avoid all public engagements. He politely described my illness as 'nervous exhaustion caused by a physical breakdown', and recommended that I visit him at his clinic as soon as I was able. I took his prescription, said that I would rest and showed him the door with an equal amount of politeness. Dr Studley appeared shortly afterwards looking as harassed as ever. He read the note passed on to him by Robert's doctor and, after pausing for a brief moment, said that I should block out all the light in the afternoons and lie down in the dark room until early evening. I should stay out of bright daylight because it made me think too much. I was on 'mental overload', and if I did not heed his warnings and force myself to take a rest in this way, I would turn into a hopeless neurotic, and he wouldn't hesitate before putting me in a rest home.

The Kinks had gone on tour without me, with a replacement to sing my part. Everybody refers to that period as the time R.D. first broke down, when in fact it was just one of a series of 'mind overloads'. But this was the first time anybody else had been affected by it.

Later that week we had another meeting with Freddie Beinstock under the chandelier in his Savile Row office. Everybody could see that I was emotionally unbalanced, and they carried on as if I was not there. I was wearing a new brown hunting jacket made by Dege of Savile Row, and I was admiring its fine buttons on the cuffs when Grenville asked Freddie if there was any news on the suit. Why were they talking about somebody's wardrobe?

Freddie replied in his usual tone, which had a lilt to it as if he was about to tell a joke, 'Well, you know I spoke to Rubenstein and Nash.' I still thought he was talking about a suit, and that Messrs Rubenstein and Nash were his tailors. Freddie continued in his Swiss-Austrian-American accent: 'They say no news is good news, and the amount of money they are holding for Raymond is earning interest every day.'

It was only then I realized that they were talking about the status of the litigation – meaning law-suit. I looked over at the painting by Francis Bacon, a man trapped in a square cylinder which was transparent, as if he had deliberately done it to himself. It seemed possible that he could escape if he wanted to, but he preferred to remain a prisoner in a hell of his own making. I contemplated my situation and my own stupidity for being in this position. I was either a genuine fool or had deliberately put myself in a similar cage. Self-imposed torment. The meeting concluded and I was taken home by Robert. I was still not considered well enough to make my own way home.

Brian Somerville resigned as the Kinks' publicist immediately after my showdown with him. The official press release stated that it was a mutual parting; the truth was that the whole relationship had run out of steam. In any event, Somerville had found the Beatles a much more cooperative bunch of young men: keen to please, amiable and much more marketable than the Kinks. My dislike and distrust of the press was something he found repellent.

Somerville obviously took offence because I had taken issue with the way he was representing us. Before that unhappy time, I had looked upon Somerville as a slightly eccentric uncle who felt happier playing with the younger children at Christmas than he did mixing with adults. He always dressed in a very conservative, sombre manner, completely at odds with the way many publicity men dressed in that era of flamboyance and extravagance. Perhaps he would have enjoyed dressing up like all the other sixties dandies in flowered shirts and skin-tight trousers, but probably thought that it would have made him look ridiculous.

In fact, most of Somerville's exterior and behaviour were correct to the point of being drab, except for one notable occasion after the Kinks had played a concert at the Opera House in Blackpool. We had been supporting his former employers, the Beatles, and perhaps Brian was over-excited about being reunited with his old playmates and Brian Epstein, as well as being exhilarated by our own success at the concert. Most of the hotels and Bed and Breakfasts in Blackpool were full and, as a result, all the Kinks had to share one room. Somerville burst into our communal bedroom wearing spotted silk pyjamas and tried to provoke a pillow-fight. We were so used to seeing the lantern-jawed, balding publicist dressed in dowdy business suits that we were completely taken aback: he now resembled a tubby circus clown.

The only accusation I can level at Brian is that when on that regrettable day I rushed into his office full of anger, instead of acting like a man when I threw a punch at him he ducked to the floor and squeaked like a mouse. But perhaps he had seen that I was distraught, had taken pity on me and pretended to faint. Perhaps, like so many people who encountered the Kinks, he expected more from a group with such an outrageous name. Perhaps the Kinks were too dull for Brian Somerville.

Much as he would despise me for saying so, when he left I quite missed him.

After that incident, I stopped doing any interviews and saw very few people. In the music press they were saying that I had become a recluse and there were even rumours that I had left the group. But the break allowed me time to stay at home and write songs, some of which were therapeutic, others for the next Kinks album. The sunny days of early spring 1966 consisted of getting up, writing a song, playing with my daughter, lunch in the back garden, the afternoon resting in a dark room, then back in the sun, more song-writing and bed. Bliss. 'Oh yes it is, oh yes it is.'

'A Dedicated Follower of Fashion' was just beginning to move slowly down the hit parade when a delegation consisting of Robert, Grenville and, to give them emotional clout, my brother Dave all arrived on my doorstep. They said that unless we went into the studio and made another single and album, any impetus that the last single had given us would be lost. I said I had several ideas, but nothing as good as the last record, that I was not ready, both physically and mentally, and that I wanted to leave the group and become a painter. A week later I was in the studio recording tracks for the new album. I had a few ideas left over from the American tour the previous summer, songs like 'Holiday in Waikiki', 'House in the Country', 'Party Line', along with more recent ideas such as 'A Most Exclusive Residence for Sale', 'A Rainy Day in June' and a strange ballad called 'End of the Season'. All these songs seemed to be influenced by my current circumstances. Songs about a man who had become wealthy, and, after travelling the world for the first time, returned home to buy a house and settle down. It was a character that was outside my experience and background, but the only way I could interpret how I felt was through a dusty, fallen aristocrat who had come from old money, as opposed to the wealth which I had made for myself.

Robert and Grenville had become 'new' money in the sense that they had opted out of the establishment world of stockbroking and banking and found careers for themselves as managers of a successful pop group. They kept up the public-school image, and dressed in pin-striped suits. The fact that they managed us must have made them radical and anti-establishment in their own circles. And, like the character singing my songs, Robert had become an unrepentant money-waster. While I had bought a modest semi in N2, Robert had gone straight for the Rolls-Royce and maintained his Belgravia life-style. Perhaps each person has his own idea of what success will buy, according to his background, but Robert was not unlike my brother Dave in the sense that they were going to blow the lot on cars, booze and babes. And why not? They were flush

During my 'recovery', I listened to a lot of old Frank

Sinatra records sent to me by Reprise. I had also bought a
book on arranging by Glen Miller, and I had started writing a
song on my recently acquired upright piano. I called it 'The
Tax Man's Taken All My Dough'. It was meant to be a
topical song about the new taxes the Labour Government was
bringing in to relieve the wealthy of all their hard-earned
cash. Again, it was my imaginary character singing through
me, just as he was in all my other new songs. As this was my
first year of being a success, I could sympathize with the sad,
decadent character I had invented. I was brought up believing
that all Conservatives were cruel slave-drivers who took
advantage of the poor and cared little for the unfortunates on
whom their whole financial empire had been built. Here was
I, newly rich (on paper), singing about the woes of having
money taken away from me by a Labour Government. To
take the curse off of this aspect of what was otherwise a good
song, I turned the narrator into a scoundrel who fought with
his girlfriend after a night of drunkenness and cruelty. I also
kept repeating 'in the summertime' over the chorus, to make
the song more seasonal. By the time it came to make the
record, I was back doing dates with the group, and for the
time being my 'retirement' plans had been scrapped.

We recorded 'Sunny Afternoon' on Friday, 13 May 1966.
The four Kinks plus Nicky Hopkins on piano put a back track
down in three or four takes, and I sang the lead vocal in one
pass. I had bad hayfever and could not have managed to sing
it twice. We had just finished putting on the back-up vocals
when I noticed that Pete, our bass-player, had played some
wrong notes in the last few bars. I wanted to record the track
again, because we had no way of separating the bass from the
rest of the instruments. The whole group looked shocked as I
suggested this to Shel Talmy. He refused point blank.

'Nobody will notice, its just a fluff on the bass.'

I pointed out to Shel that my voice sounded wobbly, but
Shel was in no mood for an argument. I reluctantly let him

get on with the last overdub on the record, which was a melodica solo by Nicky Hopkins. This gave the track a 'good-time', music-hall feel, and I soon forgot about the mistake on the bass.

The record had taken three hours to make and a decision was made by the record company later that day to bring out the single by the second week in June, to take advantage of the hot summer which was forecast.

Just prior to the release of 'Sunny Afternoon' we secured the services of Alan McDougal as publicist. McDougal was a short, jovial Scotsman with a broad Glaswegian accent, and his Dickensian Soho office combined with his laid-back attitude were a complete contrast to the public-school air of Brian Somerville. Alan arranged for me to give the *Melody Maker* an exclusive interview, where they would be the first to review the record.

As I played the white-label acetate to Bob Dawbarn, I saw a smile come over his face as the jazz-like intro started. Dawbarn was himself a trombone player, and as a musician and journalist he had watched the traditional jazz boom of the early sixties get pushed aside by Beat music. In those days the whole staff of *Melody Maker* was primarily jazz-oriented, as was most of the music press. Dawbarn commented on the sweet acoustic sound and said that the drum playing actually had dynamics in it. McDougal seized upon the opportunity. 'That's because Avory was a jazz player himself, and knows all about dynamics, so let's all have three cheers for Mick Avory'.

Bob Dawbarn was totally enthusiastic about 'Sunny Afternoon'. The other reviews, however, were less than complimentary, saying the record was sluggish and dreary. It didn't bother any of us because we knew we had a hit. I gambled on it being a very hot summer, and the longer the sun stayed out, the more records we would sell.

I went back to McDougal's office. Alan was speaking

eagerly about the great press we would get from the record
and said that one of his associates, Frank Smythe, was anxious
to work with me. As I looked down into Old Compton
Street I saw what I thought was a down-and-out tramp lying
in the gutter. I called McDougal over to the window and was
just about to comment on the tragic plight of the alcoholics
and the homeless in London when the keen Scotsman informed
me that the man trying to crawl on to the kerb was none
other than Frank Smythe.

'Ah, the poor laddie must have stumbled on his way to
DeHems Bar.'

We went and helped Smythe up to the office, where he
seemed to sober instantly. Frank was a born-and-bred
Yorkshireman, who had been an accomplished skiffle singer in
his college days. A poet and writer, with a huge, robust
physique and features that could have allowed him to be
mistaken for Oliver Reed – depending on how many drinks
the onlooker had consumed, and how smoky and dark the
drinking club was. Frank Smythe took me under his wing,
which meant a tour of most of the pubs in Soho, where he
introduced me to everybody from Dominic Behan, who
immediately boasted of his brother, Brendan, the great but by
now deceased Irish playwright, and of a mysterious and
hitherto unknown sister called Les, who was a dyke. Francis
Bacon's ravaged face loomed up in a drinking club, as did a
large-breasted woman called 'Mighty Margaret', who as well
as being a last-minute carnal watering hole for Smythe at the
end of a long piss-up, was a screenwriter. When the pubs
closed, Frank knew all the right drinking clubs. It was a
superb but somewhat protracted binge and, although it resulted
in a fearsome headache the following morning, it rekindled
the memories of art college – all that might have been, all I
could have been, all the pictures never painted.

Anyway, I don't want to talk about this any more. Let's
have a look at the diary. Let's see . . . 'Friday, 3 June. "Sunny

Afternoon" was released. The Central Pier Ballroom in
Morecambe. A good show.'

Good show? Why did Rasa write that? She wasn't even
there! What does she mean, Good show?

That was the night Quaife's life started to shift away from
the group. All because of a girl he wanted to chat up after the
show. We got into the van and shouted at Pete to bring the
girl with him. We were driving back to Manchester to this
old Bed and Breakfast that we knew. It had a reputation as a
raver's paradise, and the owner allowed us to take in as many
girls as we wanted. Before that we had been in numerous
rows with various hotels up and down the country, and were
bored with using fire escapes to avoid the hotel night-porters.
The B and B, on the outskirts of Manchester, was a private
boarding house run by a raunchy widow who must have been
in her late forties. I remember her always being somewhat
scantily clad, in a see-through dressing-gown under which
were equally revealing undies. She must have been a trim craft
in her day, and although there were lumps where there
shouldn't have been on her body, and her legs displayed a few
broken blood vessels at the back, her breasts were delightfully
plump and bounced around freely above her paunch. In the
sitting room there was a television in one corner and a cheap
formica-covered cocktail cabinet in the other. The bar was
never closed, and if the occasion had arisen where there was
no girl to hand, I am convinced that this delightful lady of the
house would have willingly offered her services. I bet she
would have been a wonderful bang, at that.

Anyway, Pete stayed behind to wait for that stupid girl.
What a dope. He probably only did a bit of french kissing
followed by some minor sleaze at the end of the pier. He said
he would drive back with Jonah in the equipment truck.
When I woke up the next morning I looked out the window
and saw that the loading truck was not in the yard as expected.
I ordered some breakfast, which was personally delivered by

the titty madame, still dressed in her naughty nightie in case one of us got the urge for a late morning grope with Grandma. Then I went downstairs to the lounge. I turned on the television to watch *Grandstand*, a midday sports programme, and on came a brief news report to announce that one of the Kinks pop group had been badly injured in a crash. Jonah had skidded on the road on the way back from Morecambe, and both he and Quaife had ended up in hospital. We were due to play the Imperial Ballroom in Nelson that night, but of course the show was cancelled, as was the following night's show in Glasgow. The next day we managed to tape the television show *Thank Your Lucky Stars* without Pete. It was all mimed in those days, so it didn't really matter that he wasn't there.

The following Monday we were even in the studio without Pete. Robert and Grenville decided to book in a session bass player. Amazingly, from six p.m. to midnight we recorded six backing-tracks: 'Rainy Day in June', 'Rosie Won't You Please Come Home', 'You're Looking Fine', 'Too Much on My Mind', 'Fallen Idol' and, somewhat appropriately, 'Session Man'. Boy, we could really bang them out in those days. The following day, Tuesday, 7 June, the concert at Malvern was cancelled, but 'Sunny Afternoon' went into the charts at Number 22, four days after its release. Amazingly, the following Saturday, just seven days after Pete's accident, the Kinks doubled at two venues in Birmingham. How did we manage to get a bass player so quickly?

We were rehearsing in the demo room at 17 Savile Row, and I was doing a record review for the *NME* at the same time. I was also drunk, which didn't help. Keith Altham, a journalist from the EN-EM-Y, played me a record, and I made a remark about it which he would later turn into something readable. There was one record in particular by somebody I admired, a wonderfully eccentric American by the name of Kim Fowley. It was a cover version of one of my songs called 'Don't You Fret', but I was so pissed and still so angry about

Pete's accident that I took the record off and threw it out the window. At that precise moment Bill Fowler, a Carlin employee, brought a candidate to stand in for Pete. He introduced himself as John Dalton, but Dave shouted out that he looked like a fat version of Paul McCartney. Mick agreed, 'It's Pull My Cock Off!' Dave threw a bass guitar at Dalton and as I swigged back the rest of my Newcastle Brown I asked the chubby McCartney look-alike to play the scale of D minor. He willingly obliged, and the next day the unknown Beatle double was seen playing the D minor introduction of 'Sunny Afternoon' on *Top of the Pops*. Before the accident Quaife had been experimenting with a new bass guitar because he had seen John Entwistle of the Who using one on TV. Dalton inherited this instrument. I still had not heard Dalton actually play, but he convinced us that he knew all the Kinks' hits. He had been in other groups – the Creation and Mark Four – and came highly recommended by Fowler. Two days later we were to play a double header in Birmingham. Two sets of twenty-five minutes at clubs owned by a promotor called Mrs Reagan. A rehearsal was considered to be unnecessary. It wasn't until we got on stage and heard this appalling banjo-like sound coming from the bass that we realized how much trouble we were in, and how important each member's playing is to the sound of the group. Although John could play, he had his own style – and also was not familiar with Pete's equipment. It was fortunate that the sold-out shows comprised of screaming girls. Thankfully that covered up the appalling din coming from the stage.

Rasa may have written in the diary that it was not a bad show apart from faulty equipment, but I can assure you it was awful. We didn't have any choice, we had to go on playing. The following day we had to fly to Spain with a bass player we hadn't even had a rehearsal with. Our equipment boy, Jonah, was still in hospital and had been replaced by Stan Whitley, a friend of Pete's from the Coldfall Estate. I had seen

Stan at other gigs but I had never spoken to him. His brother
did occasional work as a minder for Robert and Grenville
from time to time and, like his brother, Stan gave the
impression that he was a bit of a heavy, but underneath the
hard-nut image he was a lovable softie. As we checked in at
the airport, we saw Stan dressed in his immaculately-tailored
wide-boy suit, complete with tie-pin, silk shirt and perfectly
groomed hair, ready to be a suave minder, not aware that he
had been hired simply as a band boy, to set up our stage
equipment. Robert accompanied us on this trip, and the
thought of putting the unfortunate Stan through this
humiliation probably amused him. My next sight of Stan was
of him crawling around on all fours behind a row of amplifiers
trying to set up the equipment. By this time he had taken off
his jacket to reveal his Sunday-best braces, arm-clips, cuff-
links, still with a perfectly knotted tie held down with the tie-
pin. His face, however, was a study in frustration. The most
experience he'd probably had as an electrician was changing a
light bulb. The prospect of joining cables and wires to
amplifiers was overwhelming. Eyes wide with panic, his silk
shirt so wet with sweat that it was sticking to him. The poor
bugger had no idea he had to change the voltage to the
continental standard, and so when he finally did set up the
equipment it exploded when he turned it on. This humiliation
was added to by the indignity of his trousers splitting at the
back, exposing his underpants. He was also surrounded by
annoyed Spaniards gesticulating vehemently and pointing to
their watches: we were late going on. We stood at the side of
the stage and watched as Stan tried to explain to them that he
needed help. With frustration written all over his red, sweating
face, he stormed across the stage towards me. Up until now I
had still not found it necessary to speak to Stan or he to me,
but his first utterance was one I will always treasure. In a
perfect north London cockney accent Stan uttered the
immortal words: 'Some fucker help me before I chin some

cunt!' He then fell to his knees and collapsed on the floor, his hands held up as if in prayer.

This tragic sight aside, it was obvious that there was a certain amount of disharmony between Robert and the Spanish promoter who was a small-time club owner. Somehow we managed to play a few songs and, although the fans enjoyed what little we performed, the owners of the club were far from satisfied. Before the police had arrived on the scene, however, there had been real threats of violence: both Dalton and Robert Wace had been threatened with a flick-knife. Stan Whitley had by now recovered from his earlier humiliation, and the sight had immediately drawn on his instincts as a minder. He was ready for 'bovver'. He stood rigidly, legs astride, arms outstretched, between Dalton and his aggressor. Then he uttered his second great line of the trip: 'So you want some, do you, you Spanish git? Let's have a go, then, I don't give a monkey's.' Before anything could happen the Spanish police arrived, and soon were seen dragging John Dalton away with them. The devious promoter had accused him of being a Peter Quaife impostor, and that he was not a member of the original Kinks. The promoter was not only refusing to pay us, but he had confiscated our equipment as compensation. As the equipment included the bass guitar which sounded like a banjo, it was generally considered that he had done us a favour.

Morning came and we found ourselves confronted by a Spanish solicitor, who told us that Dalton had been retrieved from the police station along with our equipment – which unfortunately still included the dreaded bass guitar. Robert decided to fly Sam Levy out to join us because, in Robert's opinion, Sam had some experience of touring on the continent, and it was obvious that his powers of persuasion would be subtler than those of the unfortunate Stan, who, only three days before, had been happily contemplating a future as a long-distance lorry driver on the M1. No

Kinks. No Spaniards. And, most of all, no amplifiers. Instead
he had found himself suddenly thrown into a war
zone.

It was also clear to me that Robert couldn't cope either.
Robert had been educated well enough to have a decent
smattering of French and German, but on a previous trip to
Paris when Grenville had been confronted by a French customs
inspector, he admitted being able to understand French, but
refused to speak it on the grounds that President de Gaulle had
refused to speak English. In other words, for Robert and
Grenville foreigners did not count for much. It is fortunate
indeed that these two aristocratic and well-educated men had
decided to manage a pop group and not enter the diplomatic
corps.

It was customary for Sam, on arriving in a new city, to
head straight for the hotel restaurant. There we found him
demolishing a steak and an entire bottle of wine. He had
brought over the English newspapers which had the latest
chart positions, and we were all excited to see that we were
Number 8. The BBC had shown our video clip of *Top of the
Pops*, which had helped to carry 'Sunny Afternoon' higher up
the charts.

Somehow we recovered our equipment from the club and
we left Madrid no richer for our endeavours, to fly to Norway.
Stan Whitley was also a nervous flyer, and his endurance was
stretched to the limit when our plane burst a tyre as we
landed. After playing a concert somewhere at the top of
Norway, literally in the midnight sun, we flew to the seaport
of Bergen for another concert. This was, incredibly, less than
two weeks after the release of 'Sunny Afternoon' and Pete's
accident.'

Raymond Douglas stopped talking. He held out his old but still
slender hands, and as he bowed his head, I could see that the crown
of his tightly cropped white hair displayed a slight bald patch.

Even so, he was still a handsome old boy. He muttered something like, 'Some faces you never forget.' I asked who he was referring to, but he carried on talking to himself as if he had not heard what I had said.

'She saw me off at the airport in Bergen. She was Norwegian, with short, thick red hair. I didn't even know her name. Everything around me was happening in such an exciting way, and I was successful again. And yet, as the girl with no name took me by the hand and told me not to go, I would have willingly given everything up to stay with her in that beautiful place where the sun stays out at midnight and the people talk backwards.'

For a moment I thought that R.D. had flipped his lid. I thought that maybe I had been driving him too hard and it was all too much for him to take, but by now my journalistic instincts were beginning to get the better of me, and I decided to take advantage of this old man who had momentarily lapsed into a senile memory warp.

'Was she *the* girl who affected you so much?' I asked, stupidly.

Raymond Douglas slowly looked up and glared at me.

'I should tell you to fuck off. But I won't. I'll just be more careful from now on. That's if you promise not to act like a little prat. Don't take me for a fool, kid, and I won't treat you like an asshole.'

I didn't find his reaction difficult to understand, but I was supposed to be in the presence of a rock poet, only to discover his language was, to say the least, blunt. At times he would speak so eloquently, only to snap and in an instant revert to the language of the gutter. Still, he was old and had been through a lot. I apologized and we moved along.

Raymond Douglas picked up the diary again and slowly browsed through the pages.

When I had looked at the diary the night before it was becoming clear that two people were writing their own versions of what was happening.

For Tuesday, 21 June, Rasa had written, 'My birthday'; Raymond Douglas had written that he was playing in Oxford. He had made no mention of his birthday. I mentioned this to Raymond Douglas who still looked bewildered.

'It's like she was living part of my life for me. I guess that's what people do when they get married, they live for each other.'

It struck me as weird that Rasa seemed to be living her life through Raymond Douglas' work. That's fine if you're a fan, but she was supposed to be his wife. But it was clearly Raymond Douglas' handwriting that announced boldly that 'Sunny Afternoon' had reached Number 1 on Monday, 4 July. Rasa, on the other hand, simply noted that she had gastric flu.

I held out the diary and showed Raymond Douglas the date. He smiled and seemed to perk up.

'Boy, I was happy, wasn't I? I didn't realize how wonderful life was. Do you know we were Number 1 just before England won the World Cup? It all looks wonderful in a diary. Rasa wrote that "Reimukas" had gone on a business trip. Reimukas? That's Lithuanian for Ray, I guess. What Rasa didn't know was that Reimukas had been to New York to meet with Alan Klein.' Raymond Douglas stopped to reflect.

'Was I really doing all this? I was so busy that perhaps I was driving myself on deliberately so I wouldn't know what was happening to me. I had recovered from the awful period where I'd been overloaded and couldn't function, but I remember sitting with Grenville and looking at the hit parade with "Sunny Afternoon" at Number 1 asking him why we didn't have any money. The basic reality was that we were signed to Pye Records at a criminally low royalty. And the law-suit between Boscobel Productions and Denmark Productions meant that all my song-writing royalties were still frozen. Grenville raised his eyebrow in a theatrical way and after pausing for a moment, spoke quietly, and his voice took on a dramatic edge, as if from a mystery play:

'"I know a man who knows another man, and together they can do something about this situation."'

At this juncture R.D. shuffled around in his chair uncomfortably.

'Another man. What other man? A few days later I found myself on a flight to New York to meet with Alan Klein. Then I was thrown back into the same old system that I had tried to escape. The lawyers get you, then the system, then the establishment has you back.'

At this point, Raymond Douglas became silent. Perhaps the recollection of this period of his life was making that dark cloud come back. I let the poor old fellow rest and left the room on the pretext that I was going to make yet another cup of tea.

I empathized with Raymond Douglas' plight. In my own humble way I had experienced the same difficulties, even if on a much smaller scale. The establishment was still running the country, the same as when he was a young man, and I was confronted by the same ultimatum: conform or fail. I had watched my own youthful optimism become dominated by the ruling classes. Perhaps that's why the music of Raymond Douglas was beginning to mean so much to me.

My mind wandered. I started to think about Julie at my office. When would I see her next? I wished I had known my parents. What sort of story would I be able to tell if I were ever in R.D.'s position? He had lived inside his work as a shelter from the world which had closed him out. It was odd, but I felt no generation gap with him. I enjoyed hearing all his pop anecdotes, but what really interested me was when he talked about his family – a family that I wish I could have known myself.

I re-entered the room quietly and sat down in my usual chair. R.D. just sat and stared at me, almost looking through me. I was beginning to think I should make my way to the door when the strangest thing happened. He stood up and walked straight into the light. He was smiling a compassionate smile. I saw his eyes for the first time. They were watering and seemed full of emotion.

'Why is it that I get the distinct impression that you understand what I'm saying, even though we are generations apart? I'll tell you why. I have this theory, I call it Navajo logic. My grand-mother, Kate Wilmore, looked like an old Navajo squaw. She was a large woman with enormous eyes that seemed to penetrate right through to your deepest thoughts. 'Big Granny' had so many grandchildren that she often mixed up their names, but she always took time to listen to the most trivial questions. She sat in a large chair in the corner of the room like a great dowager, and held court over the rest of the family in true matriarchal tradition. Meeting Big Granny was like going to confession, and that's exactly what I did when I was in her presence. I could swing a pretty decent lie on both of my parents, and if that wasn't convincing enough, I relied on emotional blackmail, but not with Big Granny. She eventually lived to be ninety-eight, alert and intelligent right up to the day she died.

'She had been born in another century, in the reign of Queen Victoria, grown up at the tail end of the Industrial Revolution, in the days when children went out to work in the factories. In her youth, women were expected to have babies; when one baby had been born, to get pregnant again until the husband either lost interest or, as in Big Granny's case, he dropped dead. Her family was large, probably about fifteen children, and even though she left school before any kind of education could take effect, she had an intuitive streak that enabled her to comprehend spiritual values and convey images more effectively than any textbook in a library. It was like she had a knowledge of an inner world that remained dark to most people. When Big Granny was around, a light shone inside you and exposed your darkest secrets. She had tremendous intuitive powers and, like the Navajo Indians, she thought that the problems of man were quite insignificant in nature's great scheme. When she sang old Victorian lullabies, the sound in her voice was so truthful that she took you back in time before there were radios and gramophones. When she sang, children listened attentively and somehow sensed through her spirituality some emotions that defy time. That's the logic. There's no trick to it. All you have to do is relax and feel your history, because it will never go away and there is no future without it. Let me play you some of my past. Some of my Navajo logic.'

R.D. had me completely baffled. Maybe the old man had finally gone off his rocker. Why was he telling me his theories about senses and memory, and why suddenly had he decided to take pity on me?

He put a new tape into the cassette deck. As it began to play those friendly plodding bass notes at the opening of 'Sunny Afternoon', I glanced down at another entry in the diary: 'The taxman's taken all my dough and left me in my stately home.' As I read the words, they ran simultaneously together with the lyrics on the tape. My head nodded up and down to the rhythm. I imagined my own parents and wondered whether this would have been their favourite song. It probably took them back to the summers of their youth. Sandy beaches full of families having picnics by the sea. Snapshots of people sitting in deckchairs squinting their eyes at the camera to avoid the sun. I imagined when 'Sunny Afternoon' was Number 1 in the charts in June 1966. Everybody must have related to its slow-motion world of black-and-white nostalgia in their own personal way. The song sounded blissfully sentimental, in stark contrast to the forlorn reality of my own life. I was sitting in this dark unreality, listening to the sunny truth on the tape. Was I listening to the sound of a bright smiling exterior covering up a black centre? I looked down at the pages in R.D.'s diary. The words he had written there soon told me all I needed to know.

Powerman 16

'Alan Klein, an accountant, and Marty Machat, his attorney, were already well known for their abilities to extricate artists from 'unsatisfactory contractual arrangements'. Accompanying us on the flight to New York to meet them were Robert Ransom, our accountant, and Peter Grant, the overweight concert promoter from north London who was acting as the 'facilitator' and Robert and Grenville's contact man to Klein. 'The man who knew a man.' Grant, who would later earn a reputation for himself as creator and manager of the band Led Zeppelin, was so big that he could barely fit in the economy seat of the DC 10.

We were picked up from the airport by a limousine, much to Grenville's delight, and deposited at the Edison Hotel, which was not greeted with the same enthusiasm by my managers and accountant. The Edison was at the time considered to be a hang-out for hookers and low-life businessmen. My only concern was that the television in my room worked, so I could watch *Captain Kangaroo* and the *Today* show, which I had become addicted to on my previous trips, but Grenville protested bitterly on the telephone to Klein's office about the 'squalid' quarters at the Edison. In my opinion it was palatial compared to some of the hotels we had stayed in. Half an hour later the limousine arrived again and this time deposited us at the more fashionable Warwick Hotel, where the hookers and low-life businessmen restricted their hanging-out to the hotel bar. Mick and Dave were also there, but only as what politicians call, 'official observers'.

Klein had been 're-negotiating' the Rolling Stones' contract with Decca Records, and there was a rumour that he had them sailing around Manhattan Island on a yacht while he closed the deal. That way nobody but Klein could get to them. Perfect tactics orchestrated by a couple of real professionals. Machat and Klein were the ideal combination of calm, calculating assessment full of business acumen and the pit-bull-terrier killer instinct needed to deal in a cut-throat industry. Machat went in as the quiet counsellor, while Alan interjected sharp bursts of aggressive outrage. Unsuspecting record executives were at times rendered defenceless in their presence. At first sight Avory said they looked like the comedy duo of Abbott and Costello. Machat, the taller, had a cigar-smoking intellectual image, apart from an occasional air of shiftiness, probably developed as a result of hanging around unscrupulous businessmen. Klein, a short, stocky, former accountant who had probably worked for too many so-called respectable businessmen, seemed to have decided that the only way to knock down the barrier of respectability was to steam-roller his way through. Alan Klein talked as if his jaw was continually clenched; his eyes wide open.

'What do you want?' he snapped at me.

'I want my money and a better record deal. What do you want?' I replied.

Klein didn't hesitate: 'The Beatles, of course. Who doesn't?'

After introducing themselves to the rest of my entourage, ending with Robert Ransom, Klein sniggered as if he had weighed up the whole situation in an instant: 'Ransom. Great name for an accountant.'

'I think that's what this case is all about, don't you, Alan?' Machat said, as he puffed on his cigar.

Alan sat himself down in a swivel chair behind an oversized desk that had the effect of making him look even smaller. Machat cruised the room slowly, pausing occasionally to make a legal point, while Klein dictated the conversation.

'You got talent?' he shouted across to me. I remained silent.

300

'Oh, come on, let's cut this phoney humble act. You got frigging talent, or what? Of course you've got frigging talent. So much so that you're making Reprise Records and Louis Benjamin at Pye a goddam fortune.' The room remained silent.

Grenville raised an eyebrow as he crossed his legs, took a swift but nervous puff of his cigarette and pronounced in his best, over-exaggerated English accent, 'That's why we're here, Alan. To put the situation right.'

A piece of ash fell on Grenville's perfectly tailored suit, betraying his inner nervousness. Klein sat back in his chair, clenched his teeth, waved his head from side to side as if thinking out loud, and looked up at the ceiling.

'Wrong, right, right, wrong.' He remained in this position while Machat ran through the legal issues involved and compared them to other cases that he had dealt with.

At the end of Machat's knowledgeable, if drawn out, assessment, Klein shouted, 'To hell with it, I'll get you your money. Do you know how?' The room remained silent as he picked up some legal papers relating to the Kinks.

'Infancy,' Marty muttered under his breath.

Alan's eyes opened so wide with rage and his teeth were so clenched so tight it looked as if he was about to have a fit. 'Too fucking right, infancy!' he shouted.

Ransom coughed, as if to try and interject some decorum into the proceedings.

Klein ranted on: 'Did you get advice from a lawyer – sorry, solicitor – when you signed this contract? Doesn't matter! Do you know your first record came out on two labels in America? I think I owned one of them!' Klein laughed.

Machat had circled the room and now positioned himself behind Klein. He picked up the conversation where Klein left off.

'We'll have to start this with an injunction. It seems to me that Pye did not have your best interest in mind when they signed you to Reprise Records. I doubt if you were even

consulted. I'll call Mike Maitland at Warners and tell him he
no longer has the Kinks. That'll start the ball rolling.'

Grenville raised his eyebrow and pouted his lips. Robert
guffawed in a schoolboyish manner, exposing his capped front
teeth. Klein sat back and contemplated the outcome. Now his
voice was more restrained, but it still retained its New York
gruffness.

'And then Maitland will get pissed at Pye. We'll say to
Benjamin he doesn't have a deal.'

'The Donovan case,' Marty whispered confidently.

'Exactly. We'll use the same tactics as we did on the
Donovan case. Then we'll re-sign with the same labels for a
better deal. They'll still have their act. The band will be on a
better royalty and Mr Humble here will have his money.'

Klein laughed as he finished the speech. Grenville and
Robert enthused. Ransom breathed a sigh of relief at the
apparent simplicity of it all.

'And Kassner?' inquired Grenville.

'I think his case is in the toilet,' shrugged Klein.

Ransom looked distinctly uncomfortable and checked to see
if his briefcase was beside him.

Machat began to expound with finesse, like a man speaking
at the pinnacle of his knowledge. 'It's a simple matter. Kassner
assumes he has a long-term relationship with Raymond when
all he has, in fact, is a song-by-song assignment. At the very
most he can only lay claim to the copyrights already assigned,
which he will either lose, or pay the writer a good royalty.'

Grenville sighed and stubbed out his cigarette. 'We'll get
the copyrights back.'

For the first time Klein acknowledged somebody other than
Machat. 'Goddam right. We'll take it all back. Kassner will go
apeshit.'

I asked Klein what I should do in the meantime. Klein leaned
over his desk in a very slow way, to make sure it sank in: 'Go . . .
home. Write songs. Play your concerts and we'll take care of it.'

Klein flicked through some other papers on his desk. 'And this other business with the immigration people? Marty here deals with this sort of thing all the time. Mr Ransom can go back to his office and look after his accounts.' He suddenly became serious. 'I will succeed because I believe that all men are born evil. That is how I stay in business and that is why we will win. So don't worry.' That night we felt so relieved that we met up with Mort Shuman, then went out and got plastered.

When we returned to England I told Rasa that the business trip had gone well. Then the next day the Kinks flew to Majorca to do a concert in a bull ring. The dressing-rooms were improvised in the pens where the bulls were usually kept before they went in to be slaughtered by the matadors. When I was a child my father told me that in the Second World War he had killed a bull for food and, after disembowelling it, he cut the poor creature into pieces and hung up its parts to dry in the sun. My father said that he kept the knives as a memento. In the bull pen in Majorca there was the same smell of death that I had imagined as a terrified child. Of all the tales my father had told me – swimming the Irish Sea as a teenager to impress a pretty Welsh girl; capturing single-handed the crew of a German bomber which had crashed in Kent; playing the banjo in the music-halls, or soccer for the Arsenal reserves – of all the yarns my father had spun, the story of the knives was the one that had stayed with me.

As I walked into the arena to do the concert, I imagined for a moment that I was a grand matador, entering to the applause of an adoring crowd. Then I thought back to the meeting in New York a few days earlier and quickly assumed the role of a bull going to its ritual slaughter at the hands of the matador.

The next day we flew to Scotland to do a concert. 'Sunny Afternoon' knocked 'Paperback Writer' off the Number 1 spot after it had been there for just one week. Nobody had ever killed a Beatles record off that quickly before. And, despite all the negativity in the business side of our lives, the group was once more achieving chart success. When I returned to England the world soccer cup was in progress and England were favourites to win – and on English soil. It was as though crowds were cheering the length and breadth of the country. Meanwhile in the Boscobel–Denmark case, statements were being read and writs were being prepared as the law began to take its course.

The one thing that set John Dalton apart from Quaife was that he was, like Dave and myself, a soccer fanatic, and we took every opportunity to follow the progress of the English side. While I had been in the States meeting Klein and Machat, England had drawn 0–0 with Uruguay, then had beaten Argentina and progressed to the semi-finals. 'Sunny Afternoon' was still in the English charts and we all somehow felt that we were on a winning streak. This included the England soccer team. The day England played Germany in the final, the Kinks were due to appear at an open-air festival in Exeter, but at three o'clock on that famous Saturday afternoon, we were all assembled around the television in my living room, and we were not going to leave until we knew the result. We had just started to get in the car as England were leading 2–1, when Jackie Charlton gave away a free-kick just outside the English penalty area. John Dalton, or Nobby as he had been renamed by Avory, dragged us back into the living room as Germany equalized. This meant extra-time: another half an hour. In those days before the motorway, it was impossible to get to Exeter in three hours, and we would not be on stage at the scheduled time if we didn't leave right away. But we were determined not to go until the final whistle. By now Stan Whitley had been promoted to driver, as his performance as equipment-boy in Spain had meant either instant dismissal or job relocation. In the tradition of Brian Longstaff and

Hal Carter, Stan made us laugh, and so he didn't get the sack. But the thought of another half-hour delay made him pace nervously up and down the shingle drive outside of my semi, like a father-to-be waiting for his wife to give birth. History tells us that Geoff Hurst scored two goals for England, but even when the BBC commentator Kenneth Wolstenholme uttered the immortal words as Hurst ran and scored in the final seconds: 'Some people are on the pitch . . . they think it's all over. . . It is now!' The Kinks insisted on staying to watch the victory parade, and cheered the other Nobby, whose last name was Stiles, as he danced around the pitch at Wembley with the World Cup balanced on his head. I looked over at our Nobby. He had tears in his eyes. Patriotism had never been so strong. We were all war babies, we had all seen Hungary beat England 6–3 at Wembley when we were at primary school. In the early sixties we had heard Harold Macmillan say to the country, 'You've never had it so good', while I watched my father walk to the Employment Exchange. On the soccer pitch Bobby Charlton buried his head in his hands as he fell to his knees and wept on the English turf. In an emotional moment I felt like millions of others watching on television: I wanted to be next to him to help him to his feet. England had won the World Cup and the Kinks were Number 1 in the charts. I wished that I had a machine-gun, so that I could kill us all and everything would stop there – but we had to get to Exeter for the concert.

The faster we tried to drive, the longer it took. The more Stan panicked, the more wrong turnings he went down. Stan was born and bred in north London, and it was clear that he should never have been allowed to venture beyond the bounds of N10. The M1 motorway which had recently been completed was simple to negotiate: all Stan had to do was point the car in the direction of north and in a matter of hours we would be in Birmingham. Exeter, on the other hand, was to the west, through an assortment of antiquated A and B

roads, that were completely beyond Stan's capabilities as
expedition leader. The situation was not helped by the streets
being full of jubilant soccer fans. It took us nearly two
hours to get past Wembley itself. When we eventually arrived
in Exeter, five and a half hours later, the large crowd which
had assembled to see us play was about to go home. We
rushed out of the car and grabbed our instruments, leaving
Stan sitting in the driver's seat, an emotional wreck.

Some of the crowd was booing and as we went on stage the
promoter tried to stop us performing, in order that he could
sue us for breach of contract after not turning up on time
but I pointed out to him that as long as we played before
midnight we would not break our agreement. I think we
actually went on stage at 11.45, much to the annoyance of the
promoter's staff. We completed as much as we could of our
set before the promoter, who by now was more conciliatory
towards us but looked like a man ruined, with dark rings
around his unblinking eyes, walked from the side of the stage
with the mains plug connecting the electricity to our amplifiers
in his hand. For a moment I thought he was going to commit
suicide in front of us all. He stood in front of me and said,
'I'm sorry, lads, I've got to do it. It's a curfew, they'll never
let me promote again. Forgive me.' As he uttered the final
words he pulled the plug out of its socket. There was a little
puff of smoke before the lights went out. This came as a relief
to us all, as even though the audience had stayed to get their
money's worth, they had taken pleasure in throwing empty
beer bottles at us during the performance. 'Fuck off!' Dave
shouted from the stage. 'We turned up, didn't we?' An
empty bottle of Newcastle Brown smashed against his guitar.

We made a hasty exit from the stage and ran towards our
car, to find Stan besieged by angry fans who looked as
though they wanted to drag him from his seat in order to
have him tarred and feathered. Eventually we made our getaway, and Stan finally reached the roundabout and with a sigh

of relief passed an arrow pointing to London. We had driven
for nearly two hours before we realized we had almost reached
the Welsh coast. Stan had continued on the roundabout and
taken us in the opposite direction to home. It was dawn
before we finally drove past Wembley stadium again on our
way back to Muswell Hill. Stan looked a broken man
twitching in the driver's seat. Near exhaustion, he offered
his resignation as we arrived outside my house. But none
of us responded. We were too busy trying to contain our
laughter.

But the mystical fairyland of 'Sunny Afternoon' and the
World Cup was soon to become overcast by the gloomy
onset of writs and summonses. In the meantime Rasa and I
took a little boat on a holiday around the Norfolk broads. Alan
Klein and Michael Simkins were going about their work.
Wace and Collins were taking advantage of their regained
success and formed their own publishing company with
Freddie Beinstock. They were signing several new artists, one
of whom had the unlikely name of the Marquess of
Kensington. There was a rumour that Wace, still the frustrated
singer, had recorded the song with himself as vocalist and
dragged in the first good-looking stud he saw off Carnaby
Street to create a new superstar. Kassner was presumably still
fuming with rage over the fact that his 'boy' had abandoned
him and had given another publisher a Number 1 song.
However, according to my diary, Rasa's fairytale world was
still intact. She knew about Klein, Machat, Kassner and Page,
but she imagined that a good fairy would come along and
blow the bad fairies away.

My father came up to Norfolk to join me and Rasa for a
couple of days' fishing, and after only one night on the Broads
netted a large bagful of eels. Rasa awoke in the middle of the
night as she felt a slippery sensation around her feet. I lit the
small gas lamp at the end of the bed to discover that the little
cabin where we slept was completely engulfed by black eels,

escaped from my father's keep-net. I felt that this was a
warning that all was not well. As I struggled to catch them
and throw them out of the boat, I realized there were too
many to cope with. Rasa and I abandoned the boat and left it
to the eels. The next morning my father arrived and with an
impish smile cut off the heads of the remaining eels and gutted
them and cast their entrails back into the dark waters. I wished
that he could do the same to the managers, publishers,
businessmen and accountants. But this was not to be. My
father had many knives, but they were not sharp enough to
cut off the heads of all the slippery creatures.

As Rasa and I reclaimed the boat after Dad went back to
London, we turned on the transistor radio. By now 'Sunny
Afternoon' was no longer in the Top 10, and we heard a new
record called 'Wild Thing' by a group called the Troggs. At
first I experienced the same feeling I had the first time I heard the
Who's 'I Can't Explain' – mixture of being both flattered and
enraged because somebody had apparently been inspired by
our group's sound. But any fears of the Kinks being deposed
were dismissed as soon as an ocarina solo appeared in place of a
raving Dave Davies guitar sound. Shel Talmy had done it
with the Who, and at the end of 'Wild Thing' the radio
announced that the producer of the Troggs was none other
than Larry Page. In many ways the records Larry produced
with the Troggs were as entertaining and authentic as anything
else around. I hoped that if the Troggs' record reached
Number 1, Larry might be distracted and forget about us. But
this was not to be.

On my return from holiday I was confronted by a list of
one-night stands up and down the country combined with a
list of meetings with solicitors and legal counsel. Two things
were uppermost in my mind. First, perhaps Larry and Kassner
had been so delighted by the success of the Troggs that they
had decided to drop all actions against me, which would allow
the courts to release my royalties; second, that Stan Whitley

had taken the advice Mick had given him after our trip to Exeter and bought and studied a map of England. I was delighted when Stan proudly pulled up outside the Locarno in Burnley without so much as one wrong turning on the way, but disappointed to find that Kassner and Page were pursuing their claims with relentless gusto.'

Raymond Douglas ranted on about the legal saga, as if all the bitter memories had returned to haunt him.

'I knew it was all going on around me. I felt that something bad was happening. All the legal activity, combined with the wheeling and dealing, was gradually muddling my thinking so much that it seemed to me a simple situation was turning into a complicated, twisted affair. I felt I was being slowly poisoned by it all. I had shut down emotionally after "Dedicated Follower", but when I wrote "Sunny Afternoon" it was like emerging from a black tunnel. That whole sixties thing was beginning to get to me. Things were supposed to be swinging in London. But looking back and reading between the lines it was obvious that some weird stuff was going on. Pop art had become the new opium of the people, while the politicians continued to screw everyone up. Maybe I was just pissed off that I was successful, but married, with a child and responsibilities, and there were all those supposedly fantastic girls out there in miniskirts and I couldn't get near it all without some reporter up my arse with a camera. It wasn't just sex, it was just the fact that the whole fucking world knew that I was married because I was famous, and any old girlfriends I did meet had to be in dark clubs or the back of taxi-cabs. Simple innocent reunions were turned into tawdry assignations. My feelings for Rasa were the same as ever, but something in the back of my mind said I should have waited a bit longer before I married. I remember something Larry Page said just before my wedding. It was a flippant remark but it had an element of truth in it. He said that I was the type of guy that needed security or responsibility, because guys like me usually let what's hanging between their legs dictate their lives.

Perhaps it wasn't the subtlest way of putting it, but perhaps I would have got carried away with all the success, with hangers-on catering to my every whim, that I would have ended up dead after six months' with a needle in my arm and a chic sucking my dick which was still hard even though I was dead. Way to go, man!'

Raymond Douglas paused. Then he apologized for speaking in such a way. I looked at him closely and he was shaking, as if he was remembering a traumatic moment in his life. Suddenly he grabbed me and held me close to him, without seeming to know or care who I was, just as long as he was not alone. The totally desperate way he held me somehow brought out protective feelings in me. He spoke slowly, in a whisper.

'Will you hold me for a second? I feel afraid. I don't want to be intimate or have sex with you, all I want you to do is show some affection and forget about what's good and what's bad. Right and wrong and obscene in this life. Everything is reduced to what's physical in the end, because it's the filth inside people's minds that creates all the evil. What is a body, anyway? I suppose you've got to abuse your body to understand it. If you're not prepared to humiliate yourself in order to give somebody else a moment's pleasure, I don't believe that you've actually lived. It's impossible not to debase yourself occasionally in this world, but the secret is not to lose your self-esteem at the same time, in order to make yourself pure again without guilt or conscience. I know many so-called happily married people who have never tasted that emotional freedom. It's like juice. Love fuel. So many people stay together until they die and yet even on their deathbeds they never knew total love because they were too proud to taste the filth as well as the sweetness. People are so goddam respectable, they never do or say what they really feel. Insecurity, I guess that's what drives people to do that. Remember, I am not a queer and I do not want your body.'

Then R.D. closed his eyes and kissed me gently on the lips. He whispered a name under his breath as he drew away from me – Julie Finkle.

As a human being I was a little sickened, but as a journalist my appetite for a story was getting the better of me. I was getting closer to what I had come for. When he whispered 'Julie Finkle' to me it had sounded like a clue. A lead. Or possibly a cry for help. We both remained silent for several minutes. Then I said that he shouldn't feel bad and that I understood, but deep down I knew I was dealing with a troubled person, who was haunted by something in his past. So much so that it had driven him into almost total seclusion. Maybe he needed medical help. Maybe just a good woman. He was old, but not past it sexually. Perhaps it was *the* girl. That girl he'd wanted but couldn't have. All these years she'd been locked away in a tiny corner of his mind. I thought about the newspaper stories of his sexual ambiguity. Maybe they were true after all. He had been born at a time when homosexuality was still illegal. Although not gay in my opinion, he had lived through the era of the closet queen, and his songs were some of the first to sing openly about those poor tortured souls. I thought of what he had said the first time I met him. Raymond Douglas began talking again. But now he completely changed the subject. He had become a completely different person.

'Don't you think Harold Wilson had a weird smile? They say that Hitler was a product of the twentieth century. I mean, I know he was evil, but he had to exist. He, or should I say It, had to happen. Like Marilyn Monroe, Vera Lynn, Lee Harvey Oswald, Charles Manson, Stalin, Lenin and Charlie Chaplin. They all had to exist. But old Harold Wilson, bless him, our Premier and guiding light for most of the sixties, reminded me of so many of those promoters up north who came to us after a show and expected us to thank them for giving us work. It's unbelievable that Harold Wilson was part of the 'swinging' sixties, but I think the sixties were a con: the establishment still ruled the country. Grenville didn't know too much about managing a rock group, but he knew about the establishment. The sixties were like a carrot held up to youth to distract us so that we would not rebel against the ruling classes and all the backhanders and corruption that were actually present in politics. The countryside was being eroded and trees pulled up in order to build motorways, factories were being closed, coal mines were being ear-marked for the chop. I suppose there's some Welsh in me – probably a lot of Welsh in me – basically I'm a mongrel, and being a mongrel I was becoming aware of the thousands of people who were given the shit end of the stick in the sixties. They were the people who would be left behind without work when the party was over, without a place in society. My job lasted from record to record. The sick thing was, that I was heralded as a standard-bearer for that deceitful time. I was writing songs and the country was gradually being sold out. Cheated.

'Maybe that's why I didn't go down the King's Road with the others. They thought that I was uncool, unhip. Some even called me a snob. Maybe that's also why I married somebody who was not only classless, but stateless. It was her total homelessness that appealed. I wanted to take her and find a home for her. I never wanted to live anywhere permanently, because to tell you the truth being a house owner is a terrific responsibility. My friend Barry Fantoni, who had become a TV celebrity on a teenage talk show, received an urgent phone call from me while he was at the BBC studios. We were supposed to go out and meet at a club somewhere, but it was a cold night and I thought that if I left the house my pipes would freeze. I had heard from other home-owners that the worst thing that can happen is for a pipe to burst. So that night Barry Fantoni, one-time art-school teacher and "Face of 1966", kept me company during my vigil in my darkened attic, waiting for the pipes to thaw out. His friendship was tested to the limit.'

Raymond Douglas started singing like a drunk in a public house.

'There's a crack up in the ceiling and the kitchen sink is leaking.
Out of work and got no money
A Sunday joint of bread and honey . . .
        People are living on Dead-end Street.'

Then the old rock and roller started mooching around the room like a vaudeville comedian. Posing at the end of each line.

'. . . And it stretches from the King's Road to Threadneedle Street
. . . *Yeah.*
From John O'Groats to Land's End . . . *Yeah.*
The pipes were freezing everywhere
But everybody was being too swinging, man,
To worry about what's going to happen when the pipes burst . . .
Yeah yeah.'

The Preacher was back on the soap box. R.D. was swinging. He put on an American accent that reminded me of Groucho Marx.

'And when Harold Wilson smiled like a north-country promoter, devalued sterling and passed laws behind our backs, a man's only right when he owned his own house was that he could do whatever he wanted *in* that house. Copulate, masturbate, flagellate and perpetrate all manner of sins in every room if he so wished, provided the neighbours didn't see, and only if that house was *freehold*. But no one told you that 150 civil servants had the right to enter that house without a warrant.

'Dead-end Street . . . yeah . . . Dead-end Street.'

The little variety show was over and Raymond Douglas fell exhausted back into his chair. He was out of breath but he still went on. He reverted to his maudlin Cockney drone.

'It's really scary owning a house and living under a microscope. Do you know what I mean? The responsibility is awesome.'

R.D. made me want to laugh, but the old boy was serious. 'I think so,' I replied cautiously. I thought that Raymond Douglas was cracking up. No wonder some journalists and disc jockeys had considered him to be an unpredictable crank. I let him continue. Then he completely changed the subject and started talking in a calm, coherent way.

'After the car accident Quaife totally wigged out. He had some injuries to his foot, but I think he did something to his brain as well. Or maybe it's like I was saying, it was chicks. When chicks get involved with a band, it's all over. Poor old Pete, he only wanted to be loved, like anyone else, but Pete never did anything by halves. While we were going through all that turmoil on our first visit to Copenhagen, Pete had met Annette, the daughter of a rich hotel owner. He decided that he didn't want to be part of the Kinks anymore and while we were in Copenhagen playing a gig Pete signed an official letter of resignation. I remember we were at this large, almost palatial house, where Annette's parents lived. I got the impression that Pete thought that Annette was where the real money was at. I'm not suggesting that Pete saw his relationship with this girl as some sort of leapfrog to prestige and high status, I think he was genuinely in love, but I definitely felt that he had lost all his love for the band, and that hurt me. I remembered how when we were at school together and Pete lived in a council house on the Coldfall Estate near Muswell Hill we were such good friends. Or were we? You know, I have this notion that perhaps I have never had a real friend in my entire life. It was almost as if Pete just wanted to be rid of us, like he was ashamed to be in the group. Perhaps he had just wanted to make one hit record and then give up. Perhaps he wasn't seduced like I was into going on and on. It wasn't until Pete signed that resignation letter that I realized that I had never know him at all.

I also felt that he had been freaked out by all the legal actions that were being started in the name of or against the Kinks, and he was terrified at the thought of being tangled up with the likes of Alan Klein. At first Pete had been the most show-business-conscious member of the band, but as time wore on I had taken more and more of the limelight away from him. Dave and Mick couldn't give a damn. Pete really acted as if he thought he had found a new life where he could make a clean start, in a country which considered him a

superstar and also classless. Maybe that's what he thought.
Maybe he just settled for marrying a millionaire's daughter.
Whatever his reasons, on 30 September 1966 he signed a paper
which said: 'I, Peter Alexandar Greenlaw [*Where the fuck did
the Greenlaw come from?*] Quaife, hereby resign from Kinks
Productions and cease all activities . . . blah blah blah, etc., etc.'
Grenville was fluttering around the room like a diplomat at
the signing of a peace treaty, while Annette's father looked on
dispassionately. When it came to witnessing the document
Grenville dragged in Stan Whitley, who dutifully added his
signature to the document. A sad piece of paper, which gave
one man the right to go his own way in Denmark, witnessed
by a man who couldn't find his way to Exeter.

Pete was married shortly afterwards. I don't think we even
got an invite.'

R.D. appeared to still be hurt about the departure of Peter Quaife.
He told me that Pete had been one of his best friends at school, and
so the end of the relationship was like a divorce. R.D. was full of
self-pity. I felt like telling him that he wasn't the first bandleader
to have a musician walk out on him. Quaife probably had good
reasons of his own. In all probability, he had seen the changes
in R.D. and did not want to see his old pal hoodwinked into being
somebody he wasn't. I could have said a lot of things. But I just
watched R.D. sitting there despising himself. This was not part of
the scenario R.D. had planned for his life. R.D. was beginning to
treat me like a friend and had begun to confide in me.

And round the corner was looming the big battle with Boscobel
and Kassner.

'I always thought friends would be there forever. I had known
Pete since school. We had grown up together and were
always there to help each other. Now I needed all the help I
could get because around the corner was looming the big
battle with Boscobel and Kassner.

The Michael Simkins organization had expanded from the two rooms it had previously occupied in Davies Street, and it had taken into its employ one Colin Wadie, a solicitor who specialized in litigation. Colin had gone to Highgate Public School and had lived down Highgate West Hill by Hampstead Ponds on the Holly Lodge Estate. He later told me that he had actually known Judy, one of my girlfriends from art college. Even though Colin spoke and acted in a public-school manner, our north London connections made it possible for me to trust him more than the many other legal eagles who were surrounding me at this time. Although at first he gave the impression of being plain, stalwart, fastidious and at times pedantic to the point of being almost uninteresting, he showed genuine concern for my situation, and in return I trusted him more than anybody I had known since leaving school and entering the music business. He once took me to dinner at Musto's Bistro in Belsize Village, then to his somewhat sad little bachelor flat nearby, where he showed me his prized possession, a collection of imperfect wine glasses. Whereas other people would have thrown them away, Colin had taken these distorted objects in and given them a place in a glass cabinet, as if to provide them with refuge. As he muttered something about the fact that they were flawed made one appreciate the art of glass-blowing, I contemplated the fact that Colin may have considered me to be like one of the oddities in his collection. The impressive part about Colin was that he was not afraid to show that he was human. He genuinely cared for people. Mick Avory observed that Colin held his chin up in such a manner when he entered the room that it made it seem as if he suspected that either he or somebody else had trodden in a dog turd. I did not consider this to be a fault. On the contrary, it gave him added character, and this, along with his meticulous note-taking, made him look as if he had walked straight out of a Dickens novel.

Colin was a bachelor, and as soon as it became apparent that he was going to figure prominently in the world of the Kinks, at least until the law-suit was over, Grenville and Robert decided to take him under their collective care in order to find him a suitable wife. Bridge parties, weekends in the country, dinners in Pimlico (where Grenville was now living with the stately-looking Sue Sutherland, whose family apparently owned half of Scotland). Sue not only spoke like the Queen, she looked like the Queen. All that was missing were the corgi dogs.

Colin knew that I was terrified about the up-coming law-suit, and while some advisers involved brushed it off as a 'circus', Colin made me feel that he would do his utmost on my behalf. I had to travel to New York without the band, accompanied by Colin, to give a pre-trial deposition. It was to take place in the offices of Kassner's attorney. Klein had secured the services of Barry Fredricks, a smart young attorney who interjected when the opposing attorney's questions got out of line. At first the tone of the proceedings was very formal, considering that we were not in a courtroom, but then my inquisitor got very abrasive and loud, which was probably meant to intimidate me. One question led to another. Minor details of seemingly little consequence. Major pronouncements of no relevance. When I said that, in my opinion, I was being screwed by the record companies and the publisher, the man on the other side of the desk leapt to his feet and declared in no uncertain terms that he would tolerate no outbursts that would lead to any such false accusation. To which Fredricks replied, 'Does this mean that my esteemed colleague wishes to reserve all such rights for himself?' The atmosphere was calmed down by Colin with true British diplomacy, and the deposition continued for another two days.

Colin and I were staying at the Warwick Hotel, where Klein had a suite of offices. My solicitor was wonderful company, and eased the obvious panic that was continually

inside me. 'Enjoy life, Ray!' he said as he ordered a bottle of
Löwenbräu from the waiter behind the bar. 'For the most
part, litigation of this sort is rather a game of posturing in
order to gain some tactical advantage. It's a serious business,
but try not to take it too seriously.'

We drank our Löwenbräus, and although I wanted to tell
him that I considered him to be a personal friend and that he
looked like my nephew Terry I thought better of it for some
reason. He was my professional adviser, after all.

During that week, Colin and I were driven out to Alan
Klein's house in Queens, where there was to be a small
gathering of friends for Klein's anniversary. The limousine
pulled up outside a typically ostentatious American detached
house, which was much grander than the other houses on the
smart suburban street. Inside we were greeted by Klein and his
pretty wife, who proudly showed me around the recently
decorated house. One thing which confused me was that all
the furniture and carpets had plastic coverings on them. When
I inquired as to its purpose, Klein informed me that it was all
newly decorated, and he did not want a crowd of people to
soil it in any way. The party was small because Klein preferred
it that way. In some strange way I felt privileged to be
invited, partly because I had begun to like Klein, who had
been described as not an obviously likeable person.

Suddenly there was a toast of congratulations to the Kleins,
and after glasses clinked and we sipped our Californian
champagne, a piano chord was heard and the lights suddenly
dimmed. A spotlight went on as Bobby Vinton walked into
the room singing 'Blue Velvet'. Klein had been involved in
Vinton's career, and, for all I knew, may have been the
publisher of the song. As Vinton sang his hit and gestured
towards the anniversary couple, Klein grabbed his wife around
the waist and they started to do a slow foxtrot. The assorted
guests applauded as the Kleins took centre-stage. It was a
moment of true Americana, teetering between sentimentality

and heart-felt emotion. It was also tacky as hell. Whatever. It meant a lot to the Kleins.

Colin and I soon returned to England because more concerts were waiting to be played in the wake of the success of 'Sunny Afternoon'.

One notable gig was in Rutland, the smallest county in England. Bill Collins, a likeable Welshman with grey wavy hair, was standing in as road manager and was driving us around. (Bill's son Lewis had been the bass player in the Mojos.) The gig was in a marquee which had been erected specially for the concert in a village called Oakham, and a local major (retired), David Watts, was the promoter. After the initial introductions, Major Watts explained somewhat apologetically that there were no proper dressing-room facilities, and offered to let us change in his house. Even though we were playing a summer's fair, Major Watts thought that the late-night air would be damp when we came offstage, and that it would be sensible for us to change in more comfortable quarters.

David Watts looked the part of a major, and dressed in a manner which became an ex-member of the Queen's Own Hussars. Except that he was wearing white socks. It was unusual in those days even for rock 'n' rollers to wear white socks. White socks and polo-necked sweaters were to anyone aware at the time an outward sign that you were either gay or at least prepared to venture over to the other side when the occasion demanded. This meant, in the language of Avory, 'versatile'. I thought this to be most unlikely, especially as the Major's voice was deep and masculine. Mick disagreed and shook his head.

The Kinks dashed offstage after the show and headed straight for David Watts' cottage. In the midst of changing our sweaty undies, David Watts arrived with crateloads of Rutland beer and opened a refrigerator full of pink champagne. Mick seized

319

the opportunity to prove a point and dropped his trousers in front of the Major, then proceeded to prance around like a tart. I asked the Major if he fancied Mick. He said, 'Oh God, no, not that slut. I'm more interested in that little whore,' and pointed to Dave, who was dancing with Mick. Then various members of the regional constabulary and other local dignitaries arrived to join in the impromptu festivities which, by some strange coincidence, were without women, in drag or otherwise. After downing half a bottle of Pinkers, I decided that positive action should be taken. I seized the moment and started negotiations with the Major for my brother's hand, thinking that he would be outraged at this suggestion and have us thrown out. Was he actually interested? Or was he just playing along? Here was an opportunity of finally unloading my little brother. While Mick and Dave danced tantalizingly cheek to cheek, I tried to put together a deal whereby the Major would leave Dave his entire estate, brewery included, if the two should ever break up. Mick thought I was making a deal which included himself as part of the package, and he was disappointed to hear that it was to be Dave who would be the sole beneficiary of this potential liaison. I did not think it necessary to inform Dave of the transaction.

The party went on till the early hours, and everyone was dancing with everyone else until Bill Collins sensibly suggested that it was time to leave as there was a long drive home. By this time David Watts was in full flow, romancing Dave on a swing in the back garden, and he was in a very emotional state when we dragged Dave away. David Watts realized by now that Dave was indeed a slut, and a disloyal one at that. Avory took the distraught major to one side and explained that Dave was renowned as a heart-breaker. After the tears had been mopped up and all emotions were in order, David Watts declared his fondness for the whole group and announced that the Kinks would be welcome in his house

whenever we felt like dropping by. We promised to see him
again the next time we performed in the area. What had
seemed a heady and potentially dangerous romance, turned out
to be a fond friendship. I had made a complete mistake.
Some men prefer the company of other men. It does not
necessarily mean they are gay. In a way, I looked up to
David Watts.

We did subsequently visit him at his country manor house,
and enjoyed a lunch of sausage and mash with him before
travelling to a gig in Peterborough. Visiting David became a
welcome relief from the touring and the litigation surrounding
us, and our friendship grew because we knew just where we
stood with one another. His affection, the totally genuine
emotion felt by an older man who saw his own youth
embodied in a young boy, was still there, but a romantic
liaison was never discussed again. For us the visits to the
Major's house also made a pleasant change from the usual
roadside cafés that existed up and down the A and B roads of
Britain before the countryside was carved into motorways
where Trusthouse Forte, Granada and Happy Eaters sold food
for the masses. A typical stopover was an establishment just
outside Bristol on the A4 called Flies. Flies was so named
because there were flies as big as sparrows around the food,
which was left open on the counter. Mick pointed out that the
proprietor resembled Charles de Gaulle: he was 6 feet 6 inches
tall and had a huge nose which hung from between his eyes
right down to his bottom lip. The only consolation for this
unfortunate man was that his male member assumed
proportions of an equally substantial nature. This information
was once again supplied by Mick, who had been privileged to
observe the colossus when sharing the same urinal as 'Monsieur
le President'. The group usually reached Flies by three or four
in the morning, where we found other bands enjoying, or
suffering from, the President's greasy-spoon food – except the
drummer from a jazz group called Mike Cotton Sound,

Jimmy Garforth, who travelled around with a gas stove and cooking utensils in his suitcase. (Jimmy later found his niche in life when he opened a café in the West Country when his touring days were over.)

There were other assorted characters around the band who could have really only existed in the sixties. One such was the Widow O'Brian. We had first met him in the *Ready Steady Go!* studios at Kingsway when waiting to promote 'All Day and All of the Night'. He appeared in our dressing room while the group was getting changed. 'The Widow' used to work in a boutique in Carnaby Street, and he had fallen in love with Mick at first sight when we went to have some clothes made. He used to invite Mick and his friends to the flat in Notting Hill that he shared with his mother, and he used to offer a selection of drinks that came laced with what Mick described as aphrodisiacs. The Widow always entertained lots of other friends, usually people in showbiz, with some dockers from the East End just to add a bit of rough trade. Eventually the party guests would leave, and the next morning Mick would wake up in the Widow's boudoir alongside with another of Mick's friends, a scrap-metal merchant from East Molesey, Colin the Scrap.

One night Mick dragged me along and, after succumbing to the aphrodisiac lager, we were ushered into the blue-movie room. I asked for a cup of coffee, because I felt drowsy, and then slumped back on to what I thought was a hairy cushion, only to discover that it was a naked man. I jumped up in shock, the boiling hot coffee spilled over his hairy chest and he ran screaming out of the room.

The Widow O'Brian's mother rarely made an appearance, except when Colin the Scrap took a local ladies' football team from East Molesey to have their team photograph taken by old Brian. The Widow was obviously more interested in the boyfriends and husbands that the team players had brought with them, and quickly filled their glasses with aphrodisiac lager, but the team left before the lager had had the desired effect on their unsuspecting husbands. We can only assume that they all had sex of the most erotic nature once they had returned to East Molesey.

Mick also used to frequent the Cromwellian Club in the Cromwell Road, where lots of bands and singers hung out to observe the almost endless supply of dolly girls parading in their mini skirts. Mick professed to be a bum man, but he was not averse to a bit of tit. One night he was drinking there with some of his mates and a girl singer, a delightful maiden with more than generous knockers. Somebody suggested that they should all leave the club and swim across the Serpentine for a bet. She dragged Mick and his friend Terry Collis out of the club and all three set off to swim the Serpentine naked. After reaching the other side, Mick and Terry were scaling the bank when the police arrived and put them under arrest for indecent exposure. It was only when the girl emerged from the waters like a goddess, displaying her enormous breasts, that the police relented and let them off with a caution.

On another occasion Mick found himself with the same girl, who was accompanied by an attractive male DJ. After visits to various clubs, Avory got to first base and, just as he mounted the blonde Wagnerian goddess, he felt a thrusting pain in his rear end. He screamed and turned to see that the D J had thrust four fingers up Avory's back entrance. Avory never revealed the rest of the story, but the three of them were later seen at the Widow's house, where the D J no doubt discovered that heaven can often be attained after a pint of lager.

Anyway, let's get back to the music. It was the recording of 'Dead End Street' that really put the final nail in the coffin of Shel Talmy as the Kinks' producer. Bill Collins was still our temporary tour manager, and an accomplished musician himself. Bill had been employed as a caretaker instead of Stan

323

Whitley, even though Stan had regained some dignity and by now could recite every road to Exeter by heart. Madrid had made an indelible impression on him, but it was decided that he should assume the role of 'equipment boy' until he could navigate the highways and byways of the UK with more assurance.

John Dalton still had the appalling Dan electric bass guitar inherited from Pete Quaife. On the session it was decided that John would play the normal Fender bass while Dave played an identical pattern an octave higher on the Dan electric. Nicky Hopkins, who had played piano on 'Sunny Afternoon', was not available, and so I played piano. A few years earlier Mort Shuman had seen me play the piano, and even though it was obvious I could hack it chordally, I was no virtuoso when it came to the old joanna. Mort had made the point that I had the thumping rhythmic pattern to my style that somehow drove the rest of the band. When we had recorded 'Sunny Afternoon' Shel had asked Nicky Hopkins to watch me play the song once and then copy my technique. Nicky must have been a musical masochist as well as a gentleman, because he dutifully sat down and reproduced that pounding sound which was associated with so many of our records at that time. Avory had more than earned his keep by playing on 'Sunny Afternoon', and it had been decided that he would play drums on every recording from now on. In any event, the song had a good-time traditional jazz feel to it, perfect for Mick who, from his days in the boy scouts, had been a jazz fan.

The first version of 'Dead End Street' we put down with Shel had an organ part put on by Bill Collins. While it gave it a whirlygig fairground effect, it was not bleak enough for my taste. Shel heard the playback and wrote the song off as a hit almost dismissively. He threw his overcoat on and left through the swing doors of Pye Studio number 2. I sat in the corner of the studio and willed Shel to allow us to record the track again. At that moment the sleeve of Shel's coat became entangled in the swing door, and the force of it pulled his left arm out of its socket. He cried out in pain as he saw his hand dangling somewhere by his left foot. Fortunately he had a friend with him who managed to lie him down on the floor and force his arm back into its socket. But it was obvious that he needed medical attention, and so he was taken to hospital to check that everything was in order.

After Shel had left I asked Grenville if I could have another crack at recording the song. We discussed this briefly with the rest of the band and it was decided to re-record the song from scratch. I had got what I wanted. The original Shel Talmy version had used a classical French horn player by the name of Albert Hall at the end fade-out section. But the horn combined with Bill Collins' fairground organ made the song sound too joyous. This time, at my insistence, the song was recorded slower and bleaker. Stan Whitley was dragged in to help out with back-up vocals, but a horn of some description was still needed to play on the fade-out. Grenville disappeared to the Mason's Arms pub just round the corner from Pye studios and returned with an unsuspecting trombone player who Grenville had discovered just as the pub was beginning to close. He had been doing another session nearby and although he was clearly in an inebriated state, I considered this to be a perfect condition for my purpose. The trombonist heard the fade-out once and said, 'Let's go for it. I can still get another pint before they shut.' He recorded a perfect solo in one take and in ten minutes was back in the Mason's Arms better off by a session fee gratefully paid in cash by Grenville.

The following morning I played Shel the new version of 'Dead End Street' which had been recorded without his knowledge. Talmy said in no uncertain terms that the recording was perfect and that there was no way he was going to allow the Kinks to re-do it. He did not know that he'd been listening to the version which had been recorded after he had left the studio. Nothing more was said about the matter, even though it was obvious that the two versions were totally different. Shel had said on a prior occasion that he was not interested in the glory, he was just interested in the money. In this instance he received both as the first pressings of 'Dead End Street' went out with Shel Talmy credited as producer.'

R.D. had obviously taken great pleasure in divulging this story to me. 'Dead End Street' definitely had a bleak sound to it, and the famous trombone fade-out provided a perfect ending.

I was just noting down what R.D. had said when I heard his voice in my ear. He had got up from his chair and moved right behind me. The level of his voice was reduced to a whisper. As he spoke I stared ahead at the flickering TV screen above the control desk. Raymond Douglas was in a freaky mood. His voice was deep and sinister.

'Have you ever seen the past, present and future all at the same time? I mean, you're always talking about my past. That's OK. But there are moments in life that are so vivid they stay in your present even though at the time they seemed irrelevant. An experience I had with 'Dead End Street' summed up so much about life for me. It put the true meaning of time and space completely in perspective. I want you to imagine it's happening to you now.

It is 1967. We are at the BBC television studios recording *Top of the Pops*. A large, gangling Lancastrian gentleman puts his head round the dressing-room door. He smiles a smile which exposes his nicotine-stained teeth, with several gaps where some have fallen out. His hair is long on top but cropped short at the ears, which makes him resemble George Orwell. He speaks like a vaudeville comedian. It is Harry Goodwin, the official BBC photographer at *Top of the Pops*. Harry also keeps a book on the side, laying odds on which records will make the charts. He speaks in a broad Coronation Street accent.

'Laying six to four that you'll be Top 10 in two weeks.

Won't go to Number 1 though, being it's Christmas and all. Should've put sleigh bells on end, 'stead o' bloody trombone. Can I have a quick happy snap of band before you go on?'

His voice diminishes to a whisper. 'And there are a couple of models down the corridor dying to meet you. They've been wetting their knickers all afternoon 'cos I told them you'd be here. They fancy you dead rotten. After we done the snaps I'll send them in.'

In the corridor outside the dressing room we pose for Harry as he takes his happy snaps and he talks constantly while he is taking the pictures.

'Head up, Dave . . . Mick, don't look such a miserable bleeder . . . And new bloke at back, sorry, what's your name, oh, Nobby, yeah right . . . Ray, come to the front lad.'

A flash bulb pops off and Harry shouts his catchphrase, 'That's it, lads, shot of a lifetime.'

The two models are waiting outside the dressing-room door. Harry may be a gambler, but he is certainly not a liar.

'What did I tell ya, the blonde, it could be Brigitte Bardot, but the other one's really dirty. Lay two to one each way you'll have 'em both before dress rehearsal.'

I hand my guitar to Stan Whitley and make eye contact with Brigitte Bardot and her accomplice. Dialogue is unnecessary. The situation has been accurately sized up. I feel that familiar bulge in my tight corduroys as Brigitte Bardot and friend check their lipstick in the mirror. I know that anything I wish will be their command. All three of us understand the situation. As I stroll towards the two girls I pass a television monitor which is showing a newsreel of Donald Campbell, who that day has been making an attempt to break the world water-speed record at Lake Coniston. The garbled sound of Campbell's voice is barely audible above the roaring of his speedboat. Then there is a moment when the whole world becomes a still photograph. The two girls waiting at the end of the corridor. Other musicians waiting to go on to perform their hit. A group of studio technicians staring at the newsreel. Donald Campbell's voice makes a final croaking noise, almost as if he had seen his destiny appear from the lake like a giant serpent. Campbell sees himself face to face. At that moment the powerful speedboat lifts from the water and takes off into the sky, like a giant bird. Suddenly a moment of almost exquisite irony as the world is frozen, then abruptly jerked into fast-forward as Campbell's boat turns a somersault and crashes into tiny pieces on the lake. His body shattered into atoms. I walk up to the would-be Brigitte Bardot and kiss her on her perfectly formed lips. Her tongue slips delicately into my mouth, then shoots back in order to lick her lips and keep the red gloss shiny. The thought of what might be achieved with the would-be Bardot has just been eclipsed by the extravagance of Donald Campbell's tragic but heroic departure from this world. I walk back into my dressing room and close the door behind me. I leave the two girls outside. Nothing they can do could compare to that moment on the lake. It was just like Harry Goodwin always used to say when he got what he thought was the ultimate picture: 'a shot of a lifetime'.

Raymond Douglas had walked back to his customary seat by the desk and was reaching out for the diary as he spoke.

'You see what I mean, my young friend. One minute you're there, the next you have disappeared from the planet. So fast that it's slow and it don't go away. A child is conceived just as an entire universe explodes and the rest is all in between.'

R.D. paused.

Hearing the expression 'shot of a lifetime' made me remember that my book would have to contain photographs, but I had not raised the subject with R.D. I had needed to gain his confidence before asking for access to his personal library of snapshots. Now I boldly asked the question which, needless to say, didn't go down too well: I needed some personal photographs.

'Photographs? Happy snaps? Don't mean nothing. The camera is supposed to tell the truth, that's what they say. But I tell you I would rather carry the images in my head than see a machine's interpretation of my reality. Perhaps it is the old Navajo logic again. Pictures take away some of your soul. I've hated having my picture taken ever since I was a kid, so you can imagine how I felt when I entered a business where I had to have my picture taken on a regular basis. That's why I look so goddam miserable in pictures. Did you ever hear my song, "People Take Pictures of Each Other"? Well, that lyric sums up the way I feel about the world of photographic images.

'People take pictures of the summer
Just in case someone thought they had missed it
And to prove that it really existed.
Fathers take pictures of the mothers
And the sisters take pictures of brothers,
Just to show that they loved one another.
You can't picture love that you took from me
When we were young and the world was free,
Pictures of things as they used to be.
Don't show me no more please.

'See what I mean? I think that pictures only encourage nostalgia. I like to remember people the way they were. Pictures just show the world how much a person has aged, whereas memory renders a person ageless. No, the camera is cruel. You can't have any access to any photographs. I would rather you saw a painting of me than a picture. The great painters knew how to see truth and put it on the canvas for better or worse. Artists put in all the experience; all the inner thoughts that the camera can only touch the surface of.

'Snapshot memories cannot be acquired. The camera may not lie, but it is not entirely honest. It shows only a small slice, a narrow perspective. One split second of a lifetime of such small moments. It makes events which should be ambiguous turn into absolutes, and it disallows personal interpretation. Why reduce life to a series of images that shows a bias towards the objective when a person has spent his entire lifetime creating subjective, ambiguous images? For example, the only argument I have had against rock videos is that they imposed images on to the audience instead of allowing listeners to conjure up their own ideas of what the songs are about. What would have been the point of making a video out of "Waterloo Sunset" or "Celluloid Heroes"? Some things are best left to the imagination. I enjoy making my own videos because, for better or worse, I still have control over the images I want to project to the audience.

When I was a kid I saw *The Jack Jackson Show* on TV. *The Jack Jackson Show* was in a way the first video show, in that there were people miming to songs which were in the Hit Parade. There were two performers, Glen Mason and Libby Morris, who mimed to the records, and dancers like Una Stubbs and Dougie Squires who danced their own interpretations of some other songs. I remember having a crush on one lady dancer in particular called Mavis Trail. I have no idea why I fancied her; it was just the way she moved. The good thing about *The Jack Jackson Show*, or *Cool for Cats* as it was later to be known, was that the performers allowed the artist on the record to retain a certain amount of distance from the audience, thereby retaining some glamour and mystique.

'Later there was a television show called *Oh Boy*, where British groups covered hits from America. The producer of the show, Jack Good, created a programme which became a Saturday-night institution with singers like Marty Wilde, Adam Faith, Joe Brown, Wee Willie Harris, Bert Weedon, Cherry Wainer and Don Storer, who played Anglicized versions of hits by Little Richard, Jerry Lee Lewis and Duane Eddy. Sometimes the original artists came over to perform themselves. The greatest of all was Eddie Cochran. Without a doubt Eddie Cochran was the finest rock guitarist and singer ever to hit Britain. According to folklore he sat on the drums and told his English back-up drummer how to play the drum patterns. Then he did the same to the bass player, until he got the sounds he wanted. Chuck Berry and Buddy Holly were having hits, but Eddie, along with Gene Vincent and the Blue Caps, were the first of the American bands to make a real impact on British television. But, you know, seeing him live was one thing. Seeing pictures of how he dressed and posed was another. Pictures just gave you a look at the style. To go inside his mind by judging what you see in a photograph is a totally different proposition. The music itself is the only way to do that. Because half of the reason you are attracted to the music is because it triggers something off in your imagination. It exists in your head.

'No. No photographs. This was meant to be a book about me and the worlds inside me and the dreams I carry along with me. Photos can only diminish that.'

R.D. stayed silent and stubborn. I was flabbergasted by his very thought-out argument, and a little concerned: his outburst had taken a visible toll on him.

I didn't have the courage to tell him that my contract with the Corporation required that photographs should be included. R.D. had given me a very strong argument: the Kinks had been one of the great unseen and unrecognized bands – so why shouldn't R.D. retain that privacy? I told him that I agreed, and would hand in my manuscript only if the Corporation accepted that there would be no pictures. I said this knowing that I was lying. I had no authority to make such decisions for the Corporation. But the more I thought about it, the more I began to side with R.D. He was giving me access to his dream world – the very centre of his soul – and it was like the Corporation wanted some smart-assed illustrator to come in and draw R.D.'s dreams. Show the dumb unsympathetic world what his 'Waterloo Sunset' looked like. It would be easy to print pictures of the group and the man. But how would you photograph his soul? The Corporation was beginning to seem more and more sinister in its intentions.

I went home and looked at my contract. They didn't just want his earthly life and how he wrote and lived; they wanted his dreams: the most precious thing a man possesses. It's all very well for a man to share his dreams. Artists can do that. The Corporation on the other hand wanted to *own* them, so that they could have them interpreted, or misinterpreted, and possibly destroy them, the way they had done with mine. I decided they might have control over my dreams, but they would never get to R.D.

If I was worried about the Corporation and its contract with me, I had almost reached a parallel emotional state to the one R.D. was in the following day. We both knew that we were going to have to discuss his old law-suit, and although I did my best to cover up the fears I had for my future if I failed to deliver the book, R.D. had somehow picked up on my nervous condition.

He took out a pair of bifocals as he strained his eyes to read the diary. He licked the tips of his fingers and turned the page. He started reading to me as if it were a nursery rhyme.

'The New Year was sung in as usual at the Alexandra pub in Muswell Hill. I had started drinking quite heavily at the time, particularly as my hits of the previous year had all been adopted as sing-along tunes throughout the country: everywhere I went, people offered me drinks. I remember seeing my family singing 'Sunny Afternoon' as the sound of Big Ben was heard on the radio and the rest of the world was trying to sing 'Should auld acquaintance be forgot . . .' I was seeing quite a lot of Frank Smythe too, and whether the rendezvous was in Soho, Chelsea or Hampstead, it was always in a pub. I had also started playing soccer for the Showbiz Eleven and footballers, whether they be part-time or full-time, generally like a few pints after a match.

Playing in the Showbiz Eleven gave me the opportunity to meet showbiz heroes from my youth. Sean Connery's reign as centre half had just come to an end, but singers such as Tommy Steele and Jess Conrad, who had appeared on *Oh Boy*, often played. I even got to meet Glen Mason, from *The Jack Jackson Show*. Unfortunately Mavis Trail was not attending the games and, as far as I could ascertain, had even given up dancing. Still, it was a thrill to see these famous faces from another era running up and down the soccer pitch alongside me. There are many wonderful stories attached to the Showbiz Eleven, but perhaps we can discuss these later.

Frank introduced me to an acquaintance of his who called herself Georgie. She was a former teacher at the Royal Film School, and even after a few drinks she spoke eloquently about film, music and poetry. This rekindled my interest in film, which had been abruptly stopped by my superiors at Hornsey Art College. At first I assumed Georgie was one of Frank's long-suffering girlfriends, but it soon became apparent that Georgie was with Frank in order to see me. It was reassuring to talk to somebody who was not just interested in me as a pop star, even though I was recognized nearly everywhere I went. I was talking to somebody who actually cared about art and film and who knew more about the subjects than I. Like Smythe, Georgie was four or five years older than myself, and despite being a drinkist of astounding durability, always seemed to remain clear-headed while to my eyes the universe was spinning like a merry-go-round. She mixed in many circles and said that she was a friend of many celebrities, particularly the actress Julie Christie, who according to Georgie trusted her judgement so much that she would only accept a movie part after Georgie had approved the script. If that were the case, I found it a relief to discover that there was somebody else in the world who was not only more famous, but more insecure than myself.

Georgie was a welcome change to the endless legal acquaintances that I was rapidly developing, particularly as the law-suit between Denmark Productions and Boscobel was looming on the horizon. Robert and Grenville were more concerned that I kept writing hit records. At the end of January 1967 Klein called me from the States to say that he would be over soon to organize the law-suit. There was fear inside me, but as I was twenty-two years old, it did not manifest itself in the same way that it does in me now that I am an old man. My body was strong and ready to withstand anything; I also had found an outlet in my writing. This comforted me.

On 4 February the Kinks played a concert at Stoke, and Cindy re-appeared as usual. By this time she had become, hopefully with my guidance, the most glamorous creature, with the confidence and aloofness of a celebrity. I knew that my work on Cindy was nearly completed when in the dressing room after the show she suddenly unbuttoned her blouse to reveal a black lace bra which had a see-through section where her nipples were. This was no home-made attempt; she had actually purchased the bra from a manufacturer who specialized in such designs. There was nothing cheap about her either: she went about everything with total class. I felt as proud of Cindy as I would have done if she had been a song or poem I had just completed. I took this to be a good omen, because I felt that she was lucky for me.

At this time it was like there were three people inside me: the loving suburban husband and father who happened to be a pop star; the confident celebrity who took pleasure in spreading his own form of good-will to his fans up and down the country, while at the same time preparing for major litigation; and, finally, the lost soul who was desperately insecure and looking for friendship which would not turn into some kind of betrayal and end up hurting me.

I was starting to become distrustful and afraid of nearly everybody. I would not tell anyone except Rasa and the band what I was writing about. This was partly because on the *Face to Face* album, the first 'manufactured' by Alan Klein, there was a song called 'Dandy', which we thought would be a single after the album was released. Klein had given a white label, or pre-released, copy to the record producer Mickie Most, who had been responsible for producing hits with the

Animals, Donovan and Herman's Hermits. I was flattered
until I discovered that Most had produced the song 'Dandy' as
a single with Herman's Hermits. I was informed it had been
set for release in the States. When I tried to quiz Klein about
this, he announced over the transatlantic telephone, 'Are you
gonna argue with 600,000 records sold?' I had no argument. I
suppose I should have been pleased that the single had gone
into the American Top Ten. Klein had liked the song and told
me that it reminded him of something from a musical. It had
not occurred to me before, but Klein had a good ear for a
song. Perhaps I felt frustrated because our own career in the
States had been halted by the ban imposed on us after our tour
two years before. Nevertheless it just made me feel as if
nothing was mine. After hearing their version, I was pleased
that they had done a good job but concerned because I had
not been told about it beforehand. Even so, if 600,000 copies
had been sold it did not mean that I could get my hands on
any money. All royalties were still being held in escrow until
the law-suit with Kassner was resolved. I began to think of the
royalties as an inheritance I would receive after a distant,
eccentric aunt died – and Machat and Klein were the executors
of her will.

In February we recorded two tracks for our new album, the
'Village Green' and 'Two Sisters'. When Robert heard 'Two
Sisters' he smiled for the first time in what seemed like many
months and said that I had taken my writing into another
class. 'Two Sisters' was based partly on Dave and myself. I
was Priscilla, 'who looked into the washing machine and the
drudgery of being wed', and Dave was cast as Sybilla, who
'looked into her mirror and mixed with all her smart young
friends, because she was free and single'. The song was also
drawn on images of Rasa the housewife doing the laundry,
changing the nappies, cooking the meals. Also on my own
mother and sisters, who had been tied through marriage to
children, which meant never having the opportunity to

embark on careers of their own. The final chorus of the song
had a lot to do with my feeling of being trapped by having a
young daughter and the responsibilities of marriage. When in
the bridge of the song the housewife sister would 'throw away
the dirty dishes just to be free again', it was my own reaction
in a sense, but it also came from seeing Rasa pushing the pram
down the street. The last verse started with 'Priscilla saw her
little children and decided she was better off than the wayward
lass that her sister had been'. That was me looking at my
daughter Louisa crawling on the floor and being content just
to see that. And as frustrated as I was about the legal turmoil
surrounding me and the restrictions and confines brought
about by marriage, I felt somehow redeemed by having
written the song. At this time more than any other I was
beginning to write about myself through my own
subconscious. 'Two Sisters' was a reflection of the suburban
husband. The confident celebrity manifested himself in
'Dandy', a song about a happy-go-lucky womanizer with a
girl in every port. The lost soul was finding himself writing
about a world that had disappeared forever, all the images of
childhood gone, to be replaced by a new and less caring
existence. It was a world which I thought was lost.

Pete Quaife had returned to England with his wife Annette,
and for reasons best known to himself had asked to rejoin the
group. John Dalton was very disappointed, but accepted it in
a good-natured way, knowing full well that it meant a return
to the building site and playing in the local pub at weekends.
(This didn't go unnoticed by the gutter press, who took
pictures of poor Nobby on a building site holding a guitar in
one hand and a shovel in the other.) Quaife, however, had
resigned from the Kinks company once, so on the advice of
Grenville and Robert we took him back on a trial basis – Pete
was in the habit of changing his mind overnight.

As a teenager I had stood on Waterloo Bridge and watched
the high tide nearly flood the banks of the Thames. The water

was a bright brown; almost red. This was probably caused by pollution, but it gave the impression that the water was like blood flowing through a giant vein that led to the pumping heart of the Empire. I felt that there was a bigger tide coming that would completely flood the banks and submerge the Houses of Parliament. This was a tide of reality and change that was soon to turn England on its head. I started writing a song about Liverpool that implied that the era of Merseybeat was coming to an end, but I changed it to 'Waterloo Sunset' not only because that gave me a bigger canvas to work on but because it was about London, the place where I had actually grown up. We tried recording the song with Shel, but I felt so precious about it that I pretended that it was an experiment for an album track which had not worked. We played the back track a couple of times but gave up before anybody had a chance to hear the melody or lyrics properly. *Face to Face* was released and now I felt that the group was ready for something special.

I knew that I had to make my own version, and so in early April I went back into the studio and laid down the back track. I remained so secretive about 'Waterloo Sunset' that I would not even sing the lyrics while the band played. I went home and polished up the lyrics until they became like a pebble which had been rounded off by the sea until it was perfectly smooth. A week later I went into the studio with Dave for a couple of hours to put on his guitar part, which I had carefully prearranged in my plodding piano style at home. On 13 April I took Rasa, Pete and Dave into number 2 Studio at Pye and we stood round the microphone and put on our backing vocals. I still didn't tell them what the lyrics would be about. Simply because I was embarrassed by how personal they were and I thought that the others would burst out laughing when they heard me sing. It was like an extract from a diary nobody was allowed to read. But when I finally put the vocal on later that evening everything seemed to fit

and nobody laughed. It was not difficult to mix the record
because it was only recorded on a four-track machine. The
engineer, Alan MacKenzie, was sensitive enough to realize
how much the song meant to me and allowed me to push the
faders myself. It was like painting with sound. After
the song was mixed, I had an acetate cut and I took it
home to play to Rosie and my niece Jackie. Rosie had come
back from Australia for a visit and although she was staying
with my mother she visited me almost every night to make
up for all the time we had been apart. I thought that she
would get a kick out of hearing Terry's name used as one of
the two characters in the song. Terry meets my imaginary Julie
on Waterloo Bridge, and as they walk across the river darkness
falls and an innocent world disappears.

Even when the record was finished it was still like a secret,
and for a while I didn't want it released. I met Barry Fantoni
when we were both playing a charity soccer match for the
Melody Maker. When he asked me what the title for my new
record was, rather than tell him I said that I had forgotten.
When the record was released on 5 May Penny Valentine, the
record reviewer for the *Disc Music Paper*, phoned Robert and
Grenville to say that it was the best record I would ever make.

I suppose this was just in time, because the Boscobel-
Denmark case was due to commence. It would become
one of the most referred-to cases of the period: one that set a
legal precedent, and helped lay the ground-rules for others
that were to follow.

Boscobel versus Denmark was possibly the first time such a
songwriting contract was challenged in the High Court. In the
fifties and early sixties people in the music business, particularly
the businessmen such as publishers and promoters, were not
considered in the same way as the established professional
classes. For the most part show-business had been run by
former artists turned businessmen. There were ex-band leaders
like Val Parnell, ex-tap dancers like Lew Grade and Bernard

Delfont, and ex-pop singers like Dick James, who had sung the theme tune to the *Robin Hood* series on television and was now the owner of Northern Songs (who published the Beatles). Of course there had always been horror stories connected with the music business, of writers and performers denied their dues in some cases simply because the artists were either so poor or so anxious to get a break that they simply signed on the dotted line and accepted a pittance in order to get work published.

I once met a sad old drunk in the A and R Club, a seedy drinking establishment above a shop in Tottenham Court Road. The old man was introduced to me as the man who wrote 'Sally', the Gracie Fields hit. I was honoured to meet this man, because 'Sally' had been one of the most requested songs whenever the Davies family had a singsong. However I was appalled when the sad old fellow told me that Gracie Fields' manager had purchased the song from him for £50. 'Fifty pounds! And that included all performing rights and record royalties forever. I never want to hear that bloody song again!' exclaimed the old man. I had heard many similar stories and suddenly Eddie Kassner's original offer of £40 a week for life sounded a princely sum in comparison to the tragic tale told by the man who claimed he had written 'Sally'.

When we signed the contract with Boscobel Productions there was a clause in that contract which really affected us later on. It said that in effect Boscobel had the right to assign part of that contract to a third party. We didn't take legal advice at the time we signed with Boscobel and we were not well versed in the intricacies of legal documents. According the contract, it was not my right to know. It was, legally speaking, none of my business. To this day I don't fully understand, and to tell you the truth the thought of it makes me cringe with embarrassment. I later discovered that Boscobel had an arrangement whereby Larry could participate in the management of the group. This is one thing and OK, I knew Page was involved on a management level, but the company Page used to sign us was called Denmark Productions which, as it turned out, was partly owned by Eddie Kassner. I even suspect that Kassner was the major shareholder. In this agreement, which I don't recall having ever seen, Boscobel passed on to Larry Page the rights to place the publishing of the songs – *my* songs – with anyone he chose, and that was it. Bingo. Guess who he chose? Eddie Kassner. Whammo. That's all I know. End of story. I suppose they thought it was a fair deal. Maybe it was. I don't know. Now do you understand what a sucker I feel after all this time?

Play the tape.'

I pressed the play button on an antiquated tape recorder and the old Kinks song, 'The Money-Go-Round', started playing. The lyrics were more or less a description of the Kinks early music-publishing arrangements, and the intricate deception which would inevitably lead to litigation. The vocal style reminded me of a man being driven to the verge of a nervous breakdown. On one side he is anti-establishment, making rock records, being a pop star, and, on the other, going from solicitor to solicitor in a quest for artistic and commercial freedom. I watched Raymond Douglas as the song played, and thought that in a tragic and strangely ironic way, he was fighting the same battle he had fought with the art college principal who had tried to dictate the way his work should look. One authoritarian system had just taken over from another.

I listened to the song, and wondered why he had never decided to stop fighting the system and join it, as so many of his contemporaries had done. Go on the marches, do the concerts for worthy and fashionable causes, play the game with the press and allow the media access to intimate secrets about his life. To me, the whole mystique surrounding him and his group had been created because they hardly ever did publicity, and as a result most of their more important work had been overlooked or misinterpreted by the public. Raymond Douglas stayed an outsider, supporting unfashionable causes only to move on to other things when the rest of the world finally picked up the cause he had supported years before. As a result his group always remained on the fringe of mainstream success. Difficult to categorize, impossible to package – to such a degree that their unpopularity took them to a cult status.

As the song finished Raymond Douglas regained confidence, and his willingness to communicate returned.

'At least they could not stop me writing songs, although everybody had expected me to cave in under the pressure of it all. It was a pity that the law-suit happened because, as I said earlier, we had it in us to rise above all the phoney sixties euphoria and turn the whole thing into something really different. If we could have made the thing work, we could have had it all. Instead the ideas about uniting in a classless society went out of the window because in the end everybody reverted to type. At school I was continually told I would fail. Every time I did something that did not quite fit in with the rules, a barrier was put in front of me. Then I started writing songs and was able to express myself, and as soon as I became successful I found myself in a court of law having to fight for my right to do so. My dad always used to say, 'If they don't get you one way, they'll get you another way.' I guess he knew, but I was determined that they, whoever 'they' were, were not going to stop me saying and doing what I believed in.

We were supposed to be one-hit wonders. Our first Number 1 record was supposed to have been a fluke. But I wouldn't stop. I just kept on writing. I think that's what annoyed them so much, the fact that I kept churning out the hits. I just stayed hot.

Actors work on stage, barristers inhabit rehearsal rooms called chambers and, when they finally appear on stage, they call themselves counsel. For the first time in my life since leaving college I was reintroduced to the pecking order of society. All of a sudden I was drawn back into a world where rules from another age applied. Where a person's accent and background were considered before you were judged and given your 'rightful' place in society. I might just as well have robbed a bank, or killed somebody, for all it mattered. In my opinion I had done nothing wrong, but there I was, like a criminal, fighting for my freedom. In other words the establishment had grabbed another rebel by the balls and made him kneel before them. I had become classless because of my success, but litigation put me straight back on that cold suburban street surrounded by greyness. I felt that dark cloud drift up behind me and slowly cover my head. I was right back where I started, in an emotional wasteland.

The court case was looming and the barristers were preparing for the 'circus' that was about to take place. Andrew Bateson was to be the junior counsel for Boscobel. He was a small, thin, surprisingly jovial character who would literally rub his hands at the prospect of interrogating Kassner and Page. The leading barrister, the man who would actually ask the questions in court, was to be Mr Fisher. This was considered to be a considerable coup as, according to Bateson, Fisher's father had been the Archbishop of Canterbury, and would not only give the Boscobel case a certain degree of righteous clout, but also indicated that in Bateson's words, at least 'God is on our side'. Denmark Productions' leading counsel was Mr 'Blackie' Campbell, a Second World War hero who according to Grenville was supposed to have been one of the few men to escape from Colditz.

One of our many advisers announced with glee, 'A great prospect. What a circus!' I soon learned what the term 'circus' meant to his sort: a defendant was like a clown jumping through hoops; dwarfs being humiliated; litigants like lions being tamed with the whip of justice; desperate men walking a tightrope without a safety net to save them when they fell, and the ringmaster judging and keeping a watchful eye over the proceedings.

Collins and Wace smiled with relief at the sound of the word 'circus'. I realized that they felt secure among their own kind, the so-called professional classes. For no particular reason I started to feel alienated from the two of them, and at times I wondered whether or not they were actually on my side. I even wondered what the case itself was about. Wace and Collins were only trying to sort out the situation with Page and Kassner, and get back to managing the Kinks. There was nothing, or very little, spoken about my right to take my publishing away.

Only Colin Wadie seemed to show genuine concern for my deep-rooted fears. Wadie diligently took notes in longhand, pausing only to make the occasional interjection on a point of law. Bateson told Wadie to put any such queries down in his notes and let leading counsel decide whether or not it bore any relevance to the case.

By now I was beginning to feel a certain amount of paranoia about the so-called 'case'. Whose case was it? And, more to the point, whose interests were really being looked after? It was obvious to me that this was more a dispute over management rather than who had the rights to administer my publishing. As Bateson spoke about Kassner and Page, it was clear that, this was going to be a battle of classes. West End versus the City.

I looked at Collins, Wace and Colin Wadie, and suddenly realized that nothing had changed in society. My success as a pop musician had only taken me out of that world temporarily. Now I was back in the clutches of the establishment. I had to enter court and swear on a Bible and God was my witness; I had to take the oath of allegiance to a religion that seemed far removed from my predicament. I was to be represented in court by the son of the former head of the

Church of England. The very same church that had filled me with the beauty of its hymns and compassion for the weak, while at the same time only allowing a boy to move in the world according to his class. It was obvious that all men were not born equal after all

After a meeting at his chambers, Bateson asked me whether there was another pop hit on the way. I turned and looked around Bateson's chambers: a mixture of spartan Victorianism and pious splendour, with a picture of a great lawyer on the wall. He looked like he needed a hit. The room fell silent. I didn't want these people to have access to my work as they seemed to know every other aspect of my life. I wanted to say that the new record was about something that they would never understand because they had forgotten their own innocence. Because until the record was released, the song and what it represented was for my friends only; my private world. Grenville broke the silence and announced that the Kinks had just recorded a song called 'Waterloo Sunset', and it stood a very good chance of becoming a hit.

'Will it make me laugh like "A Well-Respected Man"?' asked Bateson jovially.

I looked over at the inquisitive barrister. 'It might make you smile if you believe this country has some romance left', I replied. Nobody in the room had any idea what I was talking about.

As we left, Bateson looked at me in a way that made me feel I was on the other side of the dock. 'You're quite an enigma, Mr Davies. You must be careful not to attempt to make poetic remarks on the witness stand. Even the best judges, and Judge Widgery is one of the best, can only make judgements on facts. An enigmatic answer or inconclusive reply, however poetic, has put better men than yourself into difficulties in a court of law. Mr Campbell will jump on any opportunity to show that you are a wastrel, or quite possibly a half-wit. Vague poetic responses are dangerous ammunition for a barrister, particularly when he is your inquisitor and out to prove that you are not a man of your word. Look what such behaviour did to Oscar Wilde.'

The others chuckled and even I had to acknowledge Bateson's wisdom.

But as I left I suggested that provided I told the truth at the trial then I was in no danger. Bateson smiled. Colin Wadie muttered under his breath, 'Thomas More was a truthful, innocent man according to many, and yet even he was judged as being guilty. In the end it cost him his life at the hands of the axeman.' I was only party to a civil action, but already I was conjuring up images of going to the gallows if Boscobel lost.

My taxi took me along the Embankment, and I thought about what had been said at the meeting. All the false illusions of the sixties were being exposed. The idea of the working man and the upper-class man joining arms after the Second World War for the great battle ahead was total nonsense. Throughout the meeting at Bateson's chambers, the sound of 'Waterloo Sunset' had gone round and round in my head. The lyric told how the imaginary Julie, who suddenly symbolized England, met my nephew, Terry, on Waterloo Bridge. A reunion of past and future that had obviously never happened. I thought about Terry's father Arthur, and how his bitterness and sense of betrayal by Britain had forced him to emigrate to Australia to a new life. For the first time, I considered the possibility that Arthur may have been right.

'On 23 May 1967 the Boscabel-Denmark case started in the High Court. The case was heard in front of Judge Widgery (who later became Lord Chief Justice).

Judge Widgery sat patiently while he heard the testimony of Larry Page, followed by Sam Levy and Eddie Kassner. The following day it was the turn of Robert Ransom, David Dane, Kassner's accountant, and Robert Wace. During Dane's testimony, he produced a crumpled piece of paper, a note I was alleged to have written some time the year before when I ran down to Denmark Street in an abortive attempt to sort out Brian Somerville and the rest of the world. The letter, which was almost illegible, said that I was sorry for all the unhappiness I had caused: the type of confessionals people under stress tend to write when they are pushed completely over the edge. Denmark's counsel waved the piece of paper around, asserting that I was a confused and manipulated young person who had been swayed into leaving Denmark Productions. Then the scrap of paper was handed over to Mr Fisher, and I expected him to dismiss the note as the incoherent rantings of a tormented soul. He too waved it in the air, but as if to indicate that it was a piece of inconsequential evidence. Andrew Bateson tipped his barrister's wig forward in a cocksure manner, leaned over and joked that Blackie Campbell had been waving the note around frantically because the ink had not dried sufficiently. Dave made a particularly good impression on Judge Widgery when, cross-examined by Blackie Campbell, he replied to a devious question as to whether he was doing well financially by saying, 'Very well, Guv, can't complain.' I was astounded by the confidence of my younger brother, still only nineteen years old, and yet already a seasoned musician, playboy and litigant.

The following day, I, Raymond Douglas, was in the box. Not only did I discover that I was on oath, as if speaking in front of God, but when the end of the session came for that day, I was informed that I was not allowed by law to speak to anybody about the case, and about my evidence in particular. I was amused to see that everybody, including Grenville and Robert, turned away when I asked if they were going for a drink afterwards. That night, I went home to discover that 'Waterloo Sunset' had gone into the Top 10. I sat alone in front of the television and watched Glasgow Celtic beat Milan and become the first British team to win the European Cup.

Klein and Machat were orchestrating backstage because, regardless of the outcome of the Boscabel-Denmark case, it did not touch on the matter of the record company dispute, which was about to erupt between the Kinks and Pye Records.

The following day I was asked by Blackie Campbell why, if I had such distrust and loathing for Kassner and Page, had I, in my moment of madness after the confrontation with Brian Somerville, gone directly to their offices next door to seek refuge? It was a good question. I felt a little ashamed to say that I was being pursued by the police, and if I had said that I felt emotionally confused at the time, it would have opened a can of worms that undoubtedly would have been used against me. So I looked up at my inquisitor and explained that it had been a sunny day, and on a sunny day I will talk to anybody. This seemed to me a truthful enough answer, but it produced a slight titter around the courtroom, as if I had made some sort of blunder. I looked at Bateson, who by now had tipped his wig over so far that it completely covered his eyes, and I suddenly remembered his words of warning about being poetic and vague. Suddenly the image of the gallows loomed. But I felt that all in all, my answer was sufficient.

Judge Widgery looked me up and down, as if to study the

depth of my honesty; then he turned across to look at the so-called parties in dispute. After a short pause for thought, he pronounced wisely that 'Mr Davies is what this case is about, because what we are dealing with here is a dispute over his publishing.' I looked around the courtroom. At last somebody had grasped the truth, and it happened to be the judge hearing the case. Kassner was gritting his teeth; Page was glaring through his large black-framed spectacles ; Grenville had his usual raised eyebrows; and Robert merely stared straight ahead impassively, as if he were on a golf course somewhere trying to decide which iron to use on his approach shot to the green.

Judge Widgery added that even though this was his assessment, this was not the case which had been put before him. Later that week, after a brief adjournment, he gave his decision. Nobody had won. All I remember was that the judgement was greeted by shouts of 'appeal' and 'costs' as one counsel shouted across the courtroom to the other. I slumped down in my chair. I couldn't quite understand the somewhat ambiguous result.

The effect of this decision meant that my finances as a writer would be frozen and held in escrow until the appeal at least. We were informed later by Mr Fisher that the other side had indicated to him that they would take the case to the House of Lords if they had to. I went back to my mother's house with Dave and sat in the front room while he strummed a song we had recorded called 'Death of a Clown'. We were both shell-shocked from the courtroom dramas that had surrounded us both. I watched Dave, in the same front room where he had been born, and where I had written 'You Really Got Me', as he strummed. I suggested that it sounded a little bit like a Bob Dylan song.

As he played it through, he kept missing out the bridge. I assumed that Dave was just playing the parts of the song which comforted him after the courtroom ordeal. The lyrics were singable and heartfelt, but without the bridge

the song sounded repetitive. I went over to the old upright
piano and played the bridge in E flat. This had been the first
song Dave and I had co-written, but on the recording session
Dave had not bothered to write lyrics to my section and so
Rasa had simply la-la'd her way through.

The song still sounded Dylanesque, even with the bridge,
but Dave liked that. I had always distrusted Dylan as a
songwriter, in the same way that at college I had distrusted
Picasso as a painter.

I had the feeling that both men were great artists but
creative chameleons. In Dylan's case I suspected that he wanted
to be the new Woody Guthrie, but had deviated when he got
access to early Beatles' records. As far as Picasso went, he
dabbled with Impressionism. He tried his luck as Braque and
sometimes even surpassed him. And by the time he achieved
greatness, he was already copying himself. As a cynical art
student the only work I respected of his was *Guernica*. I was
totally bowled over by that. (Perhaps if I had seen Bob Dylan
live, I would have felt the same way.) When I saw the print of
Guernica as an art student, I imagined the actual painting to be
enormous; when I saw it many years later in New York I was
amazed at how small it was compared to the emotions and
events it depicted. Maybe, like all legendary works of art, it
did not seem as large or as small as I imagined it to be. This
started me thinking about the rest of Picasso's work, which I
had dismissed as bullshit when I was an art student. I suddenly
saw the humour in it: that he was so talented that he could
have a painting taken seriously while he was in fact laughing
at the hypocritical art world. It wasn't until later that I started
to feel the same about Dylan. He was also making fun of all
the fashion victims who were calling him a great poet. The
only thing I had against him was that he had changed his
name; but then I guess that was his privilege. Even Picasso was
usually marketed without the Pablo. Dylan and Picasso: two
giants of twentieth-century art, both giving a new meaning to

the expression 'piss artist'. Why shouldn't they take the piss? They were both masters of their art.

So there was Dave trying to come to terms with his own art by playing that sad little song. 'Death of a Clown' was autobiographical in the sense that Dave Davies, the great raver and womanizer, was contemplating marriage to a Danish cousin of Pete Quaife's wife. He made only one comment on the matter, 'I've met a girl who smiles when I make love to her.' The soon-to-be Lisbet Davies was a gentle woman and would turn out to be a long-lasting friend with seemingly perfect manners and an inscrutable, almost oriental smile that was seldom removed. In later years the ever-curling corners of her mouth constantly curled further upwards as new babies were born. Her fixed grin and slightly squinting eyes on a rounded face, accompanied by a Danish person's attempt to speak English, gave her the impression of being a Danish geisha girl. Dave was married sometime in 1967 in Denmark with none of my family there. And 'Death of a Clown' was a nominal attempt on Dave's part to become a respected married man. But not only can you not teach a dog new tricks, Dave was destined to remain a clown both to my joy and despair, because in Dave's case Mr Hyde had already taken over and Dr Jekyll made the occasional appearance as did an inferior publicist at births, weddings, funerals. 'Death of a Clown' would not mean the end of Dave Davies. It was released shortly after 'Waterloo Sunset' descended from the charts.

By this time, I was being hailed as one of the better British songwriters of the period. Upon the release of 'Death of a Clown', Ned Sherrin, producer, broadcaster and founder of the sixties satire movement, summoned me to dinner at 3 Bywater Street, in Chelsea, the habitat and general pit-stop for many of London's so-called 'swinging celebrities'. Ned's tiny terraced house was the watering-hole/confession room of some of the brightest people in London, and for me to be invited was considered a major feather in the cap of my socially

aware management. Ned Sherrin was not only the godfather
of satire but godmother to many of its aspiring young actors
and writers. As I arrived the legendary and statuesque Mr
Sherrin stood on the steps above, his monumental chest puffed
up like a giant pigeon during mating season, his eyes piercing
down at me with a hypnotic gaze. He addressed me as he
would have done a plumber or window cleaner who had just
completed their duties to his satisfaction. Sherrin had a clipped,
musical, upper-class voice that was remarkably high-pitched
for such a large man.

'Raymond Douglas, I assume. I thought "Dedicated
Follower of Fashion" worked rather well, and your baby
brother's little number is quite a singable ditty.' As he spoke
he ushered me up the stairs and into the house. The strains of
'Death of a Clown' could be heard in the background. As
Dave had been promoting 'Death of a Clown' dressed like a
regency dandy, with heavily made-up eyes, I was convinced
that the wrong brother had been invited to dinner. At the
same sessions as 'Waterloo Sunset' the Kinks had also recorded
a ridiculously camp tune called 'Mr Pleasant', about a man
who's kind to everybody on the exterior but doesn't realize
the pitfalls and traps involved in being superficially happy,
because Mrs Pleasant is having an affair. For some reason 'Mr
Pleasant' was released in Holland and went straight to Number
1, with 'Waterloo Sunset' at Number 2. Perhaps that was a
problem for many people including Mr Sherrin. I was two
people at once: a Romantic with strong ideals on one hand and
at the same time a cruel observer with no mercy. Nevertheless,
I was greeted with warmth and affection and the champagne
flowed as long as I could stand up. After a short while it was
clear that Ned had invited the right brother to dine.

Avory's pursuits, meanwhile, were of a less artistic but
equally flamboyant nature among the more squalid
surroundings of the transvestite bars of Putney and Earls
Court. Not that Avory knowingly sought out such places. It

just seemed that every large-breasted actress led, ultimately, to a late-night drinking club frequented by drag queens. In order to bed the lusty maidens, Avory invariably ended up at the Widow's apartment in Notting Hill Gate, where, after a pint of lager laced with an aphrodisiac, he would finally achieve his heart's desire either in front of a one-way mirror or with the drag queen in bed with himself and a busty actress. After several such encounters Avory had built such a reputation for himself that the Widow O'Brian decided to turn him into a male model.

Later, Avory dragged me and John Dalton to O'Brian's flat, but even after many lagers were consumed, the Widow found Dalton – to Dalton's great relief – too butch; even though she was 'mad about Dalton's thick white ankle socks', and 'mental for the Davies' limbs', ultimately she was a slave to 'the Avory body', declaring that even though she was a slut and was anybody's after a lager, 'an old queen must know where her true lust lay', and in her case, the Widow O'Brian was eternally devoted to 'Miss Avory'.

This turned out to be a disappointment for O'Brian, as Avory was straight and therefore a permanent relationship had to be sacrificed while, in the words of the Widow, Avory pursued, 'big-titted plones'.

During the summer a little hunchbacked man came to the house twice a week to do my back garden. He was the same hunchback I had seen walking the streets when I was a child. Although he was older in years, his stooping posture made him appear as young as he had always been, in that afflicted people always remain like children: his handicap outshone his age. He tended the garden with loving care, and as the seasons changed he swept up the dead leaves and prepared the garden for the next life cycle. Watching him always made me feel optimistic about the future; that there was always a better day coming. As a child he had symbolized everything that I feared. Now I was a man, he could not only be my friend, but share in my accomplishments. As I watched the friendly old man stoop over his hoe, I thought back to the Harley Street doctor who in February of that same year had suggested that in order to stop the pain in my middle back, a leather brace should be worn, similar to a corset, in order that I would not be a hump-backed cripple by the time I was thirty. Also, I was to refrain from any physical activity. I looked at Charlie as he endured his predicament and felt at one with him.

Soon after the release of 'Waterloo Sunset' Rasa drove me to a kennels where we purchased a puppy, a wire-haired fox terrier which I christened Georgie. By this time meetings between me and Georgie, the film teacher, were taking place in the absence of Frank Smythe. Georgie or Georgina as she was christened, was of Eastern European extraction, and her beauty was contained within a face that displayed a life of hard living. For all intents and purposes, the few secret meetings we had could have easily been attended by Frank Smythe, as they were inevitably held in pubs. Our entire relationship could have been held in a telephone box. It required no additional physical space as the only bodily contact, apart from the touching of hands, was an alcohol-tainted kiss of friendship at the end of the evening. I was losing touch with my world of dreams and Georgie was holding out a thread of hope that one day I might find it in myself to write the perfect rhyme. Then start making my rhymes turn into moving pictures.

Georgie the dog presented another set of problems altogether. Wire-haired fox terriers are pedigree dogs and require a good deal of attention, far more than the usual mutt that I was more accustomed to during my childhood.

Whether or not it was Georgie the person or the sudden introduction to Rasa's distant relatives (who had arrived on a short holiday from Lithuania), it cannot be ascertained, but after 'Waterloo Sunset' and 'Death of a Clown' faded from the charts, I found a new passion for vodka. I waited until Rasa was asleep and then crept downstairs to find the vodka bottle. Several glasses later, I phoned Georgie, who always picked up the telephone immediately and, without waiting to hear who was at the other end of the line, said , ''Allo, what's the matter?' After a long pause I replied, 'I'm afraid.'

I was afraid. Alan Klein had persuaded Warner Brothers and Pye to renegotiate their contracts with the Kinks. After the High Court judgement, Klein had come over to London, where he held court in the penthouse suite at the Hilton Hotel where a string of attorneys from Pye were ushered in and out. To say that he bullied them into a new deal with the Kinks would be an understatement. Doing deals was Klein's passion as well as his living. Colin Wadie attended these meetings and was disturbed by some of the tactics used by Klein and Machat. But in the mid 1960's, the gulf between the English solicitors and the American attorneys was clearly apparent, as was the manner in which they negotiated contracts. At one point Colin walked out of the meeting. I ran after him and grabbed him at the doorway. There were actually tears in the solicitor's eyes as he asked whether or not I wanted him to handle this litigation. His voice was shuddering. Klein's tactics were alien to him. I replied that of course I wanted him to continue. In the background I could hear Klein raising his voice to somebody. It was not clear if he were addressing a barrister or room service.

Colin left and I walked back into the room to join Klein, who was negotiating two deals at the same time. In the case of the Kinks the general thrust of the argument was that we'd been coerced into entering into an agreement when we were under age. Klein had formed a company called Bethevan, which on paper acted as manufacturer of Kinks records in America, as an intermediary, when in reality it was there to pass the Kinks' product from Pye to Reprise. In return for this, Alan B. Klein partially secured an advance of around \$ 16,000 to the Kinks for each Pye album delivered through Bethevan. Just before the deal was to be signed, I got cold feet. For some reason, I had always imagined that while in

London Klein would actually meet up with my mother and she would tell him in no uncertain terms to piss off. Unfortunately, that encounter never took place. It would have been a true clash of the Titans.

They call the closing of the deal 'consummation'. To businessmen it's like coming. The thought of money. The thought of tying up people's lives in contractual bliss. Copyright. Mechanicals. An orgasm of money. A contractual orgy. After I had signed the papers, Marty Machat took me into his bedroom where he was packing to go back to New York. Machat put on that characteristic rational tone of voice which was compassionate and very persuasive. As he spoke, he paused mid-sentence and took out a Havana cigar which he put into the top pocket of my jacket. As he patted my pocket, he continued to rationalize about the deal; then he took out another cigar and repeated the process. I suddenly imagined I heard the 'Star Spangled Banner' playing in an American movie as the Great Eagle swooped up and surveyed his domain. America had got me and once it gets you, you belong to it forever. The only way to get out of one deal is to get into another. Provided you have enough baggage to carry all the cigars.

The group had been restored to its position as one of the most consistent chart bands in Britain, and even though the Musicians Union ban was still in force in the United States, 'Sunny Afternoon' had become a Top 10 hit over there. They may have been able to stop us touring, but they couldn't stop us making records. Yet.

My publishing royalties were still in dispute and my writer's earnings frozen until the outcome of the management court case. I felt grateful for just being allowed to continue to write songs. I had achieved everything I had set out to do creatively and I was twenty-two years old. Perhaps the money would arrive before I collected my pension.'

*

That night after leaving R.D., I went home with every intention of starting to do some work, but I found myself listening to the *Face to Face* album by the Kinks. This album was the first recording made under the new deal which had been set up by Klein and Machat. I sat back and listened. The opening track, 'Party Line', started with a telephone ringing and the voice of Grenville Collins saying, 'Hello, who's that speaking, please?' The music sounded deceptively happy at first, but songs like 'Too Much on My Mind', 'Rainy Day in June' and 'Fancy' gave away the fact that a confused and troubled mind was at work. I imagined Collins and Wace receiving the $16,000 cheque from Alan Klein, while Peter Grant sat in their office in a large chair. I soon found myself listening to the next album under the deal, *Something Else*. The title suggested that R.D. was already on a treadmill. This album started out with the engineer Alan MacKenzie speaking down the intercom: 'This is the master.' R.D. then counted the song in backwards, possibly in honour of his lost love from Bergen, then the Kinks started playing 'David Watts'.

I look over at my message-light flickering on and off but before I can get over to it I start to drift off into a deep sleep. In my dream I hear the song 'Waterloo Sunset' being played in reverse. Then, I dream again. Pleasant images, no nightmares at all. I travel in time back before my birth to the land of green fields and warm summer days. I see R.D., who is ten years old, walking down a path carrying a fishing rod, going to join his father who is sitting by the river. This moment fades gently into another image of Rasa asleep in bed in R.D.'s semi in North London.

Rasa sleeps and dreams of having babies and a bigger house, somewhere in Cheshunt, or maybe Weybridge; of a new Lancia sports car. Downstairs Georgie, the wire-haired fox terrier, sleeps by the radiator, full stretch. He twitches in his sleep as he dreams of the pursuit during the hunt for food. I see R.D. drinking vodka from a bottle while rubbing his knees to keep out the autumn cold. I observe him as he quietly dials a number on the telephone. He whispers to the invisible Georgie, 'I am afraid.'

By now Georgina, being a woman not only of great wisdom and compassion, is beginning to display a need for physical commitment. My dream continues as on a damp afternoon R.D. attempts to get drunk enough to go back to Georgina's flat. I see him flat on his back while Georgina straddles her legs across his shoulders, like a wrestler pinning her opponent to the ground for a count of three. With amazing agility she manages to contort herself so that her head is next to R.D. From his point of view her mouth seems as large as the Grand Canyon and as he runs his hands along her black tights it is apparent that she wants this to be more than just a platonic relationship. R.D. cannot function. Georgie whispers that they both may as well wait until the next world. After realizing that any form of sexual foreplay is futile, Georgie suggests artificial insemination. Then, in my dream I think of Julie from my office, her pale white skin and thick head of hair. My dream flashes back and forth, up and down, forward and reverse as I'm thrown between R.D. and Georgie, Julie and myself. I eventually wake up covered in sweat with my bedclothes thrown on the floor. . . My mind floats as my present catches up with R.D.'s past.

I returned to R.D. at his studio later that morning. I wanted to tell him about my dream, but I preferred to let him continue without any further disturbances.

He drank his tea from his old Coronation mug and continued his tale.

'As autumn turned into winter, and Christmas went by, a few meetings with my friend Georgie took place and Frank Smythe reappeared in the scenario, along with John Philby, an old college friend of mine. Rasa had still only met Georgie the dog at this point. There were still walks in Hampstead where Georgie and I breathed alcohol on each other to keep out the cold. There were discussions about the poems I intended to write and the films I wanted to make and all my dreams as yet unfulfilled. Then it struck me. The difference between getting pissed and taking the piss. I just wanted someone to hear my

fears and talk about lost causes. For all the care and attention I
had given in return, I may as well have been talking to my
dog. On New Year's Eve I made an excuse to go out so that I
could make a telephone call to Georgie which simply said 'A
Happy New Year'. She said, knowing there was no
commitment in my voice, 'Thank you for the posh meals and
the drunken nights and unfulfilled dreams.' I felt ashamed.
'Thank you for the days.' I think it only cost a few pence to
make a telephone call in those days. That's all it cost me to say
goodbye.

A few weeks later I arrived home after a recording session
to find Rasa crying. I thought somebody had died or the
house had been burgled or, worse still, someone had stolen her
new Lancia. Rasa ran up to me and threw her arms around
me. Her voice was choked with emotion.

'Georgie. Somebody has stolen Georgie. He was a pedigree.
The police say that we'll never get him back.'

I tried to console her but unsuccessfully. Poor thing. She
didn't know that there are lots of Georgies in this world.

You've got to understand that I never manipulate situations
to achieve artistic ends. I try my utmost to depersonalize what
I write, but sometimes things stay in the subconscious and you
have to bring them too the surface. It was then that I really
began to become afraid regularly. It seemed that the law-suits
would go on forever. One night out of sheer desperation I
took a large bottle of vodka – finished it all – while I wrote
the lyrics to a song called 'Wonder Boy'. Vodka seemed to
bring out something macho in me. After writing these lyrics, I
wanted a son. I staggered up to bed. 'Wonder Boy' would be
like a parting gift to a kind soul, and to friendship, something
to be treasured.

I'd reached the point where even though I knew that
'Wonder Boy' would not be a gigantic hit, I was more
concerned with what I had written than with what it had sold.
I think the record died in the 20s, but Grenville said that

someone had seen John Lennon in a club and he kept on asking the disc jockey to play 'Wonder Boy' over and over again. I guess that approval from my peers meant that 'Wonder Boy' had not been a complete mistake. Sometimes when you write inside yourself you have no idea whether you are sane or not. When the rest of the world acknowledges your work, somehow they condone your insanity. In the case of 'Wonder Boy', it felt that the people who bought the record had not understood my own little subtext. They were buying a Kinks record. To me it was a cry for help. Later, the full impact of what had happened finally hit me.

A similar thing happened when I recorded 'Days', though I didn't realize that what I was writing would be the most significant song in my life so far. The song predicted the end of the group. Before we recorded the song I was convinced that Quaife had decided to leave the band forever. We had made the back track, I had recorded the vocals and Nicky Hopkins was putting on a keyboard part. Quaife walked over to me with the box that would contain the master tape and substituted the word 'Days' with the word 'Daze'. I think the anger that I felt for him was really anger at myself. It was conceit on my part; my work had become too precious to me. The truth was that as proud as I was of the song, I was literally in an emotional daze about where I was, who I was and who I wanted to be with. Maybe Quaife was as well.

One night, in the back room of my semi I played the finished tape of 'Days' to my mum and dad. My sister Gwen and Brian, my first tour manager, were also there with their kids. Their young daughter Janice sat and looked out into the garden with a sorrowful look in her eyes. The expression on Janice's face was telling me that something was about to end but she was probaly just upset because she wanted to go into the garden to play. I knew that 'Days' was telling the world that it was the end of the group. All that was left to do was to make *The Village Green Preservation Society*, as a farewell gesture .

When the album was written, I thought that the Kinks would never get back into the States after the ban. While everybody in the world was gravitating towards love, peace and San Francisco, the Kinks were in a London suburb making this strange little record about an imaginary village green.

You see, I think that when Quaife left the band, some of the original impetus and determination fell away. We got replacements sure enough. Dalton was a good man, but the original band was gone and when Barry Wentzel took those last cover shots outside Kenwood House in Hampstead, he was documenting the end of the band. I've got mixed feeling about the follow up L P *Arthur*. The record had some musical high spots, and was undoubtedly the first genuinely constructed musical play by a rock band, but as a whole I remember it for what it might have been, rather than what was eventually realized.

The *Village Green Preservation Society* had attracted a certain faddish following, even though the album was a commercial flop and received almost no airplay in Britain. When it came out in 1968, there were hardly any pirate stations left to act as alternative radio. The illustrious government had outlawed them, those stations that were the last of the truly independent outlets. Now the BBC monopolized the airwaves, and for many of the emerging DJs, the Kinks sounded too English. While everybody else thought that the hip thing to do was to drop acid, do as many drugs as possible and listen to music in a coma, the Kinks were singing songs about lost friends, draught beer, motorbike riders, wicked witches and flying cats.

We had also parted company with our flamboyant agent Arthur Howes, and after a brief spell with agencies whose names elude me we ended up at the MAM organization; a company that was supposed to be co-owned by Harold Davidson and Tom Jones' management. Barry Dickens, whose father Percy had run the *NME*, became responsible for us.

Although Barry became a close friend to the Kinks (he had even seen us perform at a youth club in the East End when Robert was our vocalist) and the whole organization seemed more professional, Arthur Howes' personal touch was missing. It was the passing of an era.

Before I had written *The Village Green*, Rasa and I had moved out of the little semi in north London and taken up residence in a manorial mock Tudor mansion in Elstree. This was partly at the insistence of two of my sisters, who felt that someone who had written so many hits should indulge himself in a luxurious house. The house looked grand and sprawling on the outside, but turned out to be far from luxurious, with old solid-fuel central heating which made clanging noises, and a large panelled dining room that was riddled with woodworm and dry rot. The night we moved in, I decided that the house was not suited to myself and my young family. (Louisa was just two and Rasa was pregnant with Victoria.) Eventually, I had an extension built on to the old house in Finchley and we moved back into the semi. However, most of the *Village Green* and *Arthur* had been written in that large, woodworm-infested property.

Robert and Grenville were persuaded by our new agency that a career move was in order. We were booked into a series of northern nightclubs to see how we would fare as all-round entertainers. Up north the cabaret audiences dressed up in evening clothes and gambled in an upstairs room, using cash instead of chips. Then they ate potato chips and scampi when they went downstairs to watch the cabaret.

The 'career move' proved to be an immediate and unmitigated disaster as we played too loud for both the audience and the management. On one notable occasion Dave played the opening of 'All Day and All of the Night' so loudly that the scampi and chips on a nearby table were blown off by the reverberations from the amplifier.

It was a bright spark producer called Jo Derden Smith,

who approached Robert and Grenville about the Kinks
recording the first rock opera for Granada television. Derden
Smith, who was as tall as Grenville and Robert, took us all to
lunch in a smart Soho restaurant and asked what I wanted to
write about. He was like many intellectuals of the time who
decided that they could turn rock and roll, which was the
voice of the proletariat, into an élitist art form. I thought why
not take advantage of him taking advantage of me? Derden
Smith knew so much about the pop culture and was so
incredibly well informed about current trends, that he was
a complete fashion victim; indeed, I fantasized that he changed
his musical tastes as frequently as he changed his underpants.
The only thing that remained the same was a long black
leather overcoat. I knew that *The Village Green* was about the
decline of a certain innocence in England, and when I
suggested that I go the whole way and write about the decline
and fall of the British empire everyone, without exception,
thought that it was the perfect subject matter. Derden Smith
strutted around in his full-length leather overcoat and
suggested various writers with whom I should collaborate
with on the script. To be fair, Derden Smith had the courage
to embark on subject matter which he must have known was
not fashionable, but at least I started to believe that I could
deliver the goods and that was all that mattered. I had seen
Forty Years On at the theatre and thought that Alan Bennett
would be a good choice. Someone else suggested Sir John
Betjeman, who was not only the poet laureate at the time, but
his work, in the opinion of Derden Smith, echoed my own
feeling for a world and a way of life that was disappearing.
This all seemed a little depressing and slightly melancholic,
and eventually someone suggested a writer in the mould of
Colin MacInnes who had written several cynical but well
observed novels. The other writer they suggested was Julian
Mitchell.

During this period, which can only be described as

uncertain, our new road manager was Ken Jones. He was a quiet man from Northern Ireland with a keen sense of economy, which in our uncertain financial state made us feel at ease. We began to let him make decisions about our travel plans, even though normally Grenville and Robert had done this. But Robert just laughed and referred to Jones as the travel agent. However, Ken often encouraged us to play concerts in faraway places, simply because he wanted to experience the satisfaction of going there with all travel and hotel costs thrown in.

One notable venue was Beirut, Lebanon. Robert and Grenville were sceptical, because we were in the middle of recording *Arthur* and the world was expecting war to break out any day in the Middle East. Jones said that the Lebanese promoter had promised 'the trip of a lifetime' and half the money up front. Reluctantly we went, and were greeted by a friendly promoter dressed in a western business suit. He took us to a hotel he owned, showed us the concert venue which was conveniently located outside the hotel next to the swimming pool.

Robert had disapproved of the trip, but felt that at least we'd get paid. However, problems started to surface at the television studio the next day. We were supposed to play to promote the next day's show, but neither Dave nor Dalton had arrived in time for transmission. The director told Mick and me to 'spread out'. We walked out. The promoter, now in full Arab dress, demanded that we fulfil all sorts of promotional obligations, none of which had been mentioned before. Having my photo taken in the harbour smoking a hookah was one thing, eating goats' eyes and calves' brains in the promoter's restaurant was another. He was insulted.

Beirut at this time was the Las Vegas of the Middle East, and Avory insisted that the promoter lead us on a tour of every club in the city. Our only problem was that the promoter had put guards on every floor to prevent us from taking girls to our rooms. I devised a method of distracting

the guards while Avory took a woman up the emergency
stairs, only to be foiled when two guards followed us into the
room. The promoter was now totally outraged and threatened
us with imprisonment.

Ken, meanwhile, was enjoying himself, sunbathing by the
pool. Despite warnings about the heat, he was there all day
wearing only his underpants and a pair of leather moccasins.
He said he had served in the RAF in the Far East and was
used to the climate. The morning of the concert Ken was
nowhere to be found. Eventually hotel security opened his
door and we found Jones curled in a foetal position looking
like a blown-up lobster. Poor Ken was in such pain that he
begged for someone to give him a shot of morphine – or kill
him – anything to put him out of his agony.

Robert simply said he expected him to have the equipment
set up in half an hour, and walked out of the room. This
turned out to be unnecessary when we discovered that the
promoter had decided to abandon the concert and impound
our equipment. The lobby was full of Lebanese men waving
their arms and shouting at Robert in Arabic. Eventually
someone from the British embassy came and through an
interpreter we were advised that if we did not pay back our
advance we would all be imprisoned and never see the light of
day again. The promoter had clearly run out of money and
was trying to find an excuse not to mount the concert. When
pressed by Robert for compensation, the promoter said that
he was also in the confectionery business and would pay off
the remainder of the fee with Mars Bars.

We decided to cut our losses, forget about Mars Bars and
head for the airport. At passport control an official said that as
the dispute had not been fully resolved we would have to
leave someone behind as a token of good faith. The people of
Beirut were already learning the value of taking hostages. We
immediately suggested leaving Ken Jones and offered to help
take his luggage off the trolley as his sunburnt arm was still in

a sling. However, we relented when he threatened to commit suicide in front of us. Eventually Robert managed to get us all on the plane and Ken Jones' journey of a lifetime was over.

On our return, Derden Smith and I met in Julian Mitchell's smart terraced house just off the King's Road and talked about my ideas. By now I wanted to centre the whole story around an ordinary man like myself, who had been a small cog in the empire and had watched it pass him by. After several meetings I trusted Julian enough to mention my brother-in-law Arthur. We both agreed that he would be an excellent choice, particularly as the name Arthur would also conjure up connections to King Arthur and the Round Table, the Holy Grail and all that. We were, however, convinced that our story should be about a family that was being torn apart because some of the children were emigrating to Australia. In our scenario Arthur was to be much older, he was to have served in the Great War and it was he who was being left behind in an old world that was in decline.

I immediately started writing lyrics and showed them to Julian, who then wrote scenes around them. When Robert read the lyrics to 'Some Mother's Son', a song about a young soldier killed in the war, he looked at me and exclaimed that I would probably be treated as a serious writer after this album came out; at last he had seen lyrics that showed I was back on form. He even referred to them as poetry. He added that he doubted it would sell, but to keep up the good work. I felt on a creative roll. The word back from Granada television was that the commissioning editor was very excited about what had been submitted so far and casting had already begun. A director called Leslie Woodhead had been assigned to the programme, but I suspected that the ambitious Jo Derden Smith would be firmly in control because he had all the necessary rock credentials, including a full-length black leather overcoat.

The album was finished and ready to be released. The final

script was given in. Sets were designed. Animation sequences filmed. Frank Finlay was shortlisted to play Arthur. Then, mysteriously, the plug was pulled by Granada. Grenville was livid, threatening litigation. (I was still in dispute with Kassner and so another law-suit was all that I needed.) The story was that Derden Smith, who had been involved in documentaries about the Doors and the Stones in Hyde Park, went to Granada and had fallen out with them over our programme. The upshot was that the powers that be pulled the show. A month or so later the Who came out with 'Pinball Wizard'. A month or so after that, nearly the same time as *Arthur* was to have been transmitted, the Who released the concept album *Tommy*. A record with a loose story line, not as thoroughly plotted or worked out as *Arthur*, but a record which, nevertheless, went on to be hailed as the first rock opera. Once again, we were beaten to the punch.

The critics were kind to us. 'Shangri-La', the first single, was a song that demanded the listener's attention. Tony Blackburn, a Radio 1 DJ, played 'Shangri-La' and at the end pointed out that the record, at over five minutes, was so long that you could go into the kitchen and make a cup of tea while it was playing. The same DJ had been heard to say that 'Dead-End Street' was too depressing as subject matter for a pop record. There were a few good guys left, but I got the feeling that they were playing our records for old times' sake rather than because they believed in the music. 'Shangri-La' disappeared from the airwaves after the second or third play. Later on 'Victoria' went on to become a small hit, but overall the BBC did not take to the album. Jo Derden Smith had also disappeared, along with his full-length leather overcoat. Thinking back, I suppose I was creatively conned. The work was good – I was pleased with what Julian had written – the songs were good, but I somehow felt that the music was serving the subject matter too much, and the first rule of rock music is that the music must always come first. Also, the band was not the same. Before we recorded *Arthur* I tried to persuade Quaife to stay but this time he had decided to quit for good. John Dalton played and sang well on *Arthur*, but I can't help feeling that the record would have been better if we had kept the original band. I also felt that in some strange way I had betrayed my class: ironically I had sold out to a corporation like Granada, that had built its whole empire on an image of the common man. *Coronation Street* was a classic example. Working class, hugely successful, cheap television.

But the album *Arthur (or the Decline and Fall of the British Empire)* was receiving good reviews in America. Yes, America of all places; where the Pod people from *Invaders from Mars*, the cult sci-fi movie of the fifties, seemed to use Martians as a metaphor for the 'Commie threat'. The same America with its gun laws that ended up killing JFK. The same America with its fear of rock bands who wore hunting jackets. The rednecks were waiting. The acid heads. Nuclear families. Perfect post-war suburbia. Grass-fronted houses for middle-class whites. Ghettos for the blacks. The same America that had marched to Washington with Martin Luther King and later had him shot along with Bobby Kennedy. The America that was proud of its Bill of Rights and yet lynched anyone who spoke out against it. America, where pornography and drugs was big business and preachers went on television and begged for money. America, that had banned and therefore harmed the Kinks for no apparent reason and as a result cost us the best years of our lives. America. All of it was waiting in its zoned out, freaky, pot-smoking, stupefied splendour. We couldn't wait to get back there.'

I looked over towards Raymond Douglas, who had gone silent, and I noticed that dark cloud reappear and move towards him. As it hovered behind Raymond Douglas' chair, he looked at me and said that his father had known the same darkness; when he was weak he would allow it to engulf him in total despair. Suddenly

Raymond Douglas grinned and explained how he was visited in a dream by his father's mother, who told him that all he had to do was to look the cloud in the face and smile at it. Then it would become discouraged and disappear: it is a negative force and can only thrive on despondency. Raymond Douglas looked up at the cloud, which was about to drop down on his head, and gave the broadest grin. The cloud dispersed above him and drifted into a corner of the room.

The endless hours he had spent in this room during his long career had obviously taken their toll; it seemed to be his only haven from the realities of the outside world. Time stood still in the small mixing laboratory. For my part, I felt dissatisfied with the progress I had been making. The Corporation would be reassured to a certain extent: I had extracted enough from Raymond Douglas to make a reasonable start on his life story. My only problem was that I, a Corporation employee, personified everything the old rock and roller despised. The world had changed since he was a young rebel in the sixties. My generation had been brought up to serve the Corporation in much the same way Raymond Douglas had been bred as factory fodder. My generation had learned to love the corporate ideal; total ownership of product; individual ambition satisfied as opportunities to climb the corporate ladder were clearly defined; pension schemes; sexual and marriage guidance offered as part of the school curriculum; marriage contracts negotiated by independent lawyers who all worked for different firms, but all under the umbrella of one corporate entity. My world was so well planned compared to R.D.'s and yet I felt that I had missed out on some of the independence aspects he had enjoyed during his life.

19

A promised land

I had undertaken this project with total enthusiasm, but as the days wore on I realized that I was no nearer the truth about R.D. than I had been before I met him. I should have already submitted my first draft, but as I scoured over my notes I realized that the old man had told me virtually nothing about himself. I had received two letters from Head Office asking me to hand in my manuscript, but as I had nothing of consequence to give them, I feigned illness. Then a letter came requesting an examination by a company doctor. I had to deliver soon, or risk an inquiry and possibly expulsion from the Corporation's employ. This would mean complete ruin. Why did they want R.D.'s story so badly? What was so important about an old rock singer who could do no more harm to anyone?

I decided to look back into the history of the Corporation that employed me. It soon became clear that the reason they wanted him was that they had never had him. R.D. was dangerous to them because he had never been theirs. He was a renowned crusader against corporate control of any kind; he was, in fact, one of the last of the independents. I remembered R.D.'s flip-side to 'Sunny Afternoon' had been a song called 'I'm Not Like Everybody Else'. R.D. was still running from an invisible force which he occasionally referred to as 'them'. Although he had never explained who 'they' were, it was now becoming obvious to me that they were the same people who were starting to intimidate me: 'they' were my employers.

R.D. had told me that his great fear had always been that one day the system would take away his individuality. I concluded that I had never been allowed to be an individual in the true sense; I was spawned by the system, born into that autocratic mould so feared by R.D. when he had been a child. I had been created to respond in a contrived way without the ability or desire to make my own choice. R.D. had, without knowing it, given me back the ability to dream, to think for myself; make my own rules and even consider becoming an individual. It was then that I decided that I was not going to play their game. 'They' were not going to have the life of R.D. to put in their computer so that they could close the file on him. I was going to ensure that R.D. retained his independence.

But there were still so many questions that I needed to ask. Who was *the* girl? Was she really Julie Finkle? What had motivated R.D. to keep the Kinks going and to form his own independent record company in the 1970s, and why did he write the *Preservation* album over and over, then turn it into a touring musical where he became Mr Flash, the head of a corrupt corporation? What was it like having to form a completely new band with his brother after the Kinks had finally conquered America in the 1980s and were, ironically, inducted into the American Rock and Roll Hall of Fame in 1990? What happened to make him turn into a complete recluse?

There was still so much that I needed to know, but I promised myself that the Corporation would not get what they wanted from R.D.D. The next day as I awoke fresh from a beautifully peaceful sleep, I threw my sleeping pills down the toilet and flushed them away. Project R.D. had done away with the need for sleepers. He had helped me confront my own demons. Now I had to make the decision between my obligation to the Corporation, and my newfound friendship with R.D.D.

The telephone rang. It was Julie on the other end of the line. Suddenly my confidence went. I found myself tongue-tied and making excuses. I could no longer trust her. I was still attracted to her, but I felt that everything she was saying to me was being monitored and my replies were being reported back to the Corporation. Perhaps she was an unwilling accomplice. Maybe they had something on her that was forcing her to act this way. They knew about my history, my emotional traumas and illness, God knows what they had on her. She went straight on to work as usual.

The questions were too intrusive, too pushy, so I brought the conversation to an abrupt end. She only let me go when I promised to hand in my notes and manuscripts by the end of the month. Just as I was about to hang up she said something which made me think that I was under surveillance.

'Are you still taking your medication?' she asked, almost as an afterthought.

'Of course,' I joked. 'Where would I be without my medication?'

Her reply upset me deeply. 'In an asylum for incurables and the feeble-minded, of course.'

I waited for her to laugh, as if she had been joking but she meant what she said. As if it were a statement of fact.

'Then you know about my problem,' I replied.

There was silence at the other end. She was obviously under pressure and hiding something from me. Then she spoke. Her voice was cold and to the point. 'I can say no more now. It was a risk to give you this assignment, but they thought that Raymond Douglas would recognize a similar disorder in himself and open up to you.'

'You're using me to get R.D.'s story? God knows what it will do to that poor defenceless old man when he finds out.'

'R.D., as you like to refer to him, must be exposed as a petty, inconsequential dreamer. He and his kind are totally out of step with the realism of our times. We have failed to suppress the music. There are still people who listen to it and not only aspire to write and live in his outdated manner, but actually try to emulate him. We must destroy their dreams.'

Hearing Julie talk like that unlocked a distant memory.

'Like they destroyed mine,' I replied.

'You were sick for other reasons. Now, find out anything you can to discredit him. Forget about all this *Preservation Society* nonsense. It is sentimental shit and you know it. Expose him as a corrupt person, unsuitable for any worthy place in our culture. You must succeed.'

'Why me?' And whose dreams must I destroy?'

'That will become apparent as you progress. Remember. In order to destroy their dreams, first we must destroy him.'

By now, I had lost all faith in Julie as a person. In a way, I had been writing R.D.'s book for her, but I felt that she had betrayed me.

I needed to confront R.D. on this issue. I had some serious questions to ask and I would demand some straight answers. My self-confidence was being eroded. My loyalties divided and my tolerance stretched to the limit. The following day I arrived at R.D.'s dark little studio to find him in a state of total panic. It was impossible to confront him.

He screamed out to me, 'Last night the cloud came and wouldn't go away. It hung over my head all night. It made me feel evil, as if I had corrupted all the innocence left in the world. The wretched sad world and all the sad people in it. I helped create the cess-pool that we all live in in this so-called country. All this reform and equality, what does it fucking mean? I dreamed about my father. My dad died believing that the world had given him a better deal than his parents before him. My dad choked to death with emphysema, after rolling around in agony in his bedroom at my house. He had staggered downstairs to the telephone, then into the kitchen, where his diseased lungs boiled over inside him. The poor old bugger fell over. The impact of his head against the tiled floor knocked him unconscious.'

R.D. sat down and composed himself before continuing. I handed him some fresh tea in his Coronation mug. I had questions I needed to ask, but it was obvious that R.D. needed to tell me about this time.

'This was way back in the mid-seventies, when I was working in London. I was about to watch the Wimbledon men's singles final on television. Dad phoned me up and told me to put a bet on Arthur Ashe to beat Jimmy Connors before the match started. Ashe, a black American, was a rank outsider, and Jimmy Connors was a white kid from Chicago, the darling of the centre court with all its strawberries-and-cream snobbery and class consciousness. Dad always liked to put a bet on the underdog. 'Ashe will slap the bastards in the face for us,' me old dad said. I found his reference to Ashe doing something for 'us' odd. Dad was no racist, but he rarely compared himself with black people. On reflection, I think that he must have meant Arthur Ashe was a dark horse. I tried to convince Dad that he would be wasting his money, but he shouted down the phone:

'For once, son, do as I tell you, just bloody well do it! I love you.'

This was uncharacteristic. The shouting, I mean. I was also a little surprised when he said that he loved me. I mean, he didn't even sound drunk. I picked up the Yellow Pages to find the number of the nearest betting shop. I called directory enquiries but it was engaged. Just as I put the phone down it rang. Mum was on the other end. She was weeping. She said Dad had died.

'I don't believe it,' I said.

'He's not awake, son. He collapsed on the floor in the kitchen.'

Dad loved the garden in the big house I had bought near Guildford. The house represented all the unfulfilled things in my life. All the promises not kept. It symbolized a fresh start in life after a series of disappointments. My parents used to go down to the house every weekend to look after the garden and see that the house was aired in case I ever wanted to visit. After hearing the news of my father's death, I had a slow-motion vision of him tending the rose bushes on the lawn outside in my garden. He loved his life as a gardener ever since his coronary made him give up all other work. He had started out as a stable boy when he left school at twelve, then

374

he went on to become a groom, then to work at Smithfield cattle market. Then various jobs around the country. He was so British, and yet he would have been perfectly at home in Kansas.

As I could not drive, Gwen and Brian came and picked me up to take me down to Surrey. On the car radio, we heard that Arthur Ashe had taken a set from Connors and was in the lead. We drove across the River Thames at Putney and I remembered going fishing with Dad on the River Ouse at the Offords near Huntingdon. I could still smell the ground bait as he moulded it in his hands before throwing it in the river to attract the fish. The smell of Old Holborn tobacco on his breath. The sight of him rolling his own ciggies. Lighting up his fag with a Swan Vesta match. I thought about the knives he kept and all his yarns about cutting the heads off of serpents in Wales during the war. I thought and remembered.

I suddenly asked Brian to stop and telephoned Dave, who was at the hospital with Dad's body. I told Dave to go check that Dad was actually dead and not just drunk. Once during a knees-up at home he had tried to do a somersault during 'Minnie the Moocher' and had fallen against a wall, knocking himself unconscious. All the family thought that he had had a heart attack, and my sisters were all crying. We even called an ambulance, but Dad woke up and asked where his beer was. But now Dave came to the phone. 'I've checked. Dad is absolutely dead. The doctors are moving him into the mortuary now, Ray. I've got to go.' The thought that the doctors were moving him meant that Dad was considered to be a non-person. That made me angry and aware of my own mortality. First a man with a name loses his life. Then he becomes a body. When death is confirmed he becomes 'the corpse'. As we drove down the motorway Ashe was turning the whole tennis establishment on its head. He had taken another set and Connors was getting dejected. The dark horse was moving up on the rails. As we entered the driveway of

375

my house in Surrey I saw the cars of relatives who had already arrived. On the radio Max Robertson was proclaiming in his magnificently articulate voice that Arthur Ashe had become the first black man ever to win Wimbledon and had caused one of the biggest upsets in the history of the tournament. I was elated and sad all at once. I remembered the flashbulb going off after Dad came to congratulate me after my first Number 1 record. Arthur Ashe, the dark horse, had done it and Dad had won the final bet of his life, but I couldn't tell him.'

Raymond Douglas started slowly kicking his foot against the mixing console, and for a moment, I thought that he was a sad old geezer who had gradually gone off his trolley. Then I started thinking about what he was trying to say to me. He was not just telling me about his father's death, or talking about 'Days' signalling the beginning of the end of his band, he was talking about the end of his family. The end of an age. He started talking about how he wrote *The Village Green Preservation Society* just to get away from the realization that the original group known as the Kinks was soon to be no more. My original decision to confront R.D. and burden him with my own doubts had to be put aside for the time being. The last thing he needed was to hear about my insecurities. He put on an old, scratchy *Village Green* album. The songs were deliberately under-recorded to give them an uncommercial quality. As if he didn't want people to really hear them. They were a series of nostalgic images of a disappearing world.

'We are the Village Green Preservation Society
God save little shops vaudeville and variety.
We are the Desperate Dan Appreciation Consortium.
God save the George Cross and all those who were awarded them
Preserving the old ways from being abused,
Protecting the new ways for me and for you
What more can we do?

We are the draught-beer English-speaking vernacular
God save Sherlock Holmes, Moriarty and Dracula . . .'

It was appealing but somehow unresolved. The subtext to the whole
record was more interesting than the songs themselves. R.D. talked
over the album as it played.

'This record had first been called *Four More Well-Respected Men*,
to capitalize on the hit the Kinks had had in America with *Well-
Respected Man* years earlier, but we decided against it. The Vietnam
War was in full swing, the Kinks were banned from touring the
States and from what I could ascertain, there was no room for
'Well Respected Men' in America at that time. The Woodstock
generation had arrived and the Kinks were almost forgotten.

'However, a smart promotion man at Warner-Reprise Records
came up with an unusual idea. *The Village Green* album had only
sold about 25,000 copies, but there was a groundswell of what he
called 'the underground'. *The Village Green* was an anti-war album
and there were many anti-war activists in America, particularly
among young college students. Somehow this uncommercial
record could spark off something in the American psyche. Grenville
joked that Reprise had replaced all the promotion men in black
suits and shades with pot-smoking hippies, and that Mo Ostin, the
president of the company, had been seen wearing beads and eating
organic food in a health-food restaurant in west LA. In a strange
way, things were looking up. We were not selling records but we
had become a cult band. Maybe *The Village Green* had rekindled
lost dreams to the Americans. Perhaps it was time to return.
Grenville and Robert knew that I had been disappointed that
'Days' had only got to Number 11 in the UK charts but said that
Alan Klein had an idea that would resolve the dispute with the
American Federation of Musicians so that we could get back into
America.'

Raymond Douglas paused after the word America, and for the
rest of the day I sat listening to *The Village Green* LP over and over
again. Perhaps the ban had been a blessing in disguise. It had

allowed him to make records about Britain and not get seduced by the acid-rock generation. I knew America had scared him, but I also knew that R.D. was a competitor and the thought of doing battle in order to win back the American market appealed to him.

That night I couldn't sleep. I left my apartment and wandered the streets. I heard footsteps behind me and felt that I was being followed. I returned to my apartment. I turned on the light. Tried to write but felt a presence in the room. I turned around slowly and saw a dark cloud hovering just behind my back. I watched as it started to move around me like a strange predator waiting to pounce on its prey. I made my way to my record player and managed to put on 'Phenomenal Cat' from *The Village Green*. It was as if the cloud recognized the tune. It slowly dispersed and eventually disappeared. I let the record play continuously, knowing that it would protect me from the darkness. I slept and felt secure in the knowledge that the Phenomenal Cat would watch over me.

Suddenly I heard the voice of Raymond Douglas in my ear.

'Hi there, kid.' R.D.'s voice had a touch of evil about it. 'Thinking about that Julie Finkle, are ya, boy? You and me, boy. We have this telepathic communication. I was just thinking that you should go around to Julie's place. Know what I mean? Borrow my car. It's the old Merc parked at the back of the studio. The keys are in the exhaust. Do yourself a favour, son. Go see to that Julie for me. She's a goddess; an English rose if ever I saw one.'

His voice faded away. I slept, but I was becoming obsessed by the mysterious Julie Finkle. Before long I found myself in R.D.'s beaten-up Mercedes. It was about four in the morning and I was driving through the suburbs of London. Then I realized that I didn't know where Julie lived and, more to the point, I didn't know how to drive. It didn't seem to matter though. I just kept heading where the car was taking me and the old-fashioned automatic made it easy for me. I looked in the rear-view mirror, and for a moment I thought that there was someone in the car with me – the dark, shadowy figure that had tormented me in my nightmares for so long. I looked again and the figure was gone. The car, for it was almost as if the car was taking me, stopped outside a small thatched cottage in a village that I hadn't even bothered to read the name of. There was a light on in the kitchen.

I moved towards the house and entered through the back door. Julie was in the kitchen waiting for me. Her thick hair hung down her back and she had a look of total purity. Raymond Douglas was right about her. She looked exactly like the true English rose. It suddenly occurred to me that R.D. had not met my researcher. Perhaps he was describing his imaginary Julie.

She spoke as if she knew everything. As if she had spoken to R.D. himself. 'I've made you a cup of tea. You must be thirsty after such a long drive.'

I sat down at the kitchen table and she poured the tea in the way R.D. liked it.

She continued:

'Have you ever thought about what it would be like to write without fear? Loneliness can be a beautiful thing. There is no despair in loneliness, provided you can bear your own company. You must learn how to like yourself.'

Julie was a seductive and persuasive talker. She told me things about R.D. that were a revelation to me. His love for that place between Belgium and Holland known as Flanders. How in a dream he had once taken her there, and how they stayed in an attic with a view of the blue sky overlooking the red roof tiles of the house opposite. She was so young; I wondered how she could have known him? Perhaps Julie Finkle, like a memory, never ages.

Soon I found myself in Julie's bed. I was making love to her when I heard a familiar voice outside the door, half whispering half shouting.

'Well, kid. What did I tell you? Isn't she just like May Day, Strawberry Fair, a stroll on a midsummer's evening? Aren't her thighs like strong oak trees, doesn't her hair run through your hands like the water from a fresh mountain spring? And between her legs. Isn't it like burying your face into those soft moist hills of Devon? Have you reached the valleys yet? And her lips? Like ripe fruit, mouth as cool and refreshing as a mountain stream. Her teeth as bright as the White Cliffs of Dover.'

Julie groaned with ecstasy.

'Ray, my darling, I love you.'

Julie was calling me Ray. I couldn't believe what was happening. I shouted, 'But, Julie, it's me.'

'Yes, Ray. I know that it's you. Give in to it. Accept who you are and be grateful.'

Then she started making love in the most outrageous and obscene manner. I was turned on and couldn't stop. Sometimes she spoke in a low whisper, sometimes in high-pitched little-girl voice. She told me about her other encounters with men. It was as if she was almost deliberately trying to humiliate me and prove that she was a whore. She turned on her bedside light and suddenly she looked older and wrinkled, as if she had been doing heavy drugs. She looked like another person; she kept on about this guy, who had turned into the devil. I was still making love to her but she kept on talking.

'It was so big but I couldn't get any satisfaction – it just rammed against my inside. A woman can only take so much pleasure.' Then she started to shout: 'Get harder, you useless prick. Stick your hand in the light socket for me. Electrocute yourself and die with a hard dick.'

I shouted and realized that I was crying.

'Why did you let him do it? Who was he?' I was sobbing. I got off Julie but she kept on talking as if she was still in orgasm.

'It wasn't so much like a who, but more like a what.' She screamed.

I turned to look at Julie as I spoke and saw R.D. on top of her. I threw up with disgust. The old man had used me to transport him to Julie. He was still wearing his scruffy old overcoat, but his eyes were red. He looked like the devil. He was foaming at the mouth and his voice was screeching in several octaves simultaneously.

I cried out, 'What made you do this? Why are you destroying the thing you love most?'

R.D. yelled back, 'Why boy? I'll tell you. America. *Fucking* America! That's why. And now I'm fucking England!'

In despair I crawled away from R.D. and Julie. I grabbed the lamp by the bed, took out the bulb and pushed my fingers against the live connection.

I woke up in my flat to the phone ringing. I fell off my bed. I was still clothed. I felt dried blood on my lips, as if I had fallen in the night. I picked up the telephone. It was Raymond Douglas.

'I had a dream about you, son. I was worried that something had happened to you.'

I was so relieved to hear R.D.'s voice sounding normal again.

'Are you coming over today? There's something special I feel I have to tell you. I trust you now, so please.'

'Sure. What do you want to talk about?' I asked.

'I thought that we could talk about America.'

'America.'

'Yeah. And the Corporation. Where all the corruption started. I'm not afraid anymore. I feel as though I can talk to you about it now. See you later, son. Sorry if I woke you.'

R.D. hung up and I stood there listening to the sound of the dead tone at the end of the line.

America.

I phoned Julie again and again, I must have left three or four messages on her video answer-machine, but I only got the same emotionless message: 'I am not in. But I do value your call, so please leave your code and I will call back as soon as I am able.' I had seen the video time and time again, but the more I called and the more I watched, the more I imagined she was saying something else to me. Hidden messages. I zoomed in closer. Looked into her eyes to see some truth, but the message always stayed the same. I called and called, now just to watch the video message. To look in her eyes.

I called up one more time. I put her image on freeze frame just as her lips were pouting to say 'please'. She looked as she had when I first saw her in the dream. Before she became R.D.'s succubus. His fantasy. I whispered down the receiver: 'Sometimes I wish that things could be different. But if they were, then they would not be the same.'

My message sounded trite, childish. I slammed down the phone, then called back immediately and said, 'R.D. was not one of the last independents. He was one of the last innocents.'

I left my apartment and went straight to the studio. I had still not recovered from the nightmare. I had been so terrified that I had bitten deep into my tongue, and this had slightly impaired my speech. I was also afraid, yet in a strange way excited, by what revelations R.D. would make about America. I pressed the buzzer and announced myself in the usual manner. The robotic female secretary's voice allowed me access. I arrived in the studio to find R.D. playing an old upright piano in a small overdubbing booth next to the mixing room where he and I usually sat. It was strange to see him actually being a musician. He was singing a slow version of a song called 'Sweet Lady Genevieve'. It was clear that he was in a mood to confess.

> 'Once under a scarlet sky,
> I told you never-ending lies.
> But they were the words of a drunken vagabond
> Who knew very well he would break your heart before long.
> Oh, forgive me, Genevieve.
> Now I've come back to see, sweet Lady Genevieve.'

As he sang the last line he paused and looked straight ahead. This little-known song from his second attempt at making *Preservation* obviously meant a great deal to him.

'This song always reminds me of my birthday in 1973.' His voice begged me to ask the question.

I complied. 'Has anything strange ever happened on your birthday?'

He laughed, then paused to reflect. The world wasn't waiting, but I was and R.D. knew it. He stretched his fingers out before him and I could see the signs of age. 'Yes. They always leave you on your birthday. Birthdays are the days they realize that they can't put on false emotions any more, they can pretend to be happy but inside they are crying to get out. It's also like that on Christmas, it's like any anniversary; it means they have to be with you and be happy.'

'They?' I inquired.

'Women, wives, lovers, musicians, even,' he replied. 'I was going to tell you about America and I will, because over the years America has been the source of great triumphs and failures, and somehow it has always had this corrupting effect on me. This song, "Sweet Lady Genevieve", was my last desperate attempt to apologize to my wife for all of the wrong I had done.'

'What wrong?' I asked.

'The trouble with starting a relationship because of a mistake is that a mistake is like a lie, you just keep building on it to cover up the previous one. As you can imagine, this is difficult for me to confront. That's why I almost have to step outside of myself to explain.'

R.D. looked around the old decrepit building, drawing on past memories of triumphs and failures. He looked at every tiny crack and crevice as if it were his own life.

'In 1972 the Kinks had purchased this building which later became Konk Studios. It was a run-down factory on the slopes of Alexandra Palace in Hornsey.

I suppose I wanted this studio to symbolize artistic freedom. Some kind of retaliation to the frustration I had encountered at art college. The college itself was just up the road, and it seemed appropriate that here was I, years later, after virtually being thrown out of that college, forming my own creative institution, less than a mile away, on my terms, with my money, and, of course, with the help of Mick and Dave.

Konk was to be the place where the band could hang out together, play snooker, table-tennis, rehearse and eventually record albums. We'd always been stuck with the recording bills since the Pye contract and we thought, why? Instead of buying expensive cars, or wasting our money after tours, why not just buy a tape-recorder and gradually build up a recording studio? It was a fine idea in theory. That's when a band was a band. We were still a united group of people. Just. John Dalton was firmly established as the bass player, and we had taken on a keyboard player called John Gosling, who I understood had been recommended to Grenville by John Peel, at BBC Radio. We had always used keyboards on records, but had never taken a player on the road full time, and I decided that it was time to turn the Kinks into a five-piece band. Gosling became known as 'Baptist', because he looked like the biblical character who had fallen foul of Salome's seven veils. Baptist was a strange mixture of the preacher and the comedian John Cleese. He joined the band just as we had recorded 'Lola' so he played on that, and on our subsequent recordings.

We had delivered *Lola v. Powerman and the Money-Go-Round*. We left Pye Records and moved to RCA after lengthy negotiations, which I had insisted on attending.
Colin Wadie sat with me throughout these negotiations, which were in early 1971, and was somewhat taken aback by the amount of input I had into the contract itself. To be fair, it was easy: RCA really wanted us very badly, and we got virtually every concession we wanted in the contract. The RCA attorneys had come to London to finalize the contract and, the day we signed, Ken Glancy, the head of RCA International, gave me what I thought at first was a box of chocolates. In fact it was a box of Montecristo cigars. This seemed to bring about a change in me; I had experienced my first big deal as a do-it-yourself businessman.

Yet, ironically, the first record we gave RCA was *Muswell Hillbillies*, our most working-class album to date. This was not a cruel joke, planned deliberately by the Kinks, but a coincidence – the songs just came out that way. But it did seem odd for a band who had signed for a prestigious label and for what was then a large advance.

Muswell Hillbillies was a homage to the family that used to be. All the songs, like 'Uncle Son', 'Holloway Jail', 'Oklahoma USA', were songs about people who actually existed in the lives of my parents. I really had an Uncle Son. My mother actually had a childhood friend called Rosie Rooke, who is named in the song 'Muswell Hillbillies'. I rate the *Muswell Hillbillies* album up there with *Preservation*. The song 'Muswell Hillbillies' was about a family similar to my own that was brought up in inner London. My parents had grown up in Islington and Edmonton and had later moved out to the suburbs called Finchley, Highgate, Muswell Hill, away from the inner city and the Victorian factories. It must have been unrecognizable then. There were green fields, fewer back-to-backs — it must have seemed like a new world. But on the album the songs are nostalgic for the old life. You have to take on a new set of values and adapt accordingly when you re-locate. People change. They lose touch with their roots.

The few years before the release of *Muswell Hillbillies* in 1971 were fraught with conflict in my personal and professional life.

The Boscobel management team was breaking up. Larry Page was long gone after I had reluctantly settled the Kassner dispute for a small lump sum, and a reduction in royalties due me as writer of all those early hits. It was, however, a relief to get this dispute out of the way. Kassner had threatened to appeal to the House of Lords if necessary, and while we all felt we were in the right, there was always the possibility that we might lose, and suffer the ensuing financial risks involved in protracted litigation.'

Raymond Douglas, for I must consider him to be a changed person by now, took this very hard. I knew this part of his story but I was not going to let it show.

After *Muswell Hillbillies* was released in 1971, the Kinks parted company with Wace and Collins. Instead of replacing them, they managed themselves and set up an office in north London. Their former press agent, Marion Rainford, came to work for them full time and Ken Jones stayed on as tour manager.

R.D. needn't have run through all the intimate facts about this part of his life. It was obvious at this time that he was successful but bitter. There he was, living in a suburban house in north London, with in many ways a perfect family life – two beautiful children – but at the same time trying to hang on to his marriage, which was suffering from all the attendant problems emerging as a result of post-1960s paranoia. Feminism, monogamy and the family unit were being held up and questioned by a society desperately trying to hang on to its identity. All the time R.D. was struggling with the thought of what might have been if he had gone back to America and allowed himself to go with the flow. R.D. looked younger as he told me the next part of his story. He was becoming another person.

'*Muswell Hillbillies* itself had been in a way inspired by a girl I had met on one of my visits to LA. I had been taken to a nude dancing club called the Rat Trap, near the studio where I was working. Its name was appropriate as inside the pot-bellied punters sleazed around the bar like rats as they waited for the girls. The climax of the act (if climax can be used in this context) was when each girl lay down on the floor, legs wide open, so that the punters could shine flashlights up them to get the optimum view. There was a pool table opposite the stage in case some of the good ol' boys got bored. It was there I met Savannah Molloy, an outstanding looking redhead with high cheekbones, bright white teeth and a slim, tall figure. She said she had grown up somewhere in the Appalachian Mountains and had lived in Louisiana, Paris, New York, and had once been the common-law wife of an Eskimo in Alaska. I didn't believe the name Savannah any more than I believed

most of the other baloney, and the only connection she had
with Ireland seemed to be her thick red hair which hung
down over her shoulders. Savannah was slimmer and more
agile than most of the big-titted women who paraded in the
nude around the stage. The first time I met her she was naked.
She had a grin that said both 'thank you' and 'fuck you' at the
same time. Savannah was a class act.

Ultimately one thing led to another and Savannah and I
became friends. I suppose you could say more than friends.
Let's settle for relationship, or even affair. How drab and
tawdry reality can be. I was very concerned about this
relationship, because by now I was over most of my grieving
for lost loves and searching for other girls, because deep down
I wanted my marriage to work. But after a while I ended up
at Savannah's place. The following morning she said I was a
pretty good lay for poor white trash. Her southern drawl
never faltered, even though our conversations got heated when
we drank. These are the moments of real emotion when
people forget that they have covered up their origins by
acquiring accents and revert back to their native tongue. As
well as being a class act, I was in no doubt that Savannah was
an authentic Appalachian belle who had found herself dancing
in a nude bar due to a series of lapsed loves and tragic
misfortune.

The American Federation of Musicians had lifted the ban
imposed years earlier, and the *Arthur* album had helped to
rebuild our status as a cult act in North America.
Although our career as a dominating musical force was in a
decline, we were being taken seriously as rock innovators and
so, on the surface, everything seemed to be picking up again. I
was in LA and a musician friend said that Savannah wanted to
ask me out for dinner. I thought nothing of this at the time
and anyway, it was the era of love and peace and people often
shared boy and girlfriends with one another. Savannah used to
drive me to Ben Frank's diner on Sunset after she finished

work and we sat around talking and laughing at the characters we saw in there. Ben Frank's was open twenty-four hours a day; and by the time we arrived it was one or two in the morning, and a lot of night owls and creeps were arriving.

On one of Savannah's nights off I went to pick her up earlier than usual. She was staying in a house full of people; a commune-like love and peace hang-out, and the only place we could find some privacy was in the bathroom. I guess that was a big error on my part. Before we knew it, well, one thing led to another, and we were both in the shower. I asked Savannah what she was going to do to me. She said, 'I'm going to take you for a meal, then we're going to have a few drinks, then I'm gonna drive you up to the Hollywood Hills, bring you back to my room and I'm going to give you some head, then, who knows, maybe I'll let you fuck me.'

Here I was, Raymond Douglas, far from home with a little spare time on my hands, and while there was a genuine friendship between the two of us the offer was there; my resistance was low. This was the era of love and peace, even though Charles Manson had just been arrested for mutilating Sharon Tate and others in a sadistic ritualistic mass murder in Beverly Hills, and America was becoming an ever-more terrifying place. The trips to LA became more frequent, particularly after 'Lola' was released and was in the US charts. And, when I went to LA, I always ended up back at the Rat Trap.

In 1970, our first excursions into the United States had been in short bursts of tours which took no more than three weeks each. Grenville was still with us at this time and Ken Jones was tour manager. America had changed, it had become a different animal. Kennedy's Camelot was a thing of the past, it was post-Woodstock, sex and rock 'n' roll and lots of it. Colin the Scrap, a school friend of Mick's, accompanied us on these tours as a bodyguard-cum-party organizer. On one notable occasion we encountered the famous Plaster Casters of

Chicago. Scrap, who, when in a state of sexual arousal, became part man, part donkey, decided to service several stray groupies who were hanging around the hotel lobby. The hotel security guards were called to our floor after a girl was heard screaming out, 'No more, Scrap, no more!' But it transpired that these were screams of pleasure rather than fear. (Like many beasts of burden, Scrap preferred the rear end.)

I found myself being seduced by the sheer 'Americanness' of it all. Britain was still coy and innocent by comparison to LA in particular. America had tentacles that gradually wrapped themselves around you until you were trapped. America was also the first nation that elevated debt to what was almost a status symbol. It also advocated free love as part of the package, but never allowed you to forget another Americanism – there is no such thing as a free lunch.

This came back to haunt Raymond Douglas, who I must say should be referred to as another person in order for me to retain a certain amount of objectivity about myself. I can't talk about him, me, myself in first person any more, because that person no longer exists.

In 1972 while Raymond Douglas was recording 'Everybody's In Showbiz', he accused Rasa of having a romantic fling with a mutual friend. Rasa denied it, but while Raymond Douglas was at home in the semi-detached house writing 'Celluloid Heroes', Rasa was at a pop festival with a crowd of people, including the 'mutual friend'. What really pissed R.D. off was the fact that Louisa and Victoria were there as well. What followed was a series of vicious arguments ending in the inevitable marital discord.

A continual shouting match began to emerge, and made the little suburban house a nightmare to live in. The kids started waking up to the sound of the shouting. The usual story: there would be Rasa and R.D., shouting at each other, usually in the bedroom, and they would look over to see Louisa crying by the door, holding Victoria's hand. Scenes like this continued right through the year. The only happiness R.D. remembers from that time was when he was playing the back-track to 'Celluloid Heroes' while he watched Victoria playing on the floor. There were no words on the song yet, no lyrics written, but as the first musical chorus came in, 'You can see all the stars as you walk down Hollywood Boulevard', Victoria turned and smiled at Raymond Douglas, telling him almost telepathically that the song would be wonderful and that everything would be all right. It was the sight of Victoria smiling that inspired Raymond Douglas to write the lyrics.

Life in suburban London with Rasa had long since ceased to be a source of inspiration to his songs. Instead he flew to LA more often, to stay with Savannah in a small apartment block on Hollywood Boulevard. R.D. watched Savannah perform at the Rat Trap and they walked home along the Hollywood walk of fame, with the names of famous movie-stars set in their own gold stars on the pavement.

R.D. started writing a script for a film about himself and Savannah called *Darrel and Becky*. The story was about two drifters from completely different parts of the world who come to Hollywood to become famous. They both ultimately fail and end up in dead-end menial jobs. However they still live in the hope that one day stardom will come for them. In the first draft of the story, Becky dies and, overnight, Darrel becomes successful. *Darrel and Becky* was about two people in love but who were a fatal combination. They always seem to destroy each other's talent.

It was also true of R.D. and Savannah. Savannah took R.D. up to the Palomino Club in north Hollywood, where they danced to genuine Country music. Savannah was tall and had tied up her hair to make her look like a boy. She dressed up in some of R.D.'s clothes, and some of the other patrons thought they were a couple of male gays. They drank tequila and danced to the Country music, and in the middle of the floor they stood and kissed, which infuriated the redneck element at the club, so much so that one night a pot-bellied cowboy asked R.D. if he could take Savannah outside and 'suck her dick'. R.D. explained to the cowboy that Savannah was a girl but if the cowboy would care to step outside, R.D. might oblige. The fat cowboy explained to R.D. that he was a closet queen who was after some rough homo action and considered R.D. too effeminate for this purpose. This confused R.D. and hurt his ego to such an extent that he took Savannah home and made love to her while insisting that she stay dressed in her man's suit.

R.D. walked around during the day and drew inspiration from some of the ridiculous, sad characters on the Boulevard, and at night he wrote his script while he watched Savannah sleep.

Everybody's a dreamer and everybody's a star.
And everybody's in movies, it doesn't matter who you are.

Raymond Douglas returned to London and his marriage to Rasa recovered some of its old happiness over the following Christmas, more because of the children than anything else. The Davies family was moving further away from north London and starting families of their own. R.D.'s dad was trying to keep the family parties together, but he was losing some of the spring in his step and the Cab Calloway impressions were less energetic. Soon R.D. heard that Savannah had arrived in London and was working as an erotic dancer in a seedy Arab nightclub off Berkeley Square. Eventually the two met up and for a while the relationship was rekindled, but eventually R.D. backed off when he heard that Savannah was married.

People are like wine. Some of them don't travel very well without losing their flavour. In any event I felt as though Savannah and I were like Darrel and Becky in my story. They were a fatal cocktail for each other.

As far as my marriage was concerned, I have since learned

from other experiences. You always know when it's all over when you know they don't care any more. You just get that feeling. You may as well be dead. No emotion. False smiles. No nothing.

Nothing was ever the same after 1973. 1973 was when the world really started to shake. The Arab oil embargo started, Nixon floated the dollar, the Watergate hearings were about to erupt and bring about the first cracks in the hitherto superficially perfect world of America. The uneasy feelings I had when I first went to the States in 1965 were starting to show themselves again.

The Kinks had just done a tour of North America and arrived back near the end of spring 1973, where they had finished up the tour at Bill Graham's Winterland Theater in San Francisco with Dan Hicks and his Hot Licks as their support act. R.D. arrived home jet-lagged, to find nobody to meet him at the airport, nobody at home. In an emotional crisis, any time of emotional upset, jet-lag has a worsening effect. Raymond Douglas waited up till two in the afternoon and Rasa was still not home. He went to bed and woke up at seven-thirty at night to discover that Rasa had been and gone while R.D. was asleep. There was a note on the table: 'The girls are in bed, I have gone out to meet some friends in a club.'

R.D. sat in bed and watched *Pot Black*, a snooker game. He had been home for nearly a day and hadn't seen Rasa. He remembers every shot played in that game. Suddenly, he put two and two together and remembered that Rasa's brother-in-law ran a nightclub in Chelsea. Raymond Douglas put all his cash in his pocket and went down to the club. He walked in right on cue and saw a big burly fellow with his arms around Rasa. Raymond Douglas laughed. He sat down and asked them all if they'd had a good time. They had been to see *Last Tango in Paris* and were calling it the most erotic film they had ever seen.

Raymond Douglas told them about a film called *Deep Throat*, and while it was undoubtedly pornographic, certain American film critics considered it to be the most artistic thing they had ever seen. One had even compared it with *Citizen Kane*. R.D. went into great detail and explained the plot of *Deep Throat*. This infuriated Rasa's friends so much that after a short scuffle Raymond Douglas was frog-marched out of the club, but not before he was knocked unconscious. Someone had decided to take a potted plant and smash it on the back of R.D.'s head. Rasa reluctantly took Raymond Douglas to hospital where he had X-rays for a possible fractured skull. He looked at the large picture of his skull and saw the small crack in his head. Rasa did not care anymore. 'Let's go home, let's get out of here, you make me feel ashamed. You have embarrassed me in front of my friends.' R.D. tried to rationalize about this sad time.

On reflection, nobody was really to blame. 'You slept with someone, so I'll sleep with someone.' It was all so petty. So meaningless, so modern.' The real problem was not the crack on the outside but inside the head of Raymond Douglas Davies. Rasa was practical. She knew she had got everything emotionally she could get out of him, she had no idea that he could possibly continue to make hit records. It was time for her to get out while there was still time and money enough to start a new life.

During the late spring R.D. started to write 'Sweet Lady Genevieve'. He was about to start work on a more complete version of *The Village Green Preservation Society* to take on tour to America. The Kinks had made the original record during their ban by the American Musicians Union, but this had been at the height of flower-power and Woodstock. The band felt that they had missed out on not being at Woodstock, but perhaps if they had been there, they wouldn't have made *The Village Green*. In many respects, that ridiculous ban took away the best years of the Kinks' career when the original band was performing at its peak. The only way the ban could have been lifted was for the Kinks to sign a document apologizing for things that either they didn't do or didn't know about. That's the first sign of being corrupted. R.D. would never have done that a few years earlier. The Kinks had no choice but to sign it because their records were not selling and their advisers said that they had to be more visible in the States. Common sense, I suppose, but why apologize for something they never did? To appease bureaucracy or stroke the ego of a faceless official in a tiny office.

At the beginning of June 1973 the Kinks played a concert at London's Festival Hall. Then another at Drury Lane. These gigs were somehow connected to something to do with the Common Market, which the British government was about to join. At the Drury Lane concert Raymond Douglas tried to put on a first version of *The Village Green* album he had been preparing. He was writing too many new songs and staying up all night trying to make them better. Rasa looked at him and said, 'Why are you trying so hard? All you have to do is play.' R.D. knew that she was right, but he also knew that deep down time was running out in every sense.

The Drury Lane concert featured not just the Kinks but a full blown back-up orchestra and session singers to perform a new work which had yet to be recorded. R.D. had the lyrics to most of the songs on idiot boards at the front of the stage so that he would get them right. The concert worked because, as rough as it was, it conveyed his sense of loss about the final decline of *The Village Green* – Britain. Call it what you like.

After the concert, Rasa was driving Raymond Douglas over Waterloo Bridge when he said that he couldn't take this new band any further. She slammed on the brakes, nearly causing an accident, then lit up a cigarette before continuing on. She looked drained, the same as R.D. must have looked. She had never heard him talk like that before. She knew that he was coming to the end of this creative road and she was not sure whether or not she would continue down the next one with him. R.D. continued to write the songs for the new album and recorded most of the songs from the Drury Lane show, but he later abandoned them and started recording again at the half-finished Konk studio. He tried to keep himself and his marriage together, but he knew that something was going to happen that would change his life for ever. On 20 June 1973 he returned home after a day in the studio to discover that Rasa and the children had left. There was a note which simply said: 'I've gone, please contact my solicitor.'

Raymond Douglas knew it, but he couldn't accept it. Living in a house where suddenly the people aren't there anymore. They leave personal effects behind, little clues in each corner, cups on sideboards, pieces of themselves scattered around, an ashtray full of cigarette ends. Smells. Pictures. Memories. The children's bedroom was exactly the same, they had left everything except their favourite toys. They were certainly travelling light in Rasa's Volkswagen Karmann Ghia.

R.D. wandered round the house, made a few phone calls. He was not sure what was really happening to him, he was in some kind of bewildered daze. Why was this happening? He felt elation one minute – he was actually free, alone, the person he wanted to be – and then total despair as darkness came, there was nobody in the house. There were some of the children's clothes left behind in the bedroom, Rasa's perfume in the bathroom. There was something ghostly about the house. Eventually it started to haunt him, he got out, went to a pub, met some people, went to a party and then the most absurd thing happened. There were some gay people clustered around Raymond Douglas. Some guy stuck his finger up R.D.'s backside while he was trying to pour himself a drink. R.D. couldn't believe it. He smacked the guy round the face and ran out of the building. They shouted, 'Bye-bye, Kinky!' That name. The Kinks returned to haunt R.D. He went to another pub and got blind drunk.

Relatives tried but couldn't help. Gwen and Brian came to see him and all R.D. could do was cry – what a dumb, sick fucker, crying as he stood at his piano where he had written all his songs. He looked out on to the garden at the back of the house. The garden used to be a source of inspiration, but now it just looked like an empty piece of lawn that needed cutting. A rat ran across the bottom of the garden. Raymond Douglas always considered that the sight of magpies and rats was an evil omen. He went to see his family doctor. How ironic. What a fool. Old Dr Aubrey would have advised R.D. to take a cold shower, then leave England to become a preacher and set up as a missionary in Africa. This GP only prescribed Valium. Marian Rainford, the Kinks' secretary, decided that Raymond Douglas should get out of the house and moved him into the office in Highgate. Raymond Douglas' despair took a new comic twist when he suddenly decided to become a playboy. He bought five cases of Dom Perignon champagne and had parties every night, but the parties usually ended up as sad affairs with Raymond Douglas in a crumpled heap of depression in the corner of the room. The Valium and the Dom Perignon, like the fictitious Darrel and Becky, did not make for a happy cocktail.

Ken Jones moved into the semi in Fortis Green with his own family. The house had to be lived in, and Raymond Douglas thought that with new people in the house, the evil spirits might be driven away.

There was a gig offered a month later at the White City Stadium, in Shepherds Bush, London. Everybody thought that if the Kinks played a concert then perhaps Raymond Douglas would shake himself out of the doldrums. The Kinks were also still recording another version of the *Preservation* album. This didn't help matters because R.D. was having to be creative while in this emotional, unreal state. This was not good. The mind was over-stressed, the pills were going in one end, the Dom Perignon was coming out the other, but their

combined effect was staying inside him. This certainly didn't
help his recovery. During this period of extended drunkenness,
R.D. asked Mick to find Savannah for him. After bringing
R.D. a map of the US and pointing out the city, Avory, who
had met Savannah in Los Angeles, said he would ask around
the Speakeasy Club in Mortimer Street, where he usually
spent his evenings. He looked in all the usual clubs and bars,
but he was unable to locate her.

Instead Roxy, a friend of Savannah's, turned up on R.D.'s
doorstep. Roxy had known both R.D. and Savannah from
the Rat Trap days in LA, and while not as striking as Savannah
the fact that she came from Richmond, Virginia, almost made
her a more authentic hillbilly. Roxy had dyed blonde hair
with black roots unashamedly exposed; she looked like she
had put her make-up on as an afterthought, except for her
shiny red lipstick, which never seemed to be spoiled. She had
a classic 1950s look, curvaceous apart from her thighs, which
should have been hidden beneath a large Victorian dress rather
than tightly squeezed into a pair of Levi's. Her face was a little
bloated from her bouts of drink and drugs but her features
were finely chiselled. When she smiled she exposed her slightly
nicotined-stained teeth. There was an air of cheapness about
Roxy, but her common sense and down-to-earth honesty was
a life-saver.

Because of her R.D. learned that beauty need not always be
contained in a perfect exterior, and love doesn't always have a
filter over it in order to smooth out the imperfections. Roxy
was a willing companion who arrived by sheer chance. If
R.D. had seen her in a crowd he probably wouldn't have
given her a second glance. Now she was a central part of his
recovery. She was a life-line and as they walked around
Waterlow Park in Highgate Village R.D. began to feel as if
he and Roxy might even be compatible. He had cast Savannah
as Becky in his celluloid hero's dream movie, but the real star
should have been Roxy. As a rule, in real life people don't

live up to their screen image. Savannah was always in R.D.'s mind and dreams, but Roxy was real. They spent very little time actually sleeping together. R.D. spent very little time sleeping at all. When he wasn't haunted by his own loss of family, he watched Roxy sleep in her own troubled world. She never complained to him about it. She was an angel.

By now Colin Wadie had heard from Rasa's solicitor, who had laid all the matrimonial cards on the table. There was a preliminary hearing some time the following month. Raymond Douglas decided that he wanted custody of his children. Colin sensed that this was a very emotional issue, which would be difficult to resolve amicably. R.D. had started writing about experiences in a world that did not relate to the world his parents knew. He had always played them the first pressings of his records, before they came out, but now he was losing touch with them too. The whole Davies family was moving away from the neighbourhood, losing touch. The source of much of his material was vanishing.

Times being what they were, and advisers being what they were, it was natural that Rasa decided to go for broke – why not? Raymond Douglas' life was dedicated to his music, however, this time he was having to produce and write a new album while his nerves were stretched and everyone in the small Kinks organization was uncertain of what it was going to be like. He knew he had created this character, partly from his own experience, called Mr Flash. Mr Flash was someone who had come from a very humble background. After a traumatic childhood experience, he had turned into a petty criminal, then a cruel dictator. Mr Flash became R.D.'s super villain. But that was in *Preservation* land. In the real world, Rasa's side were shaping themselves up into believing that Raymond Douglas was some sort of irrational sex-crazed tyrant. If R.D. was going to be accused of participating in drug-induced orgies in LA and Muswell Hill, why not be this

person and invent a character called Mr Flash? Perfect casting.
At the photo session for the album cover, he dressed up like
the vaudeville comedian Max Miller, in a dressing-gown
bought at the Harrods sale and a borrowed hat from the
comedian Roy Hudd. The fictitious Mr Flash would then take
over R.D.'s stage persona.

Fiction was fine but the thought of the upcoming concert at
the White City was emotionally a little bit too much to take.
Raymond Douglas had accidentally taken an overdose of
Valium and Dom Perignon a few weeks earlier, and was
found unconscious in the bath by Marian Rainford. She took
him to a local hospital and they pumped out his stomach.
R.D.'s attempts on his life turned into an almost farcical
comedy as the daily excursions to doctors and solicitors
increased. The White City concert was for Raymond Douglas
a chance to reunite himself with his daughters. Before the
split, Lousia and Victoria had become a central part of R.D.'s
life; he often played new songs to them and even did rewrites
based on their reactions. There had been a brief meeting at his
mother's house a few weeks earlier, accompanied by a
detective, and the two children, particularly Louisa, became
nervous and upset. Raymond Douglas wanted them to see
him at his best, in concert. The deal was, the idea was, the
dream was, that Rasa would bring the kids to see him play for
the last time. Then R.D. would quit the music business. He
wanted to announce to the world that this was going to be the
last Kinks concert. The scene was set for a melodramatic finale
in a draughty stadium in Shepherd's Bush.

Before this 'Last hurrah', Raymond Douglas had been sent
to a doctor in Chelsea, who prescribed some sort of 'uppers'
to keep him elated rather than sedated, in order to get him
through the concert. Everywhere Raymond Douglas went, he
was accompanied by Roxy. She had become more of a minder
than anything else, watching R.D. so that he didn't try to do
anything irresponsible like kill himself. She made sure he

had a meal every day, just to keep him going, keep the machinery going so the band could fulfil their contract. Ken Jones drove Roxy down to the White City with Raymond Douglas, who was already dressed in his flamboyant stage gear. Black blazer with red braiding and trimmings, white shirt with red flower especially made for him by Deborah and Claire in Beauchamp Place and a large floppy bow-tie and white flared trousers.

The concert was running late and rather than sit around backstage R.D. decided to sit on Shepherd's Bush Green. He looked at the fast-food shops that were beginning to spring up. All the burger and pizza houses would soon replace the fish-and-chip shops. The little shops of old England would soon be taken over by the big conglomerates. The supermarkets. The fast-food chains. The big combines and corporations.

Eventually it was time for the Kinks to go on stage. All the way through the concert Raymond Douglas was laughing one minute and then crying the next as he swallowed the pills prescribed by the doctor, hoping that they would make him feel better. But every song was like a bitter pill. Each lyric had a new meaning. The rest of the band thought this was one of R.D.'s better performances, but in truth he didn't want to be on stage at all. He was only there to see Rasa and the kids but they had not come. She was playing the perfect tactical game. Over the years she had learned her husband's weaknesses. Every song seemed to resonate inside Raymond Douglas. He sang songs like 'Holiday', 'Celluloid Heroes', 'You Really Got Me', 'All Day and All of the Night'. Each song had a meaning about his own life. There was obviously a lot of self-pity involved, but he could not escape these emotions, there was no escape, this was the real world coming tumbling down on Raymond Douglas' fantasyland. At the end of the concert he announced that this was the final concert by the Kinks, but the PA company accidentally turned off the sound system, and so nobody heard the resignation speech. It would have ended with 'The Kinks are dead, I am dead.' Well-meaning people helped R.D. away from the stage, but he wished that he had just died.

As he left the stage at the White City he was still chewing the pills given to him by the doctor. He sat motionless in the car afterwards with Ken Jones and Roxy. Roxy had fortunately had some experience with people who had taken drugs and she noticed that Raymond Douglas was clenching his jaw and grinding his teeth. 'What the fuck have you been taking?' she said. He calmly lifted up the empty vial of pills, 'Oh, these.' These were dangerous drugs, and Raymond Douglas had taken the whole bottle during the show. They immediately rushed to the same hospital that had saved R.D. a few weeks earlier. Raymond Douglas walked into the casualty department, still dressed in his flamboyant stage gear and with his stage make-up on.

'Hello, my name is Ray Davies. I am the lead singer of the Kinks. I am dying.'

The staff nurse laughed as if checking in a regular customer. 'Mr Davies, can I have your autograph, please?'

'But I am dying.'

'Well, fill out this form, tell us what is wrong with you. You look very well to me, and, please, afterwards will you give me your autograph?'

As he filled out the form he gradually saw it distort: he couldn't see his name, he couldn't see the faces of the people around him. He collapsed on the floor, still in full stage-gear and make-up. Next thing he knew he was flat on his back being attended to by nurses with tubes and stomach pumps.

Before R.D. passed out he saw ambulance men wheel in a man on a trolley. A nurse said the man was a drug addict. All R.D. remembered was the man's biker boots – oily, poor boots with holes in them – a real OD case. For a moment he heard the doctors debating which person to attend to first.

Raymond Douglas was fortunate; he got treated first. The man in the boots was not there when R.D. regained consciousness.

Later, still not out of danger, in intensive care, Raymond Douglas was approached by a stern-faced doctor. He looked down at Raymond Douglas in disgust. 'Tomorrow you will have some analysis.'

Raymond Douglas looked up at the doctor and tried to climb out of bed. 'Not if I can get out of here.'

The doctor smiled cynically. 'You'll only get out of here if you can write your name on the piece of paper which says you are well enough, and discharge yourself.'

Roxy stood by the bed, shaking, knowing that if R.D. left the hospital he might die. Raymond Douglas defiantly took the pen and paper from the doctor and signed his name, got up and staggered out to the amazement of the doctor and nurses. The doctor shouted, 'Tomorrow they'll bring you back, this time in a box. You haven't recovered yet. You're going to die if you leave.' Raymond Douglas turned and shouted back, using the voice of Jimmy Wheeler, an old music-hall comedian: 'Ta-ta for now, folks. Aye-aye. That's your lot.'

That night, Roxy took Raymond Douglas to Dave's house in Barnet, where Lisbet gave them both tea, and put Raymond Douglas to bed. The hallucinations Raymond Douglas experienced that night were grotesque distortions of all his fears, and guilty feelings which were coming back to haunt him. It was R.D.'s journey into hell. He saw faces mixed together – solicitors, Rasa, Kassner, Page, Roxy. Rasa suddenly became a vampire with razor-sharp teeth as she bit into his neck. Suddenly Raymond Douglas heart felt as though it was going to jump out of his body. He felt it pumping faster and faster as the drugs still in his system took full effect. The only way to save his life, he thought, was to think slow, count slow, one, two, three, bring down the heart-rate. Roxy sat by the bed, and when he woke the next morning she was still there. 'We nearly lost you last night, but your will was too strong,' she said. He had beaten all his nightmares but could feel only shame. He had nearly beaten himself.

Now it was time for R.D. to get ready for the fight in the law courts. They love to see somebody like him pulled down and put back in his place. He was determined to get back his daughters whatever the cost. Marian Rainford had seen a house advertised in *Country Life* that fitted Raymond Douglas' requirements perfectly. It had a large garden, was detached, and had an annex where a nanny could live with them when he won custody. They went down to the house by train from Waterloo and found the house perfect for these requirements. Marian did the negotiating while R.D. went round tapping the walls, pretending to be the surveyor, as he felt a little strange about buying such a large house. Raymond Douglas offered them what they were asking provided they left all the furniture. He wanted to avoid having any remnants of his own past around him. These people were happy, and he hoped to have part of their happiness, maybe it would give him good luck, and a much-needed new start to life. The deal for the house was done quickly and pushed through, much against the wishes of R.D.'s solicitor, who had wanted R.D. to stay 'liquid', as the fact that he had property made him an easy target when it came to the court case. Nevertheless R.D. moved into the house on the August bank holiday in 1973 accompanied by his mum and dad and sister Joyce. Lisbet arrived late in the evening to wish him good luck. Ray slept in a small single room, knowing he wouldn't really feel comfortable in the house until his daughters could be there with him.

In the world of solicitors and divorce lawyers there was a battle to fight. Colin Wadie was too emotionally involved for R.D.'s comfort and had been replaced by the solicitor who had won Dave's paternity case years before. David Sarch

looked like a burly sea-captain, displaying a large ginger
beard to match his protruding beer-belly. He was an
experienced criminal lawyer and adopted a hardball approach
to the case. He tried to explain to R.D. that this was for his
own good: divorce is one of the dirtiest jobs a solicitor has to
deal with. Sarch gave R.D. a lift in his old Jaguar car and
considered the position. He said that because R.D. had become
famous, he was classless and difficult to define. This enabled
him to break away from the establishment, but R.D. knew
that once they had him firmly by the balls they were not
going to let go. He could expect little sympathy. Sarch also
indicated that the costs would be enormous. Later he engaged
the services of Margaret Mitchelson, one of the most
prominent divorce barristers in practice at that time. She had
earlier indicated that she thought it might be possible to
obtain custody of the children, but at the doors of the court
the woman barrister had disappointing news. 'There is no way
you are going to get the children. I couldn't tell you before
now. I am terribly sorry, Mr Davies. This particular judge
will not allow it. It is in your best interests to push the divorce
through as quickly as possible. The other side would fight on
this issue and it would inevitable harm the children.'

R.D. sat through the hearing impassively as Rasa gave a
carefully rehearsed speech. The judge did most of the talking.
'How did he act, unreasonably?' 'Yes.' The judge spoke as he
wrote, 'Unreasonable conduct.' 'Would you say that this
marriage has irretrievably broken down?' 'Yes.' 'Irretrievably.'
'Do you feel that the children's interests would be best served
by staying with you and not your husband?' 'Yes,' Rasa
meekly replied as she sniffled into her handkerchief. The
judge made a swift pronouncement: 'Children to remain with
the mother. Decree nisi – granted to the wife.' Divorce was
passed through within minutes. Everybody left the court;
Rasa's side seemed quietly triumphant. Raymond Douglas sat
like a prisoner in the dock. He was officially, legally, alone.

Later he went back to the house in Surrey that now seemed larger and emptier. Now the house truly symbolized all his unfulfilled dreams; all his lost hopes and ambitions. Soon Roxy would realize that whatever unfulfilled ambitions R.D. had, she was not going to be part of them, and soon she would be gone. R.D. purchased a bicycle and cycled down a country road towards a pub. He knew that part of his life was over. As he cycled he looked up through the trees at the clear blue sky. For once he was free from all the lawyers, private detectives and even musicians, and he laughed out loud to himself. A giant lorry approached from the opposite direction, swerved over and brushed R.D. off his bicycle into a ditch. R.D. thought how wonderfully poetic and fitting it would have been if the lorry had collided with him head on and he had been killed. How flamboyant to die such an extravagant death. R.D. fell into a ditch. After brushing himself down he cycled on up the road and stopped outside a little church school. Inside there was a young woman schoolteacher getting ready for the new term. She was pretty ordinary to look at, but seemed the sort of person you could depend on. The schoolteacher and Raymond Douglas made eye contact as he sat back and rocked on his bicycle, contemplating the future. She smiled at him and, after closing the window of the schoolroom, went back to work. It may not be so bad, I'll just have to get over the initial loneliness. 'Fuck it!' he thought. I don't need anyone. Who am I kidding? I'm desperate!' Whatever else, that year was the year R.D.'s world came to an end. He dreamed that he had been killed on that warm autumn afternoon as he cycled down the country lane. Perhaps he had actually died after the White City concert?

For a time Roxy stayed on at R.D.'s house while he was trying to reorganize his life in London, to come to terms with the divorce. Finally Roxy left probably because she felt she was just a replacement for Rasa. If this was the case, who was Rasa a replacement for? You've gotta think hard. Roxy had asked for a long-term commitment and at one point R.D. had even thought about it, but this had fizzled out and when Roxy realized this she made this decision to bite the bullet and get out. She had to. She could see her life being ruined. But before she finally left she sat R.D. down and asked him to spell out the truth: who was she replacing if it was not Rasa? R.D. just looked at the stars and thought about Hollywood Boulevard. That Christmas was one of the strangest of R.D.'s life. Christmas day spent on the Circle line with a six-pack of Kronenbourg.

'It makes you laugh, it makes you laugh; you go round and round on the Circle line and come back where you started. The last can of Kronenbourg is half finished and you're dying for a pee. Eventually you get off and pee up against a wall somewhere in the station. Suddenly you realize the six-pack's run out and it's just you and a couple of drunks left on the train and there's nowhere to go because all the off-licences are closed and you need more beer. Makes you laugh, you've gotta laugh.'

Eventually R.D. made his way over to East Molesey where Colin the Scrap's local pub had an afternoon drinking extension. Scrap was at the bar talking to a fat old buzzard called Sydney Barker. Barker after shaking R.D.'s hand, continued to chat up a fat barmaid. Sydney was a likeable old bloke who revelled in being called an old bugger. In his world an old bastard was someone you could depend on. Sydney and the barmaid were both in their late fifties. On second glance the barmaid was possibly in her late sixties, and still wearing heavy make-up in a style that she hadn't changed since she was twenty. Sydney ordered drinks all round and explained to everyone that the last time he had screwed the barmaid was during the war. He was giving her one under the bar when a bomb landed nearby and blew out the windows of the pub just as he was on the 'vinegar' stroke and the barmaid was about to come. Must have been the biggest blast of their lives.

Eventually the pub closed and Colin the Scrap took R.D. to the British Legion in Molesey, which turned out to be closed. Not to be done out of a drink, Scrap then drove R.D. all around Surrey in his open lorry until he found a pub open in Thames Ditton. The rest was a blur. Thankfully. A mixture of free drinks, cigarette smoke and stale kisses from the old boilers and dossers who hang around pubs on Christmas Day because they have no family.

Scrap finally topped R.D.'s Christmas by taking him to a friend's house to watch blue movies. Unfortunately for Scrap, the friend's relatives were assembled around the television watching Morecambe and Wise and opening Christmas presents. Outraged but not to be outdone, Scrap packed away his projector and blue movies and drove off with R.D. in the lorry to another unsuspecting friend's house. R.D. was still hungover and asked Scrap why they couldn't just go back to Scrap's house and watch the blue movies without ruining everybody else's Christmas. Scrap looked over at R.D., took a giant pull on his roll-up and explained that it was because it was no good without an audience.

Colin the Scrap spoke the truth. It hit R.D. straight between the eyes. That was the key to the problem. R.D. had lost his audience. Somebody to do it for, to write, to live, to have and know that, somewhere in the world, they're going to hear your song — it's got to be a special person. Somebody worth doing it for R.D. had started off with an audience of one, ended up with thousands, only to lose them again.'

Raymond Douglas looked like himself again. This story had made me a little emotional but R.D. smiled at me across the control room in a reassuring way. There was optimism in his voice as he spoke. 'All you really need is that one person to get you started. A Julie Finkle. A muse. Go looking for her, get in the car, drive forever, just hope that you can open the door one day, look in a bar and there she looks up at you, with that look in her eyes that says, "I'm your friend." It's got to be out there somewhere, just keep searching for it. When I think about it though, perhaps Julie was part of my dream world that nobody could penetrate.

'Just like the song. Fancy that. I predicted my own end.

'All in all, I suppose I got what I deserved. I came from a family who for all their failings stayed together. Mine was the first marriage to break up. The stupidity and the shame seemed to send me on an endless spiral that I never quite recovered from. I was never fully reconciled with Rasa. With me, when it's over, it's over for good. Creatively, however, there were good things ahead. I've got a lot I want to tell you. Maybe next time I'll even tell you who that mystery girl was in Southsea!'

'Julie Finkle? Margie?' I enquired.

'No. Get out of here. I'll tell you tomorrow. I might even tell you who the real Lola was and the rest. The old brain-box is somewhat knackered and I need some sleep and so . . . go. Take the car.'

Hearing Raymond Douglas describe how his family disintegrated made me feel fortunate that I had not known my own. I had no memories, no blood ties. And yet I still miss them, even though I didn't know them. That night I began to be haunted at night by faceless people walking towards me, holding my hand, embracing me, loving me; the love that comes from the heart; the love that's all-consuming and yet lets you free. That's the most difficult love; a love that can hold you and still lets you grow. But now I wanted my family back. Raymond Douglas, what have you done to me by telling me about yourself? You made me want the impossible. I look at myself as if I were another person. In the reflection behind me I see Raymond Douglas riding down a country lane in Surrey and his narrow escape when the lorry knocked him off his bicycle. The drive was probably worthwhile just to see the schoolteacher at the end of the road. Maybe he was prepared to risk death, just to see her. There's got to be a reason for doing everything. Perhaps R.D. was too insecure just to do it for himself. His words kept going around in my head. You need to have an audience, to be connected with real human beings. There's a Julie Finkle for everyone out there somewhere.

As I drive the magical Mercedes home afterwards, I see the dark road ahead of me, the flashing lights from the on-coming traffic, the motorway that took over the world. Everybody's going somewhere. That's another line, 'the killing time, see how they stand in line', I see the black sky ahead. I drive away from the big city, I drive away from the bright lights behind. I enter the blackness. Outside there somewhere there is somebody waiting. We must all keep searching for something. The cars pass me, overtake me, flashing red lights, white lights from the oncoming traffic, it all seems so unreal and yet there are people in all of those vehicles. I wonder where they're going and I wonder who they're going there for. After a while, I start to think and wonder, do I really exist? Why am I telling this story? Did these things happen? Have I always been on this motorway in this car, driving? There seems to be no life outside of this metal machine I am in. Perhaps I've never lived at all, perhaps I have always been a sleepwalker. God knows.

I see myself in the mirror of my apartment, then in the reflection I become R.D. in a meeting with Dave Davies and Mick Avory. I am an outsider and an insider at the same time. We are discussing Dave's future and the selling of his shares in Konk Studios. Dave Davies, Mick Avory and me. R.D. Of all people, why am I there? They look at me as if they know me. They call me Ray. They're asking how much I want to pay for the shares in the studio. I don't question where I am and what I'm doing. I go along. After the meeting I tell Mick how I drove up to Rutland to try to find David Watts. I knew that David Watts was the only man who genuinely cared for my brother as much as I did, and for some obscure reason I thought that if I'd found David Watts now, he'd come back to help Dave Davies out of his financial plight, but David Watts had died some years earlier. The journey seemed wasted.

Then Mick reminisced about the time the Kinks met David

Watts. 'We had a good crack then, didn't we?' We really enjoyed life. Those were the days.' That there was a time when Dave and Mick actually got along. Maybe I had always been the problem? Mr Big Mouth, Mr Big Shot. But who am I thinking this? I'm not the person they think I am. I look in the mirror at my apartment and I see myself in this scene as R.D.

I look at Dave and listen to the astronomical figures he is beginning to quote – company shares, bottom line, profit margins. I think back to when we were just in a band in a little Bedford Dormobile, driving up and down the M1, happy to get £50 a night for playing a gig. Then to that underground journey after I'd signed my first songwriting contract, which said at the bottom of the page, 'In consideration for your signature, we will pay you the nominal amount of one penny.' One penny on that train. Suddenly I'm back with Dave and Mick, company shares, how much value can you put on a lifetime of work together? I think of Mick, Dave and me laughing in the back of that van with Peter Quaife. If only we'd known then, been smart, street-wise. We were totally innocent. I look at the guys now, well into our forties, we're totally innocent, just as we were in the back of that van. Mick only wanted to do it for laughs and the girls, and even though I thought that I had something weird to prove, we did it for fun. The songs were secondary. We celebrated a time, our youth. An escape from normality. And we made a career for ourselves in a world that offered us very little alternative.

The door into the studio creaked open the following morning. R.D. was looking old and pale. I felt an intruder, just as I had done the first time I entered his room. It was obvious that the old rocker had not slept all night. I was the one who was dreaming, and he had taken on the burden of my insomnia.

I was not afraid anymore. The Corporation did not bother me. I would lose my job and disappear into the world of the unemployed. It was worth it.

R.D. looked over at me. 'What if I said that there was a part of me that knew what I was doing all along; that perhaps I was not the innocent I said I was? That I manipulated emotions in order to get creative ideas?'

'Then I would say that you were a liar.'

'What if I said the songs came from nowhere?'

'Then I would say you were a dreamer.'

'And if I, R.D., said I was born a king, then fell to earth to become working class, then ended up in a classless occupation?'

'Then I would say that you owed nothing to no man.'

'Perhaps that is who I am — *no man*. And no man or Corporation shall have my dreams. The only things that were real were the songs. The people existed half in reality and half in my imagination.

'Perhaps everyone exists half in somebody else's imagination. No one is totally human. We are all facets of someone else's internalization. Visions of what they want us to be.'

R.D. moved closer and started to tell me about myself.

'Do you sleep near to water and trains? Stay near to those sounds of trains in the far distance. That is where we were born.

'And your loneliness when you were a confused child was because you lost your sister. Your family truly loved you.'

'And Roxy? Did she exist?'

'She was similar to so many people in my life. They exist as part reality, part invention. Roxy was as real, say, as Alan Klein, Larry Page, Alfie, Cindy ... They have one reality seen through my eyes. But the truth of what they are is theirs and theirs alone. The only perception I have of them is from my own narrow angle. Like a one-camera shoot. They are probably totally different to the way I have described them to you. If you ask me about Julie Finkle, Cindy, Margie, whatever you want to call her, I will say she is as real as I am, because to me my dreams tell me more about the real world than any newspaper or history book. I have this dream about her. I have a desperate need to write. She visits me occasionally and I give her my stuff to read. As long as she is pleased with it I have no need to show it to anyone else. She is my audience of one, her approval is all I need. Our relationship is purely platonic – there is no sexual interaction between us, there is no pressure on me to prove I am a man. I live as long as she wants to hear my songs and read my poems. Julie Finkle has no face. I am alone but not afraid. I am emotionally independent.

'Enough about my dreams. Maybe tomorrow I'll tell you about the time you saw me as a demon in your dream. And tomorrow I'll tell you about your family.

'Meanwhile, be careful. You are undoubtedly being watched. You are a danger to them now.'

'Who are *they*?'

'You know who *they* are. You have always known. Now go on your way. Be off. Do not waste the time of the last of the independents. I need to rest, I'm tired. Go now, son.'

Something inside told me not to leave him alone because, although he sounded confident, I knew he was particularly vulnerable at times like this and needed someone around whom he could depend on. I was afraid that small dark cloud might appear again and consume us both, so I tried to end our session on an up note.

'All those things happened to you so long ago. You can't still feel bitter?'

'Bitter? Not really. When you get to my age you learn to be philosophical about these things. What you never had, you never miss. As for individuals, I believe that no one person knowingly intends to injure another. They were people. Not the Corporation. Anyway, it's history now. They have their lives to live and, if you'll excuse me, I must get on with mine.'

I was still uneasy about leaving, but he seemed in a better mood.

'Don't worry, lad. I'll tell you more next time, I promise.'

He sounded sincere and I forced myself to believe him, even though my better judgement told me that this was probably another one of his false promises; the kind he would give to over-zealous fans just to get them out the door. But, being a fan, I respected his wishes.

As I entered my apartment I knew that someone else had been there. The red light on my answer-machine was flickering on and off, and as I rewound the tape, I noticed a box of newly prescribed tranquillizers: the mysterious intruder must have left them on my desk. The first message was from Julie, saying that the medical department had instructed her to tell me that I should start taking this new medication. My irritation turned to anger when I listened to the next message. It was from some busybody in the legal department who had seen the early pages of my research relating to R.D.'s contractual disputes. This person was objecting to R.D.'s references to 'a Corporation', and demanded that certain events should be 'excised from the text'. I was outraged.

I deleted all my computer disks relating to R.D. and just kept one hard copy, which I hid in a safe place. There was a second message from Julie, asking me to call, but I was far too intimidated to make contact with her. The tranquillizers went the same way as the sleeping pills, down the toilet. I put on a live version of 'I'm Not Like Everybody Else', from one of the last concerts the Kinks gave. I changed the combination lock on my door and pulled out the phone so that I wouldn't hear it ring.

I waited for word from R.D. but it never came, so I went back to his studio. Once again I was confronted by the robotic-sounding voice on the entryphone. They knew me and I was allowed in, but for the first time R.D. was not there. The control room looked the same, with a thin shaft of light coming through the ceiling. His chair was still in the corner. The castors still needed oiling and the air-conditioning still whistled from time to time, but now there were none of his songs on its breath. I looked for the tapes but they, like their owner, were not to be found.

His Coronation mug was on the control desk and, before I left, something compelled me to take it as a souvenir. I took a quick last look at the room and left.

The next day I saw in the newspaper that Raymond Douglas had died. I felt my body chill with anger, partly due to the shock of the news and partly to the fact that the paper had given him only two paragraphs. They were at the bottom of a page, underneath the obituaries of a little-known nuclear scientist and a former member of parliament. There was a small picture of him with his band, but John Dalton was credited as being Peter Quaife. At least the two brothers' names weren't confused. It was a picture that I knew that R.D. would have disliked, and the caption underneath referred to R.D. as a 'Kink'. I suppose that's what he was, but somehow I wanted him to be credited as something more.

I didn't want to read how, when or of what he died. It was there, but for some reason I didn't want to know, nor did I want to know whether he would be buried or cremated.

I made a pot of tea and decided to drink it from his mug. I prepared the tea with care, in the same way I had for him in the studio. I played some old Kinks records as I drank, and I became somewhat emotional. As I listened to the songs, I hoped that he had not been alone or afraid when he died and that his family had been around him even after abandoning him for so many years as he became grumpy, decrepit and difficult to deal with. Afterwards, I imagined that a great white unicorn would come down from the heavens and protect him on his long journey. At the end of it he would be reunited with his ancestors, and wait for his loved ones to leave this world to join him. Now he could thank his sister Rene for the guitar she had bought him on his thirteenth birthday. Now he could tell his dad that Arthur Ashe had indeed beaten Jimmy Connors in the Wimbledon final, and then probably get his ear clipped for not having gone to a bookie to place a bet. He could describe how Arsenal had beaten Liverpool at Anfield to win the 1989 Football League title and repeat the championship win two years later. There were so many stories and so many incidents to reflect upon.

And what about Julie Finkle? R.D.'s name for his mystery muse. His admirer and keeper of all his secrets and the probable inspiration for 'Waterloo Sunset'? I had to find out the truth about the elusive Miss Finkle. I decided to try to contact her via R.D.'s studio. If Julie existed, she would have heard the news and phoned in by now.

I telephoned his studio and the operator answered. I recognized her voice from the first time she quizzed me about rock trivia before letting me into the building. I spoke but she didn't know me and when I asked if there was a message form Julie she denied all knowledge of her.

'Nobody called Julie here.'

I tried an obvious, somewhat desperate ploy.

'It's me. It's Ray, it's Raymond Douglas. Julie Finkle must have phoned.'

'Raymond who?'

'This is my office, isn't it?'

'I'm terribly sorry, but I don't know who you are. Your name is not listed in our directory. Will you check to see if you have the right number?'

I considered the possibility that I could have been imagining all that had happened in the past weeks. I sensed that she was going to hang up. I tried one last time.

'Is Mick Avory there?'

'Mr Avory is not here yet. He's on the golf course and when he comes back, he is going straight into a meeting with other surviving partners.'

'Yes, I know, I should be there. I'm Raymond Douglas Davies, I'm a partner.'

By now the secretary had run out of patience.

'Sir, whoever you are, Mr Davies passed away last week and if this is your idea of a joke, then it's in very poor taste. Anyway, Mr Avory is actually no longer with the company since the new owners took over. Thank you.'

The line went dead. Terminal.

The Corporation. They had finally done it, just as R.D. always feared that they would. I vowed to myself that they would not have it all their own way. I still had R.D.'s story and there was no way I was going to let the Corporation have his life rights.

My paranoia started to get the better of me, and I cursed out loud: almost as though I had been deliberately cheated out of the rest of R.D.'s story. I felt as though he had conned me. As though after selling the Corporation the rights to his life, he had actually told me nothing before he died.

After I had taken a shower, I calmed down and became more rational. I concluded that R.D. had given me much more than a list of events in his life plus a few worn-out old anecdotes. That would have been normal, acceptable and expected, and therefore much too ordinary for him. He knew that to most of the world he had been an ordinary man who had been in the right place at the right time and, as a result, had capitalized on his good fortune and turned himself into a myth. Perhaps this was partly true, but the real value of the time I had spent with him was that he had given me an insight into his world of dreams and imagery, where past and future live side by side. He had shown me how it is possible to escape the reality and dullness of the world simply by examining, observing and celebrating it. He had helped me out of my own crisis by showing me his own. Now his songs were more valuable to me than just anthems from another age.

From a last-minute pang of conscience, I decided to go to the funeral after all. I arrived just as the last of the limousines carrying official mourners was pulling away. As I approached the row of sad, perfectly arranged flowers, a single figure appeared under the shadow of a tree. I stood back and watched her approach. She was a mature but still elegantly slim woman: Raymond Douglas would have described her as a 'nice bit of old'. She was attractive, dressed all in black and, although her head was covered by a scarf, I could see that her slightly tinted hair was pulled into a bun at the back of her head. Her face was covered with white make-up and she wore dark sunglasses. Who was she? Margie, Alfie, Anita? She was too old to be Victoria or Louisa, even though they must have been there. Maybe it was his last wife. After reaching down to pluck a small fuchsia from one of the wreaths, she turned away before I could approach her. I tried to catch her but she disappeared into a waiting limousine. As she got into the car I saw that she had well-formed dancer's legs: the sort of legs Raymond Douglas would have appreciated.

A few days later a package arrived for me. I unwrapped the brown envelope to discover a few old diaries tied together with string. They were accompanied by a note from R.D.'s solicitor. It said I was to have the diaries on condition that I did not publish them until the tenth anniversary of R.D.'s death. And on no account was I to let them fall into the hands of the Corporation. I was elated. My faith in R.D. had been restored.

R.D. must have known he was going to die for some time and had decided not to tell me. But he had trusted me enough to have access to the missing diaries and tapes. A key fell out of the envelope and on it was a label which said that it was to a trunk that contained additional notes, along with cassettes of unfinished and unreleased songs. These had been left for me to complete and have recorded. But there was no indication of where the trunk was. This was so typical: to give me the key to a box that did not exist. Then a few days later it arrived. There were storage and delivery charges: it was as if even after his death R.D. had decided to play one last trick on me and leave an outstanding bill to pay.

I opened the chest to discover it packed with old cassettes and reel-to-reel tapes from the sixties, seventies and eighties. Countless notebooks, newspaper cuttings and photographs. This was a treasure trove. My Tutankhamun's tomb, King Solomon's mines. Raymond Douglas Davies' life story was laid out in front of me for me to finish. It made me feel as though he were still alive. But now I could discover the answers to those questions I had never had the opportunity to ask. And I could re-live moments with him by working with him, listening to his voice on the tapes. R.D.'s life was like a jigsaw puzzle and it was my task to put it back together. Most people are the sum total of many parts; as varied in temperament and layers of character as there are molecules in the human body. The most explicit analysis of a person's exterior can show us only a fraction of what that person is about. An old X-ray photograph of R.D.'s injured back fell out on to the floor and I picked it up and studied it. I felt that while the physical world can see two people – the outer and inner person – there is also the third person, a spiritual driving force that constantly intermingles with the first and second person. Intangible and totally inseparable.

I also knew that if the Corporation found out what I was about to do they would stop at nothing to get their hands on these materials and my manuscript. It was obvious that they would pursue me forever; and that Julie and I were finished. I wanted to see her again so badly, but I knew that if I made any attempt to contact her it would bring about her ruin as well as my own. I had to disappear — and fast. I gathered together all my belongings and packed R.D.'s car full of his memorabilia. I drove with no destination in mind; I knew that the car would automatically point me in the right direction. Eventually I reached a far country and rented a small attic that was just large enough to accommodate me and my belongings. That night I heard the sound of a train in the distance and knew that this was near to where I had been born. The sound both comforted me and filled me with anxiety. I longed to speak to Julie to tell her about the incredible events that had occurred, but I knew better. They had taken away my dreams once, and I was determined that they would never have them again. I started to think of the image of the attic in Flanders. Of that bright blue sky above the red tiles of the house opposite that had come to both R.D. and myself in a simultaneous dream. It was our image of freedom. Loneliness without desperation. Work without frustration. Love without the fear of it being lost. I felt that I no longer existed, I was invisible and able to see people, observe and document their lives, without having to answer to anyone. To discover that truth is not a single thing and that the only way to be totally free is to be totally devoid of any identity. The inner spirit is all important, and R.D. is inside me. When I think of him he will think of me.

Through my attic window, I heard people talking in the streets below. It was a strange, backwards-sounding language and although it was a dialect I had never heard before, I was able to understand more and more of it as days went by. I felt as though I had been born again and placed into another life. I looked over my shoulder and for a moment I thought I saw R.D. sitting beside me. R.D. had become my shadowman, who would be my companion in my new existence. As the small dark cloud reappeared in my attic room I welcomed it like an old friend as well as an enemy, because now I knew that it would always be there to consume me if I let it. I smiled at it and allowed it to drift outside the attic window, and once I knew that the black cloud was safely outside, I blew it a kiss and quickly closed the window in its face.